Hand Book of Modern Bakery Products

OTHER RELATED BOOKS

- Fruits & Vegetables Processing Hand Book
- Fruit Beverages & Processing With Mango Products
- Food Processing & Agro Based Industries
- Manufacturing Technology of Snacks Food, Namkeen, Pappad & Potato Products
- Preservation & Canning of Fruits and Vegetables
- Hand Book of Food Dehydration & Drying
- Meat Processing & Meat Products Hand Book
- Technology of Food Preservation & Processing
- Hand Book of Food Packaging Technology
- Agro Based & Processed Food Products
- Potato & Potato Processing Technology
- Technology of Maize & Allied Com. Products
- Technology of Food Processing Industries
- Technology of Sweets (Mithai) with Formulae
- Hand Book of Organic Farming And Organic Foods With Vermi-Composting and Neem Products
- Hand Book of Fish Farming And Fishery Products
- Hand Book of Mushroom Cultivation, Processing And Packaging
- Hand Book of Spices & Packaging With Formulaes
- Start Your Own Cold Storage Unit
- Hand Book of Bakery Industries
- Hand Book of Confectionery With Formulations
- Breakfast, Dietary Food, Pasta & Cereal Products Technology
- Hand Book of Modern Bakery Products
- Modern Bakery Technology & Fermented Cereal Products With Formulae
- Technology of Confectionery, Chocolates, Toffee, Candy, Chewing & Bubble Gums, Lollipop and Jelly Products with Formulations
- Hand Book of Poultry Farming & Feed Formulations
- Hand Book of Pig Farming
- Agro Based Hand Book of Plantation, Cultivation & Farming
- Agro Based Plantation Cultivation & Farming
- Agro Chemical Industries (Insecticide & Pesticides)
- Modern Bee Keeping & Honey Processing
- Technology of Modern Rice Milling And Basmati Rice
- Hand Book of Goat Farming
- Floriculture Hand Book (Flowers Growing Technology)
- Aloe Vera Cultivation, Processings, Formulations And Manufacturing Technology
- Hand Book of Dairy Formulations, Processes & Milk Processing Industries
- Milk Processing And Dairy Products Industries
- Hand Book of Dairy Farming to Produce Milk with Packaging
- Hand Book of Ice Cream Technology And Formulae
- Hand Book of Milk Processing Dairy Products And Packaging Technology
- Dairy Farming for Milk Production Technology
- Ayurvedic & Herbal Medicines With Formulaes
- Hand Book of Ayurvedic Medicines With Formulations (A Complete Hand Book of Ayurvedic & Herbal Medicines)

* E-Mail: eiribooks@yahoo.com & eiriprojects@gmail.com
*Website: www.eiriindia.org & www.industrialprojectreports.com

Hand Book of Modern Bakery Products

Written By

EIRI Board of Consultants & Engineers

ENGINEERS INDIA RESEARCH INSTITUTE
4449, Nai Sarak, Main Road, Delhi - 110006 (India)
Ph: +91-11-23918117, 23916431, 45120361, 23947058, 64727385
* E-Mail: eiribooks@yahoo.com & eiriprojects@gmail.com
*Website: www.eiriindia.org & www.industrialprojectreports.com

PRINTED & PUBLISHED BY

ENGINEERS INDIA RESEARCH INSTITUTE

4449, Nai Sarak, Main Road, Delhi - 110006 (India)
Ph: +91-11-23918117, 23916431, 45120361, 23947058, 64727385
* E-Mail: eiribooks@yahoo.com & eiriprojects@gmail.com
*Website: www.eiriindia.org & www.industrialprojectreports.com

Sole Distributor:

EIRI PROJECT CONSULTANTS AND PUBLISHERS
4/54 Roop Nagar, Delhi-110007

2nd Revised & Enlarged Edition

ISBN: 9788186732618

Printed in New Delhi (INDIA)

₹ 900/-

Printed & Published by Sudhir Gupta for "Engineers India Research Institute", 4449 Nai Sarak, Main Road, New Delhi -110006

Preface

Quality production of bakery items, requires basic scientific knowledge about raw material supported by specific skills. In preparation of bakery products along with skills it is also very important to follow the rules of hygiene and sanitation. Considering these points this course is specially designed to impart basic knowledge and modern techniques of bakery and confectionery. This will help to develop entrepreneurship attitude in students and make him/her economically self sufficient.

The objectives of the bo to enable the students to : 1) Get scientific and technical information regarding basic raw material required for bakery and confectionery products and their functions and characteristics. 2) Know about equipments used in bakery and confectionery. 3) Develop & inculcate habits of hygiene and sanitation during production of bakery and confectionery products. 4) Develop scientific and technical skills for quality production. 5) Be economically self sufficient by sell of bakery and confectionery products. 6) Develop entrepreneurship attitude.

The book *Handbook of Modern Bakery Products* covers almost all the basic and advanced details to setup your own Bakery Unit. The main chapters are: *Baking, Ingredients Leavening Agents and Ovens, Biscuits, Breads and Rolls, Cakes, Cookies and Pastries, Raw Material, Processing, Bread Making Methods, How to Judge the Quality of Bread, Bread Faults, Bread Diseases, Staleness in Bread, Bread Improvers, Cake-Making Ingredients, Cake Manufacturing, Characteristics of Cakes, Balancing of Cake Formula, Cake Faults and Remedies, Cookies, Pastry, Cookies, Biscuits, Cakes, Buns, Pies, Icings Breads & Pizzas, Health Breads, Chicken Patties, Noodles, Asian Noodle Technology, Biscuits Manufacture, Bread and Bun, Compressed Baker's Yeast, Fried Snack Foods: Sev,*

Bhujia, Bombay Mix, Fried Nuts and Dal, Packaging for Biscuits, Chapati Making Unit, Automatic Biscuit Making Plant, Automatic Bread and Biscuit Unit, Automatic Pineapple Biscuit Making Plant, Bread Manufacturing, Bakery Unit (Pastries, Bread, Buns, Cake, Toffee etc.), Bakery Gel (Translucent Semi Solid Paste), Baking Powder, Mini Flour Mill (Atta), Modern Bread and Bakery Unit (EOU) (Bread, Buns, Rusk), Roller Flour Mill, Details of Plant & Machinery, Suppliers of Plant and Equipments, and Consultants for Bakery Units.

The book has been written for the benefit and to prove an asset and a handy reference guide in the hands of new entrepreneurs & well established industrialists.

EIRI Board of Consultants & Engineers

CONTENTS AND SUBJECT INDEX

Chapter - 1

Baking, Ingredients Leavening Agents and Ovens

BAKING

Baking is a process by which the food is cooked in hot air in a close oven. The action of dry heat is modified by steam which arises from the food during cooking. Bread, cakes, pastry, pudding, vegetables and potatoes may be cooked by this method. Whether baked in primitive or modern ways, wheat is to be first ground to a flour. In baking, for each purpose flour of a particular quality is required for bread making a hard wheat flour containing a high level of protein is required. For biscuits wheat flour with a low protein content is desirable. According to modern specifications, the flour should also contain minimum levels of nutrients such as vitamins and minerals or other ingredients.

INGREDIENTS

Depending on a nature of the baked products, different types of flours are milled. The types of flours made for baking are the following :

Bread Flour

Bread Flour should form good gluten when mixed with water, and form bread with a good volume when baked. Thus, bread flours should have a high protein content. They are milled from blends of hard winter and spring wheats and then moisture content, protoin content, ash content, starch quality, protein quality and particle size are all controlled.

Self-raising Flour

This flour is used domestically for making puddings, cakes, pastries etc. This is made from milling weak wheats of low protein content. Hard wheat up to 20% can also be used. The moisture content of the flour should not exceed 13.5% to prevent premature reaction between the chemicals present in the flour. Sodium bicarbonate and acid calcium phosphate or some other acid ingredients are the chemicals used in the ratio of 1.16% bicarbonate and 1.61% acid calcium phosphate on flour weight. A slight excess of bicarbonate gives rise to an unpleasant odour and a brownish yellow colouration.

All-purpose flour (household or family flour) is made from hard wheat or a blend of hard and soft wheats and has a moderate protein content. It does not contain self-raising agents. It is suitable for use in yeast and quick breads, biscuits, pastries and cakes. A variation of this flour is 'instantized flour' - an instant blending flour. This is made by a special agglomerating procedure whereby a number of individual flour particles are combined.

Biscuit Flour

This flour is made from weak wheats of low protein content. Depending on the type of biscuit, special types of flours are made. The flour should make a dough having more extensibility but less spring (resistance) than bread dough. Dough pieces should retain their size and shape after being stamped out. The extensibility of biscuit flour dough may be increased by treatment with a proteolytic enzyme, or with the reducing agent sulphurdioxide, or by the addition of sodium metabisulphite to the doughs.

Cake Flour

Cake flour is a medium-strength flour ground from soft low protein wheat of low α-amylase activity and is very fine in structure. The purpose of flour in cakes is to allow an aerated structure to be retained after the cake has been made. The stability of the final cake depends largely on the presence of uniformly swollen starch granules. Hence the starch granules should be undamaged during milling, free from adherent protein and unattached by amylolytic enzymes.

Pastry Flour

Pastry flours similar to cake flour are made of soft wheat and are fairly low in protein. They are finely ground and they can be used for all baked products other than breads.

Water

Water makes possible the formation of glutten.

Gluten : Gluten as such does not exist in flour. Only when flour proteins are hydrated gluten is formed. Water assists in the control of dough temperatures (warming and cooling). Water also makes possible enzyme activity.

Home baking is one of the easiest ways of cooking and nothing is more rewarding than delicious home-made cakes or cookies. The virtues of baked products are many. They are easy to make and are economical too. They pose no problem while packing, as they are light and could be easily carried. They are nutritious and are easily digestible. The retention of nutrients is better in baked products than that in fried products. Baked foods are suitable for any occasion and they suit the palate of the old and young alike. Incorporation of baked products in our daily diet is a must not only for nutritional improvement but also for enhancing the palatability and relieving the monotony of any food or diet.

Bakery industry in India is one of the most important processed food industries and also the fastest growing one. Every year nearly 0.35 million tonnes of cookies are produced and sold in Indian market. Baked products are popularly consumed as snacks by people of all classes and of all age groups. As such these products may be considered as ideal carriers for the supply of nutrients to the vulnerable groups like growing children, pregnant mothers and convolescents. Baked products even play a vital role in popularizing wheat in traditionally non-wheat-consuming regions of the world.

LEAVENING AGENTS

A leavening agent aerates the mixture and thereby lightens it. Leavening action may be produced by physical, chemical or biological means. The common leavening agents are air, steam and carbon dioxide (CO_2).

Air

Air is incorporated into flour mixtures by: beating eggs; folding and rolling doughs; creaming fat and sugar together; sifting the dry ingredients; and beating batters

Steam

Steam is probably produced in all flour mixtures to a certain degree, since all flour mixtures contain water and are usually heated to the vapourization temperature of water. Although the steam produced during baking causes the mixture to expand, steam alone cannot leaven a mixture. Its action must be combined with that of air and/or CO_2.

Carbon Dioxide

The principle means of leavening flour mixtures is by the formation of carbon dioxide generated by the action of chemical leaveners or produced from sugar by the action of yeast, microorganisms; chemical leaveners include baking powder, baking soda and ammonium carbonate.

Baking Powder

It is defined as the leavening agent produced by mixing of an acid reacting material and sodium bicarbonate, with or without the addition of starch or flour. Baking powders are classified according to their action rates. Fast acting ones give off most of their gas volume during the first few minutes of contact with liquid. When such powders are added to a mixture, the mixture must be handled quickly to avoid loss of carbon dioxide and volume. Slow acting powders gives up very little of their gas volume at low temperatures, they require the heat of the oven to react completely. Double acting baking powders begin to act at low temperatures and give viscosity and smoothness to the batter, but they do not go into complete reaction until they are exposed to high temperatures.

Baking soda

The reaction of baking soda is similar to the baking powder as a leavening agent. Carbon dioxide is released when the baking soda comes into contact with the liquid in the dough. The amount of baking soda must be only one-fourth of the amount used for baking powder in any recipe.

Yeast

Yeast helps in fermenting the dough, carbon dioxide is produced as a result and thus it helps in leavening. Yeast, a microscopic unicellular plant reproduces rapidly under suitable conditions of food, warmth and moisture. Yeast in 2 forms, i.e. compressed and dry forms are available. Dry yeast is used preferable in most of bread varieties.

Bread improver

The finest bread improver is a good craftsman. Flour is always of variable quality, depending on the grade. Bread improver may be divided into three main classes.

(i) Those of a mineral nature, mainly used by main classes.

(ii) Those of an organic nature, mainly enriching agents.

(iii) Those which, while coming under categories 1 and 2 are also valuable yeast foods, helping the yeast to work more vigorously.

Sodium chloride

The most important mineral addition to bread is common salt (sodium chloride). Salt lowers caramalization temperature of cake batter and aids in obtaining crust colour. Salt improves grain and texture of loaf by strengthening the dough.

Persulphates

The persulphates used are potassium and ammonium. Flours treated with persulphates take more water to allow for the tightening which takes place as fermentation proceeds; in this way increased yield is obtained.

Potassium bromate

Bromate has an estringent action on glutin, necessitiating the use of more water in the dough. It improves the gas-retaining properties of the gluten, and then increasing loaf volume.

Phosphates

Acid calcium phosphate and ammonium phosphate both have a tightening action on gluten, and since phosphates are necessary constituents of yeast food, they are both fermentation stimulants.

Lime water

As lime is alkaline, it reduces the acidity of the dough and then slows the speed of fermentation.

Organic acids

Lactic and succinic acids are natural constituents of a fermenting dough, so that an addition, within limits, can be made with perfect safety.

EQUIPMENT

Equipment used to measure dough quality or rheology

Rheology is the science of formation and deformation of dough and of flow of batter. It mainly includes viscosity, elasticity and plasticity. Doughtesting apparatus are of two types: dynamic and static.

Those which automatically record the properties of a dough over a period of up to 20 min. of continuous mixing may be termed dynamic. The static type record the stress and strain relationships during the short time taken to stretch a piece of dough until it breaks. The various instruments used are: recording dough mixers, load extension meters, extrusion meters, penetrometers and texturometers.

Recording dough mixers

These record the power needed to mix a dough at constant speed. The curves obtained yield information about changes in rheological (dough) properties during mixing. The curves usually consist of a rising part, showing an increase in resistance with mixing time, followed by a more or less slow decrease in resistance. The maximum is either flat or broad or peaked depending on the type of instruments and type of flour. The curves indicate the rate of dough development and subsequent breakdown. Maximum resistance indicates optimal development of the dough. The instruments commonly used are Brabender farinograph, Swanson and working mixograph. Some of them are explained below.

Farinograph

This is a dough-testing equipment of the dynamic type as the resistance offered by a dough to constant mechanical mixing under consistent test conditions is measured from the very moment the dough is formed. The graphical record thus obtained is an energy-time diagram and is a criterion on the general quality characteristics of the flow.

The instrument consists of a twin-bladed water-jacketed mixer, operated by an electric motor which is free to rotate about its axis when a torque is applied by the resistance of a dough to the action of the mixing blades. The motor housing is connected through a damping device to a pen which operates over a moving band of paper. During the mixing of a

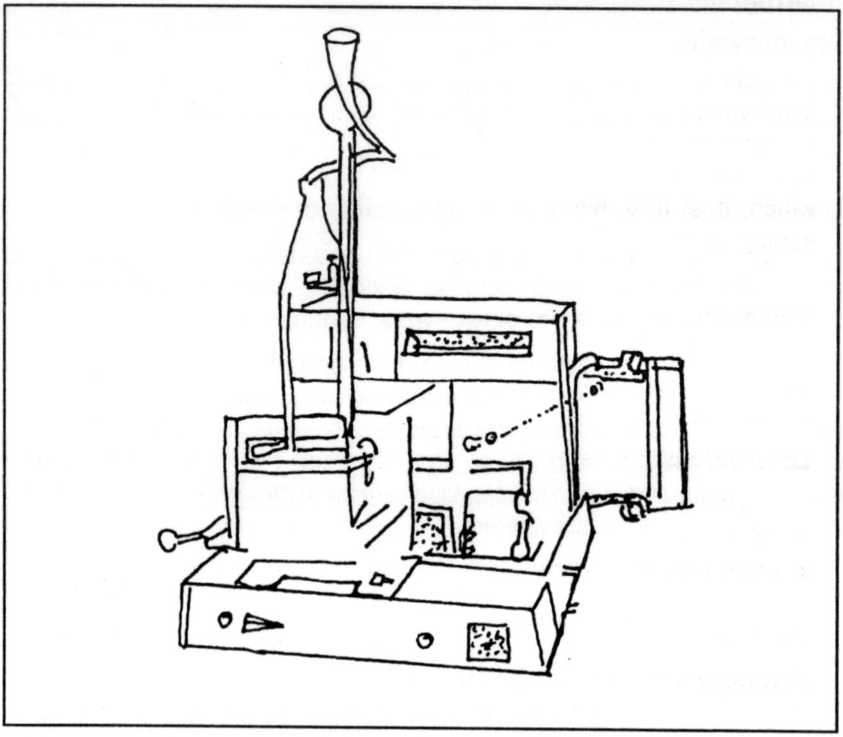

Fig. 1.1 Farinograph, a dough-testing equipment of dynamic type

wheat flour dough in this instrument, the pen traces a curve on the paper, the shape and general configuration of the curve depending on the physical properties of the dough. The paper is printed with a scale along its length indicating the time in minutes, and across its width, an arbitrary scale of 0-1,000, which measures the consistency of the dough (Fig.1.1).

A typical farinograph curve gives an idea of (a) water absorption percentage to produce a dough showing a consistency of 500 Brabender units, (b) dough developing time in minutes indicates the mixing time required by the flour, from the moment doughing up starts to the time it reaches optimal dough development and attaining at the same time maximum width of the band, (c) dough stability, in minutes, represents the time during which there are no changes in the consistency of the dough after it has reached its optimum development. The sum of dough development time and dough stability time is considered as the resistance of the dough, (d) width of the curve represents elasticity, (e) weakening of the dough is measured in farinograph units and is represented by the difference in dough compactness after a further mixing.

Mixograph

This equipment is mostly used in America and is a dynamic type. It consists of vertical cylinder (bowl), open at the top. This contains four fixed vertial pins fastened to the bottom. A head piece, which could be lowered into the cylinder also contains four pins and is rotated through flour and water kept in the bowl, dough development occurs in the cylinder which, if let free, would have rotated. This movement is restricted by a spring, so that the twist could be measured and recorded.

As the dough develops, the curve rises to a minimum. The curve then descends and as the doughing continues, a curve more or less similar to that given by a farinograph is obtained. The steepness with which the curve rises, its height and the manner in which the curve descends after the maximum are associated with above flour characteristics.

Load extension meters

These instruments measure the load required for the rupture of the dough when it is stretched. The curve of load versus stretching of dough is recorded. From these records, resistance against deformation and extensibility can be read. The instruments commonly used are Brabender extensograph, Chopin Extinsograph, Halton extensograph etc.

Alveographe (chopin extensimeter)

This is a static type of dough-testing instrument which records the stress/ strain relationships in a dough while the dough is stretched until it breaks, but it employs a different method for deforming the dough. A disc of dough is blown into a bubble by means of air pressure, and the pressure within the bubble is recorded continuously from the time the bubble starts to form until it finally ruptures. All dough tested contain the same proportion of total water. Based on the area of alveographe the flour/dough can be

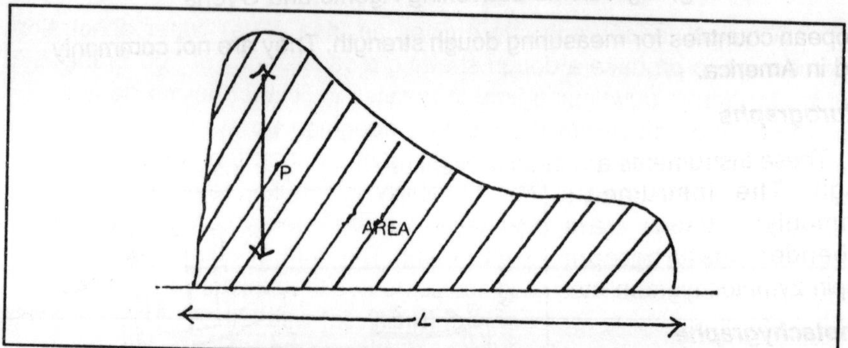

Fig. 1.2. A typical alveographe curve

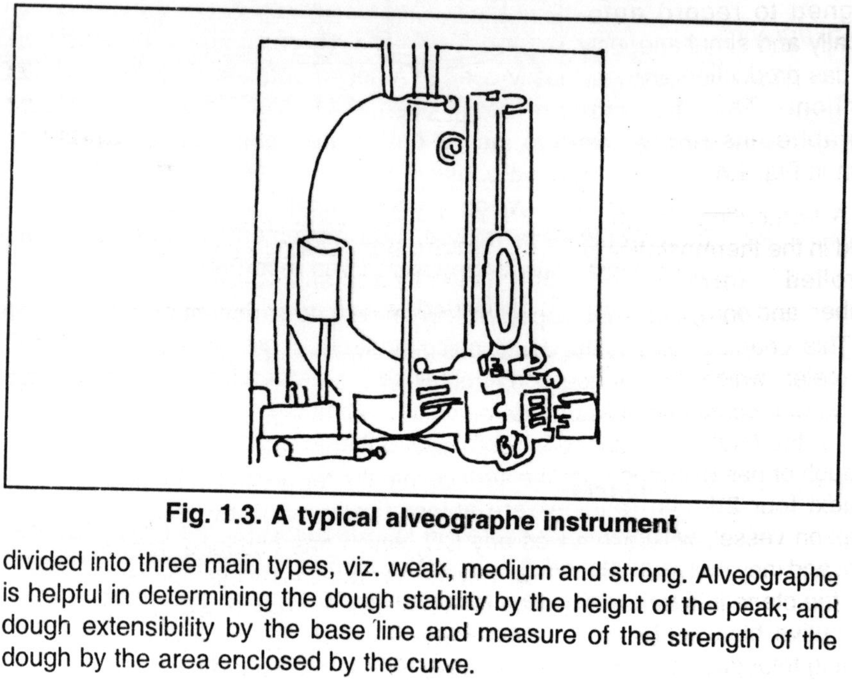

Fig. 1.3. A typical alveographe instrument

divided into three main types, viz. weak, medium and strong. Alveographe is helpful in determining the dough stability by the height of the peak; and dough extensibility by the base line and measure of the strength of the dough by the area enclosed by the curve.

A typical alveographe curve is shown in Fig.1.2 and the alveographe instrument is given in Fig.1.3.

Extrusion meters

These instruments measure the amount of force required to extrude the dough. They are not commonly used for measuring dough quality.

Penetrometers

In recent years, penetrometers are being used extensively in some

European countries for measuring dough strength. They are not commonly used in America.

Maturographs

These instruments are used to measure the properties of fermenting dough. The instruments commonly used are Brabender maturograph, Chopin zymatochygraph etc.

Zymotachygraphe

This is an instrument designed to record automatically and simultaneously both gas production and gas retention. The zymotochygraphe instrument is shown in Fig. 1.4.

Fig. 1.4. Zymotachygraphe; an instrument used to record automatically and simultaneously both production and retention of gas.

A fermenting dough is placed in the thermostatically controlled fermentation chamber, and once every 2½ min. This chamber is automatically put into connection with the water manometer, which carries a pen operating on a moving sheet of paper. The first four connections are made direct, so that the pressure recorded is that of the total as produced by the yeast, whether it is retained within the dough or has escaped from the surface into the fermentation chamber. The next four 2½ min readings are automatically made by way of an absorption vessel, which removes any CO_2 which has escaped from the dough, and they measure, therefore, only the gas retained within the dough. When the stage is reached at which dough allows the gas to escape, the consecutive blocks of four readings vary in height, the higher blocks indicating total gas produced and the lower blocks gas retained.

Barbender amylograph

The gelatinization of starch within the loaf during baking has an influence on the condition of the crumb of the baked loaf, i.e. whether it is dry, sticky or normal.

The amylograph simulates the effect of baking on starch step by step, by raising the temperature of a flour/water suspension at a constant rate, during which the starch gelatizes. A graph is recorded, the height of which is related to the viscosity of the paste. A high curve reveals a starch with a good water-binding capacity resulting in bread with a dry eating crumb. A low graph line shows a starch with a low water-binding capacity and is usually indicative of high alpha-amylase activity which will result in a damp sticky crumb. The mean between the two, shows the most suitable flour for breadmaking.

Extensometer

This instrument gives a curve which is similar in shape to that produced by the extensograph.

For the extensometer test the dough is shaped into a ball and placed upon 2 spikes, and when the instrument is set in operation the lower of these spikes moves downward while the top one remains stationary. The tension in the loop of dough that is formed, and the extent to which the

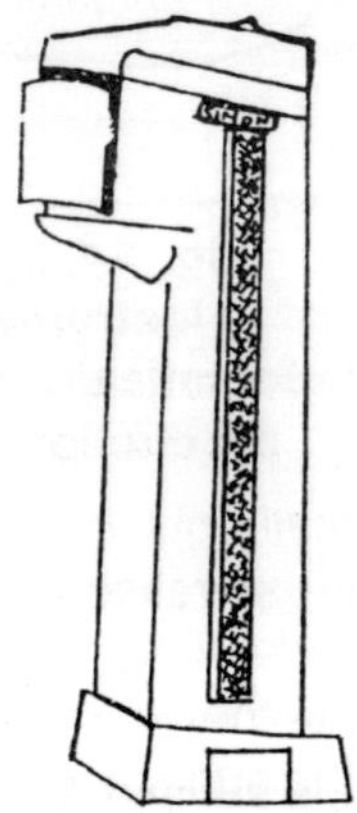

Fig. 1.5. Extensometer

dough is stretched is recorded on a moving sheet of paper until the dough breaks. As the flour is progressively treated the dough yields become progressively less extensible but more stable. This finding has led to the suggestion that the area under an extensometer curve is a measure of the potential strength of a flour. Diagramatic representation of extensometer is given in Fig.1.5.

Extensograph

The test consists of stretching a dough of culindrical form by means of a moving arm. The stress produced in the dough by its resistance to extension is recorded in a graphical form. It is suited for testing fermented dough and for studying the effect of improvement on dough.

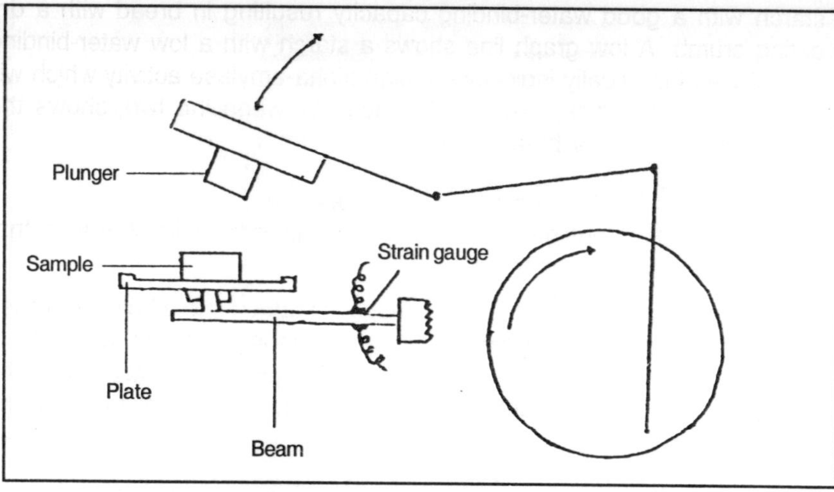

Fig. 1.6. : Principle of the general foods texturometer

Five types of doughs can be distinguished with the help of this equipment. These are plastic short dough, short and stiff dough, elastic and extensible dough, extensible dough and flowy dough.

Food texturometer

The general foods texturometer is a well-known instrument in this category. The principle of this instrument is shown in Fig.1.6.

Samples of the five biscuit types, conditioned at seven different relative humidities, were subjected to the following series of instrumental tests (a) a simple beam, centre load end support, bend test; (b) a cantilever beam, end load bend test; (c) a direct shear test; (d) a uniaxial compression test; (e) a 'bulk' compression test; (f) a uniaxial tension test; (g) a charpy impact test; and (h) an FMBRA biscuit texture meter test. The principles of tests (a) to (g) are illustrated in Fig.1.7.

TERMS COMMONLY USED IN BAKING

The terms of commonly used in Baking process as per U.S. Wheat Associates.

Aeration: The treatment of dough or batter by charging with gas to produce a volume increase.

Adhesiveness: Work necessary to overcome the attractive forces between the surface of product and adhesive material.

Bake: To cook a roast by dry heat in a closed place such as an oven.

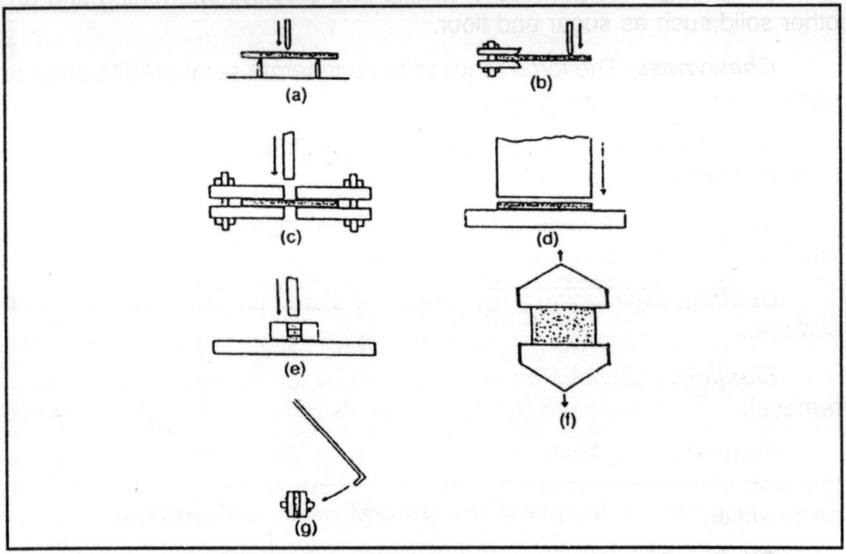

Fig. 1.7. Principles of tests applied to biscuits in the study of crispness and brittleness. (a) centre load, end support, bend test; (b) end load, end support, bend test; (c) shear test; (d) uniaxial compression test; (e) bulk compression test; (f) uniaxial tension test; (g) charpy impact test

Baking powder: A chemical leavening agent composed of soda, dry acids and corn-starch (to absorb moisture), when wet and tested carbon dioxide is given off to raise the batter during baking.

Batter: A homogenous mixture of ingredients with liquid to make a mass that is of a soft plastic character.

Bread: The accepted term for baked foods made of flour, sugar, shortening, salt and liquid, and leavened by the action of yeast.

Brittleness or crispyness: The force required to break the material

Caramelized sugar: Dry sugar heated with constant stirring until melted and dark in colour, used for flavouring and colour.

Carbon dioxide: A colourless, tasteless edible gas obtained during fermentation or form a combination of soda and acid.

Clear flour: Lower grade and higher ash content flour remaining after the petent flour has been separated.

Colours: Shades produced by the use of dyes.

Creaming: The process of mixing and creating shortening and another solid such as sugar and flour.

Chewyness: The force required to degenerate semi-solid to slaky or pasty or ready to swallow consistency.

Cohesiveness: It is the strength of the internal bonds making the body of product.

Dough: The thickened mass of combined ingredients for bread, rolls and biscuits, but usually applied to bread.

Dusting: Distributing a film of flour or starch on pans or work bench surfaces.

Elasticity: Slight deformation caused by force, retained after force removal.

Fermentation: The chemical changes of an organic compound due to action of living organisms (yeast or bacteria) usually producing a leavening action.

Gliadin: One of the two proteins comparising gluten which provides elasticity.

Gluten: The elastic protein mass that is formed when the protein material of the wheat flour is mixed with water.

Glutenin: One of the two proteins comprising gluten, which gives strength.

Greasing: Spreading a film of fat on a surface.

Hardness: Force necessary to attain a given deformation.

Hearth: The heated baking surface of the flour of an oven.

Leaveng: Raising or lighting by air, stear or gas (carbondioxide). The agent for generating gas in a dough or batter is usually yeast or baking powder.

Mix: The combined ingredients of a dough or batter.

Moulder: Machine that shapes dough pieces for various shapes.

Parker house rolls: Folded buns of fairly rich dough.

Plasticity: Material does not regain its original form even after force removal.

Proof box: A tightly closed box or cabinet equipped with shelves to permit the introduction of heat and steam used for fermenting dough.

Proofing period: The time during which dough rises between moulding and baking.

Steam: Vapour formed and given off from heated water.

Temperature: Degrees of heat or cold.

Tempering: Adjusting temperature of ingredients to a certain degree.

Troughs: Large containers usually on which used for holding large masses of raising dough.

Vienna colour: A hearth-type bread with heavy crisp crust, sometimes finished with seed tapping.

Viscosity: Rate of flow per unit force in a given time.

Yeast: A microscopic plant which reproduces by budding and causes fermentation and the giving off carbon dioxide.

TYPES OF BAKING OVENS

Various kinds of fuels can be used for heating ovens. The ovens may differ considerably in structure and they can be easily classified as coal, coke or oil-fired or heated by gas or electricity.

Internally-and externally-fired ovens

The baking chamber of an oven can be heated by the application of heat externally or internally. Internally-heated ovens of several classes still exist and all of them are to be found doing active service in various parts of the country. They are:

1. The side-flue or early prototypes of this oven
2. Small domestic gas cookers and cabinet ovens
3. Modern travelling biscuit ovens heated by gas
4. Some types of reel ovens

Other types of ovens are heated externally. This means that the fuel is burn outside the baking chamber and the heat carried by various means to inside of the oven. Goods can be baked in externally-heated ovens are being fired, and although this equally applies to internally-heated gas and electric ovens it cannot apply to those internally-heated fired with coal, coke or fueloil. The reason is that the latter produce smoke, soot, fumes, etc., which would soil the goods in the oven, whilst the flames that issue from these fuels would ignite the bread, etc. and consume it.

Side-flue and similar ovens

This class of oven may still be seen in use, particularly in India, and many people believe that bread baked in them is much better to eat than that baked in more modern types of steampipe oven. Field ovens of the kind previously used by the army, faggot ovens and Scotch chaffer ovens, as well as ordinary side-flue ovens consist of a baking chamber fitted with a door. An oven stock is present in all of them except field ovens. The method of heating varies. The field oven is filled with wooden logs which burn directly and heat the materials of which the oven is constructed as well as the clay spread thickly over the top of it and the tiled or earthen floor or sole (Fig. 1.8).

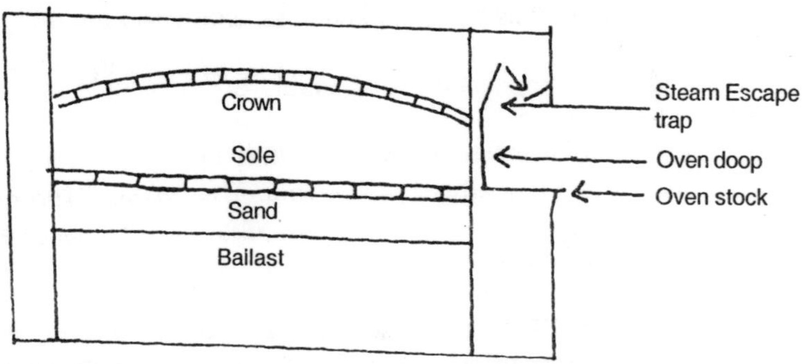

Fig. 1.8. The slide-flue oven, side elevation

When the wood has burned long enough to heat these surfaces sufficiently, the goods are placed into chamber to bake. The aperture acting as the door is closed with a metal sheet and the chinks plugged up with clay. It is very close to the faggot ovens in use in the continent in small French and Belgian village bakeries. Here the oven is usually a permanent structure, stoutly built of brick with tiled sole and arched crown. On the top of the crown a thick layer of sand is provided to act as a heat reservoir and insultator. Faggots of wood are lighted inside the oven which is also fitted with a damper and a chimney to carry off the smoke. The wood flames away whilst the dough is being scaled, handed-up and moulded and are raked out into a bin standing beneath the oven stock after proof is completed. The bin is then pushed under the oven out of the way whilst the baker swabs the sole of the very hot oven with a scuffle pole. This is a long pole to which a sack is fastened with a short length of chain. The sack is dipped into a bucket of water, then inserted into the oven and the sole well swabbed over to get rid of soot and ashes. The door is then closed for about 10 min. to allow the fine or flash heat to be absorbed by the brickwork. After this the bread is set and allowed to bake. There is no method of testing the exact temperature. The baker judges this from his experience.

The Scotch chaffer oven is similar, except that the fire is contained in a metal, basket-like affair called a chaffer. Coal is the fuel rather than wood. Another variation is the wagon oven and in this the fire is lighted in a container called a wagon which is then inserted in the oven. Finally the best form of all these ovens is the side-flue. As its name implies the fire is lighted in a furnace at one side of the oven. Coal or wood is generally used but in more recent years fuel-oil and even gas burners have been adapted to sideflue ovens. A large fire is required and good gaseous coal is needed, so that a long tongue of flame extends across and round the oven to the other side of the door where the chimney, with damper, is fitted. No method of ascertaining the temperature is available on most side-flue ovens, although pyrometers are fitted to some. The experienced baker knows when the oven is hot enough by observing that the soot-blackened back wall of the oven turns to a whitish ash colour. The baken then get rid of any flaming or smoking coals in the furnace very quickly or a lot of heat roar away up the chimney. Having a clear fire, a small bowl of water is thrown over the hot ashes which have fallen through the fire bars into the ashpit. This creates a little steam which rises, passes through the fire, becomes superheated and improves the atmosphere of the oven. The damper is closed and a period of 20 min. allowed, so that the walls, sole, and crown absorb the flash heat. The oven can then be scuffled out to clean the sole of soot and ashes before the bread is set.

Advantages of side flue ovens

Advantages of side-flue ovens are:

1. Produce bread of excellent flavour, with appetizing crusts, when skilfully operated.
2. Very cheap to maintain. Once they are properly constructed the only new fire bars occasionally and furnace-brick renewals Rarely the oven requires resoling with new oven tiles.
3. Owing to the great thickness of the walls, etc. there is a great reserve of heat which can be utilized for baking many small goods throughout the day after bread-baking completed.

Disadvantages of side-flue ovens

Disadvantages of side-flue ovenm are:

1. They are very dirty to operate.
2. Coal has to be brought into the bakehouse and ashes to be wheeled out almost daily.
3. In no sense are they continuous. When one batch of bread is drawn the oven must be refired, damped down and scuffled out before a second batch of bread can be baked.
4. When solid fuel is used they create a very unpleasant sulphury odour (sulphur dioxide) in the bakery.
5. Owing to their construction they tend to harbour hosts of blackbats, cockroaches, silver fish and crickets.

Steam-pipe ovens or steam-tube oven

The introduction of steam-pipe ovens marked a great advance on the side-flue. They rely for their heating upon a series of very strong tubes, each of which contains a small quantity of water hermetically sealed within the narrow bore running along them. By sloping the tubes slightly towards the furnace the water runs down to the end. As the tubes can be sloped towards the back, or be set transversely and therefore sloped to either side, the furnace can be arranged in any position to suit the convenience of the premises. It is not at all necessary to have the furnace inside the bakery and it is generally situated at the back of the oven in a small apartment separate from but adjoining the bakehouse.

Small pea-sized coal can be used in automatic stokers attached to these ovens, but coke, gas, or fuel-oil is quite frequently used for firing steam-pipe ovens. When the fire is lighted the water in the tubes boils and steam is produced. This cannot escape as the tubes are hermetically sealed. As heat continues to be applied more and more steam is formed, so that pressure is brought to bear on the surface of the remaining water.

As pressure increases on the surface of a liquid, its boiling point increases. Steam creates pressure which raises the boiling point of the water from 100°-100.6°C. Apply heat continuously to raise the boiling point of water as high as 260°C. This heat is equal throughout the length of the tube, though heat is applied only at one end, and the whole oven is heated. Rows of these tubes are placed under the oven crown and just under the sole to heat the top and the bottom of the oven (Fig. 1.9).

The tubes are evenly spaced apart. In some of the earlier ovens of this type the tube-ends extend into a furnace running right across the back or along the whole length of the side of the oven. In such cases, it is important that fire is spread evenly along the whole length of furnace or tubes which are not near enough to the fire will not be properly heated and

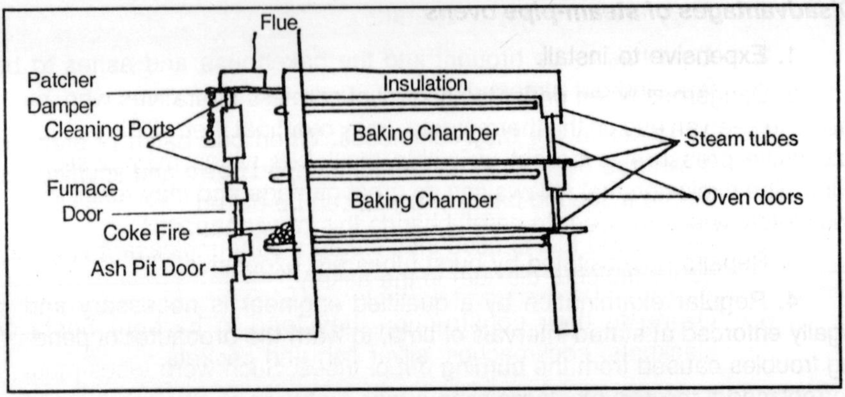

Fig. 1.9. The steam tube oven. Coke fired.

the oven will be unevenly heated. In better-planned more modern ovens the tubes are bent around to form a compact bank in a small furnace. This arrangement is excellent for all- practical purposes, evenly heats the oven and uses less fuel.

As the furnace in this type of oven is in a compartment built outside the baking chamber with which it has no connection except for the tubes which pass through the dividing wall, no fumes reach the baking chamber and baking can proceed at the same time as firing of the oven is being carried out. Thus one batch of bread can follow closely on another. No ashes or soot get into the oven so that it is not necessary to use a scuffle pole and swab after the baking of each batch, but this should be done occasionally to remove any debris accumulating in the oven.

Advantages of steam-pipe ovens

Following are the advantages:

1. Continuous baking is possible.

2. They are clean to work.

3. Thermometers and pyrometers can be used with safety and are generally fairly reliable.

4. No fumes collect in the bakery hence working conditions are more comfortable and congenial.

5. No fuel enters and no ashes have to be wheeled out through the bakehouse.

6. Economical in the use of fuel.

Disadvantages of steam-pipe ovens

1. Expensive to install.

2. Dangerous when under the control of careless operatives who, by failure to keep an eye on the thermometer, may overheat them. This causes excessive pressure to be set up within the tubes which may possibly burst. The explosion that follows can do great damage and may result in a completely wrecked oven. In careful hands this rarely happens.

3. Repairs necessitated by burst tubes are expensive.

4. Regular examination by a qualified engineer is necessary and legally enforced at stated intervals of time, to warn the proprietor of pending troubles caused from the burning out of tubes. Such worn tubes must be replaced if the oven is to maintain a high standard of efficiency.

5. Much time is needed to raise or lower the temperature to any great extent.

Hot air ovens

There are various patterns of patented ovens, heated by hot-air currents passing through ducts concealed in their soles, crowns and side walls. These ovens are continuous, for the furnace and all hot air ducts are outside the actual baking chamber (Fig. 1,10). There is no possibility of explosion, otherwise the advantages and disadvantages are similar to those of the steam-pipe oven.

Peel and drawplate ovens

Whichever form of continuous-baking oven is chosen it can be had in a variety of designs. There is ordinary peel oven which has no moving

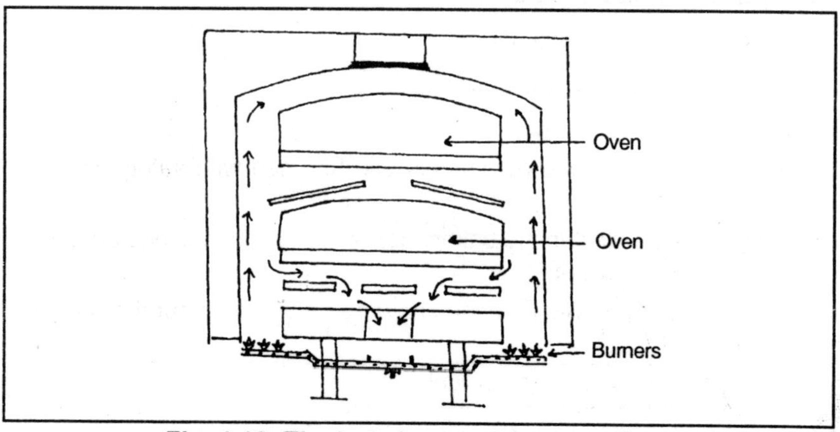

Fig. 1.10. The hot air oven (cross section)

parts and is simply an improvement on the side-flue oven. This type of oven can be had as a one-, two-, three-, four-, and five-decker. So also can be sideflue although a double-decker side-flue is generally the limit in this direction. Each deck may be arranged for independent heating, so that it is possible to bake goods which require vastly different temperatures at the same time, e.g. a batch of bread at 237.8°C in one oven and a batch of slab cakes at 182.2°C in the other.

The next variation is the drawplate. In this type the sole of the oven consists of a stout metal plate running on suitable apparatus and capable of being pulled out to its fullest extent into the bakery where it can be loaded as desired and then be pushed back gently into place again. Such an arrangement inevitably loses much heat both on account of the door having to be the whole width of the oven and the loss, by radiation, from the heated plate on withdrawal. Despite this, drawplate ovens are very good and bake bread perfectly.

Vienna ovens

The vienna oven is different from all others in that its sole slopes at a considerable angle upwards from the door to the back, though not as steeply as indicated by the accompanying diagram. When the door is opened little or no steam can escape, the latter rising so being trapped in the higher portion of the baking chamber. It is therefore possible to open the oven door and to insert bread and rolls continually without losing much steam during the process.

At the top of the slope there is a steam-escape damper. This can be opened at the appropriate time to enable the steam to be drawn off. Fig. 1.11 gives the principles of Vienna oven.

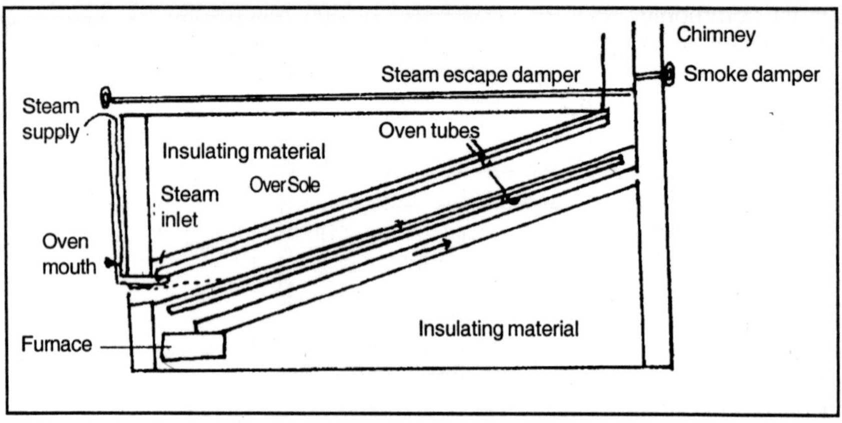

Fig. 1.11. The Vienna oven steam tube

Apart from these items of construction there is a little difference between Vienna and ordinary bread ovens. They can be fired by any of the fuels and can be of the steam-pipe or hot-air pattern. If the oven is a steampipe model then the furnace is usually at the front.

Adapting an ordinary oven for baking Vienna bread

Some form of steam trap must be devised to keep the steam back when the oven door is opened to admit the loaves or rolls. The best method is to have a metal plate cut to fit the contour of the oven mouth but leaving a gap 3.81-7.62 cm wide between the bottom edge of the steam trap and the bottom of the oven. Through this narrow space the rolls or loaves can be inserted without scraping the tops of them. In order to keep the steam trap in position two bolts must be fixed into the arch of the oven mouth but should not be screwed right home. This leaves about 0.317 cm of the body of each bolt available for forked metal clips to slide between the heads of the bolts and the metal framework of the oven mouth. The clips are riveted at right angles to the metal steam trap, so that the latter can be clipped into position when the oven is required for the baking of Vienna bread. The other point to bear in mind is that the bolts must be placed so that when the steam trap is in use the oven door can be properly closed.

Travelling ovens

The various travelling ovens, including the rotary and reel types, in which either the sole of the oven, or swinging shelves on which the goods can be placed, travel continuously through the baking chamber. All kinds of arrangements are possible. In some the ovens are of great length and the endless steel sole (usually called the 'band') travels at the required speed through the lengthy baking chamber, discharging correctly-baked goods at the opposite end to that at which they entered. This type is now most commonly used for large-scale biscuit baking and for swiss roll production. In others the goods travel on baking sheets carried along by a pair of endless chains or metal belts. The trays are placed in position, carried through the oven by the mechanism and taken off as they emerge at the other end. In this type of oven, which is largely used in confectionery manufacturing, two or three separate rows of baking sheets may be passing abreast along the oven at the same time. Still another variation, to be seen in use as part of an automatic bread-making plant, consists of an arrangement of swinging trays or shelves which pass a single aperture. At this position they are both loaded and unloaded.

All types of travelling ovens can be heated by coke, electricity, gas, fuel oil or fine coal fed to the oven mechanically by an automatic stoker. Choice of fuel, and therefore of design, needs much consideration before a new oven is installed.

Chapter - 2

Biscuits, Breads and Rolls

BISCUITS

The biscuit industry has made rapid progress in recent years in India and several other developing countries. Successful attempts have been made to enrich biscuits with proteins, vitamins and minerals. Various formulations are given in Table 2.1.

Table 36. Formula for various biscuits

Ingredients	Salt (g)	Sweet (g)	Fruit (g)	Coconut (g)
Flour	260	170	115	200
Fat	100	85	100	100
Sugar	50	85	30	100
Egg	50	-	20	50
Ammonium bicarbonate	4	-	-	-
Baking power	3	2	3	3
Milk	-	70-100 ml	-	-
Essence	-	Few drops	Few drops	Few drops
Water	25 ml	-	-	-
Coconut(desiccated)	-	-	-	50
Tuity-fruity	-	-	30	-
Cashew nuts	-	-	25	-

Method

- Sift flour with baking powder thrice.
- Cream butter and sugar till light and fluffy adding essence.
- Add flour to make pliable dough.
- Roll out into 0.31 cm thickness and cut with a biscuit cutter.
- Separate the biscuits.
- Bake at 195°C for 15 min.

Important points to remember in making different types of biscuits.

Salt biscuits : Add baking powder, salt and ammonium bicarbonate to the creamed mixture. Coat with egg before baking.

Fruit biscuits : Add cleaned and chopped fruits in the flour.

Coconut biscuits : Add desiccated coconut to the flour and some at the time of rolling.

Masala biscuits : Add 10 g masala powder in the flour, sieve twice.

Tri-colour biscuits : Sandwitch a plain biscuit with one hole using a thin layer of jam. Sprinkle with icing sugar and fill each hole with different coloured jam in each hole.

BREAD

Bread industry in India is growing rapidly to meet increasing demand of bread which has gained popularity in the Indian diet because of its availability at reasonably cheaper rate. A good bread can be prepared from four basic essential ingredients, i.e. wheat flour (maida), yeast, salt and water. Maida quality plays an important role in the production of bread. Many additives are used during mixing the dough which within limit corrects dough strength by conferring stability to the gluten to form a fine network and structure of bread. Certain additives are added to improve the nutritional quality of bread. There are common procedures

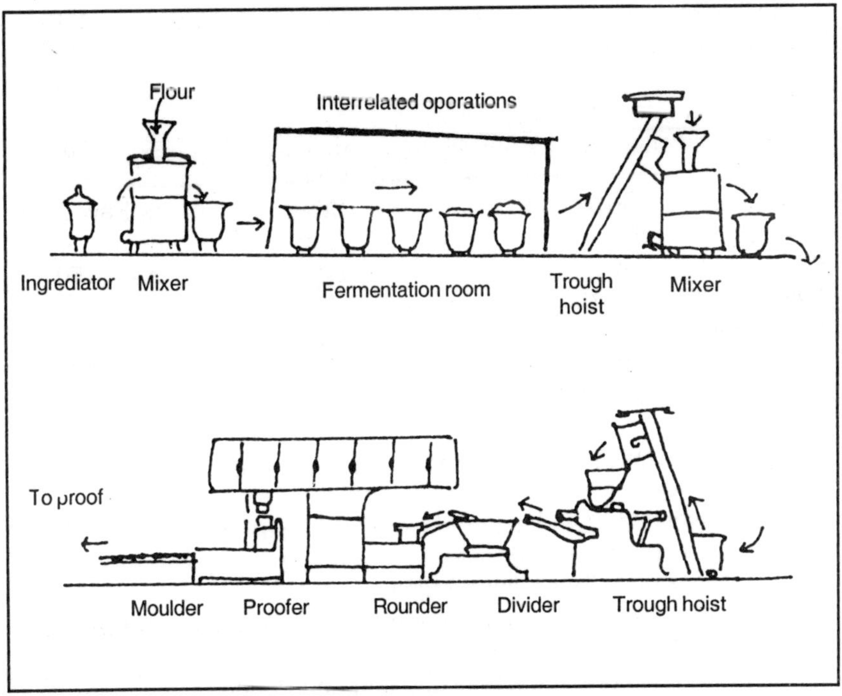

Fig. 2.1. Process of bread-making.

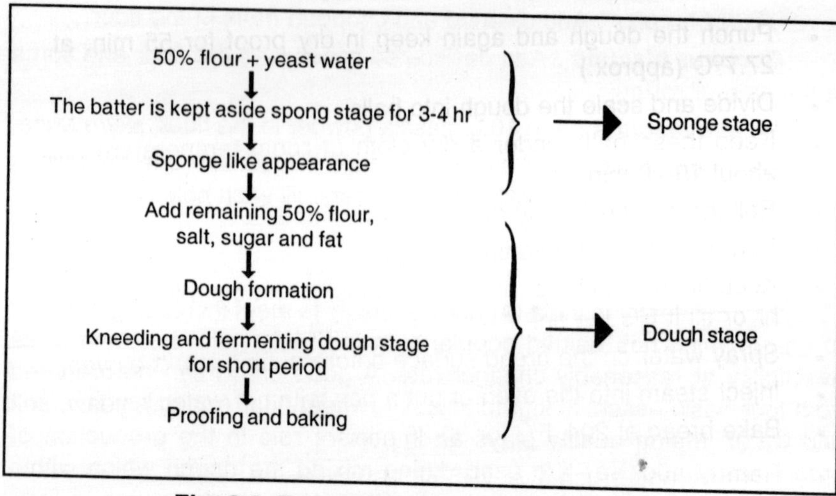

Fig. 2.2. Proces of sponge bread-making

for bread making and it includes certain steps (Fig.2.1). Sponge bread-making includes different steps (Fig.2.2).

The common method of preparation of bread using various ingredients is given below.

Bread

Ingredient	Normal straight dough	No time dough	Tin bread
Maida	300 g	300 g	200 g
Fat	8 g	10 g	6.6 g
Salt	5 g	5 g	3.3 g
Sugar	10 g	15 g	10 g
Fresh yeast	6 g	6 g dry	8 g
Water	180 ml	180 ml	180 ml

Method

- Mix yeast in lukewarm water and keep aside. Add a teaspoon of sugar.
- Dissolve salt and sugar in remaining water and strain.
- Sieve the flour. Mix water in which salt and sugar have been dissolved with the flour roughly.
- Add yeast mixture to the flour and knead to a smooth and soft dough add more water, if necessary.
- Cream the fat and knead it to form the dough.
- Keep the dough in the dry prover at 27.7°C for 1 hr 30 min. to 2 hr.

- Punch the dough and again keep in dry proof for 55 min. at 27.7°C (approx.)
- Divide and scale the dough into balls.
- Keep these balls under a dry cloth at room temperature for about 15-20 min.
- Roll the mold either by machine or by hand.
- Pour in greased bread tin.
- Keep tin in wet prover at 35°C or under a wet cloth for about 1 hr or till it fills the tin.
- Spray water on the bread surface before putting into the oven.
- Inject steam into the oven or put a pan with hot water inside.
- Bake bread at 204.4°C for 30-35 min.
- Remove and brush over with oil.

If dry prover is not available, allow dough to ferment till it becomes double the volume.

Types of bread

Whole meal bread (brown bread); wheat germ bread; gluten bread - high protein bread; high fibre bread; Granary bread; banana bread; bread rolls; short bread; white bread; dinner rolls.

Baking process involves heat transfer (Fig.2.3) and it is by conduction, convection and radiation. Various sources of enery are direct fire, indirect fire and steam.

43.3°C (110°F) oven spring

↓

62.8°C (145°F) yeast activity ceases

↓ Sugar caramelizes; protein denaturation

71.1°C (160°F) starch getalinization

↓

76.7°C (117°F) crumb structure set

↓

82.2°C (180°F) moisture loss (8-10%)

Fig. 2.3. Changes in dough at different temperature during baking of bread

Common defects in bread

The defects could be in external appearance or internal load.

External defects : The external defects are: general insufficient or excessive loaf volume, light or dark crust colour; blisters on excessive crust thickness and absence of break and shred.

Internal defects : The internal defects are : gray crumb colour, streaky crumb, cores (dense spots in the crumb), holes in crumb, poor flavour and rapid staling and poor keeping quality.

BREAD ROLLS

Formulation for rolls differ widely, however, regular bread dough may be used to make rolls of good quality. Basic formulae for rolls are as follows:

Bread-rolls formulae

Ingredient	Standard hot rolls	Quick raised yeast roils	Hard rolls (based on French bread formula)	Soft rolls (adapted from standard hot roll recipe)	Puff rolls
Flour, hard wheat (g)	100.00	100.00	100.00	85.00	100.00
Flour, soft wheat				15.00	
Water (ml) (variable)	40.00	26.09	56.67	62.00	76.19
Yeast (g)	1.24	2.85	1.85	3.00	4.76
Salt (g)	1.69	2.17	1.67	1.75	0.60
Sugar, total (g)	9.44	9.78	2.92	8.00	9.52
Shortening (g)	10.00	13.04	2.08	12.00	19.07
Milk (ml)	132.22*	65.22		5.00	9.52**

'Evaporated:**non-fat dry.

The steps in roll production are the same as for bread production. Different kinds of bread rolls available are sandwich rolls, pan rolls, winner (or finger) rolls, parker house rolls, clover leaf rolls, twin rolls, butterhorn rolls, poppy seed or sesame seed rolls. The steps in roll preparation are the same as for bread preparation like weighing and measuring of ingredients, mixing, fermentation, dividing, scaling, rounding, intermediate proof, makeup, panning, pan proof baking and cooling.

Makeup of bread rolls

Steps in making bread rolls are:

Sandwich rolls: Makeup is as follows (Fig.2.4): Divide dough into 1.5 kg pieces. Round up and let rest 15 min. From each piece of dough into a rope 2.54 cm in diameter. Cut strips of dough into pieces weighing approximately 50 g each (step1). Round the 50-g pieces into balls by rolling them with a circular motion on the workbench (step 2). Place rolls in rows on a greased baking sheet 3.80-5 cm apart. Proof for 15 min.Flatten rolls with fingers to the desired thickness and finish proofing (step 3).

Problems associated with bread-roll preparation

Temperature: Temperature control is of paramount importance.

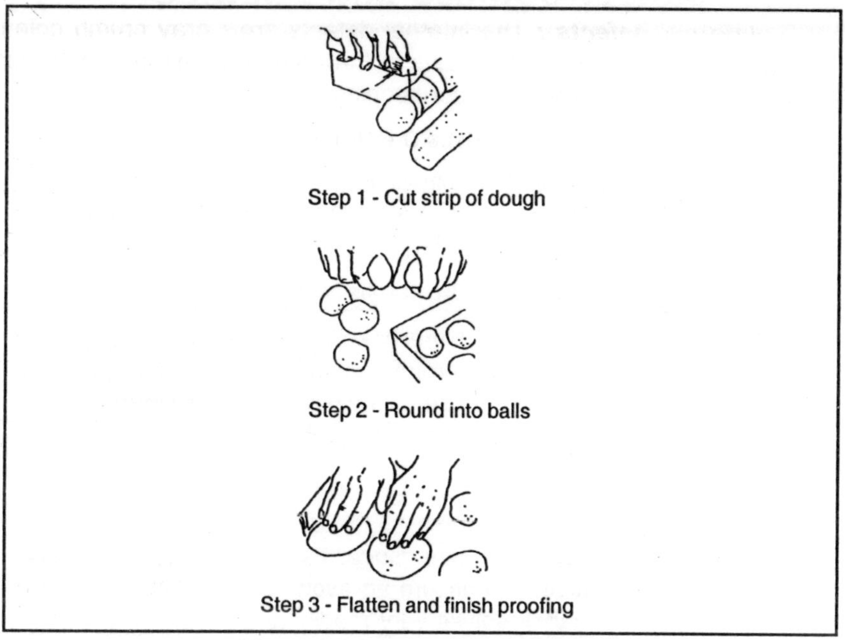

Fig. 2.4. Makeup of plain rolls

Dough temperature should remain at 26.7°C. Too high temperature will cause dough to ferment too rapidly and rolls become sour or yeasty tasting. However, too low temperature causes heavy tough rolls.

Fermentation: The amount of time needed depends on the amount of yeast and sugar used. In quick-raised rolls, for example about twice more yeast is used and only one formulation period is required because there is no makeup. Proof time is only of 30 min. duration.

Scaling and shaping : Makeup of bread rolls constitutes the major step in production. The variety of shapes possible with soft and hard rolls is most endless. Accurate scaling of dough and skilled manipulation of it in forming shapes is required by the baker.

Proofing : Since rolls are considerably smaller in size than loaf bread, proofing time is very critical in terms of volume, time required and overproofing. Other than these points discussed, problems in bread roll production do not differ from those in bread production.

Chapter - 3

Cakes, Cookies and Pastries

CAKE

The basic ingredients of a cake are divided into two types-the ones that give structure to the cake-flour, eggs and milk; and the ones that make the cake tender-sugar, shortening and baking powder.

Ingredients of cake are:

Flour

Flour provides structure for the cake as well as holds the other ingredients together. Flour with a protein content of 9%, a fine grain and well bleached is most suitable for use as a cake flour. Bleaching helps the flour carry more sugar, water and shortening. The pH of the flour should be around 5.2.

Sugar

Sugars are used as sweetners. Sugar used for all types of cakes should be of fine granulation to ensure an even grain and soft texture in cakes. This type of sugar dissolves very readily and produces a smooth creamy mass. Large sugar crystals produce a coarse texture. When creaming the sugar and shortening, best results are obtained by using dissolved sugar in milk or water. Eggs and sugar are best beaten when equal amounts of each are used. Sugar has a mellowing or tenderizing effect on the cell structure and when too high a percentage is used the cakes are quite apt to sag in the centre or fall. Shortening also has this effect. Sugars like invert sugar, honey, molasses and glucose are hygroscopic. These sugars not only help to retain moisture but also impart a characteristic flavour to the product. Sugars lower the caramelization point of the batter, allowing the cake crust to colour at a lower temperature.

Shortening

Shortening for cakes should have good creaming properties, a neutral flavour and odour. It should have excellent emulsifying properties and should be white in colour. It should be elastic when used at temperatures between 21.1° and 23.9°C. Butter is considered to be best of all baking shortenings in view of flavour. The creaming quality of butter is rather poor. Cakes made with butter are generally lower in volume and have a coarser grain than those made with a high quality shortening with good creaming characteristics.

For this reason some bakers use part butter in formula for the flavour it contributes, and part shortening for increase in volume and finer grain. Shortening also helps to retain moisture in the finished cake.

Eggs

Eggs and flour form a skelton which acts as support to the framework of a cake. Fresh eggs have pH 7.0--7.5 and if allowed to stale the pH can change to a low acid condition which will throw the leavening action of the formula out of balance. Eggs also contribute moisture, flavour and colour to the product in which they are used. Beating of eggs is very important. They should be beaten so that they will hold a fairly good crease. This is made by running a pallet knife through the beaten mass. Lecithin in yolk gives the yolk-emulsifying properties.

Milk

Milk when used as dry milk solids adds richness and structure to cake. The milk sugar lactose regulates the crust colour. Milk solids improve the flavour and are good moisture-retaining agents. The water in liquid milk contributes to the eating qualities.

Water

Water regulates the consistency of the batter. It also develops the protein in the flour which acts to retain the gas from the baking powder. The water also acts as a leavening agent, creating vapour pressure when the internal batter temperature reaches 208°F (68.6°C) during baking. Water adds moisture to the cake and in that way regulates the eating qualities of the finished cake.

Salt

Salt is one of the cheapest ingredients. It has the property of bringing out flavours. It helps in palatability of baked products and, therefore, should be used with good judgement. It also lowers caramelization temperature of cake batters and aids in obtaining crust colour.

Flavour

Due to the variations in strength of flavour it is not possible to set any given amount to be used. It is much better to use a small amount of good flavour than to load up the cake with a poor flavour. Flavouring ingredients are of 3 basic types, i.e. spices, extracts and emulsions. The spices are granular powders of roots, bark, seeds and blossoms of aromatic plants. Extracts are alcoholic solutions containing aromatic flavours.

Emulsions are colloidal systems of volatile, essential oils dispersed with water and stabilized by gum plants.

Leavening

Cakes are leavened in 3 ways, i.e. by incorporating air during mixing, by use of chemical leavening agents and by vapour pressure created in the oven. The manner of leavening depends on the type of cake being made in regard to richness of formula, consistency of batter and baking temperature.

Sponge cake

Sponge cakes depend mainly on the whipping of eggs for their lightness or aeration. This lightness is produced by a thorough beating of the eggs which causes formation of air bubbles. Due to heat, air and moisture in these, bubbles expand during baking, causing the rising action. There are 2 types of sponge cakes-one which contains eggs, sugar, flour, salt and flavour and is known as a straight sponge. The other type contains the ingredients of a straight sponge and milk, shortening, water, leavening, etc. and is known as short sponge.

Eggs are the most important ingredients in the sponge cakes, therefore great care must be taken in their selection. They must be of good quality, fresh and of a pleasing flavour. Duck eggs do not produce very satisfactory results. It has been found that when eggs are heated at 37.8°-48.9°C they will produce the best results. Care must be taken that eggs are not overheated, to avoid coagulation and production of an inferior product. Sugar has a mellowing or tenderizing effect on the cell structure of the cake and when too high a percentage is used the cakes will sag in the centre or fall. Granulated sugar gives best results. Equal parts of egg and sugar should be used for beating purposes. Any excess sugar should be either dissolved in the liquid or may be replaced by powdered sugar and sifted with the flour. When high sugar content is used a sugary crust develops. Therefore, dissolving most of the sugar will help eliminate this trouble. Soft bleached flour produced from soft wheat is generally used in the manufacture of sponge cakes. The colour of the flour though not important should be preferably white. In orde· to eliminate flour pellets in the cake, it is best to sift the flour just before adding it to the beaten eggs-sugar mixture.

Shortening provides better eating qualities to the sponge cake. However, shortening has a mellowing effect on the cells structure of the cakes and when used in large quantities will produce a cake lacking volume. Therefore, correct amount should be incorporated. When shortening is not incorporated properly streaks will be found in the cake. These streaks will give the cakes an off colour. Leavening and flour should be thoroughly sifted together so that they will be well blended. At higher altitudes it is necessary to decrease the amount of leavening agent. If the cakes contain a large percentage of acid, a coarse porous cell structure will result. Sponge cake batter breaks down readily on adding flour or other ingredients. Great care must be taken not to mix any more than absolutely necessary. When the batter is overmixed it breaks down, resulting in a tough cake which will draw away from the bottom. Likewise, undermixing results in a cake with low volume and rough texture. Therefore, sponge cake should be mixed enough, so that the ingredients are incorporated smoothly and evenly. Addition of moisture to sponge cake improves their keeping and eating qualities, but when used in excess, the cake lacks volume and may even collapse while baking. The flour used should be of good quality. The amount used must be measured carefully to produce uniform results. All ingredients should be closely checked for off- flavours. Most bakery ingredients absorb odours readily and, therefore, must be carefully stored away from any source of contamination. Many bakers overlook the possibility of boxes and wrappers having an off odour. It is wise to investigate this factor. Quality fillings should be used at all times. The keeping quality of these fillings is of great importance and should be closely checked.

When the pans are greased too heavily the fat will run over the sides of the cake on to the top crust producing an unappetizing appearance. Batter should be placed in pans ensuring that there will be no air trapped underneath the batter. Due to heat air expands resulting in hallow spots under the cake. Trapping the pans lightly will reduce this source of trouble. Sponge cakes both straight and short are baked at a higher temperature ranging from 187.8°-232.2°C, depending on the type and size of the cake.

When cakes come out of the oven they are sterile as far as mold is concerned. Mold infection is due to contamination after baking. Mold spores are present in the air at all times and their concentration should be kept as low as possible. Cleanliness is very important in eliminating this source of trouble. Cake should not be cooled in a draft or by the blowing of air by fan, as this will cause excessive drying out, unless draft is carefully controlled. Cake should be cooled so that air is able to circulate freely above and beneath them. When cakes are cooled improperly the top crust will become sticky and will peel off. Good boxes and wrappers also keep the cakes from drying out fast or excessively. All pans used be washed and rinsed thoroughly, so that they will be free from foreign odours. Many bakers overlook this important point. Cleanliness pays dividends.

Fruit cake

The term fruit covers wide area depending on the amount of fruits to be used. This amount of fruits could vary from 30 to 300% in relation to the weight of the batter. Whereas the fruit cake will not have more than 30% fruits in relation to the weight of the cake batter. The difference between the fruit cakes and cakes with fruits is that in fruit cake the batter separates the fruit from coming intimately in contact with each other and acts as a filler, while in cakes with fruit the pieces of fruits are scattered throughout. The type and amount of fruits and nuts to use will depend on several factors, mainly the price and ready availability. The cakes containing larger percentage of fruits will definitely be of better eating quality than the one with less fruit. But at the same time higher the percentage of fruits mixture, lower will be resultant volume than a cake of the same weight with a smaller percentage of fruit because of the dead weight of the fruits in relation to the lower percentage of cake batter.

There are several types of fruits and nuts which could be used in the preparation of a fruit cake. To prevent spoilage of fruits during transit and storage these are processed. Fruits like raisins, dates, sultanas are preserved by drying, while other fruits like pineapple, peaches, apples, cherries and orange peels are saturated with sugar to prevent spoilage. These are termed as glazed or candied fruits. Generally moisture in fruits is approximately 20% or less compared to 32% moisture in cake crumb structure. Therefore, almost all fruits should be soaked before use to soften and tenderize their skins, to remove the hard sugar coating and to cause them to absorb sufficient moisture for improved eating qualities. Soaking not only improves the quality of fruit but also increases the yield. Moreover, the fruits which have been soaked previously do not draw moisture from the cake structure and keep the product in good condition for a longer time. The dried fruits which have been soaked in moisture should be thoroughly drained before using. Nuts should not be soaked as they soften and become rubbery and their colour will also be affected adversely. The flour used for making fruit cakes should have enough strength to carry a high percentage of fruits, sugar, moisture and other materials. A high grade cake flour containing 7-9% proteins is recommended. This type of flour will help the fruit from sinking. Avoid the dusting of fruit mixture with flour. Dusting of the fruit will give the cake poor inside appearance. The best results are obtained when the ingredients are used at a temperature which will give the finished batter temperature of about 21.1°C. The shortening used be kept at 21.1°C and the milk and eggs at about 15.6°C. Shortening used for cake work should have good creaming qualities, neutral flavour and odour, and excellent emulsifying powers. (Emulsification is the process of blending together fat and water solutions of ingredients to produce a stable mixture which will not separate on standing). Emulsification helps produce cakes which are more tender, of finer grain, moist and with less tendency to dry out. A small percentage of butter can be used along with the shortening. Due to the presence of higher percentage of fruits of various types, nuts as well as extracts, it may be quite hard to detect butter flavour, however. The leavening content in fruit cakes is generally low. The volume is obtained through the air and moisture incorporated during the mixing of the batter.

The fruit cakes generally are decorated with various designs, made with nuts and fruits. Whether this should be carried just before the baking or after finishing baking is a matter of choice. But preferably it should be done soon after the cake is out of the oven. It will prevent the nuts from getting scorched and discoloured and the fruits will stay soft. It also produces a lively fresh appearance. Fruit cakes may be washed immediately after baking with a glucose preparation for extra gloss. The glucose preparation is made by boiling one part of glucose and one part water together and using it while cakes are still hot as they are removed from the oven. If the cakes are washed with glucose solution and then decorated at once the fruit and nuts will stick on very nicely. Another wash with glucose solution after the design is placed will enhance the appearance.

Before baking is done it is always better to check whether the batter is well packed in the pans so as to avoid holes in the cakes and unfilled corners. It is considered good practice to moisten the back of the hand and smooth the surface of the cakes before baking. This will eliminate the possibility of fruit, such as raisins exposed to the direct heat to caramelize and cause an objectionable taste.

Fruit-cakes should be baked at a temperature of 229-330°F depending on the richness of the formula and the size and shape of the cake. If oven is not equipped to inject steam during baking, place the cake pans in a shallow tray containing water just sufficient enough to cover one-fourth of the height of the cake pan. This will not only help create steam in the oven but will also prevent the charring of the fruit-cake at the bottom as well as on the surface during the prolonged baking. Trays with water should be removed when the cakes are half done. Presence of steam will produce a cake having softer crust, prevent excessive drying. In scaling allow 75 g additional batter for baking loss to each kg of batter. A good quality fruit-cake should not crumble even when thinly sliced and should be moist for good eating qualities.

Angel cake

The basic ingredients of angel food cake are flour, sugar and egg. The other ingredients are salt, flavourings and cream of tartar or an acid. The proportion of sugar in the cake mix is high because no other tenderizer is used. Sugar interferes with gluten development and thus tends to produce more tender and fragile cake. Sugar also has a stabilizing effect on egg - white foam and allows more beating without the over coagulation of the white proteins. Cream of tartar is added to egg-whites for angel food cake as it makes the cake whiter, finer in grain and more tender than it would be without it.

Chiffon cakes

Chiffon cakes usually contain a larger proportion of egg than shortened cakes and an oil. The cake is prepared by sifting together the dry ingredients followed by the addition of the oil, egg-yolk, liquids and flavourings and the whole mixture is well-blended. The whites are then beaten with the cream of tartar until the peaks just bend over; the batter is carefully but thoroughly folded into the beaten whites. The cakes are then baked in the usual way.

Off flavours in cakes: causes and prevention

Flavour and taste are the most outstanding characteristics of a good cake. The flavour and taste depend on the ingredients, proper pan care, storage and packaging, and use of icings and fillings.

Ingredients

Most of the cake ingredients will absorb foreign odours. Therefore, they must be stored carefully away from all possible contamination. In a store room the strong flavoured ingredients should be kept in an air-tight containers to avoid intermingling of flavours. A low-grade baking powder will have a residue which has an objectionable flavour. In chocolate cakes baking soda is used to produce red brown colour. The effect on the flavour is not objectionable if a correct quantity of soda is added.

Proper pan care

Dirty pans are the causes of off flavour in cakes. To overcome this defect pans should be washed after each baking. Off flavour can also be caused by improper pan grease.

Storage and packaging

Avoid storing cakes in mouldy and musty cabinets. The show-case should be spotlessly clean and odourless. Foreign odours may be due to the wrappers or boxes used for packing. Varieties of cakes soon after baking should not be cooled on the same rack.

ICINGS AND FILLINGS

Icing may mask a number of faults. But do not ice the cakes which are overbaked or burned. Icings should be made fresh each day. The use of lowgrade jams and jellies will also cause off flavours. Mouldy or rancid left-over cake crumbs when used will not improve flavour.

Besides the off flavours the baker should recognize the cake faults such as shape faults, structural faults, texture faults, crust faults, colour faults and miscellaneous faults and find the solutions by a process of eliminating the possible causes.

Icings

Icings are sweet coverings-plain or with vivid pattern in which sugar is the main ingredient. Type of an icing depends on the materials used in the preparation as well as the method of mixing. There are various types of icing which can be classified under 2 groups:

1. The icings which are like flat icings including a fondant are melted by heat and when cooled get set to a firm coating. Fondants contain a high proportion of small sugar crystals that partially dissolve on warming and recrystalize on cooling.

2. The highly aerated icings composed of a creamed mixture of shortening, confectioners sugar, water, salt, flavour, eggs and milk powder. These are more suitable for spreading and piping where aeration or whipping is used to produce icings of stiff, non-flowing consistency.

The basic ingredients of icings are sugar, shortening, dried milk powder, eggs and stabilizers.

Sugar

Various types of sugars can be included in the preparation of icings, powdered sugar or confectioners sugar, being the most common. Invert sugar, corn sugar and glucose are also used in flat icings to control the size of sugar particles.

Shortening: Emulsified or hydrogenated shortening is usually used in cream type icings. Shortening should be neutral in taste and flavour. Butter is also used in combination with shortening due to its characteristic flavour. Butter alone cannot be creamed to give an equal volume as shortening.

Dried milk powder: Milk powder provides a structure to the icing as well as enhances taste and flavour of icing. It also helps to absorb moisture. Fresh milk is not recommended due to its perishable nature. Milk powder should always be sieved along with sugar to avoid the lumps. In case lumps are present it will be difficult to pipe the icing with a fine nozzle.

Eggs: Eggs should be fresh. They constitute to the volume, taste and flavour of the icing. They should be blended carefully with creamed mixture to avoid curdling.

Stabilizers: Various types of stabilizers are used in icing, mainly to absorb excess moisture. By holding moisture a stabilizer can avoid sugar crystalization. It can also eliminate stickiness during hot humid weather. Stabilizers may be vegetable gums, tapioca starch, pectin and wheat or corn starch. Water is used to dissolve sugar in preparation of icings. Water also permits the boiling of sugar without burning. Flavours and colours should be used wisely and carefully. Salt, when used in small quantities, supplements and enhances the taste and flavour of other ingredients.

Flat icings

Flat icings are the combination of confectioners sugar, water, corn syrup and flavour. All the ingredients are to be mixed to a thick paste consistency and warmed to about 43.3°C. To avoid direct or over-heating of icing, a double boiler method of heating should be used. Many times due to overheating an icing loses its gloss after cooling. Whenever flat icing gets thickened after its make up, it should be rewarmed to bring to the correct consistency required. Do not soften the icing with water before the icings are reheated, otherwise it will cause stickiness in icings and also causes difficulties in setting. When through with immediate use of a flat icing, it should be covered with a thin film of water to prevent crust formation. Fondant is prepared by using 2 parts sugar, 1 part water and a pinch of tartar cream.

The sugar and water are placed in the pan and are heated. They should not be allowed to boil until the sugar is dissolved. When the temperature reaches 107.2°C, add the cream of tartar dispersed in little water. No stirring should be done when the temperature reaches 107.2°C. During the boiling period the side of the pan should be carefully washed down to remove sugar crystals formed on the sides of pan. The scrum should also be taken off. Boil until the moisture reaches 115.6°C, i.e. forms a soft ball when dropped into cold water. Remove from the fire and pour over a marble top. Allow to cool to 37.8°C. After cooling heat the mixture until it starts turning cloudy white, and finally into a stiff white creamy mass. Knead it till it is moulded into a smooth plastic condition. It can be stored in a cool place, properly covered. When required for use fondant is placed in a pan and carefully heated, preferably over a double boiler to a temperature of about 43.3°C. It should be made into pouring consistency by adding water or stock syrup (stock syrup is prepared by dissolving 100 g sugar to 50 g water and heated without stirring up to 104.4°C. Allow to cool. By using stock syrup, fondant will retain the gloss. Pour the fondant over the cake and allow it to set.

Creamed icings

Creamed icings are prepared with fat, confectioners sugar, water, salt, flavour, eggs and milk powder. The general procedure is to cream dry ingredients with shortenings. The beaten eggs are added gradually. The water and flavouring are added in the end, blending well. Creamed icing should be stored in a cool place and should be kept covered to avoid crust formation. Creamed icings have tendency to lose their smoothness after a long storage. In such cases icing will not have the ability to spread smoothly and evenly. In order to restore their smoothness they should be placed in warm water bath and creamed well until smooth. Do not over heat to avoid fat from melting away. Icings also help in retarding the staleness of the product. This depends mainly on the type of icing used. Flat icings which do not contain appreciable amount of shortening will have a tendency to absorb moisture from the cake. Creamed icings are much more effective in controlling the rate of staling.

Butter icing

Ingredients are: butter, 250 g; icing sugar, 500 g; vanilla, 1 teaspoon and colouring as desired.

Method: Cream butter to a smooth consistency. Add icing sugar little at a time and cream. Finally add vanilla and colour as desired. For making the cake the consistency of icing should be soft, whereas for piping it should be stiffer.

Royal icing

Ingredients are: egg-whites, 2; icing sugar, 450 g; Cream of tartar, onefourth teaspoon and colour and flavour as desired.

Method: Add cream of tartar to egg whites and beat gradually. Add icing sugar gradually and continue beating. Add colour and flavour as desired. Consistency for spreading should be softer, whereas for piping it should be stiffer.

Precautions: Egg whites should be separated neatly. Minute presence of egg yolk will spoil the icing. Utensils in use should be absolutely grease free and dry. Egg whites should be rested for sometime (3-4 hr) before using them.

Frosting

Ingredients are: Gr. sugar, 450 g; water, 150 g; egg-whites, 2; colour and flavour as desired; and cream of tartar one-fourth teaspoon.

Method: Boil sugar and water exactly as for fondant to 115°C or to soft ball consistency. Beat the egg-white with cream of tartar to a stiff peak. Add syrup in a trickle and continue beating up to the start of setting. Pour on cake quickly before it sets completely.

Cookies

Cookies are made by the same general methods as are used in making conventional cakes. The ingredients are also similar to those of cakes. The main difference is the decreased amount of liquid in cookie dough. The other differences are the increased amount of fat and egg and the smaller amount of leavening agents used. There are many varieties of cookie recipes and the different types of cookies are prepared as follows.

Drop cookies

These are made by dropping the mixture from a spoon onto a cooky sheet and baked in an oven at 190°C for 10-15 min. until nicely browned.
Bar cookies

They are also known as sheet cookies, and are baked by spreading the dough (similar to that of drop cookies) in a shallow pan. The individual bars are cut after baking.

Rolled cookies

Rolled cookies are made from refrigerated stiff dough. The dough is rolled and cut into the desired shapes and baked.

Meringue cookies

Such cookies are made with dough prepared by beating egg-whites until stiff and adding sugar slowly. Other ingredients are folded in and the batter dropped on a sheet and baked.

Sponge cookies

They are made like meringue cookies, using the whole egg rather than just the egg-white.

Pastry

Pastries include a number of baked products made from doughs containing medium to large amount of fat. These include pies, which are very popular in the United States, puffy pastries, Danish pastries, etc. The success of pie making depends mainly on the quality of crust.

Plain pastry is leavened primarily by the steam produced during baking. The ingredients in pastry are flour, salt, fat and water. Generally, the proportion of flour, fat and water is 6:2:1. This mixture gives a tender pie crust.

If a less rich crust is required, a mixture of flour and fat in a 4 : 1 ratio is used. Generally, all-purpose flour is used for plain pastry. Butter, margarine and hydrogenated vegetable oils are used as shortenings. Oil may also be used but the pastry will be crumbly and greasy.

In the preparation of the pastry, flour and salt are mixed after which the fat is cut into the flour. Water is then gradually added with stirring and worked into the dough. The dough is shaped into a ball, flattened into a circular shape, and transferred to a pie pan and baked in a hot oven at 218°C until the surface is delicately browned. Then the filling is placed on the crust.

Pizza

Pizza is consumed in place of complete meal, as it provides all nutrients needed by an individual. It is a baked product with all vegetables.

For dough	
Plain flour (all purpose)	(1Yz cup) 250 g
Dried yeast	5 g
Warm water	30 ml
Salt	5 g
Baking powder	5 g
Egg	50 g
Milk	45 ml
Vegetable oil	30 ml
For filling	
Onion (chopped)	1 large
Garlic (chopped)	10g
Cloves (powdered)	10 g
Tomatoes	250 g
Tomato puree	30 g
Salt + pepper powder	10 g
Cheese (sliced)	150 g
Any vegetable (eg. carrot)	250 g
Black olives	6 large
Olive oil	5 ml

Method: To make the dough:

- Dissolve the sugar in warm water.
- Mix yeast in warm water and sprinkle the water on top.
- Leave in a warmish place for 10 to 15 min. or until frothy.
- Sift the flour and salt and baking powder thrice.
- Cream butter and mix with flour.
- Mix dough with the yeast liquid, add a little extra flour if the dough is sticky.
- Knead for 10 min. or until the dough is smooth and elastic. Keep it in an oiled bowl. Cover with butter paper and leave it to rise to double the size.
- Turn-out onto floured surface then knead lightly until smooth.
- Roll out into a 0.63 cm thick circle and arrange on an oiled baking tray.
- Brush with olive oil and cover with slices of tomato and other veg etable slices.
- Sprinkle garlic, cloves powder. Place olives, onions, and top with slices of cheese. Sprinkle pepper and salt.
- Bake at 230°C for 25-30 min. in an hot oven.
- Serve while still warm.

Types of pizza: Ham pizza, pizza with mushrooms and olives, pizza with salaami, small pizza, and pizza Neapolitan.

Chapter - 4

Raw Material

Wheat and wheat milling process

Flour used in bakeries and biscuit factories is obtained by milling wheat. As flour is the principal ingredient for baked products, it will be in order to understand the structure of wheat kernel.

Wheat is an annual grass of the genus Triticum and it is grown in most countries in the world. Depending on the soil, climatic conditions, quality of seed and farming techniques, wheat varies widely in its properties

Wheat are generally classified according to the colour, and hardness of .grain. Hard wheat yield flour that is high in good quality protein. Such flours have high Water Absorption Power (WAP), good mixing and fermentation tolerance and good gas retention power, and are excellent for bread making. Soft wheat have lower amount of proteins and absorb less water. Such flours are good for cakes, soft dough biscuits and cookies but are unsuitable for bread making.

Physical structure of wheat consists of :

1. Bran	14.5-15%
2. Endosperm	83%
3. Germ	2.5%

Bran is made up of six layers. The fourth layer "Testa" contains the colouring matter which decides the colour of wheat and could also influence the colour of flour. The sixth layer of "Aleuron cells" contains protease enzyme, that has softening effect on flour proteins and consequently on doughs. Although bran is nutritionally rich in vitamin B, but the cellulose material of bran tends to speed up the passage of food through digestive tract reducing the total nutritive contribution to the body- The sharp edges of bran fragments have a cutting action on gluten strands reducing the gas retention power of dough. Due to these reasons, it is not desirable to have bran contamination in flour more than what is absolutely unavoidable in good milling practices (i.e. approximately 0.4 to 0.5%).

Germ contains oil which reduces the keeping quality of flour and hence it is desirable to remove germ during milling process.

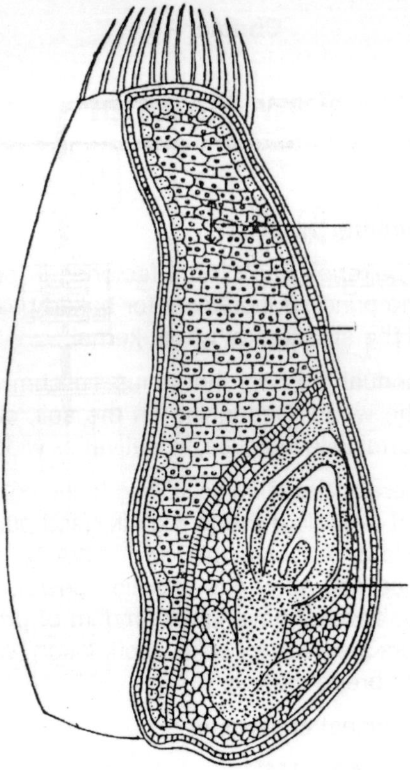

Fig. 4.1. Longitudinal Section of Wheat Grain

Endosperm is the floury portion of wheat kernel and flour for bakery / biscuit industry is produced from this part of the grain.

Milling Process

Today wheat is milled by a highly automatic and efficient system known as "Roller Flour Milling".

Wheat milling consists of:

1. Grading
2. Cleaning
3. Conditioning
4. Blending
5. Milling

Cleaning of wheat in a roller flour mill is carried out by a series of equipments:

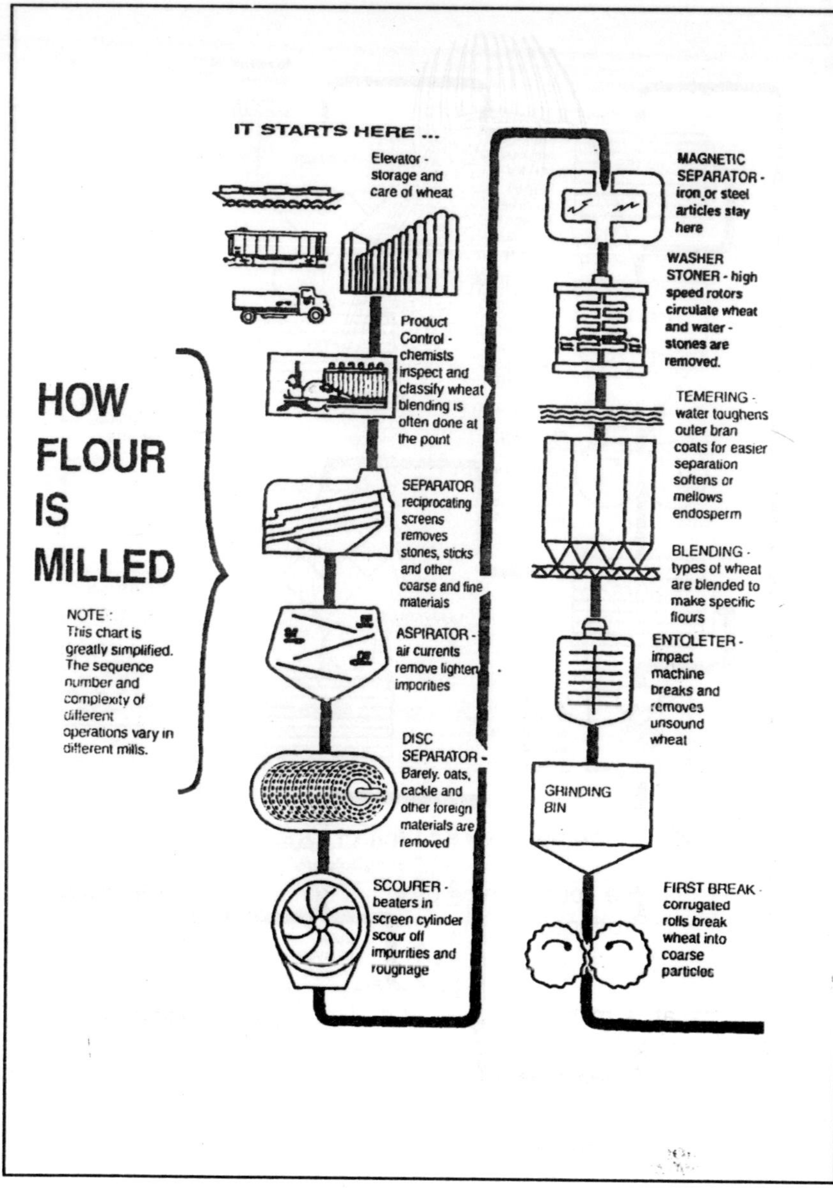
IT STARTS HERE ...
Elevator - storage and care of wheat
Product Control - chemists inspect and classify wheat blending is often done at the point
SEPARATOR reciprocating screens removes stones, sticks and other coarse and fine materials
ASPIRATOR - air currents remove lighter imporities
DISC SEPARATOR - Barely. oats, cackle and other foreign materials are removed
SCOURER - beaters in screen cylinder scour off impurities and rougnage
MAGNETIC SEPARATOR - iron or steel articles stay here
WASHER STONER - high speed rotors circulate wheat and water - stones are removed.
TEMERING - water toughens outer bran coats for easier separation softens or mellows endosperm
BLENDING - types of wheat are blended to make specific flours
ENTOLETER - impact machine breaks and removes unsound wheat
GRINDING BIN
FIRST BREAK - corrugated rolls break wheat into coarse particles
HOW FLOUR IS MILLED
NOTE : This chart is greatly simplified. The sequence number and complexity of different operations vary in different mills.

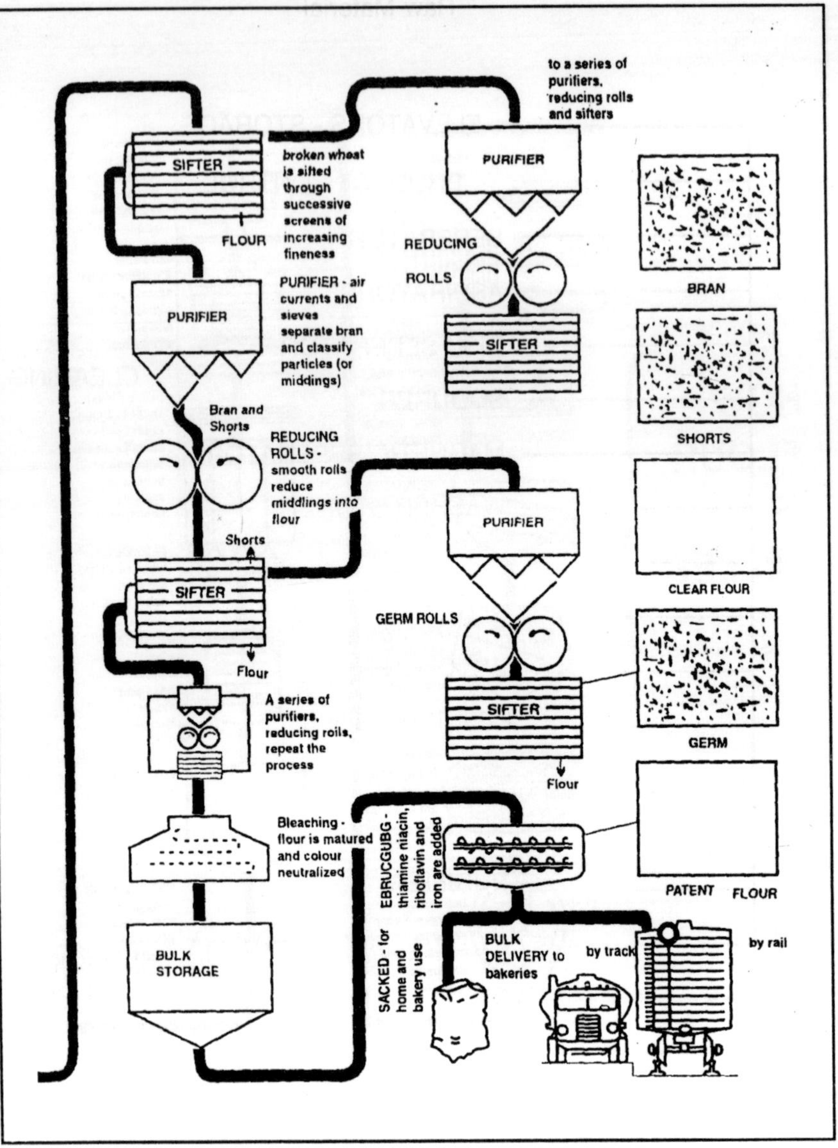
to a series of purifiers, reducing rolls and sifters
SIFTER
broken wheat is sifted through successive screens of increasing fineness
FLOUR
PURIFIER
REDUCING
ROLLS
BRAN
PURIFIER
PURIFIER - air currents and sieves separate bran and classify particles (or middings)
SIFTER
SHORTS
Bran and Shorts
REDUCING ROLLS - smooth rolls reduce middlings into flour
PURIFIER
Shorts
SIFTER
CLEAR FLOUR
GERM ROLLS
Flour
SIFTER
GERM
A series of purifiers, reducing roils, repeat the process
Flour
Bleaching - flour is matured and colour neutralized
EBRUCGUBG - thiamine niacin, riboflavin and iron are added
PATENT FLOUR
BULK STORAGE
SACKED - for home and bakery use
BULK DELIVERY to bakeries
by track
by rail

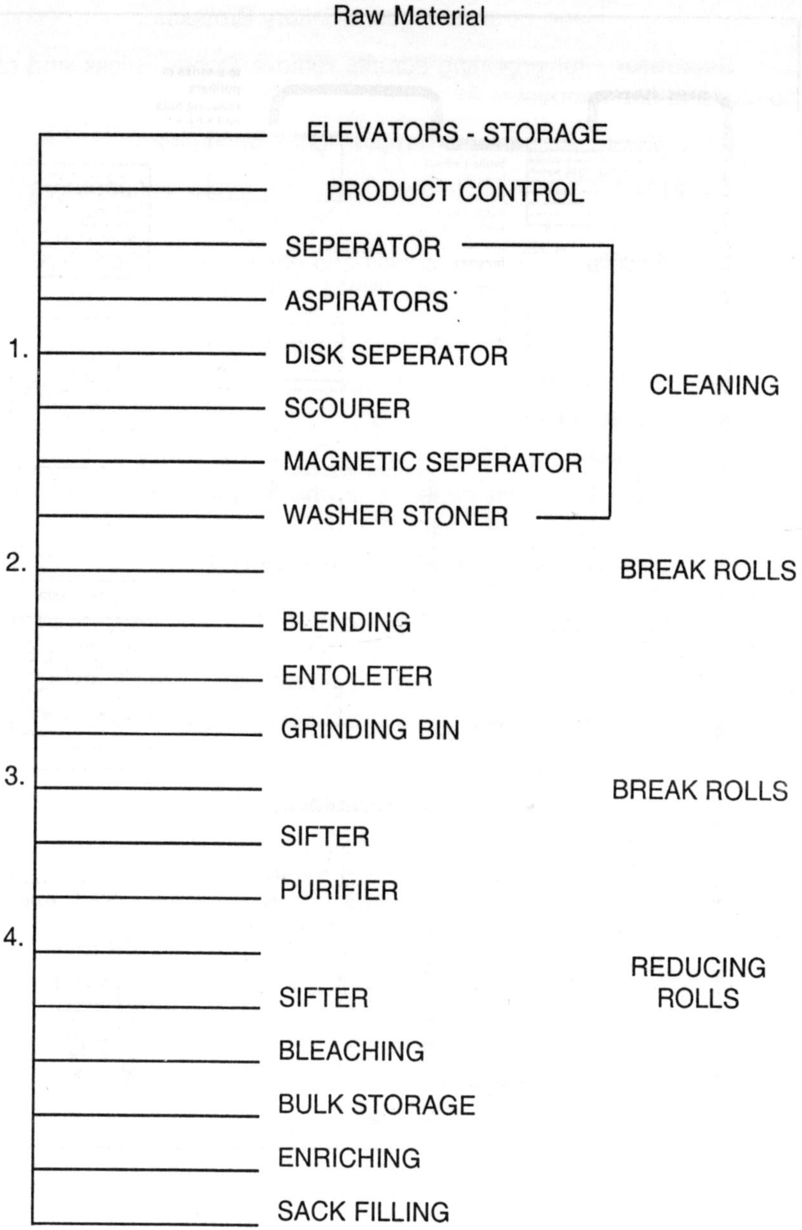

WHEAT MILLING PROCES FLOW CHART

Separator : reciprocating scrums remove stones, sticks and other coarse and fine material.

Aspirators : Air currents remove lighter impurities.

Scourer : Beaters in screen cylinders scour off impurities and roughage.

Disc Separator : Barley, cockle and other foreign material is removed.

Magnetic Separator : Iron objects are removed.

Washer- Stoner: High speed rotors circulate wheat and water.The process removes the stones.

After washing, the moist wheat is conditioned in silos for a predetermined time which depends on the original moisture content in wheat. For proper milling of wheat 16 to 17% moisture is considered ideal. During conditioning, the bran gets tough. Toughening of bran helps in its easy removal as it peels off in big chunks, which can be easily separated, rather than small fragments, which are difficult to separate. Conditioning also mellows the endosperm which helps its milling property. During conditioning germ is also rendered tough and flaky for easy removal.

After conditioning, different types of wheats could be blended to obtain flour of a particular specification.

After blending, wheat passes through sets of break-rolls. The set of break-rolls have two rolls which have diagonal grooves and which move at different speeds in opposite direction from each other. The grooves are so designed and speed of break-rolls so adjusted that wheat kernel is broken only gradually.

After the wheat passes through first break-rolls, some bran is separated and lifted off by air current. Very small amount of flour is milled and separated. Large chunks of kernel are further directed to second set of break-rolls where similar process takes place as above till finally pieces of wheat kernel are almost devoid of bran. The product so obtained is known as Sooji, Rava or Semolina from which flour is milled.

After wheat passes through the first set of break-rolls, it breaks into pieces of different sizes which are separated by Plan-sifter. Plan-sifter contains a set of sieves where the uppermost sieve has largest holes and in descending order the lower most sieve has the smallest holes. Each sieve separates the chunks of similar size which are directed through channels to join with the similar size chunks from other break-rolls for further processing.

We have seen that during break-roll operation some flour is produced. This flour is from the center part of wheat kernel and has minimum bran contamination. Although the quantity of protein in this flour is comparatively less but quality is superior. This flour is known as Patent Flour.

Refined semolina is passed through reduction rolls to obtain white flour. Reduction rolls are smooth and granularity of flour will depend on the adjustment of pressure between these rolls. However, excessive pressure will cause more damaged starch which will be detrimental to the quality of flour for bread making. Normal quantity of damaged starch in flour is approximately 6%.

We have seen above that at each stage of milling some quantity of flour is produced till finally semolina is milled. If the various streams are collected separately, these flours will be known as Fancy Patent, First Patent -etc. depending on which stream it is collected from. After Patent Flour is separated the remaining flour is termed as clear flour which is dark in colour due to higher bran content. If all the streams are blended together, the end product is termed as "Straight Run" Flour. Presently the flour available generally in the market is "Straight Run" type which is used by bakery and biscuit industry for making all kind of products.

The flour is then bleached and matured either chemically or naturally by storing it for 10-15 days. It is believed that storing improves the flour.

Flour in good condition should have a creamy white colour. When observed under bright light it will reflect light rather than have a dead appearance like chalk powder. It should have pleasant smell and slightly sweetish taste. When squeezed firmly in hand, it should tend to cling together yet should easily fall apart.

Storage :

A baker has to store flour for many reasons. When prices of flour are low, he may buy more than his normal requirement. If the shortages are anticipated he may buy flour to tide over the period of shortage. Also it is supposed that flour matures and improves in colour on storing.

Flour bags should be piled off the flour on skids to enable free circulation of air all around the piles. The storage area should be well ventilated. Flour should be kept away from direct sunlight. Temperature of storage area should be 65 - 75 deg. F or 19 - 24 degC and relative humidity, between 55 - 65%. Too low or too high relative humidity are both detrimental to flour quality. Flour has a tendency to pick up foreign odour, and should be stored away from such ingredients which may impart odour. While storing, it must be ensured that the flour is free from insect infestation.

Composition of Flour

Composition of flour will vary depending upon the types of wheat used in the grist.

A typical analysis is given below:

Starch	71.5 to 74.5%
Moisture	13.5 to 14.0%
Protein(gluten forming)	7.0 to 10.0%
Protein (soluble)	1.0%
Sugar	2.0 to 2.5%
Fat	1.0%
Ash (mineral salts)	0.5%

STARCH

Starch consists of microscopic granules or cells. Although starch is not soluble in water, it absorbs moisture through its cells and hence the necessity of protecting flour from too humid atmosphere.

When starch is heated to about 140 deg F with about six times of its weight of water, starch cells swell and cell wall bursts. Starch becomes soluble in water and in concentrated form will form a gel. The process is known as gelatinisation. This quality of starch is made use of in making fruit pies where fruits are kept in suspension in starch gel. Degree of gelatinization influences the water holding capacity of starch cells. Completely gelatinised starch will hold more water for longer time than partially gelatinised starch. For complete gelatinisation of starch, there should be sufficient (six times of the weight of starch) water available and it should be heated to 140 deg. F. In case of bread, water available to starch is insufficient and inner temperature of bread does not reach gelatinisation point until the last stages of baking and when the temperature does reach gelatinisation point the bread is taken out of the oven. Due to these reasons, starch in bread is only partially gelatinised.

When bread is hot, the starch cells are in swollen state. Position of starch cells is unstable. This is the reason why a very fresh bread can not be sliced neatly. As the bread is cooling down, starch cells shrink and become more rigid and slicing becomes easier.

During the cooling process starch cells.give away some of its water, which is partially held by gluten framework and partially evaporated. When such bread is heated, starch cells again absorb available water and become swollen. This is why a stale bread becomes softer when heated.

During the process of milling, about 6% of starch cells are crushed and damaged due to impact of rolls. Such starch is also known as soluble starch. The enzyme Beta-amylase present in the flour acts on soluble starch and converts it to Maltose sugar. During baking operation, as the loaf is gradually gaining in temperature, yeast becomes more active and requires plenty of food to produce gas. Enzymes also get activated with the rise in temperature and convert more starch into maltose sugar. Thus the need of yeast for more food is fulfilled and due to increased gas production, bread acquires desired volume. However, the presence of excessive damaged starch cells will cause production of undesirable amounts of maltose sugar, only a part of which Will be needed by yeast. In such cases, doughs become slack, sticky and difficult to handle. The bread produced from such a dough will have dark crust and crumb colour and poor in volume and texture.

Alpha amylase is another enzyme of amylolytic group which is found in flour. This enzyme partly breaks down the sound starch cells to form dextrins which, in limited amount, give sheen to bread, improving its eye appeal. However, if the starch conversion is higher than desired levels, excessive dextrin formation will make the crumb sticky. Such bread will be difficult to slice and slices will stick together and will break when separated.

This activity of Alpha and Beta amylase is known as Diastatic activity. We have seen that limited diastatic activity is not only good but necessary for bread production and excessive activity is detrimental to bread quality. A practical baker should understand it very clearly that the flour for bread making should nave reasonable amount of diastatic activity because it results in the production of maltose sugar which provides two units of glucose which is a preferred sugar by yeast as against fructose which is the end product of sucrose break down. Hence increasing sucrose sugar in the formula is no substitute for diastatic activity in the flour.

When flour lacks in diastatic action, it can be supplemented by using Diastatic malt in the formula. If flour has excessive diastatic activity as in the case of flours made from sprouted wheat it may be useful to take the following precautions in order to reduce to some extent the harmful effects of excessive diastatic activity.

1. Use plenty of yeast for vigorous fermentation of dough, as overall reduction in production time will give less opportunity to enzymes to remain active.
2. Keep the doughs cool as high temperatures will promote the amylase activity.
3. Use emulsifiers (i.e.G.M.S.emulsion etc.) liberally to prevent stickiness in the crumb. Use of soya flour could also be helpful in this regard.

4. Keep strict control on fermentation and prevent the doughs from becoming acidic. Enzymes are more active in acidic medium.
5. Bake the bread thoroughly so that it has even golden brown colour all around.
6. Slice the bread only when it is thoroughly cooled.
7. Potassium aluminium sulphate has retarding effect on diastatic action. A small lump of potassium aluminium sulphate rotated three to four times in doughing water will give: enough of this chemical to control the diastatic action at least to some extent. After turning the lump of potassium aluminium sulphate the water should be used the next day as this chemical is banned in some countries, it will be appropriate to ascertain the legal position in this matter.

MOISTURE

The next important constituent of flour is Moisture. A level of 13 to 14% moisture content in flour is ideal from bakers point of view. If moisture in flour is higher, the baker will be getting less solid material and more of water for his money. Higher moisture will warm up the flour during storage and will induce insect infestation, reducing its storage life. If the moisture content of flour is high, it will reduce the Water Absorption Power (W.A.P).of the flour, resulting in less yield. This can be understood by the following example.

Supposing a flour has 14% moisture content, and its WAP is 60%.

(1)	Flour	100
	- Moisture	14
	Solid material	86

Now supposing that the moisture content of the same flour is

increased by 1 % ,

(2)	Flour	100
	- Moisture	15
	Solid material	85

(1)	86 solid material takes up water i.e. WAP	60
	+ moisture content OF FLOUR	14
	Total moisture held by 86 solids is	74

Therefore total moisture held by 85 solids

$$\frac{85 \times 74}{86}$$

= 73.13 (WAP + Moisture content)
- 15.0 (Moisture content)

= 58.13 W A P

Thus it can be seen that when the moisture content of flour is higher by 1%, it reduces the WAP by approximately 2%, giving less yield and monetary loss to the baker.

PROTEIN

Maida contains soluble and insoluble proteins. Soluble proteins are useful in providing nourishment to yeast for its growth and reproduction during fermentation process. Two insoluble proteins Gliadin and Glutenin form a rubbery material when water is added to flour and it is mixed. This rubbery material is known as "Gluten" and is responsible for formation of structure of baked products. High structured products like bread will require stronger quality of gluten while lower structured products like cakes, cookies do not require strong gluten.

Glutenin gives strength to the dough in order to enable it to hold gases during baking operation and, Gliadin gives elastic or stretching properties to dough. The quantity and quality of these two proteins present in the flour determine the quality of the flour which is termed as strong, weak or medium. These terms should not be confused with "Hard" or "Soft" because these terms specify the type of wheat from which the flour is milled.

An understanding of the quantity and quality of gluten will be of great help to a baker in adjusting his formulation / processing most suitable for a particular type of flour.

It does not require any elaborate equipment to estimate the quantity of gluten. Just an accurate weighing scale, a small bowl, a plastic spatula or a spoon, a small burette or a small measuring cylinder, and a wire sieve.

Weigh accurately 100 g flour in a bowl and add 50 ml. correctly measured water. Mix with a plastic spatula or a spoon. If the dough so formed is still stiff, add more water 1 ml. at a time until the consistency of the dough is pliable but not. too soft or too stiff. While doing this, utmost care should be taken that flour is not spilled out of the bowl and it does not remain sticking to the bowl or spoon. Note the quantity of water taken up by flour for making a pliable dough. This quantity of water is known as Water Absorption Power (W.A. P) of that particular flour. Higher the WAP, better the flour is likely to be.

Now mix the dough ball between palms until it is very smooth. Put this dough ball immersed in water (tap water at room temperature) for 30 minutes.

Next step will be to wash out the starch under running water. Keep a sieve underneath to catch any gluten fibers which might escape while washing. To test whether all the starch is washed out or not, squeeze the gluten in a glass of clean water. If the water shows white streaks, washing should be further continued.

When the entire starch is washed out, press the gluten with palms and squeeze out as much water as possible until gluten starts sticking to hands. This mass is called "WET" gluten.

Weigh the wet gluten. If it weighs 30g., then the weight of dry gluten will be 10 g.(30/3) which means that the flour contains 10% gluten (i.e. gluten forming proteins). Such flour should make good bread. However; if gluten content is more it is still better, but it should be remembered that higher amount of gluten will require more fermentation time to mellow properly. By the same token flour with lesser amount of gluten should be fermented for lesser time otherwise structure of product will be adversely affected. A rough estimate of the quality of gluten can also be made by the baker. When the day's production is over and oven is cool enough (about 100 deg.C), place the smoothened gluten ball in a tray and keep it in the oven. After one hour observe the volume of the gluten ball. Bigger the volume, better the quality of flour for bread making.

Gluten quality can be fairly estimated by observation of colour, toughness or elasticity and smoothness. If the gluten is gray without any creaminess in colour, it is quite possible that the flour has been bleached chemically. If the gluten is rough and does not form a smooth ball, it shows excessive bleaching or weak flour. The toughness or elasticity will indicate flour strength and coupled with gluten quantity is a very fair guide to flour suitability for bread making.

Ash content

Ash content of flour is indicative of the degree of its purity with respect to bran fragments. Higher ash content means that the flour contains too much of bran fragments. Apart from darkening the colour of flour, the bran fragments also have a cutting action on gluten fibers. Such flour will not retain gas during different stages of processing and the product thus made will have a low volume and poor texture. The protease enzyme present in the "Aleuron Cells" will also weaken the flour.

On a small glass plate (6"x2") place a small heap of flour and with another similar glass plate press the flour to smoothen the upper surface. Gently cut out rough sides, and form a neat wedge (slick). Now dip this wedge gently in slanting position in a bowl of water so that the surface of flour is moistened. Now observe the moistened surface minutely. Colour of bran fragments will be more pronounced in wet condition.

Sugar

Small quantity of sugar which is naturally found in flour is of sucrose or maltose type. Even if sugar is not added to bread formula, it should be possible to make bread as the sugar naturally occurring in flour will provide sufficient food to yeast to produce Carbon dioxide gas. However, apart from providing food for yeast, sugar has other functions to perform viz. retaining moisture in bread, imparting golden brown colour to crust, improving taste and flavour of bread etc. These beneficial effects cannot be achieved with the limited amount of sugar naturally occurring in flour. Hence the necessity for using additional sugar in bread formula.

Flour Tests

Moisture: Flour should have 14% moisture. Higher moisture content is detrimental to flour quality and a monetary loss to the baker as has been demonstrated in previous paragraphs.

Ash : Ash determines the mineral matter in flour. Minerals are concentrated in bran. Hence by knowing the ash content, degree of bran contamination can be determined. Higher bran content of flour will not only darken the flour but bread volume will also be affected as bran has a cutting action on gluten strands.

Protein : Quantity and quality of insoluble (gluten forming) proteins can be determined in the laboratory. For bread making, both, quality as well as quantity are important.

Falling Number test : It indicates the amylase activity in the flour. Higher falling numbers indicate reduced amylase activity and vice versa.

Ferinograph : Measures strength of flour for commercial mixing.

Extensograph : Indicates the loaf potentialities.

Mac Micheal Viscosimeter : Indicates the amount of bleaching the flour has undergone. Bleaching of flour weakens proteins.

pH Value : Indicates the acidity or alkalinity.

Pekar ColourTest : Indicates the degree of separation.

Baking Test : Although the above tests will give a fairly good indication about quality of flour, actual laboratory scale baking test gives the best overall evaluation of the flour quality.

A baker would like to have a flour which has the following characteristics:

Colour : Colour of flour should have a creamy tinge. Greyish, yellowish or dead appearing flour like chalk powder are not desirable, specially for fermented goods. A good flour will reflect light in a peculiar shining manner.

Strength : Flours are usually referred to as Strong or Medium or Weak. Such description of flour refers to the strength of flour which is capable of producing large volumed, well risen loaf. Strong flours have tough gluten which requires longer fermentation time to mellow properly. The quality of flour is decided by the amount of fermentation it will stand.

Tolerance : If a flour requires, let us say, 2 hours fermentation time for proper maturing of gluten and if it still can produce similar quality of bold, large volumed loaf when fermentation time is extended by 15-20 minutes (as may happen in bakeries due to upsetting of schedules for various reasons such as power failure, machine break down etc.), then such flour is said to have tolerance. Tolerance of flour is its ability to withstand the fermentation process in excess of what is normally required to mature its gluten properly.

High Absorption : This refers to the ability of flour to take up and hold maximum amount of water without any change in mixing time requirement and without deteriorating the quality of dough in any way with regards to its handling qualities. Higher absorption means higher yield and that is what a baker would always desire to have.

Uniformity : A baker has to plan out his production schedule according to the type of flour which will stand a particular fermentation time. If the quality of flour varies, readjustment of production schedule will be required to be made. If such variations occur too often, it will be an additional exercise for bankers to alter the fermentation time every now and then. Majority of bakeries do not maintain flour testing facilities and the only way for them is to actually produce bread in order to verify the quality of flour. Any failures in such cases will result in monetary losses. Hence it is very necessary that whatever quality of flour is available to bakeries it should be of uniform quality so that the baker does not have to vary the processing schedule too often and the product is also of uniform quality.

Yeast

After flour, yeast is next important ingredient for bread making. In olden days most of the bakers used barm method of bread making. A liquid media was made with hops decoction, boiled potatoes, sugar, flour

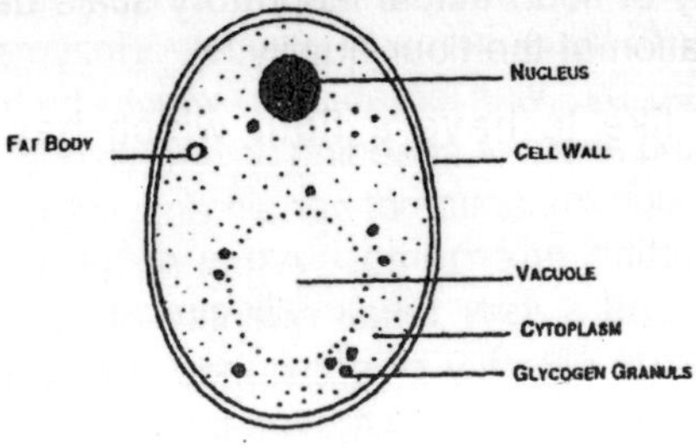

YEAST CELL

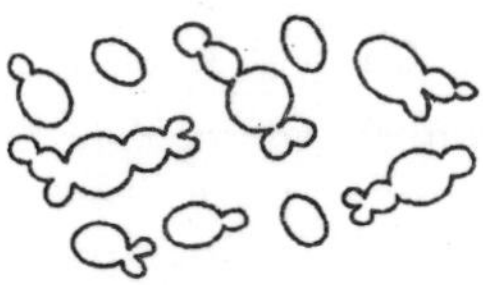

BUDDING YEAST CELL

etc. in which wild yeast was cultured. It was necessary to use prolonged fermentation. Due to prolonged fermentation periods, bread had that peculiar fermentation flavour which is still remembered by people nostalgically. However times have changed, bakers yeast is easily available and bakers botherations about uncertainties of fermentation have been eliminated.

For practicing bakers, it is necessary to understand the functioning of yeast, so that he is in a better position to control yeast activity in doughs and thus control the quality of bread and other fermented products.

Bread doughs are fermented basically for two reasons i.e.

1. Production of carbon dioxide gas which gives volume to the product, and
2. For maturing or conditioning the dough (gluten) so that it attains sufficient mellowness to stretch under the pressure of CO_2 gas and form the structure of the product.

These functions are performed by yeast. Let us see, how?

Yeast is unicellular microscopic plant. Its structure consists of a cell wall, protoplasm, and vacuole. It requires food (in the form of simple sugar), moisture and temperate climate for its growth and reproduction. Yeast multiplies by budding. When yeast cell is placed in a liquid medium at optimum temperature (80 deg.-85 deg.F) containing simple sugar (dextrose or fructose), then the cell starts growing buds on its cell wall which keeps on growing until daughter cells acquire the same size as mother cell. Then the buds separate from mother cell and start producing other buds.

The protoplasm of yeast contains certain enzymes by which fermentation activity of yeast is made possible. Enzymes are very minute substances produced by living organisms, which, by its mere presence, are capable of bringing about or speeding up certain changes. For example, food is digested through the action of certain enzymes, starch is converted into sugar by the action of enzymes. Although an enzyme does affect chemical changes, and a very small quantity of enzyme is capable of converting a very large quantity of substance from one form to another form, but enzyme itself is neither destroyed nor changed. Hence enzymes are known as catalytic agents.

There is no organism known other than yeast which contains the same combination of enzymes in the same proportion. That is why there is no substitute for yeast as a fermenting agent.

The following are most prominent enzymes which take part in fermentation process:

Invertase : Converts cane sugar or sucrose into a simple form of sugar known as invert sugar which is a combination of dextrose and fructose.

Maltase : Converts maltose sugar into dextrose which is directly fermentable by yeast.

Zymase : Is actually the specific fermenting enzyme in yeast. Zymase attacks the invert sugar and dextrose which had been previously produced by the action of invertase and maltase, converting them into carbon dioxide gas, some pure alcohol, very small amounts of glycerin, succinic acid, acetic acid, lactic acid and other substances which make up for the peculiar, pleasant fermentation flavour.

Protease : This enzyme has a mellowing action on flour proteins, thus conferring better stretchability (on gluten) for bread to acquire volume and form structure.

Thus we see that function of yeast is to raise and condition the dough so it turns from a heavy mass into a light, porous, elastic product, which when baked, is appetising, easily digestible and nutritious. Without yeast, it is impossible to think of bread, buns etc. as we know these products today. Average analysis of yeast is as follows:

Proteins	14.00%
Carbohydrates	10.20%
Fats	0.46%
Mineral matter	2.34%
Moisture	73.00%

Raw Material

Enzymes	Present
Vitamins	Present

Although the amount of yeast in bread is not large, but it is worthwhile to note that yeast itself is one of the finest foods. It supplements bread with proteins of the highest order, certain valuable nutritive minerals and particularly vitamin B and C which are so essential for the growth and the health of human body.

It is the action of yeast which converts the raw flour into a light, well risen mass, which, when properly baked, is practically 100% digestible. Simultaneously, it creates the characteristic pleasant bread flavour, which probably, more than any other characteristics, is responsible for acceptance of bread for every meal.

Compressed yeast, when in fresh condition, should have a pleasant aroma like that of ripe apples, should be firm, springy and moist to touch, should break with a sharp and clean fracture without crumbling. It should not have butter like consistency. When yeast gets old it develops brownish colour, gives an off odour and will crumble when broken. Compressed yeast should be used 2 to 2.5 times of dried yeast.

It is difficult to assess the fermenting power of dried yeast by its appearance. It should be tested for its activity before use. Take a small quantity of luke warm water (around 90 deg.F), mix one tea spoon of sugar and sprinkle a tea spoon of dried yeast. Let it rest for 5 to 7 minutes. Yeast granules which, initially sink to the bottom, will disintegrate and start floating on surface. Then add sufficient flour to make a thick paste and let it rest for about 7 to 10 minutes. During this time there should be visible rise in the volume of the ferment. If it does not show signs of gas production, such yeast should not be used.

When yeast becomes stale or old, its cell wall becomes weak and ruptures, spilling out the protoplasm. As discussed earlier, protoplasm contains proteolytic enzymes which can convert insoluble proteins into soluble proteins, robbing the gluten of its strength to make a bold, well risen loaf. Such yeast should not be used as it will cause more harm than good to the dough.

Storage of yeast

Compressed yeast can be stored in refrigerator which should be maintained at 45 deg.F Although it is claimed that dried yeast can be stored at room temperature it is advisable to store it in refrigerator if it is desired to stock it for any appreciable length of time in order to meet any emergency requirement.

Quantity of yeast to be used

In a normal straight dough bread formula containing approximately 2% salt, 2 to 3% sugar and 1 to 2% fat, the amount of yeast should be about 1-2% (dried yeast about 0.5-1.0%). However; the following points should be remembered while deciding the quantity of yeast in any formula.

1. Salt has a controlling effect on yeast fermentation as well as it also has a tightening action on flour proteins. In the presence of higher amounts of salt, quantity of yeast should also be increased and vice versa (For similar fermentation periods).

2. It is difficult for yeast to derive its food from a concentrated sugar solution. If sugar is increased in a formula beyond 5-6%, yeast content should also be increased.

3. Fat exerts a dead weight on the fine web like structure of dough. Increased quantity (more than 6%) of fat in dough will necessitate use of enhanced quantity of yeast to produce sufficient gas to raise the excessive weight of fat.

4. Milk and egg proteins have a tightening action on flour proteins. To countermand this action, more yeast will be necessary.

5. At times doughs are required to be fermented for prolonged periods in order to develop flavour in bread. In such doughs yeast content should be reduced.

6: During summer, yeast content should be reduced to prevent souring of doughs. Conversely, during winter, yeast content should be increased.

7. Tight doughs are normally fermented for longer periods and in such case yeast content should be kept low, However if such doughs are required to be taken up fast, then yeast content should be increased in order to make the dough light and spongy. The quantity should be so balanced that the dough does not tear off due to excessive gas production.

8. In many bakeries, bread is made by over night sponge method. Next morning when dough is mixed, in most cases, yeast is not added. Yeast has a definite life cycle. When the sponge is fermented overnight, very few active yeast cells are left by next morning. When fresh quantity of flour is mixed in the morning without corresponding amount of yeast, the speed of fermentation of the dough is very slow and proofing of bread also takes unduly long time. Hence, it is necessary to add sufficient quantity of yeast while mixing the dough next morning so that the proofing time is not unduly long.

It may be pertinent to mention that these days most bakeries use High speed mixers wherein fermentation time is either totally eliminated or reduced to bare minimum possible. In such cases yeast content is generally kept high {2 - 3.5%}.

Water

Water binds together the insoluble proteins of flour, which form gluten. Any water which is fit to drink can be used for bread making. However; it should be remembered that water, being a very good solvent, is rarely found in nature without any minerals dissolved in it. Hard water contains more minerals than soft water. These minerals in limited quantities, have a beneficial effect on gas production as the yeast requires minerals for vigorous fermentation. The gas retention of the dough is also improved as minerals have a tightening action on gluten. For this reason precisely, very hard water should not be used for bread making. With very hard water, it may be necessary to increase the quantity of yeast and reduce salt (to appropriate level) and / or any other constituent mineral yeast food (MYF). Lactic acid could be used which will have a mellowing effect on gluten. The quantity of lactic acid should be carefully regulated because it has a very pungent odour which may interfere with the pleasant flavour of bread. Very Soft water is also not desirable as it is not conducive either to good gas production or gas retention and in such cases it may be necessary to increase the content of MYF Medium hard water (Hardness about 17 ppm) is considered to be most suitable for bread production.

Salt

Salt imparts taste to bread. It is also one of the most important constituent to bring out the flavour in bread. It has a controlling effect on yeast activity (by virtue of controlling enzyme activity) and thus keeps the fermentation speed under check. As the salt has a tightening action on flour proteins, it improves the gas retention power of the dough. Being a hygroscopic substance, it helps to keep the bread fresh and moist for longer time. The colour of crust is largely dependant on the amount of sugar present in bread at the time of baking, and this amount of sugar will depend on the speed of yeast activity, which, in turn, is controlled by salt. Therefore, if there is less salt in the formula, yeast action will be more than normal and there will be less sugar left for caramelisation resulting in poor crust colour. Conversely, more salt in formula will produce a bread with harsh red crust colour, as there will be more sugar left at the time of baking due to check on yeast activity. The quantity of salt in a bread formula will vary between 1.25 to 2.5% depending on the strength of flour, length of fermentation time, hardness of formula water, the level of flavour desired in the product and the constitution of M.Y.F (if it is included in the formula). In sweet fermented products, the salt content generally varies from 1.0 to 1.5%.

Sugar

The main function of sugar in bread making is to provide food for yeast, which, in turn, produces $C0_2$ gas, that raises the dough fabric. It also helps in enhancing the flavour of bread and being a hygroscopic substance, helps in retention of moisture in bread. It' contributes to the familiar golden brown crust colour of bread. Apart from the sucrose sugar added in the formula, there is also another source of sugar in a fermenting dough and that is by the activity of diastase enzyme on the starch. The capacity of flour to produce sugar from starch is known as diastatic capacity and is carried out by a group of enzymes known as diastase which are contained in flour. Diastase enzyme converts starch into maltose sugar and dextrins. Maltose is broken down by another enzyme maltase into dextrose (glucose) which provides food for yeast at the critical time of final stage of fermentation ie. during initial stage of baking. Dextrins impart bloom to the bread.

At times, flour may be deficient in diastatic activity and bread may not get oven spring. To correct such condition one of the following remedies may be tried.

1. Make a small quantity of overnight sponge and add to the dough. This will reduce the pH of the dough. Diastatic activity is better at low pH (Acid medium).
2. Use diastatic malt at the rate of 0.225%
3. Blend with flour having good diastatic activity.
4. At times, even though there is no lack of diastatic activity, yet due to large size of starch granules, it does not have desired effect. In such cases, make the dough leaving out yeast and let soak for 2 to 3 hours. Then add yeast and ferment for less than normal fermentation time.
5. Soak wheat in water for 12 hours. Remove water and tie the wheat in a piece of cloth and rest in a warm place for 12 hours or until it starts sprouting. When all the wheat is sprouted, dry it in the sun or in a cool oven. When absolutely dry, make it into flour and sift through very fine sieve. Use this flour at the rate of 0.25% or more.

Fat

Fat is used in bread doughs at the rate of 1 to 2%. To that extent it improves the nutritional value of bread. In small quantities it has lubricating effect on gluten strands, thus improving their extensibility which enables the bread to acquire good volume. In larger quantities (more than 6%) fat exerts a dead weight on fine web like structure, thus hampering the volume of bread. Fat also helps in retention of moisture in bread and improves its sliceability. Fat should be added during the last stages of mixing. If it is added in the beginning, it will have an adverse effect on water absorption power of the flour. If it is desired to use G.M.S. emulsion, fat can be added to emulsion while emulsion is still hot and mixed thoroughly to make it a homogeneous mass.

Milk

Apart from improving the nutritional value of bread, milk has a beneficial effect on the physical qualities of bread. It has a tightening effect on flour proteins which improves the gas retention power of dough, thus, producing a very fine web like structure which is soft and silky. Milk improves the flavour and taste of bread. Due to the presence of lactose sugar, the crust colour and water retention power of bread is improved. Addition of milk in a formula necessitates addition of extra water to bring the dough to a soft and pliable consistency. Milk has a drying effect on the eating quality of bread. To counter this drying effect, the quantity of fat should be increased in the formula. Milk can be used in bread in any form ie. fresh liquid milk, condensed milk, whole milk powder, skimmed milk powder etc. However in each case it is necessary to know the constitution of the type of milk used so that the quantity of milk solids in the formula could be regulated. In case the type of milk used contains sugar or fat, necessary allowance should be made in the formula so that the formula does not become imbalanced. However in a bakery it is always advisable to use (spray dried) skimmed milk powder which has a better shelf life, reconstitutes readily with water, does not require any adjustments in the formula for fat content and is comparatively more economic to use. If fresh liquid milk is used it should be boiled and cooled to room temperature before use. Butter fat of milk acts in the same fashion as any other fat except that it also imparts unique butter flavour to the product. A bread dough containing milk should be guarded against over fermentation. Although milk has a buffering action on dough but excessive fermentation may produce undesirable quantity of lactic acid which may break down the gluten resulting in bread having a very coarse and dark crumb and unpleasant sour taste and flavour.

Chapter - 5

Processing

After the raw material for bread making is correctly selected, the formula should be correctly balanced. Strength of flour, type of product to be made, fermentation time to be given, are some of the basic factors to be taken into consideration while balancing the formula. After balancing the formula, the raw material should be weighed accurately. Importance of correct weights of raw material cannot be over emphasised.

Whether dried yeast is used or compressed, it is advisable to make a ferment as a first step in dough making. Take a small quantity (minimum six times of the weight of yeast) of water (from total doughing water), add little sugar, and mix. For dried yeast, it is advisable to use luke warm water. Add yeast. Compressed yeast should be broken and dried yeast should be sprinkled. Let it soak until all the yeast starts floating on top which should not take more than 5 to 7 minutes. Add enough flour to make a thick paste, whisk it slightly in order to incorporate some air and leave aside (preferably in a warm place) for 10 to 15 minutes to allow it to rise. This batter is known as flying ferment and serves the purpose of invigorating the yeast activity in a thinner medium which is congenial to yeast activity before it is added to stiffer medium ie. dough where it will be less active in the initial stage. The quality of yeast is also ensured by the speed with which a flying ferment rises. If there is not enough rise within 15 to 20 minutes, the yeast is unsuitable for use and should be discarded. Small quantity (0.1-0.2%} of ammonium chloride will help speed up fermentation process.

Yeast activity is optimum at the temperatures between 78-80 deg. F(26 -28 deg.C). Water is the only medium which can be heated or cooled in order to bring out the dough at desired temperature for proper fermentation. Water temperature above 120 deg.F is harmful to yeast while temperature below 78 deg.F will slow down yeast activity considerably.

Method of calculating desired water temperature for dough making in order to have the dough at 78 deg.F is as follows.

Desired water temperature = (Desired dough temperature x 3) - (FT +RT+FF)

FT denotes Flour Temperature

RT denotes Room Temperature
FF denotes Friction Factor

For example:

Desired dough temp. is 78 deg.F

Let us assume that FT is 86 deg. F
RT is 84 deg.F
FF is 12 deg.F

Now substituting figures in our formula we will get;
(78 x 3) - (86 + 84 + 12)
= 52 deg.F will be the desired water temp.

Friction Factor (FF} is to be calculated by actually running a trial dough where temp. of water used for dough making and the temp. of the finished dough is recorded. Thus we can use the same formula in the following form,

Tap water temp. = (Actual dough temp. x 3) - (RT + RT + FF)

or

FF = (Actual dough temp. x 3) - (FT + RT + WT)

For example let us assume that;

Tap water temp	(WT)	-	84 deg. F
Flour temp.	(FT)	-	82 deg. F
Room temp.	(FIT)	-	80 deg. F
Dough temp.	(DT)	-	94 deg. F

By substituting these figures in the above formula we get;

FF = (94 x 3) - (82 + 80 + 84)
= 282 - 246
= 36 deg. F

In order to bring down the temperature of water, ice is used. Following is the formula for calculating the quantity of ice to be used in order to bring down the temperature of known quantity of water to desired level.

$$\text{Wt. of ice} = \frac{\text{Wt. of water (tap water temp. - calculated water temp.)}}{\text{tap water temp.} + 112}$$

For example;

Wt. of water	-	60 kg.
tap water temp	-	88 deg. F
Calculated water temp.	-	68 deg. F

Then wt. of ice required to bring down the temp. of 60 kg. water to 65 deg. F will be calculated as follows :

$$\text{wt. of ice} = \frac{60\,(88 - 68)}{88+112}$$

$$= 6 \text{ kg.}$$

In case of sponge and dough method of bread making, the formula for finding the desired water temp. is as follows;

Desired water temp. = (4 x desired dough temp.) - (ST + FT + RT + FF)

ST is sponge temperature

For example;

Desired dough temp.	78 deg.F
Sponge temp. (ST)	84
Flour temp. (FT)	82
Room temp. (RT)	80
Friction Factor (FF)	24

Then desired water temp.= (4 x78) - (84 + 82 + 80 + 24)
= 42 deg.F

Having discussed the scientific method for calculating the desired water temperature, it may be said for the benefit of retail bakers existing in remote areas where ice may not be available that as a general rule, during summers doughs should be made cool by the use of cold water and water should be sufficiently warmed during winters to allow for loss of temperature through atmosphere or cool equipments. A baker is well advised to make use of thermometer in order to get even results.

Mixing

While the flying ferment is under way, other ingredients are weighed and prepared. Flour is sifted, salt and sugar are dissolved in water and if any foreign matter is present should be strained through cloth; If the fat is granular, it should be melted without effecting any appreciable rise in temperature.

The dough could be mixed by hand as well as by machine. If machine is used, water with salt, sugar, bread improvers is added to the bowl first, then flour is added and mixed at low speed. Then ferment is added and dough is developed.

Flour contains gliadin and glutenin which join together and form gluten when water is added to flour and it is mixed. Initially this gluten does not have much elasticity and appears to be wet. As the mixing proceeds, elasticity and water absorptive capacity continue to improve until the dough reaches the final stage of development. As the texture of bread is very much dependent on proper development of gluten it is very necessary that the mixing operation is carried out properly in order to obtain optimum development of gluten.

While commencing the mixing operation, it will be observed that the machine does not labour initially. This is known as "Pick up" stage when flour picks up water and all the ingredients are in the process of distributing themselves evenly throughout until the whole mass becomes homogeneous. During this stage the dough seems to be slack but as the mixing proceeds, the gluten takes up water and the dough seems to be drying up. This is termed as "Drying up" stage. The dough is still sticky and adheres to the sides of the bowl as well as the mixing arm. As the mixing proceeds, the dough cleans the sides of the bowl and pulls away from the mixing arm. This is known as "Clean up" stage. Shortly afterwards comes the "Development stage" when the dough is considered to be properly mixed. In case of flour having very strong quality of gluten, dough may require longer mixing time to reach development stage. At this stage mixing operation should be stopped.

Many bakeries follow delayed salt method of bread making, which involves two mixing operations.

All the flour, yeast, water, yeast food is mixed sufficiently to make a homogeneous mass. At this stage, aim is not to develop gluten which is accomplished in the second operation. The dough is fermented for a short period. The remaining ingredients i.e. salt, sugar, fat is added during second mixing. Fat should be added at the last stage of mixing allowing just sufficient time for its even, thorough dispersal. If fat is added at the early stage, it will adversely affect the water absorption, and also the gluten development.

Quantity and quality of gluten will decide the length of mixing time. Strong flours as a rule require more mixing time. In case of sponge, it is not necessary to mix to clean up stage. It should be mixed just enough to distribute the ingredients evenly throughout the mass.

Although, dough making by hand is a laborious job, the operation should be carried out to the right stage without let-up in order to ensure quality of product.

When the dough is properly mixed, the surface of the dough becomes smooth (which had been rough at earlier stage of mixing), and surface may show some round, coin shaped gas bubbles trapped under very thin film of dough. A small piece of correctly mixed dough can be stretched between fingers into a (paper like) very thin, translucent film.

Weak flours and freshly milled flours are mixed for shorter time. With such flours quantity of salt and yeast should be raised and fermentation time should be reduced.

If the dough is over mixed, the gluten structure will break down and the rise during fermentation time will be very poor resulting in slow speed of fermentation. The dough will heat up, be sticky and will tend to flatten out during intermediate and final proofing. Bread produced from excessively mixed dough will have less volume, and dark, crumbly texture.

Conversely, under mixing will not develop the gluten sufficiently and the dough will be less elastic. The resultant bread will have less volume and a rough break shred. There is possibility of collapse of bread during proofing or in the oven as the gluten will not have enough elasticity to extend with expanding gases.

FERMENTATION

After the dough is correctly mixed, it is fermented for a predetermined time. Although "Fermentation" has been discussed under the paragraph on "yeast" it is worthwhile to repeat it again.

Fermentation is a process whereby yeast organisms feed on sugar and produce CO_2, gas and alcohol. CO_2 gas raises the dough fabric. Part of alcohol evaporates, part is converted into acetic acid and the remaining contributes to the characteristic flavour of bread.

There are three sources of sugar in a fermenting dough;

1. Natural sugar present in the flour,
2. Formula sugar added in the mix, and
3. Sugar produced from the starch of flour through enzyme action.

Apart from gas and alcohol, some quantities of glycerin, lactic acid, acetic acid and succinic acid are also produced. These acids and protease enzyme together have a mellowing effect on the gluten thereby imparting extensibility to it. The balance between elasticity and extensibility of gluten in a properly conditioned dough should be such that the gluten should remain strong enough (elastic nature) to hold the gases and still mellow enough (extensibility) to expand with the expanding gases. This condition in gluten is achieved by fermenting the dough in the right environment (temp. 78 to 80 deg.F, relative humidity 70 to 75%) for the right time which is decided according to the strength of flour and formulation of the product. An experienced baker can make out by the feel of dough when the right degree of fermentation is achieved.

If the dough is allowed to over ferment, it becomes soft and sticky due to over action of protease enzyme and acids. The structure forming capacity of gluten will weaken and depending on the degree of over fermentation, the bread may have an excessive volume with very open texture, or it may collapse during proofing or baking. In any case, the water binding capacity of bread will be reduced resulting in crumbliness and quick staling of bread. Such bread will have a pale crust colour and dark or greyish crumb. The bread will have irregular appearance with rough top. and / or caved in sides and bottom. The bread will have a sour taste and aroma. Over fermentation can take place due to a number of factors i.e. use of too much yeast for the method followed, prolonged fermentation time without due consideration to the strength of flour, very slack doughs, lack of salt, fermenting the dough in a warm place and so on.

An under fermented dough will produce bread with less volume and a harsh redish brown crust colour. The texture will be close and compact. The bread will dry out soon and will have a tendency to be crumbly due to insufficient conditioning of gluten. Taste and aroma of bread will be flat. The dough will have a tendency to flatten out which could be observed during intermediate proofing and due to this fluidity of dough the bread will have sharp edges.

Under fermentation may be caused due to a number of factors i.e. less fermentation time given according to the strength of flour, less yeast used for the method followed, too much salt, too tight a dough, dough chilled during fermentation and so on.

Knock back

After the (straight) dough is fermented for two third of its estimated fermentation time, it is knocked back. The process of knocking back should be carried out correctly by extending the sides of the dough and putting it in the center, so that the whole mass of the dough comes in contact with fresh air and the dough is virtually turned upside down.

1. When the dough is fermenting, the temperature of the upper surface is lower than the temperature of the bottom part of the dough. This variation in dough temperature causes variation in the speed of fermentation in different parts of the same dough. By knocking back correctly the temperature of the whole mass of dough is fairly equalised and fermentation speed becomes even.

2. After a dough has fermented for some time, the gluten is in a stretched condition and if it is allowed to remain so, it will collapse by itself. But this natural collapse will not put the dough in its original compact position and the mass of the dough will have an uneven distribution of gas pockets thereby affecting uneven fermentation after the collapse. By knocking back, the condition of dough becomes even and the fermentation speed remains even throughout the mass.

3. When the dough has fermented for some time, the yeast cell is surrounded by gas and other fermentation products which slow down its activity, as it is drawn away from its food by surrounding gas. By knocking back, the gas is expelled and yeast cell is again in position to carry out its function efficiently.

The stretching action to which the gluten is subjected during knocking back operation has a beneficial effect on the finished product as this stretching action helps proper conditioning of gluten.

After knock back, the dough is again fermented for the remaining one third period during which the dough is filled with gas and the gluten becomes pliable and in a fit condition for further processing.

Dividing and rounding

The dough is cut into pieces of desired weight according to the size of the mould. While dividing the dough by hand, it is desirable to cut the dough with a regular dough cutter. Pulling and breaking the dough should be avoided as it disturbs the trend of gluten strands thereby adversely affecting the final texture of the product.

When dough is cut, the cut surface is exposed while the remaining surface has a stretched gluten film. It is obvious that some gas will escape from the cut surface (technically known as bleeding) and the condition of the dough piece will be uneven. If the piece is moulded in this state, the texture of bread will also be uneven. Therefore, the dough piece is rounded in order to make it uniform. The process is known as rounding or handing up.

In large bread factories, dough is divided by Divider machine. Machine divides the dough by volume and not by weight. Therefore it is very necessary that dough is correctly fermented. Otherwise, in case of over fermented dough a particular volume of dough will weigh less due to excessive gas in it and the same volume of under fermented dough will weigh more due to lack of gas in it.

Intermediate Proofing

Whenever a fermented dough is handled, some of the gas escapes and gluten strands collapse, making the dough tight. If the dough piece is manipulated when it is in tight condition, it will tear off leaving a rough surface. The torn surface will allow escape of gas which will have adverse effect on the texture of bread. Therefore, before manipulating the dough further, it should be rested for 10 to 15 minutes. During this period, the piece is again filled with gas and gluten comes back to its pliable condition making further handling possible without tearing. This resting of the rounded dough piece is known as "Intermediate Proofing."

Moulding and panning

The dough piece, soft and pliable after intermediate proof, is moulded according to the desired shape of the finished product. While moulding the dough piece, it should be remembered that the moulding pressure is even through out the dough piece. Uneven pressure will leave gas pockets of uneven size in the dough piece which will eventually result in uneven texture. Secondly; the dough piece should not be moulded too tight or too loose. Too tight moulding may tear off the surface which should remain smooth and may also increase the proofing time.Too loose moulding will open up the texture to an undesirable extent. Moulded pieces are put into clean and well greased pans of appropriate size. Too little or too much dough according to the size of pan will spoil the texture. The ratio between the size of the mould and weight of the dough should be 35 cc per 10 g. of dough (6 cu. in. per oz. of dough).

Proofing

After panning, the bread is proofed, under suitable conditions (temperature-95 to 98 deg.F, Relative humidity-80 to 83%) to allow it to rise again and acquire volume. The process is known as proofing. During fermentation time, the gluten should be so matured that it expands with the expanding gas and still retains sufficient strength to hold the gas. When gluten is in such perfect condition, and the temperature and humidity of proofing cabinet are ideal, the rise of bread is faster without taking unduly long time. If the dough is under fermented, the gluten will have less stretchability and more resistance, which may result in excessively long proofing time. If there is crust formation on bread due to lack of humidity, or if there is lack of temperature in proofing cabinet then also the rise will be very slow. Under all these circumstances, the texture of bread will suffer. On the other hand, if there had been excessive fermentation of dough, the bread may rise faster and then collapse. If there is excessive temperature, in the proofing cabinet, there may be partial coagulation of gluten which is immediately in contact with the walls of the bread-mould. That, along with faster rise of the rest of the bread, will adversely affect the texture. During proofing operation, the yeast should have sufficient food to affect a faster gas production, Therefore it is necessary that there is sufficient diastatic activity in the flour in order to produce fermentable sugars for yeast to carry out its function efficiently during the critical stage of proofing. If there is insufficient diastatic capacity in the flour, the proofing period is unduly prolonged affecting the texture adversely. Excessive diastatic action will also adversely affect the texture as there will be excessive gas production and gluten will also be excessively mellowed causing it to collapse.

Baking

After the bread has acquired full volume, it is baked. The temperature and humidity of the oven should be well maintained in order to get good results. The temperature of the oven is set according to the quantity of product to be baked, its size and its formulation. Normally, bread products are baked between 400 - 480 deg.F Open top loaves are baked at lesser temperature than sandwich bread. Further, if a formulation contains more than 6% sugar or any amount of milk solids, the product should be baked at lesser temperature. Similarly, large size products are baked at higher temperature than small size products.

When the bread is kept in the oven, it acquires heat gradually. Due to increase in temperature, the yeast starts functioning vigorously producing gas which raises the volume of the product. The difference in the size of a product from the time it was kept in the oven to the time it is properly baked is known as "oven-spring." During this period of baking, yeast should get appropriate quantity of food in order to produce gas. This, much needed food, is provided by the breakdown of starch into maltose sugar. As the temperature further rises the yeast cells start getting inactive and completely cease functioning at around 140 deg.F

The enzymes still remain active up to about 170 deg.F, producing sugar from starch. This activity is enhanced due to the fact that the starch is partially gelatinized making it more susceptible to enzymatic action. As the yeast, which had been consuming sugar, is already inactivated, this sugar remains in bread and performs its usual functions of retaining moisture in the product, imparting colour to the crust, improving flavour and taste.

As baking proceeds further, the proteins are coagulated (at about 172 deg.F) setting the structure of the product, after which there is no further rise in the volume of bread. Once the structure of the product is set, it starts gaining temperature. Weight is lost due to the evaporation of moisture from the product and the crust starts acquiring golden brown colour.

1. SELECTION OF RAW MATERIAL
2. WEIGHING OF RAW MATERIAL
3. PREPARATION OF RAW MATERIAL
4. MIXING
5. FERMENTATION
6, KNOCK BACK
7. FLOOR TIME
8. DIVIDING AND ROUNDING
9. INTERMEDIATE PROOFING
10. MOULDING AND PANNING
11. PROOFING
12. BAKING
13. COOLING
14. SLICING AND WRAPPING

BREAD MAKING FLOW CHART

The temperature of the oven for baking bread is very important. If the oven is very hot, the coagulation of protein, (forming of crust) on the outer surface will take place very soon. This crust formation will block the easy transmission of heat inside the bread. As a .result when gas expands in the inner portion and crust being nonstretchable, there will be an exaggerated break in the bread. The crust colour will be too dark and the bread may not be baked properly from inside. Since the early crust formation will check full rise of bread, the volume will remain small and due to uneven expansion, there will be poor shape.

Conversely, if the oven is too cold, coagulation of protein will be delayed and yeast will remain active for longer period, which will result in excessive volume of bread. Due to lack of temperature, bread will be required to be baked for longer duration, resulting in evaporation of more than necessary amount of moisture. Resultant product will be crumbly and will stale faster.

When there is sufficient humidity in the oven, expansion of bread will be even, enabling the bread to acquire proper volume. Lack of humidity in oven will cause faster evaporation of moisture from external surface of bread. As a result, there will be faster formation of crust which will eventually result in small volumed loaf.

There will be uneven expansion and poor shape. If bread is baked in excessive humidity, the crust will become tough and leathery and adequate amount of moisture may not bake off from bread, making the crumb over moist and vulnerable to mould infection.

If the oven is over loaded (in relation to the temp. of oven, which may usually happen with fire wood oven) each bread will get lesser share of heat. As a result yeast activity will continue for longer time and coagulation of protein (i.e. setting of structure) will be delayed. In such condition, texture of bread will open up excessively, promoting crumbliness and early staling. Crust colour will also remain dull. In case of under loading, the effect will be same as in case of baking bread in too hot oven. If it becomes necessary to bake a small batch of bread in a large oven, humidity should be sufficiently increased and bread should be protected from fierce heat by covering it suitably (with baking trays etc.).

Bread moulds should always be placed in oven at a distance of about half an inch from, and parallel to, each other which will ensure proper circulation of heat and evenly baked product. If moulds are loaded too close to each other, the sides of the bread which are in close contact, will be insufficiently baked, without proper crust colour. Whitish sides give a poor appearance and usually get infected by fungus very soon. However; present day practice of using set of three or four moulds strapped together at appropriate distance takes care of such problems.

When an open top loaf (without putting the lid as in case of sandwich bread) is baked, it should get a break on the sides of the loaf and the characteristic of this break (shred) should be smooth. This break-shred is a test of good bread and is the result of proper processing, mainly fermentation and baking conditions. Adequate fermentation creates such a balance between the gassing power of the dough and condition of gluten that the dough has capacity to expand with expanding gas and still has sufficient strength to retain it (and not give way to expanding gases). When this condition is achieved in the dough and bread is placed in the oven for baking, the crust formation takes place first on top and sides of the bread. The junction point of top crust and side remains the weakest part where from the gas escapes creating a smooth break. In hearth type products (French bread, Vienna bread etc. which are baked without any mould) this break could be predetermined by docking or scoring (cutting with a sharp blade) the product.

If the dough is under matured, there will be less stretchability and more resistance in it. In such case, depending on the degree of under maturing. there could be blind appearance (if too much under fermented) or a wild break or flying tops where the upper crust is separated from the crumb body of the bread like a lid with hinge. Over fermentation will mellow the gluten excessively which will have little resistance power. In this case bread will have blind appearance without any break. Bread will also have sunken appearance.

COOLING

Bread should be released from the mould immediately after baking, otherwise the moisture trapped between the bread and surface of the mould will make the product soggy, technically known as "Sweating". When the bread is withdrawn from the oven after baking, the process of moisture evaporation continues as long as it is warm. If the bread is wrapped during this stage, the water vapours will be absorbed by the bread itself (specially crust) and will remain as free moisture. This free moisture will be conducive to fungus infection. Therefore, the bread should be packed only when it is thoroughly cooled (especially center of crumb) to room temperature.

When the bread is hot, starch granules are in a swollen state and held unstably by gluten framework. If the bread is sliced in this state, the unstably positioned starch granules will lump up together giving a very poor appearance to slice. After the bread is brought down to room temperature, the starch granules will shrink and stabilise in gluten framework and then only bread could be sliced in neat slices.

PACKING

Bread is packed in order to preserve its freshness and to protect it from the hazards of external contamination. Air tight wrapping is not advisable in tropical climate. The bread should be allowed to breathe but not unduly exposed. Wax paper or indented poly propylene material will serve the purpose satisfactorily.

Chapter - 6

Bread Making Methods

Present day bread production scenario has changed to a very large extent in comparison with conventional methods. High speed machines and modern technology has made it possible to produce more, of a better quality and within shorter time. However; in spite of the benefits of modern technology, it is necessary for a student to understand the conventional methods which is like a stepping stone to modern day practice.

Straight Dough Method

In this method all the ingredients are mixed together, and the dough is fermented for a predetermined time. The fermentation time of a straight dough depends on the strength of flour. Strong flours require more fermentation time to mature adequately.

Flours which require 2 to 3 hours for maturing should be used for making bread by straight method. Flours that take very long period for maturing should not be used in straight method because during prolonged fermentation periods it is very difficult to control the temperature of dough and rise in temperature will invariably cause acid taste and flavour in bread. As temperature rise has immediate effect on fermentation speed, it is very necessary to control the temperature of a straight dough by;

1. Using shorter fermentation periods,
2. Adjusting the temperature of doughing water
3. By fermenting the dough at optimum (room) temperature i.e. between 78 deg. to 80 deg.F.

When it is desired to ferment a straight dough for longer period, it should be remembered that gluten will soften up to a greater extent and is likely to become sticky: therefore the dough should be made tighter. Yeast content should be reduced but sugar content should be increased in order to provide food during prolonged fermentation. Salt content is increase= as it provides stability to the dough and keeps the fermentation speed under control which is necessary during long fermentation period.

Salt-delayed Method

This is a slight variation of straight method, where all the ingredients are mixed except salt and fat. As the salt has a controlling effect on enzymatic action of yeast, the speed of fermentation of a salt less dough will be faster, and a reduction in total fermentation time could be affected. The salt is added at the knock-back stage. The method of adding salt at the later stage may be according to the convenience of individual baker. It may be sifted (dry) on the dough and mixed. It may be creamed with fat and mixed.

Whatever way is chosen for mixing the salt, only three-fourth (of the actual mixing time) mixing should be given initially and onefourth mixing at the time of adding salt. The method is specially suitable if strong flours are to be used for bread-making by straight method. Due to absence of salt, the fermentation speed is enhanced and gluten is matured in a reasonably shorter time.

No-dough Time Method

In this method, dough is not fermented in the usual manner. It is just allowed a brief period (about 30 min.) for it to recover from the strains of mixing. Since dough is not fermented the twin functions of fermentation (i.e. production of gas and conditioning of gluten) are achieved to some extent by increasing the quantity of yeast (2 to 3 times of original quantity) and by making the dough little slacker and warmer. Although it is possible to make fairly acceptable bread (during emergency) by using this method the product has poor keeping quality and lacks in aroma. Due to absence of fermentation the gluten and starch are not conditioned sufficiently to retain the moisture and there is no flavour because flavour producing bi-products of fermentation are absent. As there is increased quantity of yeast present, the bread may have a strong yeast flavour.

Sponge and Dough Method

Previously, in this chapter it has been mentioned that strong flours take too long for conditioning and should not be used for making bread by straight dough method. For such flours sponge and dough method is more suitable where the problem of controlling the dough temperature is not so acute as the total fermentation time is divided in two separate segments. For the sake of convenience and proper identification, a sponge- dough is indicated as 60 /40 sponge- dough, or 70 / 30 sponge - dough, where the first numbers i.e. 60 or 70 indicate the percentage of flour used in sponge and the second numbers ie. 40 or 30 indicate the percentage of flour mixed at the time of dough making.

In this method, as a first step, a part of flour, proportionate amount of water, all the formula yeast and yeast food are mixed together. Longer fermenting sponges may contain some amount of salt also. Mixing operation is carried out just sufficiently to incorporate all the ingredients evenly. This sponge is fermented for a predetermined time. Sponge fermentation time depends on the amount of flour in the sponge and flour quality. The quantity of flour in sponge depends on the strength of flour. If the flour is too strong, more quantity should be used in sponge and in turn the sponge should be fermented for longer duration.

It is advisable to test the sponge physically for its readiness before mixing it into dough. The following methods of sponge testing could be used;

1. Take a small piece of sponge and try to break it with both hands. If the piece breaks with a clean fracture the sponge is ready for mixing. If the sponge is not ready, the piece will stretch to some extent and will break in unevenly stretched shreds. In such case sponge should be allowed more fermentation time.

2. Tear the sponge apart from the center with both hands and examine the web structure. If the web structure is very fine, the sponge is ready.

3. An adequately fermented sponge feels dry to touch without any stickiness present.

When the sponge is ready, it should be broken down properly with formula water, so that its even mixing in the dough is assured. Uneven mixing of sponge in the dough should be avoided as it produces uneven results in the bread. Broken down sponge is mixed with the remaining flour, sugar, salt, fat etc. Mixing operation should be carried out to the right degree. If two different kinds of flour are at hand, the weaker flour should be used at the time of dough making.

After the dough is mixed, it is rested for 30 to 45 min. during which time it relaxes from the stress of mixing operation. Preconditioned gluten of the sponge hastens the conditioning process of the gluten of fresh flour during this period and the dough is in perfect state for further manipulation i.e. cutting, moulding etc.

Ferment and Dough Process

This is a variation of sponge and dough method. Very often a (bread product) formula may contain milk, eggs, substantial quantity of fat and sugar as in the case of sweet bread, Danish pastry and other sweet fermented products. All these formula ingredients will have a retarding effect on yeast activity. If all the formula yeast, part of flour, yeast food and sufficient water (to make a fluid batter as in the case of flying ferment) are mixed together, the yeast gets initially an environment which is conducive to vigorous activity and at the end of fermentation time (of ferment) it is in a fit condition to take on the extra load of fermentation in the presence of milk, eggs, excessive fat etc. Fermentation time of a ferment depends on the formulation of the product desired to be made and the flavour desired in the product but very often it becomes a matter of individual preference eg. some bakers may take the ferment (for mixing) after it is dropped by itself, while others may take it just prior to dropping and some may allow time even after it has dropped. A ferment containing milk should be guarded against over fermentation as it will develop more than desirable quantity of lactic acid which in turn will affect the flavour, taste and texture of the product.

When a ferment is ready, it is mixed into dough, along with the remaining ingredients and allowed to ferment for the second stage of fermentation before the dough is taken up for make up. This method is used for making enriched bread, buns, Danish pastry, sweet dough, doughnuts etc. where the speed is very necessary.

Advantages of sponge-dough method of bread making

One basic advantage of sponge - dough method is that the total fermentation time is divided into two stages which makes it possible to have better control on the fermentation activity. For the same reason, there are lesser chances of the production schedule being thrown out of gear. Any possible minor delays during the first stage of fermentation can always be remedied during second stage of fermentation.

If too strong flour is used in straight- dough method, it will take too long time to mature. During this prolonged fermentation time there will be more rise in dough temperature which will produce more acidity in the dough as well as in the bread. The same flour, if used in sponge-dough method, where all the yeast and only a part of flour is present, fermentation time will automatically be lesser than in the case of straight dough and chances of significant rise in temperature are much less.

Secondly, if a straight dough is delayed, the defect cannot be remedied and the bread will have all the characteristics of bread made from over fermented dough. If a bakery is producing more than one batch of bread then all the subsequent doughs will also be delayed. While, in case of sponge dough, if a sponge is delayed, the dough time is proportionately adjusted and production schedule is not much disturbed.

In sponge and dough method, all the formula yeast works only on a part of flour, effecting better maturing of gluten. Therefore, not only there is superior texture of bread but also the moisture retention capacity and flavour of bread is better. It may not be out of place to mention that by using sponge and dough method, a baker can ward off a number of minor irritants like temperature variations due to weather conditions, lack of diastatic capacity in flour, too harsh gluten in flour, and so on. Although, there are disadvantages also eg. each batch is to be mixed twice, ingredients are to be weighed in two lots, more floor area may be required, but these small disadvantages are far outweighed by better quality of product.

In large bakeries, present day practice is to use a short sponge and dough method, where all the flour, yeast, water and mineral improvers (if any) are mixed and fermented for a short duration (about 30 to 45 min.). Later, salt, sugar, fat and emulsifiers etc. are added in right order and dough is cleared. Substantial saving in total production time can be achieved by using this method.

With the advent of high speed mixers, the fermentation time is totally eliminated. In this method the mellowness in the dough is achieved by high speed mixing which softens the gluten to the desired extent and to have sufficient gas production, quantity of yeast is increased to 2-3.5%. If enhanced flavour is desired in such products a small portion of flour is replaced with corresponding quantity of sponge. For example in a bowl size of 30 kg. of maida the quantity of maida can be taken 27 kg. and 5 kg. sponge can be taken. Five kg. sponge will contain approximately 3 kg. maida. Thus the total quantity of maida in one mixing remains 30 kg. only.

"Continuous" bread making process was used in U.S.A. to a considerable extent in sixties. However bread made by this method is too soft and lacks in aroma and taste as compared to bread made by conventional method. Only very strong flour {gluten forming proteins more than 12%} can be used in this method. However the process, as the name suggests, is continuous which is quite different than the batch method.

In this method a liquid containing water, yeast, MYF, milk solids, salt, liquid sugar and small quantity of flour is made in steel tanks which are maintained at 86 deg.F and the mixture is constantly stirred by mechanical stirrers. A number of brews can be made where yeast is held back and added at scheduled time. This broth is fermented for a predetermined time, and then pumped into the incorporator (pre mix) where other ingredients i.e. shortening, oxidants and flour (similarly pumped) are roughly incorporated together. This mass is gradually pumped into the developer where it passes through fast rotating spindles which mellow the dough by mechanical action. The same condition is achieved in batch method by fermentation. The dough is extruded through divider, in measured quantity and in the shape of moulded bread. It falls in the bread moulds which travel at a constant speed on a conveyer belt. This conveyer belt passes through overhead proofers, and by the time the bread moulds complete their journey through overhead proofers, the bread is fully proofed where from it enters the tunnel oven and after being baked, emerges through the other end of oven. After the bread is released from the moulds, it continues its journey through cooling chambers and then to slicing and wrapping area.

Chapter - 7

How to Judge the Quality of Bread

Most of the commercially produced bread in the country is sandwich type and open top loaves are rarely seen in the market. Reasons for this change may be many eg. non availability of sufficiently strong flour to produce open top loaves, consumer preference for streamlined square slice of bread, convenience of bakers in producing sandwich bread, convenience in storing sandwich bread and so on. However; for judging the various characteristics, an open top bread should be tested as it may not be possible to notice some of the finer points of distinction in case of sandwich bread. When lid is put on sandwich bread before baking, the expansion of bread during baking operation is restricted, which, in turn, will affect the crumb structure of bread and some other characteristics also. The appearance of an open top loaf will convey quite a bit of information (about its characteristics) to an experienced baker while the appearance of a sandwich bread may often prove to be delusive. However; in order to make a complete assessment of the quality of bread, it should be examined both for external as well as internal characteristics which are as follows.

External Characteristics	Internal Characteristic
1. Volume	1. Colour
2. Symmetry of shape	2. Structure
3. Bloom	3. Texture and sheen
4. Crust colour	4. Flavour and aroma
5 Evenness of bake	5. Crumb clarity and elasticity
6. Oven break	6. Moistness
	7. Cleanliness

Volume

When we see a bread, the first thing to catch the eye is its volume.The volume of bread should always be considered in relation to its weight (i.e. specific volume) and for a particular weight of bread, the volume should be neither too big nor too small. Too much volume for the weight of bread indicates too open a texture which entails crumbliness, early staling etc. On the other hand, a small volume for the corresponding weight of dough is indicative of too close and compact crumb structure, lack of flavour etc. Factors conducive to acquiring good volume in bread are; sufficient strength in flour, adequate fermentation to achieve proper conditioning of gluten, sufficient diastatic capacity in flour to maintain the gassing power of the dough at the time of baking, proper proofing and baking conditions.

Symmetry of shape

This is another characteristic of bread (like volume) which will be affected only in the case of open top loaf as a sandwich bread is bound to have symmetry of shape (like constant volume). The lower part (Trunk) of a bread is guided by the walls of the mould, while the upper (dome shaped) part has free expansion. There should be such a harmony between these two parts of bread that it presents a pleasing appearance. Even in case of other bread products, i.e.French loaf, Vienna bread, rolls etc., this harmony between its different parts is very important without which the product will present a very poor sight. If a piece of dough having (proportionately) more weight is placed in a mould, the lower part will be guided by the walls of the mould and will remain as usual but the expansion of the top part will be exaggerated so as to present a non symmetrical shape. Excess use of bread improvers, too much under or over fermentation, excessive/ insufficient proofing, inadequate proofing and baking conditions, are some of the factors which are responsible for imparting round shoulders, caved in sides or bottom, jagged upper crust, thereby spoiling the symmetry of shape.

Bloom

This is such a delicate characteristic of bread that it requires a very fine judgment to differentiate it from crust colour. Just as a healthy plant or a healthy human being has a different appearance from unhealthy ones, so is the natural bloom of bread different from artificially acquired shine. If a bread having natural bloom is kept besides another bread having artificial shine (acquired by brushing with fat), the difference can easily be made out. Bloom is that natural flush which can be acquired in bread only by the use of good raw material and proper care at each and every stage of processing.

Crust colour

Crust of bread is supposed to have a pleasing golden brown colour. Since caramelisation of sugar is responsible for imparting such colour to the crust, the. intensity of colour will depend on the quantity of sugar available for caramelisation at the time of baking. Yeast also requires sugar for gas production. Therefore, availability of sugar for caramelisation is influenced by the activity of yeast during fermentation time. For whatever reason (such as slack dough, lack of salt, high temp. of fermentation room etc.), if more sugar is consumed by the yeast during fermentation time, the crust colour will be pale or light brown. Conversely, if there is lack of yeast activity (as may happen in case of insufficient fermentation time, stiff dough, excessive salt content, chilling of dough etc.),there will be more sugar left in the dough, which will make the crust colour reddish brown (foxy red, harsh brown) that is again not very pleasing to the eye. Apart from over or under fermentation, some other factors also influence crust colour such as proofing conditions, oven temperature, milk content of the formula, type of bread improvers used, consistency of dough, diastatic activity of flour, amount of bleaching flour is subjected to etc.

Evenness of bake

A bread should have even golden brown crust colour all around. Since the top crust remains in direct contact with hot air, it will naturally acquire slightly darker colour, but this darkness of top crust should be in consonance with the colour of remaining crust. In case if single bread moulds (as against striped set of moulds) are used in a bakery, bread is likely to have uneven crust colour if the moulds are set in the oven too close to each other. In that case, the side of the bread which is in close contact with the other mould will not get proper colour as there is no gap in between for circulation of heat. Precisely, for this reason, the moulds should be set in oven half an inch apart and parallel to each other in order to allow free and even flow of heat. In ovens also there are likely to be hot and cold spots. In that case too, bread will have uneven crust colour. Over fermentation or over proofing will create a condition where large gas pockets will remain entrapped between walls of the mould and body of bread. In that case the whole body of bread will not remain in touch with the mould and heat absorption will be uneven and crust colour will also be uneven.

Oven Break

When an open top loaf is being baked, crust formation on the side and top of bread takes place earlier while there is still no crust formation on the portion of bread which is nearest (and parallel) to the upper edge of the mould. When the expansion takes place in the inner part of bread, the gas stretches this weaker part (where there had been no crust formation) and escapes through the opening thus created. This is called Break. At this break, stretched and coagulated gluten strands could be clearly seen. The characteristic of the break (smooth, rough, exaggerated) is known as shred. If the flour is of good strength, dough is correctly fermented, and proofing and baking conditions are proper, then the break must be smooth which is invariably a sign of good bread. It had been discussed earlier that the gluten of dough should be so conditioned during fermentation that (during baking) it could stretch with the expanding gas and still have sufficient resistance to retain gas. It is the adequate balance between these two conditions which comes from proper fermentation and which is responsible for giving a smooth break. If the dough is under fermented, the gluten will have more resistance and it may tear apart under pressure A expanding gas giving an exaggerated break or even a shell (flying) top. Conversely, if the dough is over fermented, there will be no resistance left in the dough (excessive mellowing due to over fermentation) and there will be blind appearance i.e. there will be no break. Apart from proper fermentation, the "Break Shred " is also affected by correct moulding, adequate proofing, and sufficient humidity in the proofing room and the oven.

Internal colour of bread

Obviously, the internal colour of bread will be influenced by the grade of flour (use of patent flour will produce whiter crumb while in the case of whole wheat flour the crumb will be darker) but it is also true that different batches of bread made from the same flour may have different internal colour. This is so because the visual effect of whiteness of bread crumb is decided by the amount of light reflected from the crumb surface. If more amount of light is reflected from the crumb surface, the crumb will appear whiter while if the crumb surface absorbs more light and very little is reflected the result will be darker appearing crumb. A crumb structure, made up of small, even sized, oblong and shallow gas cells, will reflect more light in comparison with another crumb which has a structure made up of uneven sized, deep and round shaped cells, because, in this case more light will be absorbed by the crumb and reflection will be very poor. If the cell walls are thin, a part of light falling on a cell will pass through into the neighbouring cell and the intensity of reflected light will increase thereby enhancing the visual effect of whiteness of crumb. A bread having thick cell walls will not allow this refraction of light into the neighbouring cells and the crumb will appear to be comparatively darker. Factors which influence the crumb structure (and ultimately its whiteness) are quality of flour, degree of fermentation, manipulation of dough (knocking back, dividing, handing up, and moulding), proofing and baking conditions.

Structure

If the crumb structure of different kinds of bread products is closely observed, it will be seen that shape and size of gas cells varies considerably eg. regular white bread will have oblong shaped small gas cells which are evenly distributed throughout the crumb, while a French loaf will have round gas cells of uneven size and unevenly distributed in the crumb. In case of whole meal (brown) bread, the gas cells will be very small due to presence of bran which has a cutting action on gluten strands thus preventing them from stretching. Structure of different kinds of bread products must vary due to difference in formula, fermentation, manipulation, baking condition and so on. For example, hearth type products are made from strong flour, lean formula is used, make up is of different kind and baking is done on a flat surface without the support of a mould which will result in a structure having round, uneven sized and unevenly distributed gas cells. While in case of white bread, although same strong flour is used, but the formulation, make up, proofing and baking conditions are different which produce a structure having even sized, oblong gas cells. But the structure of similar kind of product will be influenced by the quality of raw material, degree of fermentation, manipulation of dough and proofing and baking conditions. Slack doughs will produce bread having open structure and large holes while a tight dough will produce a bread with close structure.

Sheen and Texture

If the crumb structure of bread is made up of small, oblong, shallow and evenly distributed gas cells having thin cell walls, the cut surface of the bread slice will not only appear bright but will also appear to be full of small sparkling objects which is nothing but increased intensity of reflected light due to thinness of cell walls. This characteristic is known as Sheen. If a cut surface of bread slice is gently pressed with finger tips, the sensation could be that of smooth silkiness (like velvet), or hardness (like a drum) or coarseness (like jute bag) and so on. This sensation of touch is known as texture of bread. The texture which is soft, silky and still with certain degree of firmness is considered to be good. A slack dough or too much final proofing will produce a bread having open crumb structure which will be soft to touch but will be coarse. Such texture is known as Wooly. Excessive tightening action on flour proteins as in the case of too much milk in the formula or high levels of potassium bromate will produce a bread with such a compact crumb that it will appear almost like a block of cheese. This is known as Cheesy texture. Bread made from under fermented or too tight dough will have a texture which is very tight, hard to press and rough, known as Drummy texture.

Flavour and Aroma

Taste of any bakery product could be fully appreciated only when it is accompanied by matching flavour. A cake or cookie or bread product cannot be enjoyed if there is no flavour present. In case of bread, a number of acids and other bi-products are produced during fermentation time. When these acids etc. come in contact with heat during baking; they impart special flavour to bread. Therefore the bi-products of fermentation have a major roll to play in deciding the flavour of bread. If dough remains under fermented, there will not be enough bi-products present and consequently bread will lack in aroma. On the other hand, over fermentation will produce excessive quantities of acids etc. and the flavour will be too strong (sourish) some times termed as gassy. High temperature of dough during fermentation or too much temperature in the fermentation room will produce acidic flavour. Excessively long fermentation period will produce a flavour similar to that of rancid butter. Some of the ingredients used in bread making, also, either impart flavour to bread or enhance the natural flavour of other ingredients thereby improving the overall flavour of bread. Such ingredients are salt, sugar, malt and milk. Salt is one ingredient which exerts a considerable influence on the flavour of bread; therefore, optimum quantity of salt should be used in bread formula.

Crumb clarity and Elasticity

When a thin slice of bread is held against bright light, the whole surface should appear translucent. But at times dark spots are likely to be seen through which light will not pass. Such a dense spot feels hard to touch and is known as Core. Improper mixing of dough is a major cause for having cores in bread. Scrapings of dough (collected from table, mixing bowl etc.) should be properly mixed with the rest of dough before it is set for fermentation. If dough has crusted at fermentation or make up stage, this crust will get folded during moulding operation and will form hard cores in the crumb. Dense layers in the crumb structure are known as seams. If a fully expanded loaf is mishandled while placing it in the oven, some portion of web like structure may collapse resulting in the formation of seams. When the crumb of bread is pressed (gently), it should not break and when the pressure is released, it should come back to its original shape. This quality of bread is known as Elasticity. If a bread does not have the quality of elasticity, the pressure of slicing blades will break the crumb rather than cutting it in neat slice. Such a bread slice will not be easy to butter also, as the pressure from butter knife will also break the crumb. Good quality flour and adequate fermentation are the important factors which influence the elasticity of bread.

Moistness

Quality of freshness of bread is judged by the degree of its moistness. Moistness is influenced by the condition of gluten and starch in the bread. A bread may contain more amount of moisture and still be devoid of the quality of moistness. If the gluten is adequately conditioned during fermentation stage, it will form a very fine web like structure having thin cell walls thereby enhancing the moisture holding capacity of bread. Similarly, the proper conditioning of starch which is influenced by the action of diastase enzyme, will also improve the moisture holding capacity of bread. Some of the bread making ingredients eg. salt, fat, sugar, malt help in retaining moisture in bread. Baking and storing conditions also influence the moistness of bread. !f the bread is baked at low temperature it will have to be baked for longer time which will result in evaporation of more moisture from bread. A bread store should have relative humidity of about 60%. Lack of humidity will rob the bread of its moistness.

Cleanliness

This is such a characteristic of bread which is hardly, if ever, has any bearing with quality of raw material, or inadequacies during processing. Cleanliness of the product depends on the care a baker takes in handling the production. All the labour put in producing a good bread may be wasted if the baker is not careful in handling the finished product. Absolute care is necessary during baking, depanning, cooling, slicing and packing operations as these are the stages when bread is likely to loose its quality of cleanliness. No object, which is not absolutely clean, should ever be allowed to come in contact with the product. It is the sacred duty and social obligation of a baker to maintain perfect standards of personal hygiene as well as cleanliness of his establishment.

Chapter - 8

Bread Faults

There are a number of factors which may be responsible for creating faults in bread. However; some of the major factors which adversely influence the quality of bread are as follows:

1. Inferior quality and inadequate quantity of gluten in the flour.
2. Poor or excessive diastatic activity.
3. Disproportionate quantities of raw material ie. imperfectly balanced formula.
4. Inferior quality of raw material specially yeast.
5. Incorrect time and temperature of fermentation.
6. Incorrect methods of manipulation of dough i.e. knocking back, dividing, and moulding.
7. Improper proofing conditions i. e. time, temperature and humidity
8. Improper baking conditions, i.e. temperature, humidity and time.
9. Inadequate cooling of bread before packing.
10. Improper storage conditions.
11. A general lack of understanding of principles of hygiene on the part of baker.

A thorough knowledge about raw material and its functions, adequate understanding of bread making procedures, necessary control on timing, temperatures and humidity conditions at different stages of bread making and above all personal skill and experience of the baker goes a long way in avoiding faults in bread and also in finding out remedy, should any fault occur. A skilled baker should examine the bread carefully, and by reasoning, deductions, elimination, and if necessary, by experimentation, should be able to detect the cause of fault and subsequently find the solution.

The overall quality of bread is dependent on the degree of perfection of its various characteristics like volume, crust colour, flavour etc. (as discussed previously). These characteristics are influenced by various factors as follows:

Volume

Proper volume of bread is the outcome of adequate conditioning of gluten and sufficient gassing power of the dough at the time of baking. For many reasons as listed below, if these two conditions are not fulfilled the volume remains small.

1. Too tight a dough without commensurate adjustment in the yeast content and fermentation time.
2. Too little or excessive yeast content for the procedure followed.
3. Under fermentation of dough.
4. Too cold {Chilled} dough, or too cold temperature of fermentation room.
5. Crusting of dough at any stage of processing.
6. Excessive quantity of salt, sugar or fat in the formula.
7. Excessive temperature in the oven.
8. Under proofing of bread.
9. Lack of or excessive diastatic activity in the flour.
10. High bran content in flour (ash content more than 0.5%)
11. Overuse of chemical bread improvers.
12. A badly over fermented dough.
13. Use of too weak or too strong flour.
14. Over mixed or under mixed dough.
15. Absence of fat in the dough.

Reasons for excessive volume in bread

1. Over fermentation of dough. However, if the over fermentation is excessive, the volume may be small because the gluten will be excessively mellowed and not in a position to support the structure.
2. Too slack a dough.
3. Lack of temperature in the oven.
4. Lack of salt in the formula.
5. Excessive quantity of yeast.
6. Excessive proofing.
7. Excessive quantity of dough for the size of mould.
8. Loose moulding.

Crust colour

Crust colour is controlled by the amount of sugar present in the dough at the time of baking, presuming that the bread is baked at right temperature. If for any reason, there is more activity of yeast, more sugar will be consumed by yeast and bread will have a light, pale brown colour as in the following cases;

1. Excessive fermentation time given to dough.
2. Lack of salt in the dough.

3. Too slack a dough.
4. Excessive yeast for the process used.
5. Too high a dough temperature.
6. Too high a temperature of fermentation room.
7. Lack of sugar in the formula.

Some other reasons which, although, do not enhance the yeast activity, they do reduce the crust colour such as; low diastatic capacity in the flour, crusting of bread during proofing and use of excessive dusting flour. Insufficient oven temperature will certainly cause lack of crust colour.

Too Dark Crust Colour

If more sugar is present in the dough at the time of baking, bread crust will acquire dark colour. Following are the likely reasons for this fault:

1. Excessive sugar in the formula.
2. Too much diastatic activity in the dough.
3. Young (under fermented or over mixed) dough.
4. Too high oven temperature.
5. High milk, or/and salt content in the formula.
6. Chilling of dough during fermentation or proofing.
7. Lack of humidity in the oven.

Exaggerated break, wild break or flying tops

A smooth break-shred is a desirable quality of bread. If the gluten is not adequately conditioned during fermentation, the top crust, instead of rising gradually, will burst open under the pressure of expanding gas. Depending upon the degree of under fermentation, the bread will have exaggerated or wild break or flying top (shell top). Some other reasons for having wild break are; insufficient proofing of bread, excessive heat in the oven, lack of diastatic activity in flour, and lack of humidity in the proofing room or oven.

Lack of break shred

If the dough is over fermented, the gluten will loose its resistance power and will have excessive stretchability Such a condition of gluten will not produce any break-shred during baking operation. A bread having no break-shred is said to be having blind appearance. Some other reasons for the absence of break-shred are under matured dough, over proofing, extreme under proofing too high temperature in the oven, and very slack dough.

Holes and tunnels in bread

If for any reason, some gluten strands break, either during proofing or initial stage of baking, it has a chain reaction and neighbouring gluten strands also continue breaking until the proteins are coagulated under the action of heat and the structure of bread is set. The reasons for breaking of gluten strands could be as follows:

1. Too weak flour. Weak flour will not be able to hold expanding gas specially if there is excessive gassing due to high yeast content.
2. Too strong flour with high yeast content. Normally strong flours should be fermented for longer periods with lesser amounts of yeast. If the quantity of yeast is more and fermentation time is reduced, then there will be more gassing power in the dough but gluten will not be adequately conditioned resulting in its poor stretchability causing holes.
3. If the ingredients like fat, milk solids, salt, sugar, yeast are not mixed properly in the dough, the continuity of gluten strands will be broken wherever the lumps of these material are present.
4. If the oven sole is too hot, there will be faster set of structure on the lower surface of bread which is in contact of oven sole, while the inner part will rise as the heat penetrates in the bread creating holes in the bread.
5. If the dough is not knocked back at all or knocking back is not done thoroughly, the large gas cells present in the dough may also find their way into the bread specially if care is not taken during moulding operation to apply sufficient pressure to break the larger gas cells.
6. If excessive dusting flour is used at the time of moulding, this flour will be folded in the bread and will create elongated slits. Other reasons for creating holes in bread are: Too hard and granular fat, too little salt, Excessive use of oxidising agent (i.e. potassium bromate etc.). Undermixed dough, slack dough, crusting of dough at any stage.

Cores and Seams

When the cut surface of crumb is gently pressed with finger tips, it is likely that entire surface may not be evenly soft and presence of occasional hard spots may be felt. These hard spots are known as cores, and are formed due to:

1. Uneven mixing of dough specially hand mixed dough.
2. Incorporation of bits of dough collected from machine bowl, or work-bench, after the bulk of dough has been set for fermentation.
3. Skinning of dough during bulk fermentation or intermediate proofing. This crust is folded into the bread and will show as hard core.

Bread Faults

Very often a sandwich bread may show dense layers on the outer periphery of the crumb specially near the top crust. This happens because the expansion of dough (during baking) is restrained by the side walls or the cover of the bread mould. Due to the pressure from expanding gas, the outer structure of bread is formed into dense layers. If the cut surface of bread is observed, it could be clearly seen that the central part has a open soft structure while the outer periphery has very close and compact structure. These dense layers are known as Seams.

Reasons for having seams in bread are as follows:

1. Weight of dough more than the capacity of the mould.
2. Too hot or too cold bread moulds; in both the cases the yeast activity will be checked at the point of contact with mould.
3. Careless handling of a fully expanded bread while loading the oven, or disturbing the bread in the oven before structure is set.

Condensation marks

If the bread is not allowed to cool properly before packing, some of the water vapours will deposit in the crumb structure causing dark colour patches known as condensation marks. Bread should be thoroughly cooled before it is packed.

Rapid drying (staling) of bread

If the gluten is not conditioned adequately, it cannot acquire the quality of moisture retention and bread will dry out fast. Under fermentation due to any reason whatsoever, will promote rapid drying out of crumb. Other reasons for rapid drying out of bread are as follows.

1. Baking in too cool oven, in which case the bread will take longer to bake with the resultant evaporation of more moisture.
2. If the dough temperature is too high (hot dough) there will be undesirable evaporation of moisture during fermentation as well as proofing stage. When the dough temperature is high, usually doughs are fermented for lesser time resulting in inadequate maturing of gluten which will not acquire moisture retention capacity. If fermentation time is not reduced then dough will over ferment. Bread made from over fermented dough will have open structure which will cause rapid drying out of bread.
3. Too tight dough unless the fermentation time is adequately increased in order to allow proper mellowing of gluten.
4. Ingredients like salt, sugar, fat, have moisture retention capacity. If these ingredients are not used in the formula at desirable level the resultant product will dry out faster.

5. Use of milk in the formula without making related changes in water and fat content.
6. Excessive use of mineral improvers will cause rapid drying out of bread.

Over moist or sticky crumb

If flour is milled from sprouted wheat, it will have excessive diastatic capacity. When bread is made from such flour, there will be excessive formation of sugar and dextrin which imparts gumminess to the crumb of bread. Due to this gummyness, the normal amount of moisture will not be baked off leaving the crumb over moist. Presence of excessive sugar and dextrin will also hold moisture, making the crumb over moist. If bread is proofed in excessive humid condition or if bread is under baked then also crumb will be over moist. A crumb that is over moist, sticky and smells like rotten pineapple, denotes the presence of Rope disease (described in detail elsewhere).

Close crumb

Milk has a tightening action on gluten and if it is used in the formula without compensating with enhanced quantity of yeast, water and fat, the bread will develop a very close crumb. In plain white bread, excessive quantity of fat will break down the crumb structure making it close and compact. Over use of potassium bromate or any other oxidising agent will tighten up the crumb. Some other reasons are: Use of hard water, mould too small for the weight of dough, young dough, under proofing, tight dough, and too high oven temperature.

Crumbliness of crumb

When a dough is adequately fermented, the gluten strands develop elasticity and crumb also becomes elastic. If there is no elasticity in the crumb, the bread will not slice neatly and may break into fragments by the pressure of the slicer blades. This characteristic is known as crumbliness of the crumb: Such a crumb will also break while applying butter to the slice. Crumbliness is almost always related to the degree of fermentation given to the dough. Gluten of an under fermented dough will not be conditioned adequately to develop elasticity while the gluten of over fermented dough will be weakened to the extent that there is no elasticity left in it. Apart from the degree of fermentation, some other factors may also adversely affect the elastic nature of crumb such as;

1. Too slack dough
2. Too tight dough (without due amendments in yeast content and length of fermentation time)

3. Excessive use of fat
4. Excessive use of mineral improvers
5. Low salt content of the dough
6. Poor quality of flour
7. Undermixed dough
8. Under baked bread
9. Over proofing of bread

Leathery crust

The crust of bread should be tender and should easily break when pulled. However, at times, for various reasons, a crust becomes tough and leathery. This normally happens when a dough is under ripe or a strong flour is used without making due amendments in fermentation time. In both the cases, the gluten will not be sufficiently conditioned and will retain some of its toughness. Secondly, if, for any reason, the crust absorbs moisture unduly either during baking or after baking, it will acquire leatheriness. Excessive humidity in proofing room and oven should be avoided and bread should be thoroughly cooled before packing. Too slack a dough will produce leatheriness of crust because adequate amount of moisture will not be baked off and some of it will be absorbed by the crust causing the fault.

Runny or Sticky Doughs

It is rather difficult to process a sticky dough either by hand or by machine. A dough piece should have an alround expansion during intermediate proofing. However; at times for various reasons, it will spread only horizontally rather than have an alround expansion. Such doughs are known as runny or fluid. Bread made from such a dough will have sharp edges because due to excessive fluidity the dough will fill the corners of the mould. Bread will also have dark bottom and sides due to close contact of the dough with the mould. When a dough is adequately fermented, small gas cells are created in the dough. This is made possible because, during fermentation gluten acquires stretchability, and there is enough gas production to create cells under the framework of stretched gluten, as a result of which there is all-round expansion of dough. If the dough is not sufficiently fermented, there is neither sufficient gas production nor adequate mellowness in gluten and the dough tends to flatten out. Gluten of an over fermented dough will be too mellow to have much strength to support an upward pressure of expanding gas and in that case too, dough will be runny.

A weak flour will produce runny dough because its gluten does not have sufficient strength to support the structure. If there is excessive diastatic action in the dough, the excessive sugar and dextrines produced in such case will make the dough runny and sticky. Freshly milled flour is also likely to produce runny and sticky dough unless some oxidizing agent is used in the formula.

Sourness

Pleasant flavour and taste, developed as a result of fermentation, are considered to be very desirable characteristics of bread. However; sourness in taste or flavour is not desirable. A strict control on the temperature of the dough and fermentation room as well as on the fermentation period will allow only as much acid production as is desirable for mellowing of gluten, and for developing the right strength of flavour in the product. However; if the dough temp. or the temp.of fermentation room is undesirably high (more than 85 deg.F) or the period of fermentation is too long, the yeast will work itself out, but the acid producing bacteria will still remain active thereby increasing the acidity in dough and affecting the flavour and taste of the resultant bread. A bread, only slightly affected by rope (disease), will also have sour smell (inspite of proper fermentation condition) but this smell will be nauseating and entirely different from normal sourness which is caused by excessive fermentation.

Irregularity of Shape

While moulding bread by hand, an even pressure should be applied so that a moulded piece of dough has an even oblong appearance. Expansion during proofing of such a piece of dough will be even ,and the resultant bread will have regularity of shape. However; in case of loose moulding or moulding with uneven pressure, there will remain large air pockets in the folds causing irregularity of shape.In case of wood fired oven, normally, live coal is pushed in one corner and left there while baking operation is carried on. The side of bread facing live coal should be protected against fierce heat, either by covering the live coal or by covering the bread with some kind of protective shield such as a baking tray. If protection is not given, the shape of bread will become irregular due to uneven absorption of heat by bread. For the same reason, a small batch of bread should not be baked in a large oven without due care (such as keeping a bowl of water in the oven prior to baking). Bread should always be set in the oven at an even distance from, and parallel to, each other in order to ensure even absorption of heat by each unit of bread. A badly loaded oven will affect the regularity of shape.

Since hearth type products (like French bread, Vienna bread) are baked directly (without mould) on the hearth of the oven, their expansion is not guided by the side walls of the mould as in the case of pan bread. Such products should be docked or scored prior to baking, so that the expanding gas may escape through these openings without affecting the regularity of shape of the product. In case of insufficient or absence of docking, the expanding gas may create bulges at the weaker spots spoiling the shape of the product.

Blisters

If bread is proofed in excessive humidity, the moisture deposits on the surface of bread in the form of small droplets. Due to this increase in the moisture content, the gluten of the affected spot acquires more stretchability just as it will happen in the case of slack dough. Such spots form blisters under the pressure of expanding gas during baking operation. In case of moulding by machine, if the pressure board is adjusted too closely, the moulding will be too tight and some air bubbles will get entrapped on the surface under a very thin film of gluten.These air bubbles will expand during proofing as well as during baking causing blisters. Other reasons for having blisters are; very slack dough, loose moulding, under fermented dough, excessive top heat in oven.

Deficiency of bloom

Bloom could be affected by a number of factors like quality of raw material, faulty formulation, inadequate fermentation, faulty conditions during proofing and baking and so on. Allowing rest of the conditions to be adequate, the most important factor responsible for imparting bloom to bread is the diastatic capacity of flour. Sufficient sugar production and formation of dextrin during baking operation impart this desirable characteristic to bread. If the flour is deficient in diastase, it should be supplemented with addition of malt to remedy this defect. Malt flour can also be useful and can be made by the baker himself.

Hard (flinty) crust

At times bread has crust which is hard and breaks like an egg shell. Such crust is known as flinty crust, and is usually related to products made from very strong flour which is insufficiently fermented, specially if the dough is also tight. As most of the wheats grown in the country do not contain gluten of such strong nature, a baker is less likely to encounter such problem on this score. However over use of oxidizing agent will also produce flinty crust.

Colour Spots

Brand names etc. are printed on the flour (jute) bags and occasionally particles of dye may penetrate through into the flour. When water is added to flour, colour spots develop, and if not detected during dough stage, the bread will show these colour spots. Except this (apparently) inherent reason, colour spots are entirely the result of lack of care by the baker. While greasing the moulds, if excessive quantity of fat is taken in the brush, some of it will deposit in the corners of the mould which will ultimately, create dark spots. Unclean moulds, handling of bread with unclean hands or unclean gloves while depanning, unclean cooling racks, falling of soot from the chimney (in wood fired oven), presence of sugar crystals, milk pallets, unclean work-benches specially if cake decoration is also done on the same benches and a number of such other factors are responsible for creating colour spots in bread.

Too thick crust

When expansion of bread in the oven (oven spring) is insufficient, or bread is left in the oven for too long a time, there will be more concentration of heat on the outer surface of bread rather than heat penetrating in the bread. This condition results in bread having a thick crust.

Reasons for lack of oven spring are;

1. Lack of diastatic activity in flour
2. Lack of sugar and fat in the formula
3. Poor quality, or too strong flour
4. Over fermented dough
5. Lack of moisture in the oven

Over baking of bread will invariably result in bread having thick crust or if oven is cool, the bread has to be baked for longer time which will produce thick crust.

Chapter - 9

Bread Diseases

The two diseases which affect bread are :

1. Rope and
2. Mold

Bread is not affected by these diseases all through the year but only when the weather is warm and humid as is the case during the period April to August in major part of the country. The bacteria responsible for causing "Rope" is known as "Bacillus mesentericus vulgatus". This is soil borne bacteria. Since the "crease" and "beard" of wheat contain some amount of dust, these are generally recognised as the places harbouring bacteria, wherefrom it is transferred to the flour inspite of the cleaning operation to which wheat is subjected prior to milling. Apart from this basic source, the bacteria may also find its way to the product from some of the ingredients (such as salt, sugar) or if unhygienic conditions are prevailing in the bakery premises. It is peculiar characteristic of this bacteria that it is not destroyed during baking operation and an initially infected bread remains as heavily infected even after baking.

The speed with which a bread shows signs of infection depends on;

1. Concentration of bacteria present and
2. Warmth and humidity conditions of the bread storage room.

A bread may show symptoms of disease even within 8 to 12 hours of baking or as late as 24 to 36 hours.

When bread is only slightly infected, initially, it develops a peculiar smell variously described as sickening sweet, resembling rotten fruits, over ripe pineapple and so on. The crumb of bread may become discoloured and little sticky. However, as the time passes, the smell becomes overwhelmingly unpleasant (nauseating), the crumb becomes discoloured and sticky. When an infected slice of bread is broken, a number of threads can be seen stretching between two pieces probably that is why the disease gets its name "Rope". Very heavy infection may almost liquify the crumb.

Once this disease makes its appearance, the product becomes unsaleable which means financial loss to the baker. Therefore, it is advisable that some precautionary measures are adopted when the weather conditions are favourable for this kind of infection.

Growth of "rope" bacteria is considerably checked in an acidic medium (low pH). Acetic acid of 10% strength could be used at the rate of one percent based on the weight of flour. If still the disease is not controlled, this quantity may be doubled. For the similar action, calcium propionate can also be used. To begin with, it may be used at the rate of 0.1 % based on flour and according to requirement this quantity may be increased upto 0.32%. Although maximum quantity of calcium propionate at the rate of 0.5% is recommended at times but it should be remembered that higher levels of this preservative may also subdue the yeast activity, and proofing time may be unduly prolonged. Calcium propionate is effective in acidic medium which is provided by the fermentation process. However, when sufficient acidity is not created in the doughs (as in short time doughs), it should be supplemented by addition of acetic acid or mono acid calcium phosphate at appropriate levels.

Most of the retail bakeries in the country produce bread by overnight sponge method. This method can be standardised by individual baker, in a fashion that the dough develops sufficient acidity to inhibit the growth of "rope" bacteria and still the flavour and taste of the product is not adversely affected. Principles of "Longer fermenting sponges" may be followed in this case.

A bakery should be kept spotlessly clean all the time. There should be no accumulation of dust anywhere in the premises. The utensils, tools, equipments, machines etc. should be kept absolutely clean. Floor, walls, and ceilings should be regularly checked and maintained in a dust free condition. The premises should be well lighted and adequately ventilated. All these steps are not necessarily meant for controlling "rope" but standard hygienic conditions should always be maintained in a bakery.

A bread having well developed crumb structure is less likely to go ropy than a bread having close, compact and over moist crumb. Full complement of yeast should be used to affect a vigorous fermentation. Under fermentation and under proofing should be guarded against.

An under baked bread has an over moist, soggy crumb which is a condition conducive to rope development. Bread should always be well baked having even golden brown colour on all the sides.

Bread should be allowed to cool down thoroughly before it is packed. If a warm bread is packed, the moisture evaporating from the warm bread will not escape and will be absorbed by the crumb, making it over moist. This moisture and warmth of the crumb will form ideal medium for the growth of rope bacteria. For proper cooling, bread should be kept on racks spaced about half an inch apart from each other. Cooling room should be well ventilated to ensure that water vapours escaping from bread do not saturate the atmosphere. It may be desirable to install exhaust fan in the bread cooling room, if the production is large enough to warrant the added expenditure.

Although, bread is not supposed to be stored by the baker for any considerable length of time, still the storage room should be well ventilated. Warm and humid conditions should be avoided. Temperatures between 70 deg. to 95 deg.F and humidity between 65 to 75% are quite suitable for bread storage. Bread should never be stored superimposed on each other as the bread at the bottom will be unduly compressed and a close crumb is conducive to rope infection.

Mold

Spores of various kinds of molds are always present in the atmosphere and these spores start growing whenever they find suitable conditions of warmth and moisture in the crumb of bread.

Spores enter through the cracks on the surface of the bread and proliferate inside spoiling the entire crumb.

At times it is likely that an under baked bread may pass through the slicer blades. As the crumb of an under baked bread is not firm enough, some of it may smear the slicer blades. If such a situation goes undetected, it will form an ideal ground for mold growth and the infection will also be passed on to other breads which are subsequently sliced. Bread is normally infected by three kinds of mold:

1. White - Mucor mucedo,
2. Greenish or bluish - Penicillium, Aspergillus and
3. Black - Aspergillus niger.

When a customer complains of moldy bread, the matter should be carefully investigated. Although it is likely that the bread storage conditions in the house of the customer himself may be responsible for the spoilage, but a baker can not have any control on those conditions. It is advisable for a baker to take all necessary precautions to forestall, as far as possible, any occurrence of mold infection.

Chapter - 10

Staleness in Bread

Staleness in bread is rather a vague term and may convey different meaning to different persons. Some people may prefer to eat bread on the same day as it is baked. For them any product more than 12 hours old is stale. On the other hand, some people enjoy bread only after 12 hours of its being baked. However; in order to be recognised as fresh, a bread must have a tender crust, reasonable softness of crumb and a pleasant taste and aroma. If the crust has lost its tenderness, crumb is hard (tough) and bread is devoid of pleasing taste and aroma, we recognise the product as stale. It must be clearly understood that staleness of bread is quite distinct from microbial infection responsible for bread diseases (Rope, Mold) which have been discussed in detail in the previous chapter.

Some of the characteristics of a stale bread are as follows:

1. Crust of fresh bread is tender and breaks easily but when the bread becomes stale the crust becomes leathery (tough) or hard.
2. There is no elasticity left in the crumb of a stale bread and it becomes crumbly.
3. While eating a stale piece of bread, it feels very dry and requires considerable chewing, and even then it feels dry while swallowing.
4. Flavour and aroma that are characteristic of a fresh bread, are lost.

Staling of bread has two aspects:

1. Crust staling,
2. Crumb staling

Crust staling

There is continuous loss of moisture from bread crumb to the atmosphere. Due to its hygroscopic nature, the crust absorbs some of this moisture. Similarly, if warm bread is packed or the bread is stored in excessive humid conditions (R H more than 75 %), moisture percentage of the crust will increase. If warm bread is suddenly transferred to cold atmosphere moisture will condense on the crust. Under all these circumstances the crust will lose its tender nature and will become tough and leathery. It will also not retain its nutty flavour which is characteristic of fresh bread. A strong flour insufficiently fermented, an under fermented dough, under baking of bread, excessive humidity in the proofing room or oven are also some of the conditions which will produce leathery crust.

Following measures can be taken to prevent crust staling.

1. Dough should be fermented adequately.
2. Bread should be baked thoroughly.
3. If there is excessive humidity in the oven, the damper should be opened to allow escape of moisture. In case of wood fired oven, the moisture should be allowed to escape through chimney.
4. While baking some of the hard crusted products like hard rolls, French loaf etc. steam is injected in the oven. There should be sufficient drying out of the crust before the product is drawn out of the oven.
5. The bread should be allowed to undergo a steady, gradual and thorough cooling before packing.
6. Bread should not be stored in excessively humid conditions.

Crumb staling

When starch is heated with sufficient quantity of water, at a particular temperature (155-170 deg.F) the starch granules swell and the whole mass becomes a thick paste called "gel". This process is known as gelatinization. Starch in such a swollen state is soft and carries plenty (about six times of its own weight) of water. But, when the gel is cooled down, the starch granules loose some of its water, shrink and become harder. The migration of moisture away from the starch is known as "Syneresis". In bread, the starch is not completely gelatinized because:

1. Bread does not contain sufficient quantity of moisture required for complete gelatinization.
2. Until the last stage of baking, the temperature inside the bread is lower than that required for complete gelatinization and when the temperature does reach gelatinization point, the bread is not left in the oven for sufficient time for complete gelatinization as the bread is pulled out of the oven soon.

Although starch is not completely gelatinized in bread, yet there is sufficient water, temperature and time to bring out partial gelatinization in which case, the starch granules will be considerably swollen and hold water. That is why the starch of a freshly baked bread is soft. These soft starch granules are held very unstably in the gluten frame work of bread. When the bread is cooled down, the starch granules shrink, loose some of the water, become hard and stable. This change in the nature of starch is responsible for hardness and crumbliness of a stale bread. During fermentation period and initial stages of baking, diastase enzyme acts on starch. Due to the action of alpha amylase (a constituent of diastase), sound starch is partially converted into soluble starch which has good water holding capacity. Thus, an adequate diastatic activity in flour should produce sufficient quantity of soluble starch in bread and contribute in maintaining softness of bread for reasonable time. Similarly, a fine web-like gluten framework of bread will hold moisture for longer duration maintaining softness of bread.

A product starts staling as soon as it is cooled down after baking. The rate of staling is maximum when the product is very fresh. Storing bread at low temperature (lower than 70 degF) will increase the rate of staling. Although the rate of staling process may be slightly delayed by storing bread at about 110 deg.F as the loss of moisture from starch is minimum at this temperature, yet there is danger of microbial infection of bread. Such high temperature will also promote browning reaction between protein of flour and simple sugar (present in bread) darkening the crumb colour apart from it being very expensive to maintain such high temperature. Bread stales sooner or later; but certain measures can be taken to ensure that the bread remains in fairly soft condition for reasonable time so as to be acceptable by consumer. Such measures to delay the staling process are:

1. Flour must be sufficiently strong to produce a bread having fine texture and thin cell walls.
2. Sufficient quantity of yeast should be used to give a vigorous fermentation.
3. Adequate quantity of water must be used according to the strength of flour.
4. Dough must be properly mixed to ensure even distribution of all the ingredients, then only the action of yeast cells will be even throughout the mass.
5. Speed of fermentation should be controlled by keeping a check on temperature of the dough, temp. of fermentation room and fermentation time.
6. Manipulation of dough, specially moulding of bread, should be carried out correctly. Improper moulding will adversely affect the texture of bread.
7. Correct proofing and baking conditions should be maintained in order to ensure even distribution of gas cells which are separated from each other by thinnest possible wall made of partially gelatinized starch and extended gluten strands.

8. Bread should be cooled gradually and it should never be transferred to very low temperature like that of refrigerator.
9. Bread should not be stored superimposed on one another, as it will have a crushing effect on the crumb structure. Humid conditions (RH more than 75%) for storing bread should be avoided.
10. Suitable emulsifying agent like GMS emulsion should be used in order to ensure greater water holding capacity of the crumb.

Chapter - 11

Bread Improvers

If the quality of raw material is good and the baker knows his job well, it is hardly necessary to use any bread improvers. However, ideal Conditions for bread production do not always exist. Quality of flour varies from consignment to consignment, mineral content of water varies from place to place, and with the complete mechanization of bread production process, it has become unavoidable to make use of certain chemicals in order to ensure consistently good quality of the product. Gluten forming proteins of flour is the basic factor for making a good Bread. Strength and extensibility of gluten is the two main Characteristics responsible for bread making quality of flour. Flours, always do not contain desirable quality of gluten forming proteins. Any added material which can improve the strength and extensibility of gluten of flour is known as Bread Improver. Inorganic salts which affect the nature of gluten are known as mineral Improvers. Mineral Yeast Food (MYF) is a general term used to describe a combination of inorganic salts, some of which affect the nature of gluten while others act as food for yeast. Potassium bromate is one of the earliest known chemical used by baking industry to improve the quality of bread. It oxidises the gluten, giving it more strength, which has direct bearing on oven spring and other related characteristics of bread. After reaction is complete potassium bromide remains as end product which is considered to be a harmless substance. The quantity of potassium bromate to be used ranges from 10 to 40 ppm (parts per million), depending on the strength of maida, formulation of the product and process used. In conventional method of bread making 15 to 30 ppm of potassium bromate gives satisfactory results. Being a very potent additive, it should be used in very accurate quantity, as, even fractionally excessive quantity may render the whole batch of dough in a condition which can be very difficult, if not impossible to handle.

For convenience, a definite quantity of potassium bromate can be dissolved in measured quantity of water and the solution can be used to provide potassium bromate at desired level. For example:

Potassium bromate	10 g.
Water	1000 ml.

If 100 ml. of this solution is used in 100 kg. maida, the quantity of potassium bromate will be 1 g. which will amount to 10 ppm. Potassium bromate can also be diluted with maida in desired proportion as given below

1.			
1.	Potassium bromate		10 g.
	Maida		4990 g.
	Improver Flour	Total	5000 g.

500 g. of this improver flour per 100 kg of formula flour will provide potassium bromate at the level of 10 ppm. Potassium bromate is more effective in acidic medium which is provided inherently by fermentation process or by additives like mono acid calcium phosphate (MACP) or acetic acid or ammonium chloride. However the effect of excessive acidity and potassium bromate will break down the dough which may become almost irretrievable. For this reason the baker has to be cautious while using potassium bromate with over night sponge and also guard against over fermentation of doughs. In the event the dough does break down, retrival could be tried (may be with limited success) by remixing with additional flour, sugar and milk powder and processing the dough within shortest possible time. Another chemical which is used as flour improver is potassium iodate. It is considered to be a faster acting oxidizing agent than potassium bromate and hence it is more suitable for short time doughs. It is specially useful with such flours which tend to produce "bucky" dough as it improves the extensibility of gluten. Ammonium chloride acts as food for yeast. It has very beneficial effect on the growth of yeast cells. During its activity in the dough, the ammonia component becomes part of new yeast cells and chloride component forms hydrochloric acid in the dough which, in limited quantity, enhances the action of potassium bromate as described in the previous paragraph. This increase in acidity in the dough serves the useful purpose of inhibiting rope and mold producing spores, and enhances the effectiveness of added rope and mold inhibitors like acetic acid and calcium propionate.

Although calcium per oxide is also an oxidizing agent, its action differs from that of potassium bromate or potassium iodate. Calcium per oxide has a drying effect on the skin of dough piece, and in highly machanised bakeries, where it is necessary that dough pieces are not sticky during moulding, use of calcium per oxide is very beneficial.

Some of the combinations of different bread improvers are as follows:

2.	Potassium bromate	20 g.
	Ammonium chloride	600 g.
	Flour	9380 g.
	Total improver flour	10000 g.

3. Potassium bromate	12 g.
Potassium iodate	8 g.
Ammonium chloride	600 g.
Flour	9380 g.
Total improver flour	10000 g.
4. Calcium peroxide	10 g.
Flour	9990 g.
Total improver flour	10000 g.

All the above combinations can safely be used at the rate of 500 g. per 100 kg. of maida. However; this quantity can be increased gradually according to the requirement.

Acid calcium phosphate serves as yeast food as well as stabilizer of gluten. This acid salt is very useful on soft gluten. It increases the acidity of dough and can be used as rope and mold inhibitor. It is used at the rate of 0.1 to 0.35% (based on flour) as bread improver. This quantity may be doubled for inhibiting the growth of rope and mold spores. In the same fashion, sodium and potassium acid phosphate can be used. Ammonium phosphate is used at the rate of 0.2% based on flour. Ammonium persulphate has a tightening action on gluten which eventually improves the texture of bread. When ammonium persulphate is used as bread improver, quantity of water in the dough should be increased by 2 to 3 percent in order to offset the tightening action on the dough. Extra water will increase the yield also by the same amount. It is used at the rate of 0.01 % based on flour. In order to avoid any error in weighing such a small quantity, it is advisable to dilute it with flour as in the case of potassium bromate.

Flour milled from sprouted wheat has excessive diastatic action and dough made from such flours will be sticky. With such flours, potassium aluminium sulphate, which has a retarding effect on diastatic activity, can be used to improve the machinability of the dough. However; as this chemical is banned in some countries, it will be essential to ascertain the legal aspect before it is recommended for use. A lump of potassium aluminium sulphate can be rotated 4 to 5 times in doughing water the previous evening. Next morning, clean water should be carefully separated (leaving out the residue), and used for dough making. Lime water, being alkaline in nature, has a controlling effect on yeast fermentation. Specially during summers, lime water can be used to keep the fermentation speed under check. It also nutralises the excessive acidity which, otherwise, will adversely affect the taste and flavour of bread. It is particularly useful in making overnight sponges which generally tend to over ferment. As a starting point, clear lime water may be used at the rate of 450 ml for making overnight sponge which is to be remixed to make a dough of (total) 100 kg. flour. A note of caution will be in order that is alkalinity is harmful to the strength of gluten and any deterioration in the quality of dough should be carefully monitored.

Although lactic acid is a natural product of fermentation, still this chemical may be used in doughs made from flours having very tough gluten which, otherwise, will take very long to achieve correct ripening. It can be used at the rate of 0.15% based on flour. Lactic acid should be measured very carefully as it has a very strong odour which may interfere with the pleasant aroma of bread. Ascorbic acid (vitamin C) is a very good bread improver which has milder oxidizing action on gluten than potassium bromate. It has extremely beneficial effect on the texture of bread, making it soft and silky. It can be used at the rate of 15 to 25 ppm. For emergency requirements, it can be purchased from local chemists shop in the form of tablets of definite weight, although it should not be made a regular practice and supplies in pure form should be ordered with chemical suppliers. For accuracy in weighing small quantities, it should be diluted with flour in the following proportion;

Ascorbic acid	30 g.
flour	9970 g.
Improver flourTotal	10000 g.

500 g. of this improver flour in 100 kg. of formula flour will provide ascorbic acid at the level of 15 ppm. There is another class of bread improvers which, apart from improving the physical qualities of bread, also increases its nutritional value. Such improvers are known as enriching improvers.

Milk

Milk has a tightening action on flour proteins which eventually improves the texture of bread. Inclusion of milk in the formula necessitates addition of extra 2 to 3% water in the dough thereby ihcreasing the yield by that amount. Milk improves the flavour and taste of bread and lactose content of milk improves the crust colour. In regular white bread 1 to 2% milk (solids) can be added for improving the quality of bread which will also subscribe to its nutritional content. However; to qualify as milk bread, it should have higher amounts of milk solids content. Milk can be used for bread making in any form i.e. fresh liquid, evaporated, condensed or powder form. However; in bakery trade it is convenient to use milk in powder form. Skimmed milk powder (SMP) is preferable because;

1. Due to absence of fat it has better shelf life,
2. Adjustment in formula for its fat content need not be made and
3. It is less expensive than whole milk powder.

Spray dried milk powder is to be preferred as it has better solubility in water than roller dried milk powder. To be better effective in bread making, milk powder should be reconstituted with water. In order to avoid lump formation, dry powder should be mixed with dry sugar before adding water to it. Water should be added gradually so as to make a lump free paste initially. Then only all the remaining water should be added.

While using milk in bread dough, it is necessary to keep a strict control on the speed of fermentation. Although milk does act as a buffer and protects the dough from becoming acidic, but over fermentation will inevitably produce excessive amount of lactic acid, which will mellow the gluten to the extent that it will produce a very open and coarse structure and a dull crumb colour. Bread will also have acidic taste and flavour. While using milk in bread, the following points should be given attention to.

1. As milk has toughening action on gluten, the yeast content should be increased. Sugar should also be increased to provide food for additional yeast.
2. Malt has a very beneficial effect on the fermentation of milk bread dough and should be incorporated in appropriate quantity. It also enhances the crust colour and flavour of bread.
3. Milk has a drying effect on the eating quality of bread. Fat content should be increased to offset this dry eating quality. Malt also improves the eating quality of bread.
4. If milk bread is baked at normal bread temperature (450 degF), there will be excessive crust colour as it contains higher amount of sugar. Therefore it should be baked at lower temperature (400 deg.F) and in order to get it thoroughly baked, baking time should be increased to 45 min. approximately.

Malt

There are two kinds of malt which can be used in bread making

1. Plain malt - acts as yeast food and
2. Diastatic malt - apart from supplying food for yeast, it also assists in modification of starch.

If flour is deficient in maltose sugar, the rate of gas production during the last stages of fermentation is insufficient and as a result, the bread lacks in volume and crust colour. With such flours, use of diastatic malt makes up for the natural deficiency in the diastatic capacity of flour. Diastatic malt breaks down (Partially) the insoluble starch into soluble starch which has better water retention capacity and assists in keeping the bread moist and fresh for longer time. Malt has a softening action on gluten which improves the softness of the crumb. Specially with milk bread, the drying effect of milk proteins is offset by the use of malt. Due to its modifying action on gluten, it improves the texture and brightness of crumb. It improves the crust colour, flavour and shelf life of bread. Quantity of malt to be used is as follows:

Liquid malt (plain) - 0.25 to 0.35% based on flour

Diastatic malt (dried) - 0.125 to 0.225% based on flour

Fat

Use of fat improves the volume of bread as it has lubricating effect on the fine gluten strands. It is normally used at the rate of 1 to 2% based on the weight of flour. Excessive amount of fat exerts weight on fine web like structure. With such doughs which call for higher amounts of fat, yeast content should also be increased to offset the dead weight of fat so that volume does not suffer. Fat helps in retaining moisture in bread and thus improves its shelf life. It also improves the sliceability and eating quality of bread.

Sugar

Although flour contains natural sugar, the quantity of natural sugar is not sufficient to carry out the whole process of fermentation. Therefore, sucrose sugar is added to the dough to supplement the natural sugar of flour. Basically, sugar is used to provide food for yeast but it also improves moisture retention capacity of bread. It has softening effect on crumb and improves the crust colour and flavour of bread. In plain white bread, sugar is used at the rate of 2 to 3% based on flour. However higher quantities can also be used as in the case of sweet fermented products. Higher concentration of sugar will retard the yeast activity and hence yeast content should be increased in the formula. Doughs with higher sugar and yeast content should be guarded against over fermentation to avoid any acidity in taste and flavour.

Eggs

Egg contains proteins, fat and lecithin. Fat and lecithin help in keeping the bread moist and soft due to their modifying action on gluten. Protein of egg has strengthening action on flour proteins which improves volume and crumb structure of bread. While using egg, necessary allowance should be made for its moisture content. As an improver egg can be used at the rate of 4 to 6% based on flour. In rich, sweet fermented products it is used at higher levels (10 to 20%). Under the action of heat, egg white coagulates faster than egg yolk and beneficial components like fat, lecithin are found in egg yolk only. Hence it is advisable to use only egg yolk in fermented goods. However; egg as an improver in bread should be used with caution as it may not be acceptable to majority of bread consumers.

Soya flour

Soya flour has a modifying action on the bread crumb, thereby improving its moisture retention power. It is very rich in proteins and contributes to the nutritional value of bread. As an improver, it can be used at the rate of 1 to 2% based on flour. However higher quantities can be used for fortification of bread. It may be necessary to conduct experiments to determine the optimum quantity of soya flour which can be used without adversely affecting the quality of bread specially its flavour. It increases the water absorption power of flour and consequently yield of bread. For optimum results it should be hydrated before adding to the dough.

Emulsifiers

Glycerol Mono Stearate (GMS) is the most commonly used emulsifying agent in bread making. It has a softening effect on the bread crumb and holds the moisture for longer period and thus acts as an anti staling agent. GMS is used in the form of emulsion which is made in the following manner:

GMS flakes	1 part
Water	10 parts

Boil the water. Add GMS flakes. Stir till all the flakes are completely melted. Take it off fire. Cool, stirring all the while till it comes to room temperature and has an appearance like cream. Fat can also be included in the emulsion. For example:

GMS flakes	1 part
Water	5 parts
Vanaspati	5 parts

Boil the water. Add G M S flakes. When flakes are completely melted, add fat and take it off fire. Cool it stirring all the while as described above. In whatever manner the emulsion is made, it should be added in the dough at a rate so that the dry GMS content is not more than o.2% based on flour. For example;

If emulsion is made with 1:10 proportion, then 1 kg. of this emulsion will have approximately 90 g. of dry GMS. If 2kg. of this emulsion is used in 100 kg. maida then dry GMS content will be approximately 180 g. which will be well below the maximum quantity which can be used i.e., 200 g. (0.2 on flour). Logically GMS emulsion should be combined with fat and then added to the dough which will ensure even dispersal of both the ingredients whose functions are complementary to each other.

Chapter - 12

Cake - Making Ingredients

Cake making ingredients are classified as:

1. Essential ingredients i.e. flour, sugar, shortening and eggs,
2. Optional ingredients i.e. baking powder, milk, fruits etc.

Above ingredients are also classified according to the function which they perform in cake making. This classification is as follows:

1. Structure builders - flour, eggs, milk,
2. Tenderizers - fat, sugar, baking powder,
3. Moisteners - milk, egg.

Flour

Flour builds structure of cake and holds other ingredients together in an evenly distributed condition in the cake.

1. Flour for cake making should have protein content of 7 to 9 percent and the protein should be of soft nature. Short patent flour made from soft wheat is ideally suited for cake making.

2. Cake flour should have fine granulation which has beneficial effect on the fineness of the grain structure of cake.

3. Cake flours are bleached to a greater degree in order to brighten its colour. This extra bleaching has also a modifying action on gluten forming proteins under low pH conditions, starch gelatinizes faster and thus affects a faster set of the cake structure in the oven which is desirable in the case of cakes having high amounts of sugar and moisture such as high ratio cakes.

4. Cakes made from too strong flour will peak in the center, be tough and dry eating. In case of too weak flour, the cakes may flatten out or even sink. However, the following guidelines may be useful while selecting flour for making specific types of cakes:

   {a} Medium type flour is used for making small queen cakes and Madeira cakes.

   {b} Slab cakes and pound cakes are made best with soft flour.

   {c} For cherry cake or heavily fruited cakes, medium flour should be used in order to prevent fruits from sinking and also to avoid crumbliness in cakes.

{d} For rich cakes like wedding, christmas or special birthday cakes, a combination of medium and soft flour gives good results.

Although some flour mills do possess necessary technology to produce cake flours but its availability is very limited. Addition of 5 to 10 percent corn flour in general purpose flour may be tried to tone down the strength and make it somewhat suitable for sponges and pound type cakes. However it has been experienced that cakes made with addition of corn flour or corn starch have holes on the top crust.

Sugar

1. Sucrose is most commonly used sweetening agent in cake making.
2. Due to its tenderizing action on flour proteins it makes the cakes tender.
3. Being hygroscopic in nature, sugar helps to retain moisture in cakes, improving its shelf life.
4. The golden brown crust colour of cakes is due to caramelisation of sugar.

Dextrose-mono-hydrate is used where it is desired to cut down the excessive sweetness of cakes. Dextrose caramelises at lower temperature and thus imparts a darker colour to cake crust. Due to the browening reaction the cake crumb also acquires a darker colour. A dark crust and crumb is desirable in certain cakes such as Devils Food cake or fruit/ plum cake. Browning reaction or Millard reaction is the action between protein and simple sugar {Glucose} in the presence of heat as takes place in the cake during baking operation making the product darker in colour. Dextrose-mono-hydrate contains 8% moisture which should be taken into account while adjusting the cake formula so that the total moisture content of the mix remains unaffected. Normally dextrose is used only in part with sucrose and not as a total replacement of sucrose. Whichever sugar is used in cake making, its granulation is very important while using sugarbatter method of cake making. When fat and sugar is creamed together, small air cells are incorporated in the mix. Too large grain of sugar will have a cutting action on fat which will prevent entrapping of air cells during creaming operation. Too fine a grain of sugar will also not produce desirable aeration. A coarsely powdered sugar is most suitable for cake making.

Liquid sugars like invert syrup, corn syrup, molasses, honey, sorbitol etc. can be used in part with powdered sugar for their special characteristics. Liquid sugars have better moisture retention capacity and improve the shelf life of cakes. Liquid sugars impart specific flavour to the cake and improve its crust colour. Sorbitol has its own value as it does not produce browning reaction.

Relative sweetness of Sugars

Cane Sugar	-	100.0
Invert Sugar	-	125.0
Dextrose	-	75.0
Fructose	-	175.0
Lactose	-	15.0
Maltose	-	32.5
Galactose	-	32.5

Shortenings

1. Fats have a tenderizing action on flour proteins and thus make the cake tender.

2. It is the fat part of the batter which holds innumerable air-cells incorporated during creaming operation. These air cells also have a tenderizing influence on cakes.

3. As a moisture retainer, fat helps to keep the cakes moist and thus improves the shelf life of cakes.

Fat used in cake-making should be:-

1. Plastic in nature which could incorporate and hold minute air cells during creaming operation. Granular fats do not fulfill this function and should be avoided.

2. Fat should be able to maintain its plasticity within working temperature range i.e. 60 to 85 deg.F Too hard fats will not cream up well while too soft fats will not be able to retain the aeration.

3. Use of emulsified type of shortening makes it possible to add more water in the batter. Such cakes retain their moist eating quality for longer time. In the absence of emulsified type of shortening, a judicious use of emulsifiers such as glycerol mono stearate, sorbitol mono stearate, poly sorbate, lecithin, either singly or in combination should be considered.

Egg

1. Most important function of eggs is to provide structure to the cake.

2. Although eggs by themselves do not act as aerating agent, air incorporated during mixing (whipping) operation performs this function.
3. Eggs provide moisture to the cake.
4. Lecithin present in the egg yolk acts as an emulsifier.
5. Lutin, also found in yolk, imparts colour to the cake.
6. Egg improves the taste, flavour and nutritional value of the cakes.

Milk

1. Milk solids perform the function of structure formation of cakes.
2. Milk proteins have a binding action on flour proteins which creates toughness in cakes. However, adequate quantities of fat, sugar and water present in the formula keeps the cakes tender and moist.
3. Milk enriches the cakes nutritionally.
4. Lactose sugar present in milk improves the crust colour and moisture retention capacity of cakes.
5. Milk also improves flavour and taste of cakes.

   Apart from eggs, milk is the only other ingredient providing moisture in cakes. Therefore, even though in actual practice skimmed milk powder is normally used, but, for the purpose of formula balancing, skimmed liquid milk should be considered which contains on an average 9 percent solids non fat.

Water

1. Water, whether added as such or in the form of liquid milk, hydrates flour proteins, forming gluten, which builds up the structure of cakes.
2. Formation of gluten, release of CO_2 gas from baking powder and formation of vapour pressure are made possible by the presence of water. These factors are important in regulating the volume of cakes.
3. Sugar, in order to be effective, should be dissolved in water.
4. Water regulates the consistency of batter which affects the volume and texture of cakes.
5. Shelf life of cakes is determined by the amount of moisture retained in the cake which eventually depends upon the amount of water used in the formula.

Salt

{1} Salt enhances the natural flavour of other ingredients used in cake making and thus improves the overall flavour of the cakes.

{2} It also improves the crust colour of cakes by lowering the caramelization temperature of sugar.

{3} Certain cakes contain more sugar either in the formula or in the form of icing. Since sugar helps to keep the cakes moist for long time, it may not be desirable to reduce the quantity of sugar. Salt helps to cut down the excessive sweetness of such cakes.

{4} Salt being hygroscopic in nature, helps in retention of moisture in cakes.

{5} Functions of salt and sugar are considered to be complementary to each other.

{6} Salt can be used at the rate of 0.7 to 1.2% depending on the flavour and taste desired in the cakes, and the amount of sugar in the formula. In some sweet products salt content could be as high as 1.5%.

Leavening Agents

Leavening action in cakes is achieved by three means

1. **Mechanical aeration** : When fat is whipped with sugar or flour, the mixture is filled with minute air cells which expand under the action of heat giving volume to the product.

2. **Chemical aeration** : Baking powders of various types, when moistened with water and heated, evolve CO_2 gas which expands during baking and imparts volume to cakes.

3. **Vapour pressure** : Water, which is evenly distributed in the batter, forms vapours under the action of heat. This water vapour exerts pressure as a result of which the cakes are leavened.

Among the above three different kinds of leavening actions, mechanical aeration is considered to be necessary. Only chemical aeration or vapour pressure or these two actions together will not have adequate leavening action on cakes. When the batter is filled with innumerable tiny air cells, CO_2, gas released from baking powder, diffuses into the air cells which expand together with water vapour and impart volume to cakes.

Quantity of baking powder should be carefully regulated in the formula in order to achieve good results. If a formula calls for use of more liquid, the quantity of baking powder should be increased and the product should be baked at higher temperature so that it acquires desired volume before the structure is set. Higher moisture content tend to close down the texture due to excessive availability of liquid to starch.

Cakes baked as small units, should contain more baking powder in comparison with cakes baked as large units. A large cake has to be baked at low temperature for longer time which allows it a slow, even and gradual rise resulting in a perfectly baked product. If such cake contains excessive quantity of baking powder, there will be fast evolution of CO_2 gas which will escape from the cake before the structure of cake has chance to set, resulting in a sub standard product. On the other hand, in the case of cakes baked as small units, the heat penetrates faster resulting in early setting of structure. During this short period, the cake should achieve full volume which necessitates increased quantity of baking powder.

Products containing more fat or more eggs (known as rich formula) will have sufficient aeration during creaming or whipping operation. In both the cases, the quantity of baking powder should be suitably reduced in order to achieve perfect aeration. Egg white has better whipping properties and can contain more air cells. Cakes which call for use of egg white should not contain much baking powder as during mixing operation egg white will incorporate more aeration. The quantity of baking powder is also related to the altitude of the bakery from mean sea level (MSL). Upward pressure of expanding air cells, CO_2 gas and water vapours during baking is counteracted by atmospheric pressure and a balance between the two results in perfect volume of the cake. As the altitude increases the counteracting pressure of atmosphere is reduced creating an imbalance if the upward pressure within the cake remains the same. Hence, a reduction in the quantity of baking powder will enable the cakes to acquire desired volume. Baking powder is a combination of sodium bicarbonate and an acid salt which, when moistened and heated, will evolve CO_2 gas which leavens the product giving it volume and making it light and easy to digest.

Baking powders are of three different kinds:

1. **Fast acting** : This type of baking powder releases most of its CO_2 gas during bench operation and very little gas is released during baking.

2. **Slow acting** : Such baking powders do not release much of gas during bench operation and all the gas is released when it comes in contact with heat.

3. **Double acting** : This type of baking powder is most widely used by bakers. This baking powder releases a part of gas during bench operation, increasing the fluidity of cake batter.This action makes the weighing operation easy, enabling the baker to apportion the batter in moulds correctly. The remaining CO_2 gas is released in the oven

which imparts volume to the cake. If fast acting or double acting baking powders are used, these should be incorporated in the mix as near to the last mixing operation as possible and the product should be loaded in the oven immediately in order to avoid any loss of gas.

Flavour

Flavour is a very important aspect of a quality product. A pleasant flavour is usually indicative of good taste also, as these two characteristics i.e. taste and flavour are correlated. The natural flavour of the raw material, effect of salt on the flavour of raw material, the flavour developed during baking are, although, important factors in deciding the flavour of the finished cake, but the total effect of these flavours is insufficient and it is necessary that some flavouring material is used in the formula.

While selecting a flavouring agent, the baker should ascertain that its effect is not impaired either by heat during baking or during normal storage period. Cheap flavours often breakdown under the influence of heat giving sub standard flavour to the product. It is always wise to use a small quantity of a good flavouring material rather than to overload the cake with a cheap essence. Flavouring agent should always be measured carefully as even a slight excess of essence will not only be a wasteful practice but it will spoil the gastronomical appeal of the product.

Emulsifiers

If water and oil are put into a bottle, oil will form a layer on top and water will remain down. After shaking the bottle vigorously, water and oil will break into small tiny globules and it will appear as if water and oil have mixed together. But after standing for a short duration oil globules will come together again and start floating on top while water phase will come down. In this mixture of water and oil if some object is added which can keep the oil and water fragments from coming together again and keep them in evenly distributed form, such an object is known as an emulsifier.

Among all the baked products cake batter has maximum amount of liquids which is necessary to dissolve higher amount of sugar present in the formula. There is always a risk of liquid phase and fat phase of cake batter to separate out and present a curdled appearance. When a cake batter is curdled, there is always loss of aeration which affects the quality of cake in many ways. When emulsifiers like mono and diglycerides are added to the shortening, the shortening is dispersed in a larger number of smaller sized particles and mixes more readily with the liquid phase of the cake batter.

Since fat has the ability to entrap air cells, and entrapped air cells are basically responsible for giving volume to the cake by virtue of expanding along with chemical aeration and water vapour, distribution of larger number of finer size fat particles serves to improve volume, grain and texture of the cake. Cake acquires good eating quality and extended shelf life. Finer dispersion of fat particles throughout the batter and use of mono and diglycerides strengthens the batter sufficiently to allow addition of more sugar and necessary liquid which makes the cakes sweeter and moist eating. By the same token it becomes possible to replace a good portion of sucrose with High Fructose Corn Syrup (HFCS) which is comparatively cheaper. Some of the emulsifiers used in cake making are

1. Mono and diglycerides
2. Poly sorbate
3. Sorbitan monostearate
4. Lactylated mono and diglyceride
5. Propylene glycol monostearate
6. Lecithin

However, these days a number of different brands of cake emulsifiers are available in the market in the form of "Gel". These gels are used along with eggs in creaming method or at a suitable stage in "All-in-one" process to ensure thorough dispersal. The quantity to be used is recommended by the manufacturers. However, its quantity will depend on a number of factors such as amount of fat, liquids, leavening agents, method of cake making, etc.

Chapter - 13

Cake Manufacturing

Following methods are used for making cakes.

1. Sugar - batter method.
2. Flour - batter method.
3. Blending method.
4. Boiled method.
5. Sugar - water method.
6. All-in process.

Sugar - batter method

In this method, all the fat and sugar is creamed together. Shortenings used for cake making should be plastic in nature. Granular fats should be avoided which have very poor whipping quality. Very often a combination of fats like hydrogenated shortening, butter or margarine is used in order to acquire specific characteristics in cakes. It is very necessary that all the fats are at room temperature i.e. 70 to 75 deg.F. Very hard shortenings will not cream up well, while too soft shortenings will not be able to retain aeration. If cold and hard fat is creamed with soft fats, the hard fat will break into small pieces which will be scattered in the whole mix. These hard lumps will be difficult to break and will adversely affect the process of aeration. Shortenings used for cake making should not melt by the heat produced due to friction during creaming process. In practice, all the fats should be first blended together {either by machine or by hand} thoroughly. Then sugar is added gradually continuing the creaming process. All the sugar should not be added to fat at a time as this will adversely affect the aeration process and it may take extra time to achieve the desired results. When adequate aeration is achieved, the mixture becomes very light, fluffy and brighter in appearance.

When adequate aeration is achieved in the fat-sugar mixture, eggs are added gradually. Eggs should be at room temperature (70 to 75 deg.F) at the time of adding to the cream. For small batches mixed by hand, it is good practice to whip the eggs to a stiff consistency before adding to the creamed mixture, although, while using a mixer, it is not necessary.

Although cake shortenings are emulsified type, emulsifiers in the form of gels Can be used for better results. These can be added after about half of the total egg is added or even earlier if the batter shows any signs of curdling.

When eggs are added to the creamed mixture little at a time and mixed just sufficiently, the air cells of whipped eggs either diffuse into the air cells already present or increase the number of air cells in the cream and the liquid part of egg is evenly distributed in the mixture giving it a smooth, velvety appearance.

However, if the eggs are stale, or too much egg is added at a time or after each addition of egg, it is not mixed properly, the perfect blending does not take place and the fat is broken into small fragments separated by liquid component of egg. If too cold eggs are used, the fat will solidify soon as it comes in contact with eggs and perfect amalgamation of fat and egg will not take place. In this case also, the fat will break down into small lumps which will be coated with egg. The break down of fat into small fragments separated by egg is known as "Curdling" of batter.

Whenever and for whatever reason the batter is curdled, there is loss of aeration which results in low volume and poor texture of cakes. Whenever, signs of curdling are apparent the following remedial measures should be taken immediately.

When batter is curdled due to low temperature of eggs, the mixture should be slightly warmed over a pot of hot water, taking care that the bowl containing mixture does not. touch hot water. Direct heating of mixture is not advisable as the fat will melt or egg may coagulate. In both the cases there will be loss of aeration.

If the batter is curdled due to poor quality or improper mixing of egg, an adequate quantity of flour should be added and mixed quickly. This flour will absorbed the excessive moisture and the mixture will again become smooth.

When all the egg is amalgamated, the mixture should have a smooth, light and velvety appearance.

A part (one half to two third) of liquids such as liquid sugars, water, milk, fruit juices, fruit pulp etc. along with essances, colour, and salt can be added at this stage. This is done in order to have sufficient moisture in the mix to prevent toughening of gluten while mixing flour.

Next stage is to incorporate flour in the mixture. Flour should be sifted with other dry ingredients such as baking powder, corn flour, sodium propionate etc. in order to ensure its thorough dispersal. Incorporation of flour in the cream is an important stage in cake making and even slight mishandling of the mixture will spoil the cake. Whether flour is mixed by hand or by machine, the operation should be carried out in a fashion that the flour is evenly mixed with minimum possible of mixing action in order to avoid toughening of gluten. Flour should not be added all at once, but it should be divided into two or three portions and each portion should be added at a time with minimum possible movements of hand or machine. Each portion of flour should be added alternately with water at low speed. If any fruits are to be mixed, these should be added alternately with flour. When all the flour is mixed, the remaining liquid is added. This liquid brings the batter to a definite level of fluidity which is necessary for even and gradual rise of cake during baking operation. This liquid also serves an important function of easing the strains on gluten which are affected during mixing operation and which, otherwise, may cause toughening of cake. Precisely, for this reason, even during earlier stages when the flour is being mixed, if the mixture appears to be tough, little water should be added to avoid toughening of gluten. The batter is now ready for panning and baking.

Flour - batter method

In this method, fat and a quantity of flour not exceeding the weight of fat is creamed together. Fat should be in smooth and plastic state and the flour should be added gradually. The whole mass is whipped till it becomes light and fluffy. Eggs and an equal quantity of sugar is whipped to a stiff froth. This is added to the creamed mixture of fat and flour. Although, there is less risk of curdling of the batter, still the egg mixture should be added in small portions at a time and after each addition it should be mixed thoroughly and then only the next portion should be added. At this stage, the remaining sugar is dissolved in milk or water and added to the mixture. Any colour or flavour is also added along with this liquid. Lastly, the remaining flour sifted with baking powder, is added and mixed. During last stage of mixing, if the formula is rich, the mixing operation should be carried out gently. In case of rich cakes, most of the aeration is achieved in the fat during creaming operation of fat and flour. A vigorous mixing will knock out the air cells and the cake will have poor volume. On the other hand, lean cakes acquire most of the aeration due to baking powder and there is no risk of loosing aeration achieved in fat. A thorough treatment of batter ensures smoothness of the batterwhich is desirable for obtaining good texture in cakes. As, all the liquid is already present in the batter, it is possible to give it a vigorous mixing without the risk of toughening the gluten. In case of very lean cakes specially, where there is less quantity of fat and eggs and more of flour and sugar, some difficulty may be experienced in mixing large quantity of flour and sugar. In such case, milk (or water), part of sugar and part of flour equal to that of milk is mixed into a smooth paste and added. The remaining flour should be sifted with baking powder and added at the last stage of mixing.

Advantages of Flour- batter method of cake making

As, a major portion of flour is coated with fat before any liquid is added, the development of gluten is avoided. This fact makes it possible to use slightly stronger flours which, otherwise, are unsuitable for cake making. Very small quantity of flour remains to be added at the last stage of mixing, which avoids possibility of much gluten development. Egg and sugar is whisked to a stiff consistency and fat and flour is creamed to a light and fluffy consistency. Chances of curdling of such a mixture are minimal. Flour- batter method is specially suited for making lean cakes which do not contain much fat or egg and most of aeration is achieved through baking powder. Initial creaming of fat and flour, thorough whisking of egg and sugar, presence of enough moisture during last operation of mixing are some of the factors due to which toughening of gluten is avoided and cake acquires a good texture.

Blending method

This method is suitable for making high ratio cakes in which quantity of sugar is more than the quantity of flour. Usually emulsified type of shortening and special cake flours are used for making high ratio cakes. In this method, emulsified shortening, flour, baking powder, and salt are whipped together to a very light and fluffy consistency. Sugar, milk or any other liquid, colour and flavour are mixed together and added to the previous mixture. Eggs are added next and the whole mass is mixed to a smooth batter.

Boiled Method

This method is used for making good quality Madeira cakes and genoese sponge. Butter or margarine is placed in a bowl and heated till it melts and water in them actually starts to boil (hence boiling method). Remove the bowl from heat and add about twothird (or less) flour and mix thoroughly. Egg and sugar is whisked to a stiff sponge. Colour and flavour may be added while whisking the sponge. This sponge is added to the fat-flour mixture in about four to five equal parts. After each addition of sponge, it should be mixed thoroughly. Remaining flour can be added at this stage. When the mixture is smooth, it is scaled off into paper-lined baking sheets to about one inch thickness for making genoese. For making Madeira cakes, mixture is baked in moulds lined with grease-proof paper.

Sugar-Water method

In this method, all the sugar and approximately half the quantity (of sugar) of water is agitated in a bowl till all the sugar is dissolved. Then the remaining ingredients except egg are added and the mixture is well agitated to acquire aeration. Lastly, egg is added and the mixture is cleared. Due to more aeration and better emulsification obtained in this method, the cakes so produced have better texture and longer shelf life.

All - In process

In this process all the ingredients are put into the mixing bowl together. Aeration of the mixture is achieved by controlling the speed of the mixer as well as the mixing time. Wire-whip is used for this operation which ensures a faster breakdown of ingredients and helps to achieve good aeration. For making cakes by this method, it is necessary to use emulsified type of shortening and special cake flours (having soft gluten forming proteins, fine granulation and low pH). Non-emulsified type of shortening will not be able to hold excessive moisture present in the formula. Similarly, special cake flours will tolerate the amount of mixing given to the batter without toughening the gluten. After adding all the ingredients in the mixing bowl, the mixing operation is carried out as follows:

1. Half a minute at slow speed. This is done at slow speed so that all the dry ingredients are moistened without flying off from the bowl.

2. Two minutes at fast speed. At this stage, all the ingredients break up and are incorporated evenly throughout the mass.The batter is also well aerated.

3. Two minutes at medium speed. Aeration achieved during the second stage is not evenly distributed in the batter. By mixing at medium speed the larger air-cells break up into smaller cells and the aeration of the mixture becomes even.

4. One minute at slow speed. This is done in order to eliminate any possible large air pockets and still finer breaking down of air-cells.

Panning of cake batter

When the batter is ready, it is weighed in the moulds. Moulds should be lined with grease-proof paper or should be greased and dusted with flour. Excessive greasing of moulds is undesirable because it will have a frying effect on the bottom part of the cake and the cake will have a greasy feel. After dusting the mould with flour, the mould should be turned up-side down and tapped gently in order to remove excessive flour which, otherwise, will adversely affect the appearance of the cake. The mixture should be put in the moulds in as large portions as possible. Putting the mixture in small portions at a time may cause entrapping of air pockets between one portion and the other. These air pockets will create holes in the cakes. Moulds should be filled only two-third of its height leaving sufficient space for cakes to rise during baking. After the batter is weighed in the moulds, it should be leveled properly in order to have an even expansion of cakes. Back of hand moistened with milk may be used for leveling the batter. Slight moisture on the upper surface prevents early crust formation and allows the cakes to expand evenly and due to caramelisation of milk sugar, the crust acquires a desirable golden brown colour. It is very necessary to load the cakes in the oven as soon as the weighing operation is completed, otherwise part of gas from baking powder will escape which will have an adverse effect on the volume and texture of cakes.

Baking of cakes

Different kinds of cakes are baked at different temperatures. The oven temperature is adjusted according to richness of formula, size of cakes and number of units required to be baked at a time. Regarding richness of formula, the basic principle should be remembered that is, "Richer the formula lower the temperature of baking". Rich cakes contain more amount of fat and eggs, and they acquire all its aeration during creaming of fat and sugar or by way of whipped eggs. These cakes contain very little baking powder, if any at all. The batter does not contain much moisture and is comparatively less fluid. Such cakes should have a very slow and gradual rise in the.oven in order to have thorough baking and this is precisely the reason for baking them at low temperature. If rich cakes are baked at high temperature, there will be faster crust formation on cakes. The crust will prevent heat from penetrating inside the cake resulting in an under-baked product. There will be much concentration of heat on the crust giving it too dark colour. When, ultimately heat does reach inside the cake, the internal part will expand bursting the crust and spoiling the appearance of the cake. Lean formula contains less amount fat and eggs. All the aeration in such cakes is achieved by baking powder. Lean cake batter is more fluid in comparison with rich cake batter. Such cakes are baked at high temperature so that evolution of gas from baking powder, acquiring of volume by cake and setting of structure of cake takes place simultaneously. If such cakes are baked at low temperature, there will be evolution of gas from baking powder which will expand the cake, but due to low temperature the structure of cake will not set and the cakes will collapse. Cakes baked as large units should have a slow and gradual expansion in the oven which is possible only when the baking temperature is low. Smaller units require less baking time. Faster setting of structure is made possible by baking at higher temperature. When oven is not filled to the capacity, it is necessary that the temperature of the oven is reduced. Good results are achieved by placing a pot of water in the oven. The water will absorbe some of the excessive heat and at the same time the water vapours will delay the process of crust formation on cakes thus allowing the cake to rise evenly and acquire proper volume. Lining the moulds with paper, covering the cakes in the oven with moist brown paper, placing the moulds on baking sheets while baking, are some of the means to cut down absorption of heat by cakes and these measures should be adopted while baking such cakes which require too long baking time or while baking a small batch of cakes in large oven.

Baking and Cooling Loss

Normally there is about 12% baking and cooling loss in cakes. Excessive baking and cooling loss will result in dry-eating cakes. If there is lack of temperature in the oven, the cakes will take longer time in baking and consequently there will be excessive evaporation of moisture resulting in dry-eating cake. But most important factor in determining baking and cooling loss in cakes is the amount of batter filled in a given size mould and the depth of the mould. A mould should be filled with sufficient amount of batter so that when due expansion has taken place during baking, the mould, more or less, contains (filled with) the cake. If a small amount of batter is baked in a large pan, there will be excessive baking and cooling loss which will result in not only a dry eating cake but also will mean economic loss to the baker.

Baking Temperatures

Most cakes are baked between 375-400 deg.F (190-200 deg C). If cakes are baked at too low temperature. The gas evolved from baking powder will escape before the structure has a chance to set resulting in small volumed, flat appearing cakes. On the other hand, if the cakes are baked at too high temperature, the cake will peak and burst in the center, will be tough and may also not be baked adequately. As a rule, large cakes and rich cakes should be baked at low temperature while lean cakes and smaller cakes should be baked at higher temperature.

Chapter - 14

Characteristics of Cakes

Chief characteristics of cakes are as follows:

External		**Internal**	
1.	Volume	1.	Grain
2.	Colour of crust	2.	Colour of crumb
3.	Symmetry of form	3.	Aroma
4.	Character of crust	4.	Taste
5.	Texture		

Volume

It is rather difficult to set standards for volume of cakes which will vary according to different types of cakes and also according to consumer preference. However, the cakes should not have a pinched appearance and should not appear over extended too. A well risen cake will have a pleasing appearance with slight convex top surface. Although, the relative weight of a particular volume of cake will differ in different types of cakes, but a cake should not appear too small of too large for its weight.

Colour of crust

The crust should have a pleasing golden brown colour. Too dark or too light or dull colour is not desirable. Crust must have a uniform colour, free from dark streaks or sugar spots or grease spots.

Symmetry of form

Cakes should have a symmetrical appearance. Peaking, crack on top surface, low sides, sunken or high center, burst, caved in bottom or uneven top are undesirable characteristics of cakes.

Character of crust

Crust of a good cake should be thin and tender. Thick, rubbery, sticky or over moist, too tender, tough or blistery crust is indicative of poor quality of cakes.

Texture

Texture denotes the pliability and smoothness of the crumb as felt by sense of touch. It depends on the physical condition of the crumb and type of grain. A good texture is soft and velvety without weakness and should not be crumbly. Rough, harsh, too compact, lumpy or too loose texture is not desirable.

Grain

The grain is the structure formed by the extended gluten strands including the area they surround. Grain will vary according to the type of cake. However; uniformity of the size of cell and thin cell walls are desirable qualities. Coarseness, thick cell walls, uneven size of cells, large holes and tunnels are indicative of poor grain. Grain should not be too open or too close.

Colour of crumb

Crumb should have a lively, lustrous and uniform colour. It should be free from any streaks or dark patches. Grey, non-uniform, dark, light or dull colour of crumb will be undesirable.

Aroma

Aroma of good cake should be pleasant, rich, sweet and natural. It is not desirable to have any foreign aroma i.e. aroma not produced by normal ingredients of cake. Flat, musty, strong or sharp aroma is indicative of poor quality of cake.

Taste

Taste of a cake should be pleasant, sweet and satisfying. Cakes should not leave any unpleasant after taste in the mouth, should not have a blend taste and should also not have any foreign taste i.e. taste which can not be acquired by the use of normal ingredients of cakes. Use of excessive salt or soda will also adversely affect the taste.

Chapter - 15

Balancing of Cake Formula

Basic requirement of a cake is that it should have a pleasing appearance, with thin and tender crust, should be light, even textured and pleasant to eat. In case of fruit cakes, fruits should be evenly dispersed in the crumb. Each ingredient of cake making has certain definite function e.g. flour and egg give structure, sugar, fat and baking powder act as tenderizing agents, egg and milk impart liquid to cakes. If haphazard quantities of these ingredients are used in a cake, the resultant product will vary from day to day. Therefore, in order to have consistently good quality of product, it is very necessary that all the ingredients are used in definite proportion and in a definite manner. Such proportions of raw material which can produce a desirable cake are termed as "Cake Formula". It will be desirable to understand the difference between "High ratio" and "Low ratio" cakes and "Rich cakes" and "Lean cakes", before attempting to balance cake formula. A "High ratio" cake has more sugar than flour while a "Low ratio" cake has either equal proportion of sugar and flour or sugar is less than flour. Different high ratio cakes have different quantities of sugar which varies from 110 to 140 percent for yellow layer cakes (in which whole egg is used) and 110 to 160 percent for white layer cakes (in which only white of egg is used) and 110 to 180 percent for Devils Food cakes (in which cocoa is one of the ingredient). Sugar helps in retaining moisture and thus improves the shelf life of cakes. Higher percentage of sugar in cakes will further add to the shelf life of cakes. Addition of more sugar will necessitate additional quantity of liquid in order for sugar to be effective in cakes. A normal cake formula will not tolerate additional amount of liquid without deteriorating the quality of cakes. However; incorporation of additional moisture is made possible by the use of emulsified fat (which can accept and hold more water without breakdown), and use of special cake flours with finer granulation. Such cake flours are well chlorinated. Chlorination of cake flour improves the crumb colour of cakes and also lowers the gelatinization point of starch, making it possible to have a faster "set" in the oven and thus minimising the possibility of escape of leavening gas. Liquid egg and liquid milk are the two ingredients which act as moistening agents in cakes. In the case of low ratio cakes, total quantity of eggs and milk should be equal to sugar while in case of high ratio cakes total quantity of egg and milk should be more than the quantity of sugar i.e. Total liquid = Liquid egg+ liquid milk = Sugar + 25. In the case of low ratio cakes, shortening should not exceed egg, while in the case of high ratio cakes, eggs should be equal to or higher than shortening (by about 10%).

Shortening in high ratio cakes ranges from 30 to 80%. Thus we know the quantity of fat (between 30-80%) and the quantity of sugar (say 110-140%) for a particular formula. Quantity of egg can be calculated which should be more (say by 10%) than the quantity of fat. By substituting the figures for sugar and egg in the formula;

Liquid egg + Liquid milk = Sugar + 25

We can find the quantity of milk which should be used in the batter. In this formula, 25 is an arbitrary figure which gives desirable results in the product. In case of white layer cake, in which only egg white is used (which has more moisture content), the milk content will be automatically reduced while applying the above formula. In devils food cake, cocoa is used, which, due to its drying effect on cakes, necessitates addition of more liquid. Hence the formula to be used in this case is:-

Total liquid = Liquid egg + liquid milk = Sugar + 30 + (1 .5 x Cocoa)

Thus the liquid content of batter will be directly related to the quantity of cocoa in the mix.

Rich cakes and lean cakes

Cakes having more fat in the formula are known as rich cakes and cakes having less fat are known as lean cakes. Since, more fat will incorporate more air during creaming operation, the quantity of baking powder should be reduced in rich cake. More baking powder will be required in lean cake formula as less air will be incorporated in lean cake batter due to lesser quantity of fat. Due to less fat in a lean cake batter there is possibility of gluten development during mixing operation. Therefore liquid content should be increased in order to avoid development of gluten. Since a lean cake batter is more fluid, such cakes should be baked at higher temperature in order to have a faster "set" in the oven, otherwise CO_2 gas released from baking powder will escape leaving the cake flat appearing. In rich cakes, most of aeration is achieved during creaming operation and very little baking powder is used. Such cakes should be baked at low temperature in order to allow a slow, gradual and full expansion of cakes. High temperature in case of rich cakes will form a crust on top before the cake has a chance to expand fully, and the crust will inhibit heat penetration in the cake. At a latter stage, when heat does penetrate, the upper crust of cake will develope an unsightly crack due to expansion of air cells.

Balancing of Cake Formula

Following are some of the points which should be followed while balancing a cake formula.

1. Salt content will vary between 0.8 to 2.0 percent depending on the quantity of sugar in the formula and the amount of flavour desired in the product. Very minute quantity of salt can influence the flavour of the cake a great deal.

2. As the percentage of sugar is increased, the percent of egg should also be increased by approximately the same percent. This will be necessary in order to make up for additional structure builders and moisteners (to match the tenderising action of sugar) required in the formula. In order to compensate for the dryness and toughness created by additional egg, it may be necessary to increase the quantity of fat.

3. When liquid sugars such as invert syrup, honey, corn syrup etc. are used in the formula, their moisture content should be known and necessary amendments should be made so that the total moisture content of formula does not change.

4. When cocoa is used in the formula, it is necessary to increase the moisture content, because cocoa acts as a dryer. For the same reason it may be necessary to increase the fat content also.

5. When using cocoa, sodium bi-carbonate is used. This soda reacts with the natural acidity present in cocoa thereby imparting leavening action and also darker crumb colour. However it should be remembered that alkalinity of soda will be conducive to microbial spoilage of cake and calcium propionate as a preservative will be less effective in alkaline medium.

6. Slight acidity in egg whites improves its air entrapping capacity. Cream of tartar, citric acid, monoacid calcium phosphate, acetic acid or lime juice may be used at desired levels (o.1 to o.5%) while whipping egg whites.

7. When egg yolk is desired to be used, additional moisture will be necessary, as moisture content of egg yolk is less than that of whole egg.

8. Too much milk solids will give undesirable results in cakes unless compensated with necessary amount of water.

9. When using sugar with low caramelization point, it may be necessary to use some amount of acid salt (such as MACP) in order to prevent too dark crust colour.

Chapter - 16

Cake Faults and Remedies

Reasons for faults in cakes may generally be grouped as follows:

1. Wrong quality of raw material
2. Improper balancing of formula
3. Operational mistakes

1. Wrong quality of raw material

Flour

If strong flour is used in cake making, gluten development will take place during mixing operation resulting in cakes of small volume, peaked top, unsightly crack in the center and an uneven texture. Such cakes will be dry eating and will stale rapidly. With slightly strong flours it is advisable to use flour-batter system of cake making. Liquid content may be slightly increased and mixing operation should be carried out to minimum possible extent in order to avoid undesirable development of gluten. Use of 5 to 10 percent (based on flour) corn flour will dilute the gluten and to some extent may remedy the defect. Too weak flour will not be able to carry sugar and fat and the cakes will be poor in volume. Weak flours will be unable to carry the normal amount of liquid. This will cause the crumb at the base of the cake to remain compact showing as wet streak. In the case of cakes with fruits, structure will not be strong enough to hold the weight of fruits which will sink to the bottom. While cutting such cakes it may crumble rather than cutting into neat slices.

Sugar

Very large crystals of sugar will not dissolve during mixing operation and the resultant cake will have all the defects as if lack of sugar has been used in the formula i.e. harsh crumb, poor eating quality and rapid staling. For sugar to be effective, there must be sufficient water in the formula to dissolve the sugar. If there is lack of water in the formula, then also the cakes will have the above defects. When sugar is not completely dissolved, it appears as white specks on the top crust which spoils the appearance of cakes. Too large or too small crystals of sugar are not desirable as they do not cream up well (resulting in poor aeration) and thus adversely affect the volume and texture of cakes.

Shortening

For use in cake making, shortening must be smooth and plastic. Such shortenings cream up well and hold the air cells which are incorporated during creaming operation. Granular shortenings will not cream up well and are not capable of holding the air cells. Resulting cakes will be poor in volume and have a coarse texture. If the shortening melts during mixing operations, aeration will be lost, affecting the volume and texture adversely. Special emulsified type of shortenings for cake making give best results in batter type cakes.

Egg

Weak and watery eggs should never be used in cake making as such eggs have very poor whipping quality, and cause curdling of batter. If the batter is curdled, the aeration will be lost and the cakes will have poor volume and texture. In most bakeries eggs are used by count which is a wrong practice. Eggs must always be weighed (without shell) for use in any formula.

Baking powder

Baking powder should not be stored in warm and humid place where it,looses its aerating power and will be incapable of aerating the cakes. It should be stored in cool, dry. place in airtight containers.

Fruits

Fruits must be washed before adding in the cake batter. Unwashed fruits or fruits with syrup sticking to them will discolour the cake batter and may also imbalance the formula by increasing its sugar content. Fruits must be properly prepared so that these are of even size. Too large pieces of orange peel or citron peel or glaced cherry will sink in the cake.

2. Improperly balanced formula

Sugar acts as a tenderizing agent and has to be balanced with structure forming ingredients such as flour and egg. When excess sugar is used, it opens up the structure too much which is not supported by flour and egg and as a result the cakes collapse (Mfault), have white sugar spots and dark and thick crust. As sugar delays the setting of structure, in the presence of excess sugar, fruits will sink in the cake. Excessive sugar may also cause excessive volume with very open texture. Such cakes may be too tender to cut. Too little sugar will produce a very close grain and texture. Cakes may pull away from paper lining. Too little sugar will cause setting of top crust earlier than the inner portion. When inner portion expands, it will cause an ugly crack in the top crust and the cake will have pale brown crust colour.

Fat acts as a tenderizing agent. It has lubricating action on flour proteins. Quantity of fat should be balanced against quantity of egg which should be either equal to or higher by 10% than fat. If fat is higher, egg will not be able to support structure and cakes will have a flat top, dark and thick crust, gummy and greasy eating quality and will be too tender to cut (Crumbly). In the case of cup cakes the paper cases will separate out from cakes. Excessive fat can not be retained by protein and starch network and will squeeze out when cakes are handled.

Cakes having lack of fat will have coarse grain, holes and tunnels, be dry eating and will stale rapidly. Crust of such cakes will be sticky due to insufficient bake off of moisture in the oven as less fat will result in poor volume of cakes and poor heat penetration.

Eggs subscribe to the structure, moisture and aeration of cakes. If the egg content of the formula is less than fat, the cake will not be able to carry extra fat and will collapse having flat top. This condition will also make the fruit cakes crumbly. Lack of egg will make the cakes too tender to cut specially high ratio cakes. Lack of eggs will result in less air incorporation and reduced volume of cakes. Grain will be close and compact. Due to lack of volume, heat penetration will be poor. There will be insufficient bake off of moisture and the crust will be light coloured, thin and sticky.

Excessive eggs will impart abnormal volume to the cake. The crust will be dark, thick and will peel off as a flake. Grain will be open and coarse. Texture will be rough and dry. Excessive volume will cause more moisture evaporation from the cakes, rendering the cakes dry eating.

Baking powder

Lack of baking powder will produce cakes having less volume and flat on top. Due to lack of volume, there will be poor heat penetration which will result in light coloured, tough, thin and sticky crust. As there is not enough heat penetration, grain will be like solid unbaked mass.

Excessive baking powder will produce excessive gas during baking. Volume will increase initially but as the crumb becomes over extended, it will not be able to hold gas and will collapse. Due to higher pH and good heat penetration, there will be more caramelization of sugar giving a dark coloured, very tender and dry crust. Grain will be very open and coarse. Texture will be very crumbly due to excessive evaporation of moisture and weakening of structure. Excessive baking powder will cause the fruits to sink in the fruit cake.

pH:

pH of cake batter should be about 6.5. Higher pH weakens the proteins resulting in collapse of cakes. There will be excessive caramelization of sugar as well as browning reaction in the presence of higher pH resulting in dark and flaky crust. Grain will be open and coarse due to weakened protein. Cake will have a soapy taste and aroma due to saponification. Higher pH will also encourage bacterial spoilage of cakes. Low pH will give lack of volume to cakes. Due to lack of heat penetration and low pH, crust will be light coloured and sticky to touch. Texture will be almost smooth. Cake will have a blend aroma.

Batter temperature

A cake batter should have a temperature of approximately 72 deg. F in order to have best results. At low temperature, shortening will be rendered too hard for creaming, resulting in lack of aeration in the batter and consequent lack of rise in the oven. Crust will be thin, light coloured and moist. Grain will be coarse and tough due to insufficient aeration. Higher temperature of batter will cause much loss of gas from baking powder during bench operation resulting in small volumed and fiat appearing cakes. In this case also the crust will be thin, light coloured and moist. At higher temperature, fat will not be able to hold aeration resulting in a close and compact grain.

The Following formula can be used to calculate the desired water temperature in order to get the batter at desired temperature of 72 deg.F

Desired water temp. = (6xdesired batter temp.)-(FT+ST+Sh.T+ET+RT+FF)

For example:

Desired batter temp.		=	72 deg. F
Flour temp.	FT	=	76
Sugartemp.	ST	=	78
Shortening temp.	Shot	=	72
Egg temp.	ET	=	50
Room temp.	RT	=	78
Friction Factor	FF	=	18

Therefore the desired water temp.

=(6x72)-(76+78+72+50+78+18)
= 432 - 372
= 60 deg. F

In this case also the Friction Factor is calculated by running a trial batter and using the following formula:

FF = (6 x actual batter temp.) - (FT + ST + Sh.T + ET + RT + WT)

For example.

Actual batter temp.		86 deg.F
Flour temp.	FT	82
Sugartemp.	ST	80
Shortening temp.	Sh.T	80
Egg temp.	ET	65
Room temp.	RT	80
Water temp.	WT	82

Then, Substituting the values in the formula

FF = (6x86)-(82+80+80+65+80+82)
= 516 - 469
= 47

For calculating the quantity of ice in order to have water at desired temperature the formula used is as follows:

$$\text{Wt. of ice} = \frac{\text{Wt of water (Tap water temp.- Calculated water temp.)}}{\text{Tap water temp.+112}}$$

Improper amount of moisture in the formula:

Insufficient amount of moisture in the formula will considerably reduce the stretchability of flour proteins and cakes will collapse in the oven. Crust will be dark, thick, dry and tender. Grain will be coarse and texture will be dry and rough. Excessive moisture will weaken the structure reducing its gas retention power. Cakes will have small volume and flat top. Crust will be light coloured, thin, tough and moist. Grain will be very close and compact. Texture will be very moist, smooth and prone to fungus infestation.

3. Operational mistakes

1. Flour, baking powder and any other dry ingredients should be sifted sufficiently in order to ensure even blending. Uneven blending will result in substandard shape and texture.

2. While creaming fat and sugar, all the sugar should not be added to fat at a time. Gradual addition of sugar in small portions will ensure better and faster aeration.

3. Creaming operation should be carried out till the mixture is light and fluffy. Lack of aeration during creaming operation will adversely affect almost all the characteristics of cake. Similarly, excessive aeration (during creaming operation) will break down the cream resulting in loss of aeration.

4. Eggs should be added to the cream gradually in small portions. When one portion is completely amalgamated in the cream, then only the next portion should be added. If too much egg is added at a time or subsequent portions of egg added too quickly, the batter will curdle and aeration will be lost. The resultant cake will have small volume, coarse and crumbly texture and other related faults. About four to tive eggs per kg. Of fat can be added at a time.

5. While mixing flour in the cream, mixing operation should be carried out efficiently so that undesirable gluten development does not take place. Over mixing will develop gluten rendering the cakes having small volume with peak in the center and an unsightly crack. Texture will be compact with holes and tunnels. Undermixing of batter will impart uneven texture to cakes. It is advisable to add flour in two or three small portions rather than all the flour at a time.

6. While flour is being added, the (formula) liquid should also be added simultaneously. If there is lack of liquid content during mixing of flour, gluten development will take place resulting in poor quality cakes.

7. A fruit cake batter should not be aerated too much and should be sufficiently stiff to support the weight of fruits. Too much aeration or too soft a batter will cause the fruits to sink in the batter during baking.

8. When the batter is ready, it should be stirred gently in order to break any large air pockets which might have been formed during mixing. While weighing the batter into moulds, care should be taken to avoid entrapping air pockets. Large air pockets entrapped in the batter will cause holes and tunnels in the cakes.

9. Soon as the batter is weighed into the moulds, it should be loaded into the oven immediately. If the moulds are left out for any appreciable length of time, there will be undue loss of gas which in turn will adversely affect the qualities of cake. There will be loss of moisture from the top surface which will render the top crust dry, too dark and possibly having sugar spots.

10. When the cakes are in the oven, these should not be moved unless the structure of cake is set. During the initial stage of baking the batter is in a very delicate condition. Any movement in this condition will result in collapse of cakes.

11. Scrapings from the bowl should be evenly mixed with the batter or it can be used with the next mix. Scrapped batter put on top of batter in the mould will produce unsightly streaks.

12. Normally cake batter will produce enough water vapour in the oven so as to enable the cakes to have a slow and gradual rise.

    However; lack of humidity in the oven will cause lack of volume, crust will be dry and will peal off. Crust will also develope an unsightly crack. In such situation it is advisable to put some water in the oven at least 15 minutes prior to baking. .High humidity in the oven will not allow normal bake off of moisture from the cake which will render the cake prone to fungus infection. Crust will be light coloured because steam will act as an insulator.

13. Presently, most of the bakers produce cakes by All-in-one process. In this case also it is highly recommendable that the ingredients are added in a particular sequence only. This becomes necessary because the ingredients which are available may not be in right condition (For example sugar may have too large a grain which may not dissolve during normal mixing time or fat may be too hard and may not break up and mix thoroughly) or the cake mixer may not be very efficient to produce the right kind of batter within normal mixing operation.

Some common cake faults and their reasons

1. Collapsed or Sunk Cakes

A. Too much sugar

B. Too little liquid

2. Cake with peaked top

A. Flour too strong

B. Insufficient aeration

C. Too much top heat

3. Cake with flat top

A. An excess of opening ingredients

B. Too little liquid

C. Oven too cool

D. Incorrect balance between egg and fat

4. Sheet cakes "Blowing" (like balloon) in the oven

A. Too much bottom heat

B. Too much steam in the oven

C. Use of badly worn baking sheets

5. Shrinkage in cup cakes

A. Too little baking powder

B. Too little sugar

C. Too much mixing

D. Toughening of the batter

E. Too much bottom heat

6. Under baked area under top crust

A. Under baking

B. Bumping the cake during baking

C. Faulty testing

7. Dense streak at the base of the cake

A. Excessive use of liquid

B. Too little baking powder

C. Protein weakness (of flour or egg)

8. Tunnel like holes in the cake

A. Toughening of the batter

B. Lumps of unmixed fat in the batter

C. Pockets of air entrapped during scaling

9. Fruit falls to the bottom of the cake

A. Thin batter

B. Lack of structure

C. Too much sugar

D. Too much baking powder

E. Incorrect baking temperature

10. Fruit cake crumbles when cut

A. Weak or wrong type of flour

B. Unbalanced mixing

C. Use of unsoaked fruits

D. Incorrect baking

11. Texture (Dense) too close

A. Insufficient baking powder

B. Too much liquid

C. Too little sugar

D. Hot batters

12. Coarse texture

A. Too much baking powder

B. Insufficient liquid

C. Too much sugar

D. Too little mixing

E. Oven too cool

13. Cakes too tender for cutting

A. Overmixing of the batter

B. Too little egg

C. Too much sugar

D. A slow bake

14. Thick crust on cake

A. Too much sugar

B. Too little milk or other liquid

C. Too hot or too cool oven

D. Cakes standing too long before baking

15. Cracks on surface of the cakes

A. Too hot oven

B. Lack of moisture in the oven

C. Too little sugar

D. Toughened batter

E. Too much batter in the tin

F. Insufficient air in the batter

16. Top crust peels and flakes off

A. Over mixing

B. Oven too cool

C. Insufficient steam during baking

D. Cooking in dry condition

E. Handling cakes before they are cool

17. Discoloured crumb

A. Slow baking

B. Too .much bottom heat

C. Type of sweetening agent

D. In fruit cakes, high sugar content of fruits

E. Too much soda

18. Very pale crust colour

A. Too little sugar

B. Lack of milk

C. A very slow bake

D. A wet oven atmosphere

19. White spots on cake surface

A. Batter standing too long before baking

B. Use of very coarse sugar

C. Too ittle liquid

D. Slow baking

20. Mold growth on cakes

A. Excessive moisture

B. Contamination

Chapter - 17

Cookies

Cookies or most often classified as biscuits in common Parlance are a substantial portion of bakery business in India. In Delhi more than 50% of share of biscuit market is fed by hand made biscuits produced by small bakeries. However, in most cases the difference between two types of cookies is so little that they may very in shape, size, colour but there is hardly any difference in taste and flavour. In order to produce cookies having their own special characteristics, an understanding of raw material, process and special attention for extended shelf life is very necessary.

Cookies can be divided into following categories.

1. Sheeted type known as short dough biscuit

   a. Having more fat in the range of 60-75%

   b. Having less fat in the range of 45-50%

2. Drop Cookies

   The mixture of such cookies generally contain high amounts of fat which makes it easier to pipe through a nozzle such as fingers or stars or to shape them between palms of hand as in the case of melting moments or nan-khatai.

3. Some cookie doughs are shaped and kept in the refrigerator. When it becomes hard, it is cut into desired thickness and placed on baking sheet. These cookies are known as Ice box cookies.

4. Some cookies are made by foaming method in which egg whites or even whole egg is whisked to wet peak stage. Then three fourth of the sugar is added gradually, whisking all the while. Finally coconut or coarsely grated cashewnut or peanuts or almonds along with remaining sugar and flavour is folded gently. These are known as macaroons. Macaroons should be baked at a very low temperature. Some macaroons are left overnight to dry out before baking.

Cookie Ingredients

Flour : Requirement of flour quality will vary according to the type of cookie. A cookie having higher fat content will require stronger flour in order to prevent unwanted spread and also to maintain the design of the cookie. Cookies made with egg and very little fat as in the case of fingers require soft cake flour. Flour should be sifted to aerate it and for easy mixing operation.

Sugar : Granulation of sugar is very important in cookie making. Coarse grain of sugar will cause more spread of cookie affecting its texture, eating quality etc. It will also create problems in packaging and there could be too much breakage of packaged goods. Very fine granulation will not incorporate enough aeration resulting in dense texture, toughness and poor eating quality. Coarsely powdered or a fine granulated sugar should be used. However, in some recipes a small portion of granulated sugar is added to give the product a particular snappy bite. Some cookies are moist eating in which case part of sugar is replaced with liquid sugar such as invert sugar, honey or corn syrup. Dextrose sugar will have reduced sweetness and will impart darker colour to the cookie.

Fat : Most cookies are rich in fat content. Fat improves the eating quality for prolonged period. Generally smooth, plastic hydrogenated shortenings are used for cookie making. Granular shortenings are unsuitable as they do not aerate sufficiently and distribution of fat in the cookie remains uneven. The fat used for cookie making should be able to cream and incorporate aeration, and should not melt at working temperature. Addition of part butter improves the taste and flavour of the cookie and also does not affect the creaming quality. However, butter should be softened before blending with hydrogenated fat otherwise it will break into lumps which will be difficult to homogenize. Hard butter lumps may also cause curdling of mixture.

Eggs : Eggs form structure of cookies, impart flavour and taste. Eggs help in maintaining the shape of cookies. Eggs must be fresh. Stale eggs may give bad odour and spoil the overall flavour of cookie. Whole eggs are best used at room temperature while egg white whip better when it is cool.

Milk : Milk is generally used in the form of dry milk non fat. It imparts good colour, flavour and a very creamy eating quality. One to two percent of milk solids achieve very desirable results. Dry milk is best used after dissolving in water if, water is an ingredient of the formula. Milk powder should be mixed with equal quantity of 'sugar in dry state and then small quantity of water should be added to make a lump free slurry. It is very undesirable to find lumps of milk powder in the finished product. It can also be sifted along with other dry ingredients, in case if sufficient water is not part of formula.

Flavour : Choice of flavour in cookies is very limited. Generally use of butter and milk as the ingredients of the formula perform the function of flavourig agents which is further fortified with vanilla which is used within limits of 0.5 to one percent based on flour. Artificial butter and milk flavours should be used with utmost care as even slightly enhanced quantity may impart very strong and unacceptable flavour to the product.

Mixing of cookie doughs

Mixing operation of cookie dough is very important in deciding the nature of cookie. Over mixed doughs will produce a tough cookie. If the fat content in the formula is low, then creaming operation should be performed properly in order to aerate the mixer. Doughs having higher fat content require only a homogenous blend of fat, sugar, flour and eggs. Flour should be mixed very gently to avoid any gluten development. In sheeted type of cookies, any gluten development will make it very difficult to sheet the dough as it will have a tendency to shrink. Biscuits will also shrink after cutting. In bagged out cookies, if the dough is over mixed the mixture will become tenous and may not come out of the nozzle easily. During piping, the fat may squeeze out of the mixture. Under mixed doughs of sheeted type of cookies will produce brittle and rough surfaced cookie while an under mixed dough of bagged out cookie may not retain the sharpness of design.

In foam type cookies the eggs should be whipped to wet peak stage. If the eggs are whipped to dry peak stage, mixing of flour will be difficult and will take longer time. Some aeration will also be lost. The resultant cookie will be tough.

Sheeting of cookie dough should be very even to ensure even size cookies. Piped cookies should also be even in shape and size. Cookies must be placed on baking sheets at even distance allowing sufficient space for expansion. Bagged out cookies or macaroons are best baked on paper lined sheets which prevents sticking. Trays for baking cookies should be greased very lightly. Excessive greasing will cause too much spread of cookie. If the trays are not greased at all or ungreased spots are present, it will cause sticking of cookie and cookie spread will also be restricted. If the cookies are to be garnished with any nuts, seeds, cherry or jam, it should be done immediately after make-up and before any dry skin formation. If dry skin is formed on the surface of the cookie the garnish will not stick and will come out after baking.

Baking of cookies should be done very carefully. Cookies are small units baked for short period. If the temperature is too hot, spread of cookie will be arrested. Too low temperature will result in too much spread of cookie and dry eating quality. Cookies having more sugar should be baked at low temperature while cookies having high fat content and low in sugar should be baked at high temperature. Cookies are tested for proper baking by the top and bottom colour. As soon as right colour is achieved, it should be removed from the oven. After removing from the oven, the baking action in the cookie still continues for 3-4 minutes. This is the reason that cookies are removed from the oven at the right time to prevent over baking. Paper lining of trays will prevent charring of cookie bottoms and edges.

Following points are important regarding different type of cookies.

1. Short cookie dough should be chilled before sheeting. If chilling is not possible, atleast relax the dough for atleast half an hour before sheeting.
2. Do not use too much dusting flour for sheeting the dough.
3. Small portion of the dough should be sheeted at a time. Scrap dough from previous sheeting should be mixed with fresh dough immediately. This will avoid toughness from excessive scrap dough.
4. Dough should be sheeted to even thickness. The centre of sheeted dough is generally thicker than the edges. Centre portion should be given special attention.
5. Bagged out cookies should be spaced evenly on the baking sheet. Leave enough space in between cookies for spread.
6. If bagged out cookies are to be garnished do it immediately and before cookies form dry skin on surface.
7. Ice box cookies, after cutting and placing them on baking sheet, should be allowed to come to room temperature before baking.
8. Top heat in case of baking of Ice box cookies should be controlled, otherwise delicate colours of biscuit design will become brown and unattractive.
9. Macaroons should be baked on paper lined sheets or alternately on lightly greased and dusted sheets.
10. Macaroons should be allowed to form a crust before baking. Some macaroons are dried out overnight before baking.
11. Macaroons should be baked at very low temperature.

Chapter - 18

Pastry, Cookies, Biscuits, Cakes, Buns, Pies, Icings, Breads & Pizzas

A paste of flour, fat, salt and water is known as pastry. Optional ingredients may be added such as sugar, flavour, Milk solids, egg yolk and so on. Method of mixing differs for different kind of pastries. Pastry is actually only a base for making different kind of products such as puff, vaul au vent, Palmiers, French hearts, pie crust, tarts, turn-overs, cream rolls etc.

Based on the method of mixing pastries are classified as follows:-

1. Short crust pastry
2. Puff pastry
3. Flaky pastry
4. Choux pastry

SHORT CRUST PASTRY

In this type of pastry, fat content is generally 40-80 percent. If the fat content is low, small quantity of leavening agent (Baking Powder) should be used to impart tender eating quality. Flour is sieved (with baking powder, milk solids). Chilled fat is cut into small pieces and mixed with the flour.Then flour and fat are rubbed gently with the tips of fingers till the Whole mass resembles bread crumbs. If sugar is desired to be added, it should be added and mixed now. Sugar content in this pastry varies from about 10%. (For pie crust, tarts, turn-overs etc.) to 50% (for short dough based cookies). Salt is dissolved in part of chilled water and added. Remaining water, with the flavour is added gradually and mixed with a pallet knife by "Cutting & Mixing" method. If egg yolks are desired to be added, water should be reduced proportionately and yolks should be thoroughly blended before mixing to ensure even mixing.

Mixing operation of short crust pastry is very important. It should be carried out in a manner that gluten is not unduly developed, otherwise pastry will become hard and not remain tender as it should be. Small doughs could be mixed with a pallet knife by, what is known as "Cutting and folding" movements of pallet knife. It should be mixed just sufficiently so that water is evenly distributed and taken up by the flour and the whole mass joins together. Any undue mixing operation will toughen the pastry. Moisture (Water, Egg yolk, Fresh Liquid Milk etc.) content should also be accurately regulated so that the dough mass does not remain crumbly nor does it become sticky. Larger doughs can be mixed in a vertical mixer at slow and medium speed. After mixing, the dough should be rested in cool place (refrigerator) for Half an hour to one hour before sheeting for make up. While sheeting short crust pastry, it should be remembered that the pastry is subjected to as little frictional heat (Generated by rolling pin) as possible. Otherwise fat will melt and get separated from dough mass making the pastry tough eating. During the entire operation of making short crust pastry the aim should be to keep the fat evenly distributed in the dough mass till the product goes to oven for baking. Baking of short crust pastry is done at medium temperature (190-195 Deg.C) and the baking time will depend on the type of product being baked. If the pastry is to be baked without any filling it is advisable to prick the pastry with a fork in order to avoid any bubble formation which may spoil its appearance.

After sheeting and cutting, the scrap should be neatly placed one over the other and pressed for second sheeting. In this manner gluten development will be minimal and resultant product will remain tender eating.

PUFF PASTRY

Fat used for making puff pastry should have high melting point in order to withstand the frictional heat to which it is subjected during sheeting and folding operations. Dough for making puff pastry should be mixed with chilled water in order to prevent fat from melting. Some food acid like lemon juice is used in the dough in order to impart better extensibility to the dough. Fat should be added last in the dough because if fat is added before flour has a chance to take up and absorb water, water absorption will be reduced and gluten may not develop sufficient strength to undergo so many sheeting and folding operations.

Dough for putt pastry is made with flour, salt, lemon juice, chilled water and shortening. Consistency of the dough should be such that it could be sheeted easily without being too hard or sticky. Too tight or too loose dough will be difficult to process.

After mixing, the dough should be relaxed in cool place covered with moist cloth which will prevent it from crusting. Puff margarine is made into a square block and chilled in the refrigerator.

After half an hour of relaxation period, dough is sheeted into a square Shape somewhat larger than the margarine block. Then the chilled margarine block is placed in the center of the dough so that the sides of the margarine block face the corners of the sheeted dough. Now one end of the Dough is folded over the margarine block so as to cover it completely. Then the opposite end is brought over and folded over it. Similarly the remaining two ends are folded so that the margarine block is covered by four folds of the dough on the top side. This block should be relaxed in cool place for about 20 min. This relaxation period will ease the stress on the dough to which it is subjected during sheeting and folding operation. After proper relaxation of the dough, it is turned upside down (so that the top side having four folds is down in contact with the table top) and sheeted into a rectangular shape and folded into a book fold that is both the ends are brought in the center and again folded over so that the entire sheet forms four layers. In the similar manner four more folds are given interspersed with adequate relaxation period in between folding. Now we have a dough and fat mass in which very fine layers of dough are interspersed with very thin layers of fat. This mass is known as "PUFF PASTRY" from which various products are made such as vegetable/jam puffs, Cream rolls, palmiers, vaul au vents, etc. After final sheeting and folding, the pastry should be relaxed in cool place for a minimum of one hr. before sheeting for make up. If at any stage pastry becomes too hard (if stored in the refrigerator), it should be allowed to thaw at room temperature until it acquires sheetable consistency.

Following precautions should be observed while sheeting puff pastry.

1. Margarine should not become too hard when the dough is relaxed in the refrigerator. Very hard margarine will break into small pieces while sheeting and the desired layering effect will not be achieved.

2. Margarine should not be too soft, otherwise during sheeting it will be squeezed out at one end. This will also prevent formation of desired layers.

3. Relaxation of dough in between two sheeting operations is very important. During sheeting operation, gluten of the dough is subjected to stress and strain and its extensibility is reduced. During relaxation period extensibility is regained and further processing becomes easier.

4. Under no circumstances the pastry should be subjected to undue pressure while sheeting. This may break the continuity of gluten strands and also break the fat into small pieces. Both the conditions will disturb the pattern of layers. It will also compress the layers too much which will adversely affect its rise during baking.

5. The entire operation of making puff pastry should be carried out at cool temperature. Frictional heat from sheeting action or the atmospheric temperature (warm table top) should not make the

margarine loose which, as explained earlier, will be squeezed out and proper layer formation will not take place.

6. While relaxing the pastry, it should be covered with moist cloth in order to prevent it from crusting. If pastry is crusted during processing, it will loose its stretchability and its rise in the oven will be poor.

FLAKY PASTRY

Flaky pastry can be used for making pie crust, vegetable puffs, Bombay khara (As popularly known), cream rolls etc.

Proportion of fat could be 50-70% for layering and 5-10% fat could be mixed in the dough. Higher amounts of fat either mixed in the dough or layered will make the pastry too fragile to handle.

Dough is made with flour, salt, food acid, chilled water and fat. Dough is relaxed for about half an hour. Then the dough is sheeted into a rectangular shape and marked into three equal parts lengthwise.

Fat is divided into three portions. One portion of fat is evenly spread onto two-third portion of sheeted dough leaving out half an ihch space on the edges. Now one-third part of the dough (on which fat is not being spread) is folded over the middle one-third part (on which fat is being spread). The remaining one third portion (with fat) is folded over it. We have now alternate layers of dough and fat. Relax the dough for 20-25 min. in cool place covered with moist cloth in order to prevent it from crusting.

The dough is again sheeted into rectangular shape and the process is repeated twice more to use up the remaining two portions of fat with adequate relaxation time in between sheetings.

Similar two folding are given without fat. Now we have very thin layers of dough interspersed with very thin layers of fat which will rise during baking to form a light and crisp product. After final sheeting and folding, the pastry should be relaxed for about an hour before sheeting for make up.

After make up and before placing it in the oven the pastry should be relaxed on baking sheets for 20-30 min. This will stabilize the position of layers and rise of the product in the oven will be even. During this relaxation period the product should be protected from crusting. Some products like Bombay khara are drenched with water which is drained out just before baking. Other products like puffs or palmiers can be washed with milk or egg and covered with moist cloth.

Note:- Puff pastry in some form or the other is produced in the entire country like Bombay khara or cream rolls or vegetable puffs etc. Majority of bakers sheet the dough and spread all the fat at one time, give it a book-fold length wise and at the same time give another book-fold breadth wise. After relaxation period the same process is repeated again without fat. For this method the dough should be sheeted in larger dimensions so that necessary folding can be given easily. In this method time and labour is saved and product quality is also quite satisfactory.

CHOUX PASTRY

Choux pastry has altogether different kind of characteristics. This is an almost hollow shell which is crisp eating. Shells can be filled with fresh cream or butter cream or custard cream and then coated with fondant icing. Pastry can be made in the shape of eclairs, swans, cream puffs etc.

Water and fat is boiled together. The pan is taken off heat and all the flour is added at a time and mixed thoroughly to avoid lump formation. The entire mass is again cooked for some time on slow heat till the mixture starts leaving the bottom of the pan. Now the pan is taken off fire and whisked eggs are added gradually beating the mixture thoroughly so as to form a homogeneous smooth paste of piping consistency. Adequate whisking of this paste will ensure desirable rise of the pastry during baking.

Baking operation of choux pastry is very important. Initially it should be baked at high temperature (230 deg.C) so that it achieves maximum rise. Then the temperature is reduced: to about 150 deg.C and it is baked until structure is stabilized and shells become crisp.

Pastry should not be subjected to unnecessary movements or sudden temperature variations until its structure is stabilized otherwise it will collapse. Shells can be stored for short periods and used as required.

PROJECT PROFILE ON BAKERY

Before starting a bakery, it is necessary to survey the market for bakery products in the area in order to decide the size and scope of the project. For a large project it is advisable to hire the services of marketing agencies who are well equipped to undertake such studies. However; for small scale bakery, the following points should be studied;

1. The population, food habits and purchasing capacity of the people.
2. Availability of raw material such as flour, shortening, chemicals, yeast etc. If raw material is to be brought from distant places, it will add to the cost factor.
3. Transport and communication facility.
4. Availability of power and fuel.

5. Availability of local labour force.
6. Number of existing bakeries and their performance.

Location

The following main factors should be taken into consideration before making a choice of location for a bakery.

1. Industrial development taking place in the surrounding area.
2. Schools, colleges, hotels, Hospitals are located nearby. While selecting the site it is generally considered as advantageous when state transport bus stops, railway station, or military bases are in the vicinity of the bakery.
3. If any bakery is enjoying large volume of sales in a particular area, it does not mean that a new bakery will also be able to sell equally well. However in a developing economy it should not be difficult to tap the market.
4. Information regarding volume of sales, production capacity of other bakeries in the area and the type and quality of products they are making.
5. The possibilities of getting contract under school feeding programme or from industrial canteens.
6. Whether it is residential or industrial area.

Statutory procedures :

The knowledge of government procedures and legal aspects of the industry are as important as the technical know-how of the project.

The detailed information can be obtained from the State Directorate of industries and Small Industries Service Institute. However; in general the following formalities are to be observed.

1. Registration as a small scale industry at the state directorate of industries, and availability certificate for maida from the Department of Civil Supplies if maida is a controlled commodity.
2. Compliance of Municipal licensing regulations.
3. Compliance of prevention of Food Adulteration Act.
4. Compliance of Factory Act and other Labour Laws.
5. Compliance of Smoke Nuisance Act.
6. The premises should be such that it could be kept clean and free from dust and smoke. Proper provision should be made for ventilation.

Arrangement for finance

The financial planning of the project is a very important factor specially under the conditions where the prices of raw material fluctuate vastly. Most projects cost more than the estimate resulting in a squeeze on working capital. Most financial institutions are reluctant to finance for the additional cost of the project even when it is justified by increase in profits.

The main problem which is faced practically by any entrepreneur is getting loans from banks and other financial institutions within reasonable time frame. The delay in the formalities cause delay in the project resulting in further increase in the cost of the project.

The following precautionary measures must be taken for effective planning of finances.

1. A twenty percent contingency must be added on the firm quotations of all machinery and civil construction work.
2. Allowances should be made for pre-operational expenses. They include salaries of staff employed during and before erection, installation, transport, insurance, interest, expense incurred on spoiled batches during trial operations etc.
3. The implementation of the project must be carefully planned in order to complete it in minimum possible time. For example, the construction of building and other civil works can be started as soon as the order for fabrication of machinery is placed. However, possibilities should be explored to take premises on rent or industrial shed offered on installments.
4. One should ensure the availability of the total loan from financial institutions such as scheduled banks, State Finance Corporation, National Small Industries Corporation, Small Industries development corporation, Khadi Gramodyog Commission.

Planning layout

The machinery layout can influence erection cost, operating and maintenance cost, safety and convenience. The following points may be used as guidelines for planning the layout.

1. The flow sheet indicating the flow of material should be first prepared and then it should be arranged in a proper way to get the advantage of gravity feed wherever possible.
2. Sufficient distance must be kept between each process equipment to provide enough space for the movement of men and material and sometimes the machinery to comply with the requirements under Factory Act.

3. The baking oven should preferably be located in one corner of the plant rather than in the middle. Area near the oven should be well ventilated so that the hot atmosphere surrounding the oven is dissipated.

Selection of equipment

a. It is necessary to calculate the ratio of various types of products, the volume, the size and the profitability of the products which are desired to be produced.

b: While selecting the equipment it is necessary to consider the ultimate production goal from the sales point of view which will also be the deciding factor for the size of bakery.

c. Cheaper equipments may ultimately prove to be more expensive on account of maintenance cost and breakdowns. Such equipments should be selected which are sturdy, long lasting, require minimum maintenance, and can be operated with minimum power requirement.

d. Only essential equipment should be installed in the beginning eg. for bread production only, a mixer, oven and slicer is essential. If volume of production becomes more, then moulder can be installed. If volume is more than ten thousand loaves then only a divider and rounder may be required. Overhead proofer, and proofing assembly will be necessary only for large size production of more than ten thousand loaves.

e. If it is desired to produce cakes, pastries, cookies etc. also, a vertical mixer of suitable size can be added.

f. Serious thought should be given to selection of oven. For a small bakery, wood fired oven may appear to be cheaper proposition, but ever increasing scarcity of firewood, pollution problem, and a general ecological awareness could become a serious hurdle. While considering electric oven, one must ensure the uninterrupted power supply position. Gas ovens, although, are efficient, but availability of proper gas oven, its cost and running expenditure as well as statutory requirements should be ascertained before making decision. Diesel fired ovens, although, are expensive, but operational cost may be very favourable and its performance is quite satisfactory.

g. There are a number of other equipments which could be added as and when necessity arises such as dough sheeter for making puff pastry products, wire-cut or depositor cookie machine, freezer, water chiller, cake-batter depositor, vegetable cutting machine, mincer, nut-grinder etc.

Electricity

It is essential that the local Electricity Board is contacted regarding the approximate cost of wiring, cable laying charges, and deposits to be paid to the Electricity Board. The cost of power consumption varies from place to placa and should be ascertained from the Electricity Board.

Depending on the installed equipment, a bakery may require 10 - 50 KV connected load. Considering the future expansion, one should ensure that the wiring is done in such a manner that increased load can be connected later.

Total Space Required for the Bakery

One has to plan the layout of the bakery according to the available space and the estimated volume of production. However; about 1200 sq. ft. production area may be required to produce 3000X400 g. loaves of bread or an assorted production (bread, cakes, pastries, cookies etc.) from 4X90 kg. bags of flour. It is very necessary to make provision for future expansion

While planning a bakery, the following points should be paid attention to;

1. Floor of the entire premises should be at one level in order to facilitate movements of trollies or tables mounted on wheels.
2. It is ideal practice to wash the entire floor of the bakery at the end of days work. The slope of the floor should be such that the wash water is drained out easily.
3. Windows should be covered with wire mash and wire mashed doors should be fitted with automatic door-closers.
4. Wash basin should be provided for workers to wash their hands before starting work or after visit to toilet.
5. Raw material store and finished goods store should be so situated that these could be kept locked without any interference in normal production work.
6. Tables can be mounted on wheels for easy movements. Use of appropriate trollies saves pressure on floor area.
7. Exhaust fans should be installed wherever there is no natural ventilation.
8. Walls should be tiled upto a height of six feet in order to ensure cleanliness of premises.

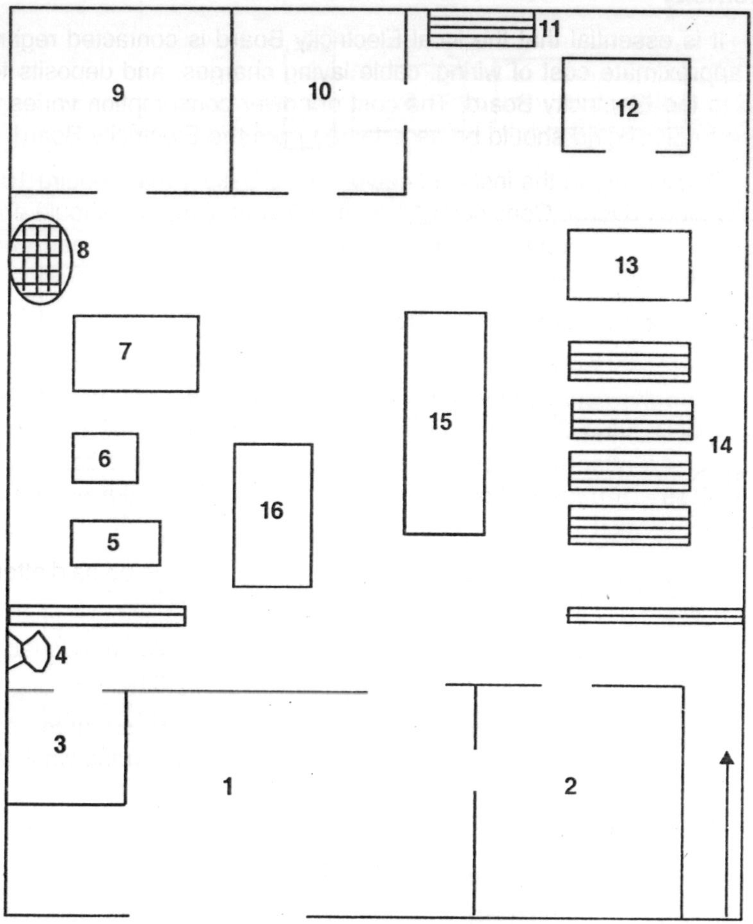

Plan Layout of a Small Bakery

1. Store
2. Slicing/Wrapping area
3. Toilet
4. Hand-wash
5. Cake mixer
6. Cookie dough mixer
7. Bread mixer
8. Water trap
9. Fermentation room
10. Proofing cabinet
11. Wall rack
12. Electric oven
13. Depanning table
14. Cooling racks
15. Work bench 10"x3½"
16. Work bench 6"x3"

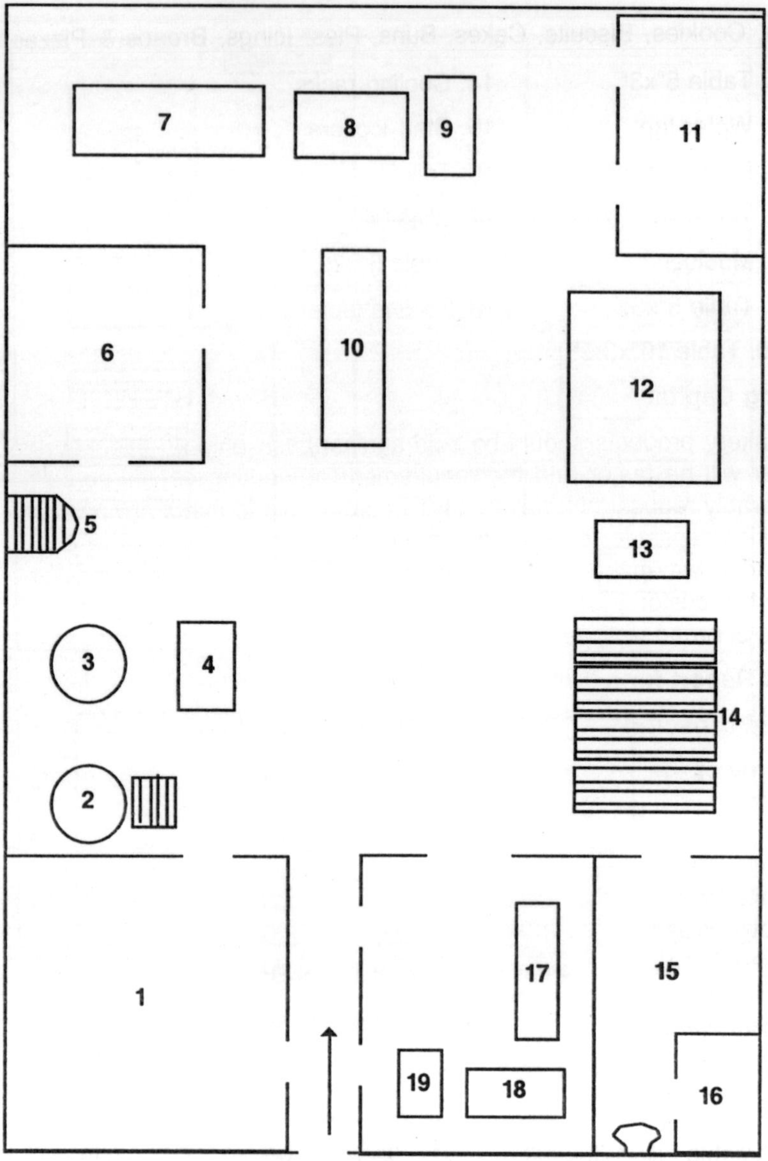

Plan Layout of a Bread Bakery

Fig. DESCRIPTION

1. Store
2. Sifter
3. Mixer
11. Proofing room
12. Oven
13. Depanning table

4. Table 5"x3"
5. Water tap
6. Fermentation room
7. Table 10"x3½"
8. Moulder
9. Table 5"x3½"
10. Table 10"x3½"
14. Cooling racks
15. Staff lockers
16. Toilet
17. Slicer
18. Table 5"x2½"
19. Sealing table

Working Capital

Bakery products should be sold against cash only. In this way the turnover will be faster and the requirement of working capital could be considerably reduced. However; it will be advisable to make arrangement for working capital for a period of three months. Bread can be wrapped in plain paper, wax-paper or poly propylene (pp) bags. Climatic conditions, cost factor, customers preference should be considered before deciding the kind of bread wrapper desired to be used.

Project Report for a small Retail Bakery

Installed capacity

S. No.	Name of the Item	Unit Wt.	Quantity	Rate	Amount
1.	White Bread	400 g.	500	8.00	4,000.00
2.	White Bread	800 g.	50	16.00	800.00
3.	Brown Bread	400 g.	50	10.00	500.00
4.	Sweet Bread	200 g.	250	6.00	1,500.00
5.	Fruit Bun	50 g.	100	3.00	300.00
6.	Sweet Rolls	70 g.	50	5.00	250.00
7.	Dinner roll	40 g.	70	3.00	210.00
8.	Danish Pastry	60 g.	60	8.00	480.00
9.	Pao Bhaji Bun	30 g.	400	1.00	400.00
10.	Vegetable Filled Bun	90 g.	60	5.00	300.00
11.	Rusk	-	25 kg.	50.00	1,250.00
12.	Pizza Base	100 g.	50	4.00	200.00
13.	Ready Pizza	250 g.	20	50.00	1,000.00
14.	Surti Khari	-	7 kg.	60.00	420.00
15.	Soup Sticks	-	2 kg.	100.00	200.00
16.	Burger Bun	50 g.	60	4.00	240.00
17.	Dough nuts	60 g.	30	6.00	180.00
18.	Vegetable Puff	70 g.	200	7.00	1,400.00

19. Special Puffs	70 g.	200	10.00	2,000.00
20. Bombay Khara	-	12 kg.	60.00	720.00
21. Special Khara	-	12 kg.	80.00	960.00
22. Cream roll	50 g.	100	6.00	600.00
23. Dil Pasand	250 g.	10	24.00	240.00
24. French Hearts	50 g.	50	10.00	500.00
25. Pastries	40 g.	450	5.00	2,250.00
26. Birthday Cakes	1 kg.	12	150.00	1,800.00
27. Pound Cake	-	20 kg.	80.00	1,600.00
28. Muffins	40 g.	100	5.00	500.00
29. Bar Cakes	200 g.	125	18.00	2,250.00
30. Sponge Cake	-	30 kg.	60.00	1,800.00
31. Cup Cakes	20 g.	12 kg.	60.00	720.00
32. Cake Rusk	200 g.	20 kg.	80.00	1,600.00
33. Plum Cake	-	7 kg.	150.00	1,050.00
34. Eggless Plum Cake	-	7 kg.	150.00	1,050.00
35. Browni	30 g.	50	6.00	300.00
36. Nan Khatai	200 g.	10 kg.	100.00	1,000.00
37. Assorted Biscuit	-	20 kg.	60.00	1,200.00
38. Fancy Biscuit	-	10 kg.	100.00	1,000.00
39. Macaroons	100 g.	2 kg.	120.00	240.00
40. Assorted Pie/Tarts	75 g.	32	15.00	480.00
41. Eclairs	40 g.	30	10.00	300.00
42. Sandwiches	-	30	10.00	300.00
		Total		**38,000.00**

Minus Sales Returns/cipples @ 5 percent	2,000.00
Net sales for one day	36,000.00
Sale for 1 year (360 working days)	1,29,60,000.00
Plus sale of empty bags/tins	40,000.00
Total annual Sale	**1,30,00,000.00**

MOTIVE POWER REQUIREMENT 45HP

FINANCIAL PROJECTION

1. Land and Building

It is proposed to acquire suitable premises measuring about 5000 sq. ft. on lease for a period of 10 years at a monthly rent of Rs.15,000.

2. Machinery & Equipment

Sl. No.	Item	Capacity	No.	Amount
A	Spiral Mixer	30 kg.	1	2,00,000
B	Planetary Mixer	50 Liters	2	1,40,000
C	Bread Slicer		1	50,000
D	Baking Oven (Rotary)			5,00,000
E	Refrigerator	300 Liters	1	25,000
F	Variable Cost			85,000
	Total			**10,00,000**

3. Testing Equipment

Rs. 10,000

4. Electrification & Installation Charges

@ 10% of the cost of Machines Rs.1,00,000

5. Cost of Tools, Fixtures, Moulds, Work Benches etc.

		Nos.	Rs.
A	Workbench 8 ft. x 4 ft. with iron frame and granite top	8	40,000
B	DepanningTable	1	5,000
C	Bread Trollies	6	30,000
D	Slotted angle racks	4	20,000
E	Show Cases	3	45,000
F	Wooden Stools	6	3,000
G	Showroom racks	3	15,000
H	Baking Trays	100	12,500
I	Bread Moulds (4008.)	250	15,000
J	Bread Moulds (800g.)	50	5,000
K	Bread Moulds (200g.)	250	10,000
L	Cake Moulds (Assorted)		10,000
M	Electronic Weighing Scale	3	45,000
N	Counterpan type weighing Scale	3	3,000
O	Platform type weighing Scale	1	10,000

P	Miscellaneous Expenses		31,500
	Total		**Rs.3,00,000**

6. Cost of Office Equipment

	ITEM	QUANTITY	AMOUNT
A	Office Tables	4	20,000
B	Office Chairs	12	24,000
C	Bureau	2	10,000
D	Computers	2	80,000
E	Printer	1	25,000
F	File Cabinet	1	5,000
G	Cash Box	2	10,000
H	Aluminium Stools	4	4,000
I	Miscellaneous		22,000
	Total		**Rs. 2,00,000**

7. Preoperative Expenses

A	Cost of preparing project report	25,000
B	Technical know how expenses	50,000
C	Cost of trial production	25,000
	Total	**1,00,000**

8. Total Non-Recurring Expenditure (Fixed Cost)

A	Plant & Machinery	10,00,000
B	Cost of Testing Equipement	10,000
C	Electrification & Installation Charges	1,00,000
D	Cost of Tools, Fixtures, Moulds etc.	3,00,000
E	Cost of Office Equipment	2,00,000
F	Pre operative Expenses	1,00,000
G	Installation of telephone	7,000
H	Sundry Expenses	33,000
	Total	**17,50,000**

9. Working Capital

A. Staff & Labour Cost Per Month

1.	Office Manager	1	8,000
2.	Cashier cum Clerk	1	6,000
3.	Factory Supervisor	1	8,000
4.	Store Keeper	1	5,000

	5. Mistrie	3	15,000
	6. Bakers	4	12,000
	7. Assistant Bakers	6	12,000
	8. Helpers	6	9,000
	9. Cake Decorator	1	5,000
	10. Salesman	3	9,000
	11. Electrician cum Fitter	1	4,000
	12. Security Guards	3	7,500
	Total		**1,00,500**
	Add 15% perks		15,000
			1,16,000
B	**Cost of Utilities**		
	1. Power		30,000
	2. Fuel		30,000
	3. Water		2,000
	4. Miscellenous		8,000
	Total		**70,000**
C	**Cost of Overheads per Month**		
	1. Advertisement & Publicity		Rs. 5,000
	2. Transport		5,000
	3. Commission to distributors on sale of Rs. 15,000 per day @ 15%*		70,000
	4. Consumable Stores		2,000
	5. Rent of premises		15,000
	6. Insurance		1,000
	7. Stationery		2,000
	8. Sales Expenses		5,000
	9. Sundry Expenses		15,000
	Total		**1,20,000**

* Part of total sale i.e. approximatly Rs. 15,000 worth of goods per day is proposed through vendors who give door delivery. Commission on this limited sale is proposed to be given @ 15%.

D. Cost of Raw Material

Sr. No.	Item	Quantity	Rate Rs.	Amount Rs.
1.	Maida	370kg.	10.00	3,700
2.	Yeast	5.5	45.00	250
3.	Salt	10	5.00	50
4.	Sugar	75	17.00	1,275
5.	Shortening	50	38.00	1,900
6.	Additives	-	-	150
7.	Candied fruits/peels	6	40.00	240
8.	Atta	6	12.00	72
9.	Kismis	2.5	100.00	250
10.	Spices	50g.	750.00	40
11.	Icing sugar	10kg.	20.00	200
12.	Potatoes	4kg.	10.00	40
13.	Vegetables	7kg.	10.00	70
14.	Masala	-	-	600
15.	Khaskhas	100g.	350.00	35
16.	Milk Powder	1.5kg.	75.00	115
17.	Eggs	1000Nos.	1.25	1250
18.	Tomato Sauce	2kg.	60.00	120
19.	Puff Margarine	16kg.	45.00	720
20.	Processed cheese	1 kg.	160.00	160
21.	Pizza Cheese	1 kg.	130.00	130
22.	Paneer	2kg.	65.00	130
23.	Cornflour	500g.	30.00	15
24.	Liquid Glucose	1 kg.	24.00	24
25.	Cream Shortening	5kg.	45.00	225
26.	Sorbitol	500g.	30.00	15
27.	Mono Calcium Phosphate	100g.	80.00	10
28.	Cocoa	250g.	140.00	35
29.	Vanilla	150ml.	400.00	60
30.	Lemon essance	150ml.	350.00	50
31.	Almond essance	70ml.	450.00	35
32.	Milk essance	50ml.	500.00	25
33.	Food Colour	10g.	-	15
34.	Butter (Processed)	2.5kg. .	120.00	300
35.	Leavening agent	-	-	20
36.	Coconuts	10nos.	10.00	100
37.	Jam	1 kg.	100.00	100.00
38.	Refined Oil	4kg.	40.00	160.00

39.	Fondant	2kg.	25.00	50.00
40.	Semi sweet chocolate	500g.	145.00	75.00
41.	Apples	2kg.	40.00	80.00
42.	Fresh Cream	2 ltrs.	70.00	140.00
43.	Desiccated Coconut	2kg.	70.00	140.00
44.	Soya flour	3kg.	14.00	45.00
45.	White Butter	1 kg.	110.00	110.00
46.	Calcium Propionate	500g.	80.00	40.00
47.	Sodium Propionate	200g.	120.00	25.00
48.	Cashew nut	1 kg.	300.00	300.00
49.	Pista	500g.	500.00	250.00
		Total		**13,500**
	Variable cost @ 3%			400
	Invisible cost			600
	Cost of packaging material			2,000
	Sundry expenses			1,500
		Total		**18,000**

Cost of raw material per month 5,40,000

10. Total recurring expenditure per month

A	Total salaries per month	1,16,000
B	Raw material	5,40,000
C	Utilities	70,000
D	Total Overheads	1,20,000
E	Sundry Expenses	4,000
	Total	**8,50,000**

11. Total Investment

A	Fixed Capital	17,50,000
B	Working Capital for 3 months	25,50,000
	Total	**43,00,000**

12. Cost of Production

A	Total recurring expenditure per year	1,02,00,000
B	Depreciation on Land & Building	-
C	Depreciation on Machinery and Equipment except oven @ 10%	50,000
D	Depreciation on oven @ 25%	1,25,000
E	Depreciation on Tools, Fix. etc. @ 25%	75,000
F	Depreciation on office equipment @ 20%	40,000
G	Interest on Total Investment @ 13.5%	5,80,500
	Total	**1,10,70,500**

13. Turnover per year 1,30,00,000

minus cost of production 1,10,70,500

Profit per year **19,29,500**

14. Net Profit ratio

$$\frac{\text{Profit per year} \times 100}{\text{Sale per year}}$$

$$= \frac{19{,}30{,}000 \times 100}{1{,}30{,}00{,}000}$$

= 14.8%

15. Rate of Return

$$\frac{\text{Profit per year} \times 100}{\text{Total Investment}}$$

$$= \frac{19{,}30{,}000 \times 100}{43{,}00{,}000}$$

= 44.8%

16. Break even point

$$\frac{\text{Fixed cost} \times 100}{\text{Fixed cost} + \text{Profit}}$$

Fixed Cost

A	Depreciation	2,90,000
B	Rent	1,80,000
C	Interest on total Investment	5,80,500
D	40% of total Salaries	5,56,800
E	40% of Over Heads	5,76,000
F	Insurance	12,000
	Total	**21,95,300**

$$B\,E\,P = \frac{21{,}95{,}300 \times 100}{21{,}95{,}300 + 19{,}30{,}000}$$

$$= \frac{21{,}95{,}300 \times 100}{41{,}25{,}300}$$

= 53%

PREFACE TO RECIPES

1. Acetic acid should be diluted in the proportion of one part of acid and 4 parts of water. Only diluted acetic acid should be issued from store.
2. Processed butter generally contains salt. Therefore while using processed butter, salt content of the formula should be suitably adjusted.
3. White butter can be used if it is homogenized. Generally white butter is sold by local dairy shops and its water content will vary from day to day. Water in homogenized form will not separate out during working.
4. Emulsifier content of the formulae is not specified. It is a matter of individual preference. The supplier of emulsifier will provide suitable information about its usage. Generally it should be added with egg in cakes. In fermented bread products, it is used in the form of (GMS) emulsion.
5. Mono acid Calcium phosphate (MACP) is included in most cake recipes. It has very beneficial effect on air entrapping capacity, providing acidity for better shelf life, it has bleaching action on the crumb colour, and acts as stimulant to preservatives.
6. Formulate for conversion from Fahrenheit to centrigrade is 5 (F-32)=9C
7. In cake recipes acetic acid, mono acid calcium phosphate (MACP), sodium propionate, sorbic acid can be used as preservatives according to requirement.
8. Yeast (C) is compressed yeast.
9. Water (V) - water quantity is variable.
10. Total fermentation time for all the yeast raised doughs are readjustable with a minimum time where dough is relaxed properly.

FERMENTED GOODS

WHITE BREAD (Straight Dough Method)

Ingredients	Percent	Actual wt. in kg.
Flour	100	100
Yeast (compressed)	1.0-2.0	1- 2
Water (variable)	60	60
Salt	1.8-2.0	1.8-2
Sugar	2.0-3.0	2-3
Shortening	1.0-2.0	1- 2

Note:-

1. These are only the basic ingredients of bread making. Apart from these ingredients a baker may like to use other ingredients also to improve the quality of his products such as soya flour, potato flour, milk solids, liquid sugars, some chemical improvers or enzymes, emulsifiers etc. These products should be added in an appropriate manner so as to ensure thorough mixing and maximum benefit out of these aids.
2. The same formula can be used for making pao-bhaji buns and sweet buns by adjusting the quantity of sugar, salt, shortening. Sweet buns generally contain 20-25% sugar, and somewhat higher amounts of shortening too. Pao-bhaji buns are placed in the baking sheet close to each other so that when these are proofed they stick to each other. After cooling. These are separated into bunch of six pieces and packed.

Procedure:

1. Take part water (approximately four times the weight of yeast), dissolve some sugar, and disintegrate yeast in it. Dry yeast should be sprinkled so that it does not form a lump which will prevent yeast from hydrating completely. Leave it for five minutes or until it starts showing signs of gas formation. Add sufficient flour to make a thin paste and whisk it to incorporate some air which will enhance the fermentation speed. This is known as "Flying Ferment". For large operations, a vertical mixer can be used for this purpose. Leave the ferment for 10-15 minutes. This procedure helps in invigorating the yeast action before it is added to the dough. It is advisable to follow this procedure for making any yeast raised dough.
2. Add water to the mixing bowl first. This prevents sticking of flour in the bottom of the bowl. Salt and sugar may be dissolved in water and strained through a cloth (If necessary) and added to the bowl. Add flour and mix. When the flour is roughly mixed, add flying ferment and mix. Towards the last stage of mixing, add shortening and clear the dough. The dough should be mixed till the gluten is well developed. Take a small piece of dough and stretch it between fingers. If it can be stretched into a paper thin sheet without tearing, the dough is considered to be well mixed.
3. Ferment the dough for two- third of the total fermentation time.
4. Knock back the dough. Large doughs can be remixed for a short duration just sufficient to expel the gas.

5. Ferment the dough for the remaining period (30-45 min.).
6. Divide the dough into pieces of desired weight according to the size of the pan. While dividing the dough by hand the process should be carried out with a sharp cutter. Breaking the dough by hand will disturb the trend of gluten strands which will adversely affect the texture of bread.
7. Round the dough pieces and let relax for 10 -15 min.This period is known as intermediate proof time. Crust formation on dough at any stage should always be guarded against.
8. Mould the bread and pan. Pans should be greased properly.
9. Proof the bread at 95-98 deg.F and Relative Humidity 80-83%, until it acquires desired volume.
10. Bake at 450 deg.F for about 30 min.
11. Cool bread completely (inner crumb temperature should be equal to room temperature) before slicing.

DELAYED SALT METHOD

In this method, the dough is made with all the ingredients except salt and shortening. Dough is allowed to ferment for a predetermined time and then it is remixed with salt and shortening.

As salt has controlling action on yeast fermentation, a salt less dough will ferment faster and thus total production time can be reduced.

Since the dough is subjected to two mixings, the first mixing need not be carried to development stage. During second mixing the dough should be mixed to develop the gluten.

SPONGE AND DOUGH METHOD

This method is. used when flour is strong (which takes more time to mature) or there are two kind of flours on hand one of which is stronger. Strong flour should be used in making sponge, and weaker one at dough making stage.

The quantity of flour in sponge is decided according to the strength of flour. As the strength of flour increases, the quantity of flour in sponge should also increase. Usually," 60:40 sponge and dough" gives best results.

Method:

1. Mix 60% flour, all the yeast, any yeast food and proportionate water.

Milk solids can be added at this stage. Mixing should be carried out just sufficient to hydrate all the flour evenly.

2. Ferment the sponge till it is ready i.e.
   a. It has fine web like structure,
   b. It breaks in clean fracture and
   c. It is dry to touch
3. Break the sponge with remaining water. This procedure ensures even mixing of the sponge in the dough.
4. Add remaining flour, salt, sugar and lastly shortening and clear the dough.
5. Give floor time of about 30 to 45 min. and proceed with dividing, moulding.

Bread made by sponge and dough method has better texture, flavour and moisture retention capacity.

A combination of delayed salt and sponge and dough method can also be used as follows.

1. Mix the dough with all the flour, water, yeast and yeast food and ferment it for a predetermined time.
2. Add the remaining ingredients (fat should be added last) and clear the dough.
3. Give floor time of about 20 minutes.

With the advent of high speed mixers and spiral mixers the fermentation time is eliminated completely. such bread lacks in aroma. A small quantity of sponge or ferment can be used with such doughs to help develope fermentation flavour in the bread.

WHOLE-WHEAT BREAD

Ingredients	**Percent**	**Actual wt. in kg.**
Whole wheat flour(Atta)	100	10
Vital wheat gluten	3-5	0.3-0.5
Yeast C	2-3	0.2
Salt	2	0.2
Sugar	2	0.2
Shortening	1-2	0.1-0.2
Water (Variable)	65-70	6.5-7

Procedure

Follow straight-dough procedure. Ferment the dough for a very short time so that the dough is just relaxed (about 20 min.). This bread should have sufficient acidity and full complement of preservative (calcium propionate) to protect it from bacterial spoilage.

Note:-

The whole wheat flour (Atta) which is generally available does not produce desired quality of bread. Hence the necessity to use vital wheat gluten which is widely available now. Alternately it may be necessary to use a certain percentage of maida.This fact should be made known to the consumer.

EMERGENCY METHOD OF BREAD MAKING

Ingredient	Percent
Flour	100
Yeast	2.5
Salt	1.5
Sugar	2
Water (variable)	58
Shortening	2

Procedure

1. Make dough as for white bread
2. Relax the dough for 15 - 20 min.
3. Divide and proceed as for white bread.

Note

1. In emergency this method can be used for making any fermented product successfully.
2. Temperature of an emergency dough should be 2-3deg. higher than the normal dough. This will reduce water absorption by 2-3%.
3. Emergency doughs should be mixed thoroughly as such doughs do not have an opportunity to condition by fermentation.
4. Sugar content of emergency doughs should be kept at low level as yeast does not have time to feed upon sugar and excessive sugar in the dough at the time of baking will give too dark colour to crust.
5. The process can be varied by making short time sponge (using all the water at sponge stage) and no time dough. Allowing fermentation time at either sponge stage or dough stage will improve the flavour.

6. If the dough pieces flatten out during intermediate proofing, rerounding will improve the quality of finished product.

7. Moulding process of emergency doughs is better done by hand rather than by machine as machine moulded bread takes longer time during proofing.

8. Use of acetic acid and other bread improvers which help in conditioning of dough in shorter duration will improve the quality of finished product.

DINNER ROLLS

Ingredients	Percent	Actual wt. in g.
Flour	100	2000
Yeast C	2-3	40-60
Water (V)	60	1200
Skimmed milk powder	2	40
Egg yolk (Optional)	6-8	120-160
Salt	1.5-2.0	30-40
Sugar	3-5	60-100
Shortening	3-5	60-100

Note

It is advisable to hydrate the SMP with water before adding to the dough. SMP should be mixed with dry sugar before adding water. This will prevent lump formation.

Procedure

1. Mix dough as for bread and ferment for about an hour.
2. Knock back the dough and rest it for 20 - 30 minutes.
3. Divide the dough into small pieces of about 50 gm.weight.
4. Round each piece and let it relax for 10 -15 min. Guard against crust formation.
5. Mould into various fancy shapes and place on baking sheet leaving sufficient space for expansion.
6. Brush with egg white when half proofed and complete proofing.
7. Bake at 400 deg. F till golden brown (about 25 min.)
8. Brush lightly with melted shortening immediately after baking while the rolls are still hot.

Note:-

The same dough can be used with minor variations for making soup sticks. The dough for soup sticks must be somewhat tight in order to have the peculiar snappy and crisp bite of the stick. Jeera or ajwain can also be added in the dough according to individual preference.

RUSK

Ingredients	percent	Actual wt.in g.
Group-A		
Flour	80	8000
Yeast	1.5-2	150-200
Sugar	1	100
Skimmed Milk Powder	1-2	100-200
Water (Variable)	56-58	4500-4700
Group-B		
Flour	20	2000
Salt	1-1.5	100-150
Sugar	25-30	2500-3000
Yeast	1-1.5	100-150
Shortening	15-20	1500-2000
Khaskhas (Optional)	1	100
OR.		
Caraway seeds	1	100
OR		
Somph (Anise seeds)	1	100

Procedure

1. Mix the sponge with 80% flour and other ingredients of group A. Let the sponge ferment till it breaks easily without stretching. Light and crisp eating quality of rusk will depend on the fine Web-like structure and even texture of the product which will depend on adequate fermentation of the sponge.

2. Return the sponge to the mixer. Add salt, sugar, flour khaskhas etc. and mix. Lastly add shortening and clear the dough. The dough should be soft and very smooth. If necessary, marginal adjustment can be made in the quantity of flour or water to achieve the correct consistency of the dough.

3. Let the dough relax for about 30 min.

4. Cut pieces of dough weighing 450g. or according to the size of the baking tray.

5. Mould like French loaf into a long oblong shape and place on the baking sheet leaving sufficient space for expansion. Generally these loaves are arranged in such a manner that after proofing they join each other but if desired these can be placed in a manner so that they remain separate, in which case the shape of the rusk will also be maintained accordingly.

6. Proofing of rusk is done in two distinguished ways.

   a. When it is half proofed, take water and oil in equal quantities. Dip the hand in it and press each piece flat so that each piece joins together. Let proof again till it becomes very light to touch. This rusk will have a close structure.

   b. Proof to achieve desired volume in the same shape as these are moulded. This rusk will have somewhat open structure.

7. When fully proofed, bake at 210 deg.C to a golden brown colour.

8. Cool the loaves overnight.

9. Cut the rusk of desired thickness. Arrange on baking sheets and toast at 190 deg.C till these are crisp and golden brown in colour.

Note:-

Rusk can be made in different shapes and sizes according to market requirement. These are known by different names as “Paape”, “Baby Rusk”etc. Sugar and shortening content being very high, some quantity of yeast is necessary to add along with group B ingredients.

PIZZA (BASE)

Base

Ingredients	Percent	Actual wt in g.
Flour	100	1000
Yeast (C)	2-3	20-30
Water (V)	60	600
Salt	2	20
Sugar	3-5	30-50
Shortening	2-6	20-60
Egg yolk (Optional)	6-8	60-80
Corn grits (Optional)	2	20

Procedure

1. Mix dough as for bread and ferment for about 30 min.

2. Knock back the dough and let relax for 15 min.

3. Divide the dough into pieces of 120 gm. weight or according to the size of desired pizza. Round each piece and let relax for 10 min.

4. Sheet each piece into round shape like a chapatti of about six inches diameter or according to the size of desired pizza. Place on baking sheet and dock with a fork.

5. Proof for about 10 min. and bake at 400 deg.F for only 3-4 minutes so that there is very light colour in the bottom while the top surface remains white. This pizza base can be stored in refrigerator in polythene bag for short duration of 3-4 days.

Note:-

Acetic acid and calcium propionate in normal quantities as preservative should be used if pizza base is required to be stored for longer periods.

PIZZA SAUCE

Ingredients	**Actual wt. in g.**
Tomato puree	2000
or	
Tomatoes	3000
Onion	500
Garlick	100
Salt and pepper	to taste
Tomato ketchup	200
Acetic acid (10% strength)	10 ml.
Chili sauce	100
Ginger	50
Corn flour	30
Water	50
Ajinomoto	As desired
Sugar	According to taste
Condiments & Spices	Optional

Procedure

1. Boil the tomatoes and take out the puree.

2. Chop onion and garlick and grate ginger.

3. Boil tomato puree, onibn,garlick and ginger till it becomes thick.

4. Add tomato ketchup, chili sauce, salt and pepper, and other ingredients

5. Add corn flour mixed with water and boil the sauce till it acquires spreading consistency.

It is advisable to prepare the sauce one day in advance and refrigerate it so that it sets into a thick mass which will be convenient to spread. If it is desired to store sauce for longer periods, sodium benzoate (1 gm. per kg. of sauce) mixed with little water may be added before adding corn flour.

MAKE UP OF PIZZA

1. Turn the pizza base up side down, that is, the part which was in contact with the baking sheet should be turned up. Brush the surface very lightly with melted butter or oil.
2. Spread the pizza sauce evenly.
3. Spread finely chopped onion, capsicums (cut into small pieces or into rings) or whatever other filling is desired. If desired the vegetables may be sauted in butter before placing on pizza.
4. Spread grated cheese liberally and bake at 400 deg.F

Note:

1. Different kinds of fillings can be used according to individual preference such as mushrooms, mince meat, prawns, fish, chicken etc. However; the make up of pizza sauce, more or less remains the same.

2 Pizza is also made with fresh dough. The dough is sheeted so that it is somewhat thinner in the center and edges are thick. Brush with melted butter or oil and top with sauce, fillings and cheese. If spongy pizza is desired, proof it for a while before baking.

DOUGHNUTS

Ingredients	**Percent**	**Actual twin g.**
Flour	100	2000
Baking powder	1.5	30
S M P	3-5	60-100
Yeast(C)	3	60
Water	25	500
Egg	12	240
Vanilla	0.5	10 ml.
Lemon flavour	0.5	10 ml.
Salt	1.5	30
Sugar	1	300
Water	2	500
Shortening	12	240
Oil (for frying doughnuts)		

Procedure

1. Sieve flour, baking powder and milk powder together.
2. Disintegrate yeast in part water, add some flour to make a ferment. Let it rise for 10-15 min.
3. Dissolve salt and sugar in the remaining water. Add egg and flavours.
4. Add salt and sugar water to flour and mix roughly. Add the ferment and mix to partial development stage.
5. Add shortening and clear the dough.
6. Ferment the dough for about 45 min. Knock back the dough and let relax for 20 min.
7. Sheet the dough to desired thickness and cut with a doughnut cutter.
8. Proof the doughnuts for 20-25 min. or until light to touch.
9. Fry in deep fat (at 370 deg.F) till golden brown.
10. When doughnuts are still slightly warm, roll in cinnamon sugar or dip in warm fondant.

DANISH PASTRY

Ingredients	Percent	Actual wt.in g.
Flour	100	1000
Yeast C	3-4.	30-40
Water	45	450
Skimmed milk powder (SMP)	4	40
Egg yolk	12	120
Vanilla	1	10 ml.
Lemon essence	0.5	5 ml.
Salt	1	10
Sugar	15-20	150-200
Shortening	8-10	80-100
Emulsifier		
Shortening for layering	50-60	500-600

Procedure

1. Mix dough as explained before. Gluten should only be marginally developed during mixing. Over mixing will toughen the Danish pastry. The dough should be sheetable ie.neither too tight nor too loose.
2. Ferment the dough for about 45 min.
3. Knock back the dough and let it rest for about 20 min.

4. Sheet the dough into rectangular shape. Mark the dough sheet lengthwise into three equal parts leaving about half inch edge on all the sides. Call the three parts as A, B and C.
5. Divide the shortening (for layering) into three equal parts spread one-third of shortening on two-third of the sheeted dough i.e. on part A and B.
6. Fold C over B and A over C so that there are alternate layers of dough and fat.
7. Relax the dough in cool place for about ten minutes.
8. Sheet the dough again into rectangular shape and fold- in second part of shortening. After 10 min. of rest to the dough, repeat the process for the third time using the remaining shortening.
9. Rest the dough in cool place (preferably in a refrigerator) for about 30 min.
10. Sheet the dough to desired thickness depending on the variety desired to be made.
11. Shape the product and place on greased baking sheet two inches apart.
12. Brush with egg wash and proof until very light to touch.
13. Bake at 400 deg.F for about 25 min.
14. Brush with sugar syrup immediately upon drawing from the oven and place on cooling rack.
15. If desired, top with fondant while the pastry is still warm.

Note:-

1. Layering fat can be folded in more than one way. The objective is to have a flaky and light product. Baker can use whichever method is convenient for him.
2. Fillings, Toppings and glaze which can be used in the Danish Pastry varieties are given separately under the heading "Fillings and Toppings".

VARIETIES

DANISH FRUIT ROLL

Roll the pastry to about 5 mm thickness, spread a thin layer of butter icing or poppy seed filling (leaving about an inch of lower edge uncovered, brush this edge with egg). Sprinkle dry fruits (raisins, cherry, tutti frutti) mixed with spices (nutmeg, cloves, cardamom, cinnamon) and roll into an oblong shape. Seal the edge (where egg is brushed). Cut with a thread into pieces of about one cm. thickness. Place on baking sheet and brush with egg wash. Proof. Top with butter toping or streussel topping and bake at 210 deg.C for about 25 min. or till golden brown. While still warm top with fondant icing.

DANISH CINNAMON ROLL

Roll the pastry into a rectangle of about 5 mm thickness. Brush half the portion with egg wash. Sprinkle sugar mixed with cinnamon powder. Fold the remaining half over it. Cut into strips of about one and a half cm. width.

Twist both the ends of the strip in opposite direction so as to give a rope like appearance. This can be formed into different shapes like snails, figure of 8, pretzels or just sticks. Top with streussel topping Brush with egg wash, proof and bake.

Croissant

Roll the pastry to about 5 mm thickness and out it into triangles, having base of about 12 cm. and the remaining two sides of 14 cm. each. Give a vertical cut of about 2 cm. in the middle of the base. Starting from the base, roll the croissant and place on the baking sheet in a crescent form. Brush with egg wash, proof and bake. Before rolling the croissant a filling of fruit jam or grated cheese could be placed if so desired.

BASIC SWEET DOUGH

Ingredients	Percent	Actual wt. in g.
Flour	100	2000
Yeast C	2-3	40 - 60
Egg yolk	12	240
Malt or Corn syrup	3	60
SMP	4	80
Lemon essence	0.5	10 ml.
Vanilla	0.5	10 ml.
Water	50	1000 ml.
Salt	1.5	30
Sugar	15	300
Shortening	12	240

Procedure

1. Mix the dough to development stage and ferment for about an hour.
2. Knock back the dough and let relax for 30 min. Now the dough is ready for make up into various fancy shapes.

Note:-

Fillings, toppings and glaze which can be used in these Sweet fermented products are given separately under the heading "Fillings And Toppings."

BUTTERFLY BUNS

Roll out the dough. Brush with melted butter and sprinkle with cinnamon sugar, cake crumbs and raisins. Roll into a long roll. Cut pieces of desired weight and then press through the center (with a wooden spoon handle) of each roll, pressing out the folds on the side to make an attractive roll looking like a butterfly. When about half proofed, brush with egg wash and top with butter topping. Finish proofing and bake at 210 degC. for 25 min. After baking finish with glace icing or fondant while the rolls are still warm.

NUTTY ROLLS

Roll out the dough 5 mm. thick. Brush lower edge with egg wash. Brush the remainder with melted butter and sprinkle with cinnamon sugar, cake crumbs and roasted-chopped nuts. Roll up like a jam roll and cut pieces of desired weight. Set upright in pans or in individual cup cake moulds. When half proofed, brush with egg wash and top with honey topping. Finish proofing. Bake at 210 degC. for 25 min. or until golden brown. After baking finish with water icing and chopped nuts.

JAM FILLED BUNS

Scale the dough into 30 gm. pieces. Round up pieces, dip in coarse granulated sugar and place on bun trays about two inches apart. Give half proof. Then make an indentation in the center of each bun and fill it with jam. Complete proofing and bake. Brush with warm jam immediately after baking.

CHEESE CAKE

Sheet out the dough and cut with a large cutter to the size of bun - mould. Place each piece in the greased mould and dock with a fork. Pour in the cheese filling (See under Fillings & Toppings) in each mould. Sprinkle powdered cinnamon sugar on top. Proof slightly and bake.

HOT CROSS BUNS

Make up sweet dough adding about 20-25% fruits (raisins, currents, orange peel, tutti frutti, cherry) and spice powder (cinnamon, nutmeg, cloves, cardamoms). Fruits should be added just before mixing is completed. Fruits should be soaked in warm water and drained thoroughly before being used so that the resultant buns are not dry. After proper fermentation, scale the dough into pieces of desired weight (approximately 80gm.), round up and set on bun trays so as to make individual bun or set together to make one whole sheet. When half proofed, make a cross with sharp blade on each bun. Finish by making a cross with short dough topping. Brush with egg wash. Complete proofing. Bake at 210 degC. for 20-25 min.

DUTCH BREAD

Scale hot cross bun dough or raisin bun dough in 250 - 300 gm. pieces: Round up and place on baking tray. When half proofed, cut across several times with a sharp blade and top with fruits. Brush with egg wash and complete proofing. After baking finish with glaze and vanilla icing.

GERMAN COFFEE CAKE

Fill the pan with sweet dough. Dock with a fork. Wash with water. Spread butter topping and proof. Bake at 200 deg.C. Do not ice.

GERMAN COFFEE CAKE (COCOANUT TOPPED)

After docking, spread over topping made with 500 g. cocoanut, 150 g. egg and 150 g: sugar.

YEAST RAISED FRUIT CAKE

Ingredients	Percent	Actual wt. in g.
Basic sweet dough	100	1000
Brown sugar	20	200
Butter	20	200
Egg	14	140
Mixed spices	0.5	5
Molasses	14	140
Soda bi crab.	0.3	3
Fresh liquid milk	10	100
Flour	35	350
Fruit mixture	85	850
Lemon peel		50
Currants		200
Figs		150
Orange peel		50
Raisins		250
Pineapple pieces		150

Procedure

1. Soak fruits in fruit juice thickened with starch
2. Cream butter and brown sugar and add egg while creaming.
3. Add basic sweet dough and spices.
4. Add molasses and soda dissolved in milk.
5. Add flour and soaked fruits and mix to a homogenous mass
6. Put the mixture in paper lined moulds.
7. Proof slightly and bake at 200 degC. for 45-50 min.

STOLLEN

Ingredients	Percent	Actual wt. in g.
Basic sweet dough (taken at punch time)	100	1000
Butter	12	120
Sugar	10	100
Egg	8	80
Fruit mixture	60	600
Cherries	6	60
Yeast (C)	2	20
Flour	To make a medium stiff dough	

Procedure

1. Mix the dough with above ingredients, and sufficient flour to make a medium stiff dough.
2. Let the dough come up for about 45 min.
3. Scale off desired size pieces.
4. Shape up with bottom size larger than top.
5. Give half proof, then wash with butter and bake at 200 deg.C. When baked, brush with butter again, sprinkle with cinnamon sugar or ice with water icing.

ROLLED - IN BASIC SWEET DOUGH

100 to 150 gm. butter for each 500 gm. Basic sweet dough. It is rolled in like Danish pastry. Rolling and folding is done three times as soon as dough is mixed. The following items are made from rolled-in Basic sweet dough.

FRENCH COFFEE CAKE

Fill the pan. Proof and bake.

BUTTER HORNS

Roll out the rolled-in dough to about 5 mm thickness and of sufficient width to make the desired size horns. Cut into strips, twist ends in opposite direction and make into snail or butter horn shape.

WAFFLE ROLLS

Roll out a piece of rolled-in dough, brush with melted butter, sprinkle liberally with chopped nuts and sugar and roll into a long roll. Cut pieces of desired weight and then roll each piece (with cut surface up) thin on some granulated sugar and put on baking sheet. Proof and bake. While still hot, brush with gelatin wash.

JAPANESE ROLLS

Roll out a piece of rolled-in dough approximately 5 mm thick. Spread on to it a very thin layer of butter topping. Sprinkle on it some finely ground roasted nuts and roll up the dough. Seal joint carefully. Cut off 30 gm.pieces. Place upright in cup cake pans, brush with egg, proof and bake. Decorate with butter cream or fondant.

DANISH FRUIT BISCUIT

Roll out rolled-in dough about 10 mm thick and 15 cm. wide. Place a layer of fruit filling along the center of the stripe. Fold over both the sides and seal. Turn underside up and cut off pieces of desired size. Wash top with egg wash, sprinkle with granulated sugar and powdered nuts. Proof and bake.

APPLE ROLLS

Roll out rolled-in dough to a width of 30 cm. and thickness 3mm. Spread a layer of apple filling on three-forth of the width of the surface. Wash the lower edge with egg wash or water. Then roll up like jam roll and seal edges. Cut off pieces of desired weight, pan upright separately on baking sheet or close together in small pans. Brush over with egg wash and proof. .Bake at 210 deg.C. Finish with vanilla icing.

MASTER SWEET DOUGH

Ingredients	percent	Actual wt. in g.
Flour	100	1000
SMP	5	50
Yeast	3-5	30-50
Water (Variable)	45	450

Egg yolk	15	150
Butter	20	200
Sugar	15	150
Salt	1	10
Malt (optional)	1.25	12.5
OR		
Corn Syrup	4	40
Nutmeg	0.5	5
Lemon essence	1	10 ml
Vanilla	1	10 ml.

Procedure

1. Cream together butter, sugar, malt, nutmeg, lemon essence, vanilla and salt.
2. Add gradually egg yolk.
3. Break yeast in little water and add.
4. Sift flour and milk powder and add with remaining water and mix to a soft and smooth dough.
5. Ferment for about 45 min.
6. Knock back the dough and let relax for 20 min.

MASTER SWEET DOUGH - FRUIT LOAF

Ingredients	Percent	Actual wt. in g.
Master sweet dough	100	1000
Egg	18	180
Sugar	20	200
Yeast(C)	2	20
Water	5	50
Butter	10	100
Shortening	10	100
Flour	20	200
Glace cherry	20	200
Raisins (Soaked)	30	300
Nuts (Broken)	10	100

Procedure

1. Mix together thoroughly egg and sugar.
2. Add master sweet dough
3. Mix yeast in water and add.

4. Add flour and mix well
5. Add butter and shortening and mix to a smooth dough
6. Add and mix prepared fruits
7. Weigh immediately and put into greased bread moulds.
8. Proof and bake at 190 deg.C.
9. Wash with syrup glaze and dust with powder sugar.
10. It can also be baked in cake cups..

STRUDEL
(From Danish or Master Sweet.Dough)

Procedure

1. Weigh 120 gm. of dough. Roll out 20 cm.x8 cm.
2. Place on baking sheet and put on about 200 gm. filling, (Apple, poppy seeds, pineapple etc.) keeping away from the edge.
3. Wash edge with water or egg.
4. Place another piece of dough, same size, on top.
5. Wash with egg and score the upper layer with a sharp knife.
6. Proof and bake.
7. Wash with syrup glaze and ice with vanilla icing.

FILLINGS AND TOPPINGS
(For Danish and Sweet Fermented Products)

These fillings and toppings can be made according to requirement. Some fillings and toppings can be made and stored in the refrigerator. Hence the actual quantities of ingredients are not given.

BUTTER TOPPING

Ingredients	Percent
Sugar	100
Butter	50
Egg yolk	25
Flour	75
Vanilla	1
Water	to make a smooth paste

Procedure

1. Cream butter, sugar and egg yolk.

2. Add flour and vanilla.
3. Add sufficient water to make a smooth paste.

HONEY TOPPING

Ingredients	Percent
Butter	100
Sugar	100
Egg white	25
Almond (finely ground)	100
Warm honey	50

Procedure

1. Cream butter, sugar and egg white.
2. Add ground almonds and warm honey. This topping must be warmed before using so that it could be brushed onto the dough.

STREUSSEL TOPPING - A

Ingredients	Percent
Flour	100
Butter (warm)	50
Sugar	50
Ground almonds	25
Mace or cinnamon(Powder)	as desired

Procedure

1. Rub in a bowl flour, butter and add sugar.
2. Add ground almonds and rub mixture well until crumbly. Use fine or lumpy.

STREUSSEL TOPPING - B

Ingredients	Percent
Flour	100
Sugar	60
Almonds(Ground)	25
Butter (melted hot)	80
Vanilla	1

Procedure

1. Mix flour, sugar and almonds.
2. Pour melted hot butter and add vanilla.

3. Rub through coarse sieve.

POPPY SEED FILLING

Ingredients	percent
Poppy seed	100
Water	150
Cake crumbs	100
Sugar	50
Butter	25
Cinnamon powder	1-3
Egg yolk	12
Milk	as required

Procedure

1. Boil poppy seed in water and drain.
2. Grind poppy seed coarsely.
3. Add and mix the remaining ingredients
4. Add sufficient milk to make a soft and smooth paste.

CHEESE FILLING FOR CHEESE CAKES-A

Ingredients	Percent
Cottage Cheese	100
Butter	10
Flour	10
Egg	30
Salt	0.3
Milk	25
Lemon flavour	0.5
Egg white	30
Sugar	30

Procedure

1. Put cheese through a coarse sieve.
2. Rub together cheese, butter and flour.
3. Add salt, egg, lemon flavour and milk.
4. Whisk the egg white stiff adding sugar little by little.
5. Add meringue to mixture and fold in, gently.

CHEESE FILLING FOR CHEESE CAKES-B

Ingredients	Percent
Cottage cheese	100
Sugar (Granulated)	25
Butter (Melted)	15
Flour	10
Egg yolk	25
Citron peel	10
Raisins	12
Lemon rind	0.5
Milk	as required

Procedure

1. Work together cottage cheese, sugar, melted butter, flour and egg yolk.
2. Add chopped citron peel, raisins and lemon rind.
3. Add sufficient milk to make a soft, smooth mixture.

APPLE FILLING
(For German and French Fruit Cakes)

Ingredients	Percent
Apple (sliced)	100
Sugar	30
Raisins	10
Currants	10
Nuts (Roasted & ground)	50
Citron peel (Sliced)	5

Procedure

Mix all the ingredients thoroughly.

CRUMB FILLING

Ingredients	Percent
Sugar	100
Egg	25
Cinnamon powder	2
Mace	1
Lemon juice	1.5
Lemon rind	0.75
Cake crumbs	250
Milk	As required to make paste

Procedure

1. Mix together sugar, egg, cinnamon powder, mace, lemon rind and lemon juice.
2. Add and mix crumbs.
3. Add sufficient milk to make a paste.

CREAM.FILLING

Ingredients	Percent
Milk	100
Sugar	20
Corn starch	8
Egg yolk	12
Salt	0.3

Procedure

1. Bring to boil three-fourth of milk and sugar
2. Add corn starch and egg yolk in the remaining cold milk.
3. Add paste slowly to the hot milk and continue heating on slow fire stirring all the time till mixture is thick.
4. Add salt and flavour when slightly cool.

ALMOND FILLING

Ingredients	Percent
Almond paste	100
Sugar (Granulated)	100
Butter	100
Egg	60
Milk	as required

Procedure

1. Mix all the ingredients together.
2. Add enough milk to make a medium stiff paste.

FIG FILLING

Ingredients	Percent
Figs	100
Water	for boiling figs
Sugar	100
Water	40

Procedure

1. Soak figs in water, heat until soft and then make into a pulp.
2. Heat sugar and 40 percent water to soft ball consistency (240 deg. F)
3. Add fig pulp and again heat to soft ball consistency.

SHORT DOUGH FOR HOT CROSS BUNS CROSSES

Ingredients	Percent
Flour	100
Shortening	50
Sugar	20
Salt	0.5
Water	as required

Procedure

1. Rub fat in the flour lightly.
2. Add sugar and salt and mix well.
3. Add enough water and mix to develop the gluten only slightly. This is necessary so that the crosses retain the shape.
4. This dough can be sheeted and cut into thin strips and placed on top of buns which is already scored in the shape of a cross.

APPLE MINCE MIXTURE

Ingredients	Percent
Chopped apples	100
Brown sugar	35
Cake crumbs	35
Broken nuts	10
Melted butter	5
Raisins	20
Cinnamon powder	1
Salt	0.3
Lemon juice	3

Procedure

Mix all the ingredients together.

CUSTARD CREAM

Ingredients	Percent
Milk	100
Sugar	20
Starch	8
Egg yolk	15
Butter	5
Salt	0.5
Vanilla	1

Procedure

1. Boil three-fourth of milk
2. Add Corn starch, and sugar together. Pour hot milk and keep stirring to avoid lump formation.
3. Return to slow heat and keep stirring till it becomes thick. A double boiler can be used for this purpose.
4. When slightly cool, add salt, vanilla and butter and whisk.

CAKES AND ICING

POUND CAKE

Ingredients	Percent	Actual wt.in g.
Margarine	50	2000
Butter	30	1200
Sugar	105	4200
MACP	0.5	20
Egg	90	3600
Emulsifier		
Water	30	1200
Salt	0.8	32
Vanilla	0.6	24 ml.
Lemon essence	1	40 ml.
Butterflavour	0.4	16 ml.
Almond essence	0.12	5 ml.
Flour	100	4000
Baking powder	1.5-2	60-80
Corn flour (Optional)	2-5	80-200
Sodium Propionate	0.3	12
Water	10	400
Sorbitol	3	120 ml.

Note:-

1 . The quantity of emulsifier is not specified in any of the recipes. Many different kind of emulsifiers are available in the market. Baker can get desired information about the use of emulsifiers from the suppliers of the product.

2. MACP that is Mono Acid Calcium Phosphate is an acid salt which makes the batter somewhat acidic. This acidic medium helps in better aeration of the batter and cake preservatives (Sodium Propionate, Sorbic acid etc.) are more effective in acidic medium. Many bakers use MACP in combination with Sodium bi carbonate as leavening agent instead of ready made baking powders. The nutralizing value for 100 parts of sodium bi carbonate is 80 parts of MACP However it is advisable to use slightly higher amounts of MACP to maintain the appropriate level of acidity of the batter.

3. To obviate the possibility of curdling of the cake batter about 0-15 % of flour can be creamed along with fat and sugar.

Procedure (Sugar - Batter Method)

1. Cream margarine, butter, MACP(Mono Acid Calcium Phosphate) and sugar till it is light and fluffy.

2. Add about half the quantity of egg gradually.Then add emulsifier. Add the remaining egg. Egg should always be added gradually in small portions taking care that each portion is amalgamated thoroughly before next portion is added. This is done to protect the cream from curdling. If too much egg is added at a time or one portion of egg is not properly mixed before another portion is added, the fine emulsion of fat and egg breaks down into small globules of fat separated by the liquid portion of egg thereby causing loss of aeration. However if there are any signs of curdling, it should be immediately remedied by addition of some flour.This flour will absorb the separated liquid portion and restore the emulsified form to reasonable extent although the batter will suffer aeration loss.

3. Add salt dissolved in water along with flavors and colour.

4. Sift flour, corn flour, baking powder and calcium propionate together and add to the cream in two or three portions.

5. Lastly add the remaining water and clear the batter.

6. Portion out the batter in moulds and bake at 210 deg.C.

Note:-

Baking temperature and time will depend on the size of the cake. Larger cakes will be baked at somewhat lower temperature for longer time. A baker has to use his own initiative while baking cakes. This formula can also be used for making bar cakes of different flavours.

POUND CAKE (Flour - Batter Method)

Ingredients	Percent	Actual wt.in g.
Shortening	60	2400
Flour	60	2400
Egg	80	3200
Emulsifier		
MACP	0.5	20
Sugar	100	4000
Water	20	800
Salt	0.8	32
Vanilla	1	40 mi.
Lemon essence	1	40 ml.
Almond essence	0.2	8 ml.
Glycerin	2	80
Flour	40	1600
Baking powder	2.5	100
Sodium propionate	0.3	12
Water	20	800

Procedure

1. Cream shortening and 60% flour till light and fluffy.
2. Whisk egg with emulsifier. Add sugar gradually. Whisk till it acquires ribbon consistency.
3. Add the sponge to the creamed mixture gradually mixing each portion thoroughly before adding next portion.
4. Dissolve salt in water. mix glycerin and essences and add to the cream.
5. Sieve the remaining flour with corn flour, baking powder and sodium propionate.
6. Add sieved flour in two-three portions, mixing each portion thoroughly.
7. Add remaining water and clear the batter.
8. Apportion the batter in paper lined moulds. Bake at 210 deg.C

MADEIRA CAKE

Ingredients	Percent	Actual wt.in g.
Shortening	50	2000
Butter	15	600
Sugar	65	2600
Skimmed milk powder	3	120
Egg	65	2600
Emulsifier		
Water	20	800
Salt	0.5	20
Glycerin	2	80
Vanilla	1	40 ml.
Lemon essence	0.5	20 ml.
Flour	100	4000
Baking Powder	2	80
Water	10	400
Orange peel	25	1000

Procedure

1. Use Sugar - Batter Method.
2. Chop about 800 gm. peel and add to the batter. Remaining peel should be cut into long and thin slices.
3. Weigh the batter in paper lined moulds and bake at 210°C.
4. When cakes are half baked, it will develope a break on top surface. Put thin slices of peel on the break and complete baking.

ORANGE CAKE

Ingredients	Percent	Actual wt. in g.
Margarine	60	2400
Butter	10	400
Butter essence	0.5	20 ml.
Orange oil	0.5	20 ml.
Liquid glucose	4	160
Sugar	95	3800
SMP	3	120
Egg	80	3200
Emulsifier		
Orange juice	10	400
Orange essence	0.8	32 ml.

Orange emulsion	1	40 ml.
Orange colour	If desired	
Vanilla	0.5	20 ml.
Flour	100	4000
Baking powder	1.5	60
Water	30	1200
Salt	0.8	32

Procedure

Follow Sugar-Batter method of cake making. Bake at 210 deg.C.

DATE AND WALNUT CAKE

Ingredients	Percent	Actual wt. in g.
Shortening	80	3200
Glucose	5	200
Sugar	100	4000
Egg	90	3600
Emulsifier		
Vanilla	1	40 ml.
Dates	100	4000
Water	10	400
Acetic acid (10%)	1	40 ml.
Glycerin	1	40
Flour	100	4000
Baking powder	1	40
Cocoa (Optional)	3	120
Water	5	200
Salt	0.8	32
Walnut (chopped)	25	1000
Walnut (half pieces)	10	400

Procedure

1. Wash, clean, stone and chop dates. Soak overnight in water, acetic acid and glycerin.
2. Follow sugar - batter method.
3. Mix soaked dates and chopped walnuts together and add in the cream alternately with flour.
4. Weigh out the batter in the paper lined moulds. Level the mixture and finish with half walnuts.
5. Bake at 200 degC for 45 min.

CAKE FOR MAKING CAKE RUSK

Ingredients	Percent	Actual wt in g.
Shortening	60	2400
Liquid glucose	4	160
MACP	0.6	24
Sugar	100	4000
Skimmed milk powder	5	200
Flour	15	600
Egg	70	2800
Emulsifier		
Water	20	800
Salt	0.8	32
Vanilla	0.6	24 ml.
Lemon essence	1	40 ml.
Almond essence	0.25	10ml.
Yellow colour	to give egg shade	
Flour	85	3400
Baking powder	1.5	60
Water	17	680

Note:-

It is advisable to make a solution of colour with definite quantity of powder colour and measured quantity of water. Definite quantity of this solution will always give even results.

Procedure

1. Follow sugar-batter method. Bake the cake in suitable pans.
2. Rest the cakes in the pans overnight.
3. Next day, slice the cakes in pieces of suitable size and arrange on baking sheets. Toast the cake pieces at about 180 deg.C until rusks acquire golden brown colour and are crisp.

CHOCOLATE CAKE

Ingredients	Percent	Actual wt. in g.
Margarine	70	2800
Glucose	5	200
Condensed milk	8	320
Sugar	110	4400
Cocoa	8	320
Egg	80	3200

Emulsifier		
Water	22	880
Salt	1	40
Caramel	4	160
Vanilla	0.5	20 ml.
Chocolate essence	1	40 mi.
Maida	100	4000
Baking powder	2	80
Water	25	1000
Corn Syrup	5	200
Soda	0.2	8

Procedure:

Follow sugar - batter method.

CHOCOLATE.BROWNIE I

Ingredient	Percent	Actual wt. in g.
Shortening	40	1600
Butter	40	1600
Liquid glucose	10	400
Sugar	100	4000
SMP	10	400
Cocoa	20	800
Egg	80	3200
Emulsifier		
Water	30	1200
Salt	1	40
Vanilla	1	40 mi.
Chocolate essence	1	40 ml.
Caramel	1.5	60
Flour	100	4000
Baking powder	1.2	48
Water	25	1000
Soda	0.5	20
Walnuts(chopped)	50	2000
Corn Syrup	5	200

Procedure:

Follow sugar - batter method.

CHOCOLATE BROWNIE II

Ingredients	Percent	Actual wt. in g.
Margarine or Butter (melted)	100	1000
Powder sugar	200	2000
Milk Solids	5	50
Liquid Glucose	10	100
Salt	2	20
MACP	1	10
Egg	115	1150
Vanilla	1	10 ml.
Gel	10	100
Chocolate Essence	1	10 ml.
Maida	100	1000
Bakiong Powder	1	10
Sodium Propionate	0.5	5
Cocoa	25	250
Semi Sweet Chocolate	10	100
Water	5	50
Walnuts (chopped)	25	250

Method

1. Use all-in-one process adding ingredients in groups as shown above.
2. Bake in a paper lined sheet pan at 190°-C for 40-45 min.
3. When completely cool, cut with a sharp knife into neat square pieces and wrap each piece in butter paper.

SUNSHINE CAKE

Ingredients	Percent	Actual wt. in g.
Shortening	65	2600
Liquid glucose	4	160
Sugar	95	3800
S M P	5	200
Flour	35	1400
Egg	80	3200
Emulsifier		
Water	20	800
Salt	1	40
Vanilla	1	40 ml.
Orange flavour	0.5	20 ml.

Lemon flavour	0.5	20 ml.
Flour	65	2600
Corn Starch	5	200
Baking Powder	3	120
Water	20	800

Procedure:

Follow sugar-batter method. Bake at 190 deg.C

DESSERT CAKE

Ingredients	Percent	Actual wt.in g.
Shortening	45	1800
Butter	25	1000
Sugar	80	3200
Ground almonds	10	400
Egg	90	3600
Almond essence	0.2	8 ml.
Rum essence	0.5	20 ml.
Vanilla	0.5	20 ml.
.Yellow colour		
Sultana	75	3000
Currants	75	3000
Chopped cherry	35	1400
Mixed peel	20	800
Water	4	160
Corn syrup	2	80
Flour	100	4000
Baking powder	1.2	48
Water	10	400
Salt	0.5	20

Procedure

Soak the fruits in water and corn syrup overnight. Follow sugarbatter method. Bake at 180 deg.C.

FRUIT CAKE

Ingredients	Percent	Actual wt. in g.
Fruit mixture		
Sultana	100	4000
Glace cherry	50	2000
Tutti frutti	75	3000
Dates	50	2000

Orange peel	25	1000
Angelica	25	1000
Cashew nut	25	1000
Mixed spices	0.5	20
Water (boiled & cooled)	10	400 ml.
Or		
Rum	10	400 ml.
Lemon juice	0.5	20 ml.
Lemon rind of 6 lemons		
Lemon essence	0.5	20 ml.
Vanilla	0.5	20 ml.
Corn Syrup	5	200
Acetic acid (10% strength)	4	160
Sodium propionate	0.25	10
Sodium Benzoate	0.25	10

Note:-

Quantity of water and corn syrup will depend on the condition of fruits. If fruits are too dry, it will require more liquid content and vice versa. If so desired, fruits can be soaked in rum as part or whole substitute for water. Acetic acid and sodium propionate is added as safety measure against fermentation of fruits if these are not used for prolonged period.

CAKE BATTER

Ingredients	Percent	Actual wt. in g.
Shortening	80	3200
Liquid glucose	5	200
Orange oil	0.5	20 ml.
Sugar	100	4000
Skimmed milk powder	5	200
Egg	90	3600
Emulsifier		
Vanilla	0.5	20 ml.
Almond essence	0.25	10 ml.
Coffee essence	0.5	20 ml.
Light caramel	5	200
Flour	100	4000
Baking powder	1	40
Cocoa	1	40
Sodium propionate	0.5	20
Water	10	400
Salt	0.8	32

Procedure

1. Clean and prepare the fruits. Mix with spice powder, water or rum, syrup, and essences. Let the fruits soak for 7-10 days.
2. Follow sugar-batter method. Add fruit mixture and sifted flour alternately.
3. Bake the cakes in paper lined moulds at 190 deg.C for about 90 min.
4. Rest the cakes in the moulds overnight before cutting. For mixed spices use the following proportions:

Cloves	1 part
Nutmeg	1 part
Cardamom	1 part
Mace (Javitri)	1 part
Cinnamon	2 parts
Coriander (broiled)	2 parts
Ginger powder	2 parts

CHRISTMAS CAKE (PLUM CAKE)

Ingredients	Percent	Actual wt in g.
Butter	50	2000
Shortening	50	2000
Liquid Glucose	5	200
Orange oil	0.5	20 ml.
Sugar	105	4200
Ground Almonds	10	400
Egg	100	4000
Emulsifier		
Water	10	400
Salt	1	40
Vanilla	1	40 ml.
Caramel	5	200
Flour	100	4000
Sodium propionate	0.5	20
Currants	225	9000
Sultana	125	5000
Mixed peel	50	2000
Mixed spices	1	40
Lemon Juice	0.5	20 ml.
Nutmeg (powdered)	0.3	12
Water	4	200
Syrup (plain or corn)	4	200

Procedure

1. Soak the fruits for 7-10 days with spices, water and syrup.
2. Proceed as for fruitcake.
3. After baking brush with melted butter or gelatin wash when cakes are still hot.

GELATIN WASH

Boiling water	10 parts
gelatin	1 part
Sugar	5 parts

MANGO CAKE

Ingredients	Percent	Actual wt. in g.
Butter	70	2800
Liquid glucose	5	200
Sugar	90	3600
Skimmed milk powder	4	160
Egg	80	3200
Emulsifier		
Mango pulp	15	600
Vanilla	0.5	20
Mango essence	1	40 ml.
Mango emulsion	2	80 ml.
Flour	100	4000
Baking powder	1.5	60
Water	20	800
Salt	0.8	32

Procedure

Follow sugar-batter method. Bake at 200 deg.C for about 30 min.

CHOCOLATE CHIFFON CAKE

(Using hydrogenated shortening)

Ingredients	Percent	Actual wt. in g.
Margarine	50	2000
Flour	75	3000
Cocoa	10	400
Sugar	70	2800
Corn syrup	15	600
Egg yolk	36	1440

Emulsifier		
Water	32	1280
Salt	1	40
Vanilla	0.5	20 ml.
Chocolate essence	1	40 ml.
Caramel	2	80
Flour	25	1000
Baking powder	3	120
Egg white	54	2160
MACP	0.2	8
Sugar	40	1600

Procedure

1. Cream margarine, 75% flour and cocoa till light and fluffy.
2. Add sugar and corn syrup and mix.
3. Add egg yolk and emulsifier and mix
4. Dissolve salt in water and add with flavours and caramel.
5. Sift remaining flour and baking powder and mix.
6. Whisk egg white stiff adding sugar gradually.
7. Fold in the beaten egg white (meringue) in the creamed mixture gently.
8. Bake in greased and dusted moulds at 200 deg.C.

CHIFFON CAKE
(Using Liquid Oil)

Ingredients	Percent	Actual wt in g.
Flour	75	3000
Sugar	65	2600
Refined oil	50	2000
Egg yolk	36	1440
Emulsifier		
Water	40	1600
Salt	1	40
Vanilla	0.5	20
Lemon essence	0.5	20
Corn syrup	3	120
Flour	25	1000
Baking powder	3	120
Egg white	54	2160

MACP	0.1	4
Sugar	40	1600

Procedure

1. Mix flour and sugar together.
2. Add refined oil and mix.
3. Add egg yolk and emulsifier and mix for about three min. at medium speed.
4. Dissolve salt in water and add with corn syrup and flavours.
5. Sift 25% flour with baking powder and add.
6. Whisk white of eggs with MACP, adding 40% sugar gradually till it is stiff (meringue consistency).
7. Fold in the meringue gently.
8. Bake in paper lined moulds at 200 degC.

COCOANUT CUP CAKES

Ingredients	Percent	Actual wt in g.
Margarine	50	1000
Liquid glucose	12	240
Sugar	100	2000
Skimmed milk powder	5	100
Egg	50	1000
Emulsifier		
Water	33	660
Corn syrup	15	300
Salt	0.8	16
Vanilla	0.5	10 ml.
Cocoanut essence	0.5	10 ml.
Flour	100	2000
Baking powder	2.5	50
Cocoanut (Desiccated)	10	200
Water	15	300

Procedure

Follow sugar - batter method. Bake in cake cups. After cooling decorate with butter cream and desiccated cocoanut. Place half cherry in the center.

BANANA MUFFINS

Ingredients	Percent	Actual wt. in g.
Banana (Ripe)	85	1700
Flour	35	700
Sugar	100	2000
Salt	1.6	32
Skimmed milk powder	8	160
Margarine	48	960
Egg yolk	25	500
Egg	25	500
Emulsifier		
Water	42	840
Vanilla	1	20 ml.
Banana essence	0.3	6 ml.
Flour	65	1300
Corn flour	5	100
Baking powder	2	40
Water	18	360
Soda bi carb.	0.5	10
Walnuts (Chopped)	10	200

Procedure

Follow sugar-batter method. Bake in cake cups. When cool, decorate with Cocoanut flavoured cream and chopped walnuts.*

MANGO CUP CAKES

Ingredients	Percent	Actual wt. in g.
Margarine	50	1000
Liquid glucose	5	100
Sugar	80	1600
Skimmed milk powder	3	60
Egg	50	1000
Emulsifier		
Mango pulp	20	400
Corn syrup	5	100
Water	10	200
Salt	0.8	16
Mango essence	0.5	10 ml.
Mango emulsion	1	20 ml.
Vanilla	0.5	10 ml.
Flour	100	2000

Baking powder	3	60
Water	15	300

Procedure:

Follow sugar-batter method. Bake in cake cups. When cool decorate with mango flavored cream. Place half a cherry in the center.

ORANGE MUFFINS

Ingredients	Percent	Actual wt. in g.
Margarine	50	1000
Orange Oil	0.6	12 ml.
Liquid glucose	6	120
Sugar	80	1600
Skimmed milk powder	5	100
Egg	50	1000
Emulsifier		
Orange juice	30	600
Corn syrup	6	120
Water	10	200
Salt	0.8	16
Vanilla	0.5	10 ml.
Orange essence	1	20 ml.
Orange emulsion	1	20 ml.
Orange colour	if necessary	
Flour	100	2000
Baking powder	3	60
Water	10	200

Procedure

Follow sugar-Batter method. Bake in cake cups. When cool, decorate with orange cream. Place half a cherry in the center.

DUNDEE CAKE

Ingredients	Percent	Actual wt. in g.
Butter	40	1600
Margarine	40	1600
MACP	0.2	8
Liquid glucose	7	280
Sugar	95	3800
Skimmed milk powder	4	160
Egg	90	3600
Emulsifier		

Flour	100	4000
Baking powder	1	40
Cocoa	2	80
Fruit mixture	200	8000
Water	5	200
Corn syrup	4	160
Caramel	4	160
Almonds (Blanched)	40	1600
Fruit mixture		
Sultana	100	4000
Peel	30	1200
Cherry	70	2800
Lemon cordial	5	200
Corn syrup	4	160
Water	8	320
Acetic acid (10%)	1	40 ml.
Lemon essence	1	40 ml.
Vanilla	1	40 ml.
Almond essence	0.2	8 ml.

Procedure

1. Clean and prepare the fruits. Soak for 3 - 4 days.
2. Blanch and peel the almonds.
3. Follow sugar-batter method of cake making.
4. Add fruits and clear the mixture.
5. Apportion the batter in paper lined moulds.
6. Arrange peeled almonds in an attractive pattern on top surface.
7. Bake at 190 deg.C for 45 - 50 min.
8. Rest the cakes in mould overnight before cutting.

EGGLESS CAKE

Ingredients	Percent	Actual wt. in g.
Condensed Milk	80	800
Processed butter	20	200
Powder Sugar	40	400
Khoa	40	400
Milk Solids	5	50
Glucose	3	30
Acetic Acid (1 :4)	1	10 ml.

MACP	1	10
Water	60	600
Soda	0.5	5
Salt	1	10
Vanilla	1	10 ml.
Sorbic acid	0.1	1
Maida	100	1000
Baking Powder	2	20
Cardamom Powder	0.5	5
Gel	5	50
Sorbitol	3	30

Method

Use all-in-one process adding ingredients in groups as shown above. Bake at 190°C for about 40 min. Being rich in milk products, the crust should be protected against acquiring excessive colouration

GINGER BREAD

Ingredients	Percent	Actual wt. in g.
Flour	100	1000
Baking powder	2	20
Ginger powder	3	30
Sugar	45	450
Shortening	30	300
Molasses	55	550
Water	20	200
Egg	30	300
Vanilla	1	10 ml.
Water (Variable)	20	200
salt	1	10
Soda bicarb.	0.5	5
Dates (Sliced)	75	750

Procedure

1. Clean, stone and slice dates.
2. Sift together flour, baking powder and ginger powder.
3. Add sugar and shortening and mix.
4. Add molasses and water and whisk.
5. Add egg and vanilla and whisk
6. Add salt, soda bicarb. dissolved in water and clear the batter.

7. *Fold in sliced dates.
8. Bake in well greased and dusted moulds at 200 deg.C.

SPONGE CAKE
(For Pastries, Jam Roll)

Ingredients	Percent	Actual wt.in g.
Egg	140	5600
MACP	0.3	12
Emulsifier		
Sugar	110	4400
Water	10	400
Sorbitol	5	200
Salt	1	40
Liquid glucose	5	200
Vanilla	1	40 ml.
Flour	100	4000
Baking powder	2	80
Melted shortening	10-20	400-800

Procedure

1. Whisk egg, MACP and emulsifier till it is thick.
2. Add sugar gradually and continue whisking till the sponge acquires ribbon consistency.
3. Dissolve salt and glucose in water, add vanilla and sorbitol and add to the sponge gradually.
4. Sift flour with baking powder and fold in the sponge (by hand) carefully so as not to drive out aeration.
5. Fold in melted fat carefully.
6. Apportion the sponge in trays and bake at 220 deg.C.

NB:

1. Sponge cakes can be made with different combinations of egg, sugar and flour for making tea fancies with butter cream or fresh cream or for making jam rolls.
2. White of egg can be separated and whisked to wet peak stage before adding yolk and sugar.
3. In order to protect the sponge from drying, use of humectants like glucose, corn syrup, sorbitol, glycerin is advisable. For the same reason melted shortening is used.

4. For making chocolate sponge, proper adjustment of water content should be made as cocoa acts as a drier.

5. All-in-one process can be used although order of adding ingredients will remain same to ensure disolution of sugar and proper aeration.

MOCHA CAKE

Ingredients	Percent	Actual wt. in g.
Shortening	50	2000
Sugar	120	4800
Skimmed milk powder	12	480
Egg	65	2600
Emulsifier		
Vanilla	1	40 ml.
Water	20	800
Salt	1.5	60
Molasses	10	400
Flour	100	4000
Baking powder	2.5	100
Cocoa	5	200
Instant coffee	3	120
Water	15	600
Soda bi carb.	0.5	20

Procedure

Follow sugar-batter method.

BON BON (Popularly known as Apple Cake)

Ingredients	Percent	Actual wt. in g.
Cake Crumbs (Fresh)	100	5000
Butter Cream	20	1000
Liquid Glucose	10	500
Sorbitol	4	200
Acetic acid (1 :4)	0.6	30 ml.
Sodium Propionate	0.2	10
Orange Oil	0.6	30 ml.
Cocoa	3	150
Vanilla	0.2	10 ml.
Milk Essence	0.1	5 mi.
Condensed Milk	5	250
Cashew Nut	3	150
Sultana	3	150
Choco Chip	3	150

Method

1. Put cake crumbs in the cake machine and work the machine till all the crumbs become fine.
2. Put other ingredients one by one and mix to a soft consistency adding more cream or sorbitol if necessary.
3. Break into small pieces and roll into round balls and then in fresh cake crumbs and put in paper cups.
4. Decorate top with butter icing flower and leaf.

RUM BALLS

Ingredients	Percent	Actual wt. in g.
Chocolate Cake (Fresh)	100	400
Sultana	25	100
Rum	25	100
Semisweet Chocolate	50	200
Acetic Acid (1:4)	0.25	10 ml.
Sodium Propionate	0.25	1

Method

1. Soak sultana in rum for about an hour.
2. Put chocolate cake in the mixer and mix to a smooth paste. Add sultana.
3. Break into small pieces and shape into round balls.
4. Melt semi sweet chocolate in a double boiler.
5. Dip each ball in melted chocolate and place in small paper cups.

MAWA CAKE

Ingredients	Percent	Actual wt. In g.
Margarine	50	500
Liquid Glucose	5	50
Acetic Acid (1 :4)	2	20 ml.
Sugar	100	1000
Milk Solids	3	30
Cardamom Powder	0.5	5
Egg	70	700
Gel	3	30
Vanilla	1	10 ml.
Condensed Milk	8	80
Khoa	10	100

Ammonium Bicarb.	1	10
Water	10	100
Salt	1	10
Maida	100	1000
Baking Powder	2	20
Cocoa	2	20
Sorbitol	3	30
Water	15	150

Method

Use all-in-one process. Bake in cup cake moulds at 200°C for 25 min.

CARROT CAKE

Ingredients	Percent	Actual wt in g.
Sugar	120	1200
Refined Oil	100	1000
Egg	60	600
Egg Yolk	10	100
Gel	12	120
Maida	100	1000
Baking powder	2	20
Salt	2	20
Cinnamon powder	1	10
Soda bicarb.	0.5	5
Shredded Carrot	100	1000
Walnuts (chopped)	40	400

Method

1. Use all in one process adding each set of ingredients. After each addition, mix to a homogerrous mass.
2. Bake at 200°C for about 40min.

EGGLESS PLUM CAKE

Ingredients	Percent	Actual wt. in g.
Condensed Milk	85	1700
Butter	25	500
Powder Sugar	40	800
Khoa	40	800
Milk Solids	10	200
Liquid Glucose	10	200
Water	60	120

Soda	0.5	10
Salt	1	20
Vanilla	0.5	10 ml.
Maida	100	2000
Baking Powder	1.5	30
Spices	1	20
Gel	5	100
Fruits	300	6000
Sorbitol	8	160

Method

Use all-in-one process. Soak fruits as for plum cake. Bake at 180°C for about 90 min.

BUTTER ICING

Ingredients	Percent	Actual wt. in g.
Butter (White, unsalted) or Margaine	50-60	2000-2400
Liquid glucose	5	200
Icing Sugar	100	4000
Corn starch	5	200
Milk powder	3	120
Sodium Propionate	0.25	10
Emulsifier		
Condensed Milk	5	200
Water	5-10	200
Salt	0.5	20
Acetic acid (10%)	0.5	20 ml.
Vanilla	1	40 ml.
Milk essence	0.5	20 ml.

Procedure

1. Sieve icing sugar, corn starch, milk powder and calcium propionate together to blend thoroughly.
2. Put butter/margarine and liquid glucose in the mixer bowl and run the machine at medium speed till the fat becomes smooth and free of any lumps
3. Add sieved icing sugar gradually, running the machine at low speed till all the sugar is added.

4. Add emulsifier, condensed milk and run the machine at medium speed till the cream becomes light and fluffy.

5. Dissolve salt in water and odd to the cream together with acetic acid and flavour.

6. Run the machine for few more minutes till the cream is very smooth, light and homogeneous.

Note:-

Acetic acid and sodium propionate are not regular ingredients of butter icing. These are added as safety measures against possibilities of spoilage if left over cream is inadvertently carried over with fresh batch of cream.

FONDANT ICING

Ingredients	Percent	Actual wt. in g.
Sugar	100	5000
Water	30-35	1750
Liquid glucose	4-6	200-300

Procedure

1. Mix sugar and water in a thick bottom pan and put on slow fire. Keep stirring till all the sugar is dissolved. It should not be allowed to boil until all the sugar is dissolved.

2. Increase heat and let it boil. Take out the scum without much stirring. Stirring of boiling syrup should be avoided as far as possible because it promotes grain formation which is undesirable.

3. Add liquid glucose and continue boiling till it reaches soft-ball consistency (240 deg.C). Put few drops of syrup in cold water, it should form a soft ball.

4. Turn the syrup on to clean granite table on which water has been splashed.

5. Keep turning the syrup. As the syrup is in the process of cooling it will start appearing milky white. At this stage beat it vigorously till the entire syrup turns to white, smooth, homogenous mass.

6. Keep it in air tight container and use as required.

7. For using the fondant, take the required quantity in a thick bottom pan and put on slow heat (use Bain marrie). Keep stirring slowly so that it does not catch in bottom. When all the fondant is melted, add sufficient quantity of stock syrup to thin it down to pouring consistency.

For making stock syrup take

Sugar	100%
Water	50%
Liquid glucose	10%

Heat sugar and water. Boil for 5 min. Add liquid glucose and boil to thread consistency.

ROYAL ICING

Ingredients.

Egg white	From 2 eggs
Lemon juice	half tea spoon
Icing sugar	500g. Approx.
Flavour and colours	As desired

Procedure

1. Take desired quantity of egg white, and add few drops of lemon juice. Whisk it lightly.
2. Sift icing sugar and add gradually to egg white. While continuing whisking add sufficient icing sugar till the icing acquires desired consistency for spreading on the cake or for making flowers etc.*
3. Add vanilla and desired colour.
4. Very small quantity of glycerin may be added to royal icing in order to prevent it from becoming very hard after drying.

GLACE ICING
(Also Known As Water Icing Or Vanilla Icing)

Ingredients	Actual wt. in g.
Icing sugar	500
Hot water	as required to Achieve desired consistency
Vanilla essence	few drops

Procedure

1. Sift the icing sugar in a bowl.
2. Add hot water with a spoon gradually and keep stirring.
3. Add enough hot water till the icing coats the spoon.

4. Add few drops of vanilla and mix.
5. Use immediately while it is still warm.

GUM PASTE

Ingredients	Actual wt. in g.
Icing sugar	500
Gelatin	15 (2 tea spoon)
Water	40 (4 table spoon)
Glycerin	5 (1 tea spoon)
Egg white	70 (2 eggs)

Procedure

1. Warm the water, add gelatin and let soak for 5-7 min. Stir it till all the gelatin is completely dissolved and liquid is clear.
2. Mix dissolved gelatin and glycerin together.
3. Sift icing sugar in a bowl. Add egg white and gelatin mixture and Mix to a firm dough consistency. Add more icing sugar if necessary to acquire the desired consistency.

ALMOND PASTE

Ingredients	Actual wt. in g.
Almonds (very finely ground)	250
Icing sugar	250
Egg white	as required
Almond flavour	few drops

Procedure

1. Sift icing sugar in a bowl. Mix with ground almonds.
2. Add egg white and flavour and mix to a firm, sheetable dough. Use corn flour for dusting.

MARZIPAN

Ingredients	Percent	Actual wt. in g.
Sugar	100	1000
Water	35	350
Liquid glucose	10	100
Ground almonds	100	1000
Almond flavour	few drops.	

Procedure

1. Boil sugar as for making fondant.

2. When syrup reaches soft ball consistency, take it off fire and add ground almonds and almond flavour. Keep stirring till it becomes a white solid mass.

3. When cool, put it in an air tight container and use as required. Use stock syrup to soften the marzipan to sheetable consistency.

Note:

Special grinding machine is used to grind marzipan in order to make it very smooth and pliable without becoming oily.

PASTRY & PIES

PUFF PASTRY
(For Khara biscuit, Vegetable puff, Cream roll)

Ingredients	Percent	Actual wt. in g.
Flour	100	5000
Salt	2	100
Water (chilled)	56-58	2800-2900
Shortening (for mixing in)	10	500
Puff fat (for folding in)	50-60	2500-3000

Procedure

1. Mix dough with flour, salt and chilled water.

2. Knead in ten percent shortening and clear the dough. The dough should be of sheetable consistency, i.e. neither too soft nor too tight.

3. Relax the dough in cool place for half an hour covered with wet cloth. At every stage care should be taken that crust formation does not take place on the dough surface.

4. Sheet the dough in rectangular shape. spread (50-60%) fat evenly on the dough sheet.

5. Cut the sheet vertically in 7-8 strips in such a manner that each subsequent strip is broader than the preceding strip.

6. Roll the first strip like a Swiss roll. Keep this roll on the next strip and roll. Similarly roll all the subsequent strips. Relax the folded dough for half an hour in cool place covered with a moist cloth.

7. Sheet out the dough to desired thickness depending on the product desired to be made.

For khara biscuit, cut the sheeted dough into strips of desired width. Then cut the sheet into biscuits. Twist each biscuit and place on the baking sheet. Sprinkle water on biscuits and rest the trays for 20-30 min in cool place. Drain out excessive water. Bake in hot oven (240 deg.C) for about 25 min. Dry the biscuits in cool oven (150 deg.C) till these are crisp.

For cream rolls, Cut the sheeted dough in strips of about 1.5 cm. width. Brush with egg wash. Wrap the strips around cones starting at the pointed end and overlapping each new turn of the pastry keeping the egg washed side downwards. Keep on baking sheet so that the end of the strip is in contact with the baking sheet. Brush with egg wash or milk. Bake at 230 deg. C till the rolls acquire light golden brown colour. Take the rolls out of the cones and dry them in cool oven till crisp. Fill the rolls with butter cream or whipped fresh cream. Top with cherry or roasted nuts.

For making puffs, cut the sheeted dough into four inch squares. place desired filling in the center of each square and fold over to make a triangle. Brush with egg wash and bake in hot oven (250 deg.C) till golden brown.

Filling for vegetable puffs (from 5 kg. flour)

Ingredients	**Actual wt. in g.**
Onion	1000
Potatoes	1500
Beans	1500
Carrots	1000
Green chilies	200
Coriander leaves (Dhania)	200
Ginger	100
Mint leaves (Podina)	200
Cumin seeds (Jeera)	20
Mustard seeds (Rai)	20
Salt	25
Pepper	20
Red chili powder	20
Turmeric Powder (Haldi)	10
Coriander powder	20
Garam masala	20
Acetic acid (10%)	20 ml.
Refined oil	200

Procedure

1. Boil potatoes and mesh.
2. Slice onion, dice carrots and cut beans into small pieces.
3. Boil carrots and beans and drain the residual water.

4. Heat refined oil. Add jeera and mustard seeds and as soon as it starts crackling, add sliced onion, Chopped green chilies, and grated ginger. Fry the onion till golden brown. Add dhania powder, haldi, chillier powder, pepper powder and salt.
5. Add boiled vegetables and fry till these are somewhat dry.
6. Take off fire. Add boiled and meshed potatoes and mix evenly.
7. Add garam masala, chopped dhania and podina leaves. Finally add acetic acid, mix thoroughly. Cool before using.

PUFF PASTRY II METHOD

Ingredients	Percent	Actual wt. in g.
Flour	100	1000
salt	2	20
lime juice	0.5	5 ml.
Chilled water	56-58	560-580
Shortening	5	50
Puff margarine	60-80	600-800

Procedure

1. Dissolve salt in chilled water and mix lime juice.
2. Add water to the flour and mix to a dough. Knead in 5% shortening and clear the dough. Dough should be smooth and pliable.
3. Wrap the dough in moist cloth and rest it in the refrigerator for about half an hour.
4. Make an oblong block of the puff margarine and refrigerate till it is firm i.e. neither hard nor soft.
5. Sheet the dough into oblong shape about twice in size of the margarine block.
6. Place the margarine block on one half of the sheeted dough. Fold the other half over it and seal the edges. Rest it in cool place for 15 min.
7. Sheet the pastry to rectangular shape taking care that margarine does not break out of the dough. Fold the pastry into three folds i.e. left one third portion over center one third and right one third over it.
8. Repeat the process three times more giving rest period in between each sheeting and folding operation. Relax the pastry for a minimum of one hour in refrigerator (wrapped in moist cloth) before using for make up.

Vaul au vent:

Sheet the puff pastry to desired thickness (about 6 mm.). Cut even number of pieces with a round biscuit cutter. In half of the pieces, cut a round hole in the center with a smaller cutter. Apply egg or water on the whole pieces and place on them the pieces with hole in the center. Bake at 225 deg.C till golden brown. Fill the cases with desired filling such as vanilla cream, whipped dairy cream, boiled vegetables with white sauce, chicken filling etc. This product can be used as appetizer or as snack with tea.

Vanilla slices:

Sheet the puff pastry to desired thickness. Cut into rectangular shape (about 15 cm.x7 cm.)Sprinkle little water on the baking sheet and place the rectangular pieces on it. Prick with a fork and let relax for about 20 min. Bake to golden brown colour. Cool to room temperature. With a pointed sharp knife cut each piece into three parts. Join two pieces together with custard cream. Place custard cream on top surface of second piece and place the third piece upside down over it and press together gently. Cover the top with vanilla icing made with icing sugar and hot water.

Palmiers:

Sheet the pastry to desired thickness and rectangular shape. Trim the edges. Apply egg on top surface and sprinkle sugar. Fold the longer upper side and bring it to the center. Similarly roll the lower side so that both the sides join in the center. Now fold one half on to other half again. Chill it till it is sufficiently hard to cut. Cut with a sharp knife into thick slices. Place on baking sheet (cut surface up) sufficiently apart leaving room for expansion. Let relax for about 20 min. Bake at 220 deg.C till it is golden brown.

Mille Feuilles:

Sheet the pastry thinly. Cut into round shape about 10 cm. in diameter. Place the pieces on to baking sheet and prick with a fork. Bake to golden brown colour. Cool. Whip fresh cream with small quantity of sugar. Fold in the cherries. Place one round piece of baked pastry , apply cream on top and cover with another piece. Similarly join the third piece placing it upside down. Cover top of third piece with glace icing and place a cherry in the center.

BAKLAVA

Ingredients

Puff pastry	-	2 pieces of 500g each

Coarsely grated nuts (pista, almonds, cashew nuts)	-	250 g.
Powder sugar	-	300 g.
Khaskhas (Poppy seeds)	-	30 g.
Condensed Milk	-	3 tablespoon
Cardamom Powder	-	5 g.

Method:

1. Take a baking tray 12"x6"x1 ". Grease it and line with butter paper. Grease the butter paper to avoid sticking.
2. Mix together grated nuts, sugar, khaskhas,cardamom powder and condensed milk.
3. Sheet one piece of puff pastry about 3mm thick and line the baking tray (bottom) with it.
4. Spread the mixture over it evenly.
5. Sheet the other piece of puff pastry of the same thickness and cover the mixture completely. Press the edges so that it does not come out during baking. Wash the top with water. Mark into one inch square piece.
6. Bake at 190°-C till golden brown on top.
7. Take out of the oven and brush with thick sugar syrup.
8. Turn it on cooking rack.
9. Cut carefully into pieces of one inch square when cool.

FLAKY PASTRY

Ingredients	Percent	Actual wt. in g.
Flour	100	1000
Salt	2	15
Chilled water (variable)	55	550
Shortening (for mixing)	10	100
Shortening (for folding)	55-60	550-600

Procedure

1. Sieve the flour.
2. Dissolve salt in water and add to the flour. Mix the dough till it is smooth and pliable. Add shortening and clear the dough. Relax the dough in cool place covered with moist cloth.
3. Sheet the dough in rectangular shape and mark it into three equal portions A, B and C.

4. Divide the shortening (for folding in) into three equal parts.
5. Place one part of shortening in small blobs (flakes) on two parts (A and B) of the sheeted dough.
6. Fold C over B and A over C so that there are alternate layers of fat and dough. Relax the pastry in cool place for 15-20 min.
7. Repeat the process with the remaining two portions of shortening with intermittent rest after each sheeting and folding operation. Give one more folding without fat. Cover it with moist cloth and place in cool place for a minimum of one hour before make up.
8. This pastry can be used for making pies. flans, tartlets and turnovers.

SHORT CRUST PASTRY

Ingredients	Percent	Actual wt. in g.
Flour	100	1000
Butter or Shortening	50-70	500-700
Sugar	20	200
Salt	0.5-1	5-10
Egg yolk	10	100
Chilled water (variable)	10	100
Vanilla	0.5	5 ml.
Butter essence	0.5	5 ml.

Note:-

Quantity of salt will depend on the quantity of sugar desired to be used. With more sugar, content of salt can also be increased. If salted butter is used then formula salt will need to be regulated accordingly.

Procedure

1. Cut hardened Butter or shortening into small pieces and rub in the sieved flour lightly with finger tips till it resembles bread crumbs.
2. Add powdered sugar and mix.
3. Mix together egg yolk, flavours, salt and half of water and mix in the flour (With pallet knife using cutting and folding method). Form into a smooth and firm dough adding more chilled water if necessary. Avoid over mixing as it will toughen the pastry.
4. Wrap the pastry in damp cloth and relax in cool place (refrigerator) for about an hour before using.
5. Sheet and cut as desired for tarts, turnovers, pies etc.

SHORT PASTRY DOUGH

Ingredients	Percent	Actual wt. in g.
Sugar	50	500
Salt	1	10
Skimmed milk powder	2	20
Liquid glucose	3	30
Chilled water	10	100
Vanilla	1	10 ml.
Shortening	60	600
Flour	100	1000

Procedure

1. Add together sugar, salt, milk powder, liquid glucose, egg yolk, water and vanilla and mix at slow speed to make a homogenous mass.
2. Add shortening mixed with emulsifier and mix at medium speed to break the shortening into small pieces.
3. Add flour and mix to form a dough. Do not over mix. This dough can be used for making cookies, biscuits, tart shells, pie crust etc.

APPLE CRUMB PIE

Ingredients	Percent	Actual wt.in g.
Tart apples	100	1000
Sugar	25-30	250-300
Flour	10	100
Salt	0.5	5
Cinnamon powder	0.5	5
Nutmeg powder	0.3	3
Butter	for dotting	

Procedure

1. Peel and pare apples and cut into medium size pieces. Add half the sugar and put on very slow fire, tossing occasionally till apples are slightly softened. Take off fire.
2. Mix remaining sugar, flour, salt and spices together and add to the apples stirring very gently so as not to mesh the softened apples.
3. Line the pie dish with sheeted pastry dough.
4. Arrange the apple mixture loosely on to the pastry lined pie dish. Dot with butter.

5. Cover the apple mixture with sheeted pastry. Brush with egg wash or milk and dock with a fork.
6. Bake at 200 deg.C for 30-35 min.

CHERRY PIE FILLING

Ingredient	Percent	Actual wt.in g.
Drained (Canned) cherry	100	500
Sugar	20	100
Salt	0.4	2
Butter	10	50
Red colour		as desired
Cherry Flavour		as desired
Cherry juice	50	250
Starch	10	50

Procedure

1. Combine sugar, starch and salt.
2. Stir in butter, red colour, flavour and one third cherry juice to make a paste.
3. Boil remaining cherry juice and slowly pour over the paste stirring constantly to avoid lump formation.
4. Cook over slow heat till starch is clear.
5. Add drained cherries. Cool before using.

WALNUT PIE FILLING (FOR TWO PIES)

Ingredients	Actual wt.in g.
Brown sugar	50
Granulated sugar	50
Butter	50
Egg	80
Maple, syrup or plain syrup	30
Fresh milk	30
Salt	1
Vanilla	5 ml.
Walnut (Chopped)	60
Walnut (Half pieces)	20

Procedure

1. Blend brown sugar and butter over slow heat (use double boiler). Add granulated sugar.

2. Mix together slightly beaten egg, syrup and milk and add in a slow stream stirring constantly to avoid curdling. Cook till the mixture coats the spoon. Add salt and vanilla.

3. Remove from heat. Stir in chopped walnuts.

4. Pour the mixture in the pastry lined pie dish, Arrange half pieces of walnuts on top and bake at 200 deg. C till the edges of the pie acquires light brown colour.

RAISIN PIE FILLING (ForTwo Pies)

Ingredients	Percent	Actual wt. in g.
Raisins	100	300
Brown sugar	50	150
Corn starch	10	30
Water	85	255 ml.
Orange juice	30	90 ml.
Orange rind	2	6
Lemon juice	3	9 ml.
Lemon rind	1	3
Chopped walnuts	40	120
Butter	5	15

Procedure

1. Combine sugar, corn starch, raisins, peel, water and juice and cook over slow heat till thick. Add butter and mix.

2. Add nuts.

3. Fill the mixture in pastry lined pie cases and bake at 200 deg.C for about 30 min.

PUMPKIN PIE FILLING (ForTwo Pies)

Ingredients	Percent	Actual wt. in g.
Cooked meshed pumpkin	100	400
Sugar	60	240
Starch	5	20
Salt	1	4
Ginger powder	1	4
Cinnamon powder	0.25	1
Nutmeg (ground)	0.25	1
Cloves	0.25	1
Egg	30	120
Evaported milk	80	320
Fresh liquid milk	80	320

Procedure

1. Grate pumpkin, boil in sufficient water and squeeze out water.
2. Thoroughly combine pumpkin, sugar, starch, salt and spices.
3. Add slightly beaten egg, evaporated milk, adn fresh liquid milk and cook over double boiler till the mixture becomes slightly thick and coats the spoon.
4. Fill the mixture in prepared pie cases and bake at 200deg.C for about 30 min.

Note :-

If condensed milk is used, sugar content should be reduced proportionately.

CUSTARD PIE (FILLING) (For Two Pies)

Ingredients	Percent	Actual wt. in g.
Sugar	100	100
Egg	100	100
Starch	20	20
Salt	1	1
Fresh liquid milk	450	450
Nutmeg powder	1	1
Vanila	5	5 ml.

Procedure

1. Blend together sugar, egg and starch.
2. Add hot milk gradually stirring all the time to avoid lump formation. Cook over double boiler till the mixture coats the spoon.
3. Add nutmeg powder, vanilla and salt.
4. Whip till foamy.
5. Put the custard in the prepared pie dishes and bake.

CHOUX PASTE (For Eclairs)

Ingredients	Percent	Actual wt. in g.
Water	160	825
Butter	100	375
Flour	100	500
Egg	105	600

Procedure

1. Place water and butter in a thick bottomed brass pan. Bring to boil.
2. Take off fire. Add all the flour at a time. Return to slow-fire and cook till flour leaves the bottom of the pan.*
3. Allow to cool slightly and then add beaten eggs in a slow stream, beating vigorously all the while.
4. Pipe through Savoy nozzle into eclairs, or buns or swans.
5. Bake in hot oven (220 deg.C) for 10-12 min. Reduce the heat to about 150 deg. C and bake further till structure is set and eclairs are crisp.

Eclairs

Fill the eclairs with cocoa flavoured butter cream. Dip the top portion in chocolate fondant.

BISCUITS & COOKIES

NUT SQUARE

Ingredients	Percent	Actual wt. in g.
Shortening	60	600
Sugar	50	500
Salt	1	10
Egg	18	180
Vanilla	1	10
Flour	100	1000
Baking Powder	0.5	5
Peanuts (roasted and grated fine)	20	200

Procedure

1. Sift flour and baking powder and mix with grated peanuts.
2. Cream fat and sugar.
3. Whisk egg with vanilla and add to the creamed mixture.
4. Add flour and mix to a soft and pliable dough.
5. Form the dough pieces into bar like shape of square cross section.
6. Chill until hard enough to cut.
7. Cut into thin slices and place onto greased baking sheet.
8. Brush with milk or egg wash. Bake at 375 deg.F

Note:-

If the biscuits break while cutting, little extra mixing. Can be given or in subsequent batch peanut content can be reduced and also should be made into a very fine powder. Same remedial measures can be adopted if the cookies are too fragile after baking.

VANILA BUTTONS

Ingredients	Percent	Actual wt in g.
Butter	70	700
Sugar	40	400
Salt	0.5	5
Egg	30	300
Vanilla	1	10
Flour	100	1000
Baking powder	0.5	5

Procedure

1. Cream fat and sugar till light and fluffy.
2. Whisk egg with vanilla and add to the creamed mixture.
3. Sift flour and baking powder. Add to cream and mix to a dough of piping consistency adding milk if necessary. Mixing operation should be carried out just sufficiently so as to avoid undesirable gluten development which may hinder piping process of cookies.
4. Pipe the mixture through a large star nozzle in the shape of buttons on to a greased baking sheet. Put a dot of jam in the center of each star.
5. Bake at 200 deg.C for about 15-18 min.

KAJU - PISTA BISCUITS

Ingredients	Percent	Actual wt in g.
Shortening	45	450
Liquid glucose	2	20
Ammonium bicarb.	0.4	4
Sugar	50	500
Skimmed milk powder	2	20
Egg	10	100
Water	6	60 ml.
Salt	1	10
Soda bicarb.	0.5	5
Vanilla	1	10

Cardamom essence	0.5	5 ml.
Almond essence	0.3	3 ml.
Flour	100	1000
Corn flour	2	20
Baking powder	0.4	4
Cashew nut (chopped)	20	200
Pista (flaked)	5	50

Procedure

1. Mix the dough by creaming method.
2. Sheet the dough to desired thickness.
3. Brush the dough with milk or egg wash.
4. Sprinkle with chopped cashew nuts and pista flakes. Let dry for few minutes.
5. Sheet it again lightly to fix the nuts.
6. Cut with an oblong cutter. Place on baking sheet and bake at 200 deg. C for about 20 min.

ORANGE BISCUIT

Ingredients	**Percent**	**Actual wt. in g.**
Shortening	45	450
Liquid glucose	2	20
Orange oil	0.5	5 ml.
Ammonium bicarb.	0.4	4
Sugar	50.	500
Skimmed milk powder	2	20
Egg	6	60
Orange juice	6	60 ml.
Vanilla	0.5	5 ml.
Orange essence	0.5	5 ml.
Orange emulsion	1	10 ml.
Orange colour	As desired	
Water	5	50 ml.
Salt	1	10
Flour	100	1000
Corn flour	3	30
Baking powder	0.3	3
Soda bicarb.	0.2	2

Procedure

Follow creaming method.

JEERA BISCUIT

Ingredients	Percent	Actual wt. in g.
Shortening	45	450
Liquid glucose	2	20
Ammonium bicarb.	0.5	5
Sugar	50	500
Skimmed milk powder	2	20
Egg	12	120
Water	5	50
Salt	2	20
Soda bicarb	0.4	4
Vanila	0.5	5 ml.
Jeera essence	0.5	5 ml.
Flour	100	1000
Corn flour	2	20
Baking powder	0.3	3
Jeera (Cumin seeds)	5	50

Procedure

1. Mix the dough by creaming method.
2. Sheet the dough and brush it with milk or egg wash.
3. Sprinkle jeera liberally and let dry for few min.
4. Cut with round biscuit cutter.

PINEAPPLE BISCUIT

Ingredients	Percent	Actual wt. in g.
Shortening	45	450
Liquid glucose	2	20
Ammonium bicarb	0.4	4
Sugar	50	500
Skimmed milk powder	2	20
Egg	11	110
Pineapple juice	5	50
Salt	0.8	8
Vanilla	0.5	5 ml.

Pineapple essence	0.5	5 ml
Flour	100	1000
Corn flour	2	20
Soda bicarb.	0.4	4
Baking powder	0.4	4

Procedure

Follow creaming method

CHOCOLATE WALNUT COOKIES

Ingredients	Percent	Actual wt. in g.
Shortening	50	500
Liquid glucose	2	20
Salt	0.8	8
Soda bicarb.	0.4	4
Ammonium bicarb.	0.3	3
Powdered sugar	55	550
Granulated sugar	10	100
Brown sugar	10	100
Skimmed milk powder	2	20
Cocoa	5	50
Egg	17	170
Vanilla	0.5	5 ml.
Chocolate essence	0.5	5 ml.
Caramel	1	10
Flour	100	1000
Corn flour	2	20
Walnuts (Chopped)	15	150
Covering chocolate (Chopped into large chunks)	25	250

Procedure

1. Mix the dough by creaming process.
2. Break the dough into pieces of walnut size and place on baking sheet an inch apart.
3. Bake at 200 deg.C.

COCOANUT BISCUIT

Ingredients	Percent	Actual wt. in g.
Shortening	45	450
Liquid glucose	2	20

Ammonium bicarb.	0.6	6
Sugar	50	500
Skimmed milk powder	2	20
Egg	12	120
Water	5	50 ml.
Salt	0.8 •	8
Soda bicarb.	0.4	4
Vanilla	0.5	5 ml.
Cocoanut essence	0.5	5 ml.
Flour	100	1000
Corn flour	3	30
Baking powder	0.4	4
Desiccated cocoanut	5	50
Desiccated cocoanut	10	100

Procedure

Mix the dough by creaming method. Add 5% cocoanut in the dough. Sheet the dough. Sprinkle cocoanut liberally and sheet it again to fix the cocoanut. Cut with a round cutter. Place on baking sheet and bake at 200 deg.C.

MASALA BISCUIT

Ingredients	Percent	Actual wt. in g.
Shortening	45	450
Liquid glucose	2	20
Ammonium bicarb.	0.4	4
Sugar	40	400
Skimmed milk powder	2	20
Egg	10	100
Water	5	50 ml.
Salt	2.5	25
Soda bicarb.	0.3	3
Mint leaves		as desired
Curry leaves		as desired
Coriander leaves		as desired
Green chilies		as desired
Chilly powder		as desired
Garam masala		as desired
Flour	100	1000
Baking powder	0.3	3

Procedure

Chop mint leaves, curry leaves, coriander leaves and green chilies very fine. Mix the dough by creaming method. Add masala along with flour. Proceed as for other biscuits.

SWEET AND SALTY BISCUIT

Ingredients	Percent	Actual wt. in g.
Shortening	40	400
Butter	10	100
Butter essence	0.5	5
Liquid glucose	3	30
Sugar	20	200
Skimmed milk powder	2	20
Ammonium bicarb.	1.5	15
Egg	6	60
Water	8	80
Salt	2.5	25
Vanilla	0.5	5 ml.
Flour	100	1000
Corn flour	2	20

Procedure:

Use creaming method or make by French method as follows;

1. Sieve flour and corn flour together on the table.
2. Make a well in the center of flour
3. Add sugar, salt, water, egg, glucose, Ammonium bicarb., vanilla and butter essence and mix till the sugar is almost dissolved.
4. Add butter and milk powder and mix till liquid portion and shortening form a homogenous mass.
5. Now pull in flour gently with fingers and keep mixing till all the flour is mixed forming a dough. Mix till the dough is smooth.
6. Sheet the dough. Cut with round cutter. Dock with fork and place on baking sheet. Bake at medium temperature.

CINNAMON BISCUIT

Ingredients	Percent	Actual wt. in g.
Flour	100	1000
Baking powder	0.5	5
Butter	55	550

Powdered sugar	55	550
Egg	15	150
Vanilla	1	10
Salt	1	10
Fresh liquid milk	if required	
Cinnamon powder	1	10
Granulated sugar	10	100

Procedure

1. Sieve together flour and baking powder.
2. Cut hardened butter into small pieces and mix with flour.
3. Rub butter in the flour till it resembles bread crumbs. For large quantities, vertical mixer can be used at medium speed.
4. Whisk egg with vanilla and salt and add to the flour. Add fresh liquid milk if required and mix to a sheetable dough.
5. Sheet the dough into rectangular shape.
6. On half portion of the sheeted dough apply egg or milk with a brush. Sprinkle with cinnamon powder mixed with sugar.
7. Fold the remaining half of the sheeted dough over it. Sheet again to biscuit thickness. Cut into fancy shapes of leaves and crescents. Place on baking sheet and wash with egg wash or milk.
8. Bake at 200 deg. C for about 20 min.

FANCY COCOANUT MACAROONS

Ingredients	Percent	Actual wt. in gm.
Granulated sugar	100	4000
Water	30	1200
Liquid glucose	4	160
Egg white	30	1200
Cream of tartar	0.1	4
or		
MACP	0.2	8
vanilla	0.5	20 ml.
Cocoanut essence	0.25	10 ml.
Desiccated cocoanut	100	4000

Procedure

1. Mix together sugar and water in a thick bottomed brass pan. Put on gentle heat stirring effectively. Do not allow it to boil until all the

sugar is dissolved. Increase the flame and let it boil. Add liquid glucose. Boil to 240 deg.C (soft ball consistency i.e. syrup should form a soft ball when poured in cold water. Syrup should not be stirred during boiling otherwise granulation of sugar may occur.

2. Start whisking the egg white with cream of tartar when the syrup is just about to reach soft ball consistency. Whisk the egg white to wet peak stage.

3. When the egg white reaches wet peak stage, start pouring the syrup in a slow stream whisking all the while. Add vanilla and cocoanut essence.

4. Fold in the desiccated cocoanut gently by hand.

5. Pipe the mixture on to greased and dusted baking sheet. It is advisable to bake macaroons on butter paper to avoid sticking to the tray. Put a small dot of jam in~the center of each macaroon.

6. Bake at 150 deg.C for about 90 min. or until macaroons are crisp.

PEANUT MACAROONS

Ingredients	Percent	Actual wt. in g.
Egg white	35	1400
Cream of tartar	0.1	4
or		
Lemon juice	0.3	12 ml.
Vanilla	1	40 ml.
Granulated sugar	70	2800
Peanuts (Roasted, chopped)	90	3600
Granulated sugar	30	1200
Salt	0.3	12

Procedure

1. Whisk the egg white with cream of tartar or lemon juice to wet peak stage. Add vanilla.

2. Add 70% sugar gradually and keep on whisking. The mixture should be stable enough to stand upright without spreading.

3. Mix together roasted chopped peanuts, 30% granulated sugar and salt.

4. Fold in the peanut mixture very gently taking care that the aeration is not lost and the mixture remains stable.

5. With the help of two spoons, place small portions of mixture on to greased and dusted baking sheet. Alternately mixture can be piped

through a piping bag fitted with a plain nozzle.

6. Bake in a very slow oven (150 deg.C) till the macaroons are crisp (About 90-100 min.)

CASHEWNUT MACAROONS

Ingredients	Percent	Actual wt in g.
Egg white	35	3400
MACP	0.2	8
Vanilla	0.5	20 ml.
Granulated sugar	70	2800
Cashew nuts (Roasted, grated)	70	2800
Granulated sugar	30	1200
Cardamom powder	0.5	20
Salt	0.3	12

Procedure

Follow the procedure as for peanut macaroons.-

FANCY CHOCOLATE BISCUIT

Ingredients	Percent	Actual wt. in g.
Shortening	45	450
Liquid glucose	2	20
Ammonium bicarb.	0.5	5
Sugar	50	500
Skimmed milk powder	2	20
Egg	12	120
Water	7	70
Salt	0.8	8
Soda bicarb.	0.5	5
Vanilla	0.5	5 ml.
Chocolate essence	0.5	5 ml.
Flour	100	1000
Corn flour	3	30
Baking powder	0.5	5
Cocoa	2	20
Shortening	2	20
Caramel	1	10

Procedure

1. Mix the dough by creaming method.
2. Divide the dough into four portions.

3. Mix together 2% shortening, cocoa and caramel and mix it in one portion of the dough. Divide this chocolate dough in three parts.

4. Take one portion of the white dough, flatten it out into an oblong shape. Brush with egg. Similarly flatten out one portion of the chocolate dough (somewhat smaller in size than the white dough) and place it on the white dough. Now roll both the doughs together like a Swiss roll so as to form two distinct colour rings when viewed at the ends of the roll. Similarly work with the remaining portions of the dough. Refrigerate till the rolls become hard enough to cut with a knife.

5. Cut with a sharp knife into slices of biscuit thickness. Place on baking sheet and bake at 380 deg.F to a very light brown colour.

Note:-

Number of different patterns can be made with two colour doughs.

JAPANESE CAKES

Ingredients	**Percent**	**Actual wt. in g.**
Egg white	100	1000
Cream of tartar	0.3	3
or		
Citric acid	0.2	2
Sugar	40	400
Vanilla	1	10 ml.
Almond essence	1	10 ml.
Cashew nuts (Roasted and grated to fine powder)	110	1100
Sugar	20	200

Cream required for the above quantity

Butter or margarine	200
Icing sugar	400
Skimmed milk powder	20
Coffee essence	15 ml.
Cocoa	20
Walnuts (Chopped fine)	200
Topping	
Icing sugar	500
Liquid glucose	50
Hot water	to make a thick paste
Colour and flavour	as desired

Procedure

1. Add cream of tartar or citric acid to egg white and whisk till it forms a wet peak (peak tending to fold over).
2. Add 40% sugar gradually, whisking all the while, taking care that the whisked egg white does not collapse. Add flavours.
3. Blend the remaining sugar with cashew nut powder and fold in the beaten egg white gently.
4. Pipe the mixture through a Savoy nozzle into round shape of about 6 cm. in diameter. Alternately the mixture can be spread in a greased and paper lined tray about two third cm. thick.
5. Bake at 350 deg. F for about 45 min. If the mixture is baked in the tray, cut it with a biscuit cutter into round shapes. Dry them in a cool oven (300 deg.F) till these are crisp.
6. Sandwich two pieces together with- coffee flavoured cream. cover the sides with cream and chopped walnuts.
7. Pipe a border with butter cream on each cake. Fill the centers with vanilla (Glace) icing or whipped fresh cream and place half a cherry in the center.

BASIC SCONE MIX

Ingredients	Percent	Actual wt. in g.
Flour	100	1000
Baking powder	2.5	25
Skimmed milk powder	5	50
Butter	20	200
Powdered sugar	20	200
Salt	1.5	15
Egg	12	120
Water	as required for making a sheetable dough	

Procedure

1. Sift together flour, skimmed milk powder and baking powder twice.
2. Cut hardened butter into small pieces and rub in the flour gently with finger tips. Larger quantity can be mixed in vertical mixer at medium speed.
3. Add sugar and mix.
4. Add slightly beaten egg and salt and mix.

5. If necessary, add some water and mix to a sheetable dough. While mixing, care should be taken to avoid undesirable gluten development.
6. Sheet the dough about one cm. thick and cut with a round biscuit cutter (about 6 cm. diameter). Place on baking sheet.
7. Wash with egg and bake at 450 deg. F to golden brown colour

Note:-

For sultana scones add 20% sultana before adding egg.

TRI COLOUR BISCUIT-

Ingredients	Percent	Actual wt. in g.
Flour	100	1000
Baking powder	1	10
Shortening	60	600
Sugar (Powdered)	50	500
Liquid fresh milk	for making dough	
Vanilla	1	10 ml.
Jam	25	250

Procedure

1. Sieve flour and baking powder together.
2. Cut hardened fat into small pieces and rub in the flour lightly till the mixture resembles bread crumbs.
3. Add powdered sugar and mix.
4. Add enough liquid milk with vanilla and mix it into a stiff biscuit dough.
5. Sheet the dough to biscuit thickness and cut even number of biscuits with a large round cutter.
6. In half of the biscuits, cut three holes with a Savoy nozzle so that the holes form a triangle.
7. Bake plain biscuits and biscuits with holes separately.
8. Cool the biscuits.
9. Join one plain biscuit and one with hole together with jam.
10. Fill the three holes with different colour jam.

ALMOND COOKIES

Ingredients	Percent	Actual wt. in g.
Shortening	70	700
Sugar	60	600
Salt	0.8	8
Egg	16	160
Vanilla	1	10
Almond essence	0.5	5 ml.
Flour	100	1000
Baking powder	0.5	5
Almonds (Blanched)	for topping	

Procedure

1. Cream shortening and sugar. Add salt.
2. Whisk egg with flavours and mix in the creamed mixture.
3. Sieve flour and baking powder together.
4. Add sieved flour and mix to a soft dough. If the dough is found too sticky, add some flour.
5. Chill the dough in refrigerator for about an hour.
6. Break the dough into small pieces of walnut size and place on baking sheet about two inches apart leaving room for expansion.
7. Top each piece with half blanched almond.
8. Bake at 200 deg.C. for about 20-25 min.

NUT RINGS

Ingredients	Percent	Actual wt. in g.
Shortening	50	500
Sugar	50	500
Salt	0.8	8
Egg	18	180
Vanilla	1	10 ml.
Almond essence	0.3	3 ml.
Flour	100	1000
Baking powder	1	10
Chopped cashew nuts	20	200

Procedure

1. Cream shortening, sugar and salt together.

2. Add egg and flavours and mix.
3. Add flour sieved with baking powder and mix to a pliable dough.
4. Sheet the dough and cut with a medium size biscuit cutter. In each biscuit cut a hole in the center with a smaller cutter.
5. Brush the biscuits with egg white and dip in chopped cashew nuts. Place on baking sheet and bake.

JAM BUNS

Ingredients	Percent	Actual wt. in g.
Shortening	50	500
sugar	50	500
Salt	0.8	8
Egg	20	200
Vanilla	1	10 ml.
Flour	100	1000
Baking powder	2.5	25
Jam	10	100

Procedure:

1. Mix dough by creaming procedure as before.
2. Break the dough into small pieces. Round each piece. Press slightly and place on baking sheet.
3. Make a shallow hole in the center of each piece and put a dot of jam.
4. Place on baking sheet about an inch apart and bake in medium hot oven.

ICE BOX COOKIES

Ingredients	Percent	Actual wt. in g.
Butter or margarine	30	300
Shortening	30	300
Powdered sugar	40	400
Skimmed milk powder	4	40
Salt	0.5	5
Soda bi carb.	0.3	3
Egg	16	160
Vanilla	1	10 ml.
Orange essence	1	10 ml.
Flour	100	1000
Glace cherry	10	100
Orange peel	5	50

Procedure

1. Mix both the fats evenly.
2. Add sugar, SMP, salt and soda bicarb. and cream till the mixture is light.
3. Add egg with flavours gradually and mix to a homogeneous cream.
4. Add flour and chopped fruits and mix to a smooth and soft (not sticky) dough.
5. Form the pieces of dough into oblong fancy shape and chill until hard enough to cut.
6. Cut with a sharp knife into slices of biscuit thickness and place on baking sheet.
7. Brush (Optional) with beaten egg white or milk and bake at 200 deg.C.

ROCK BUNS

Ingredients	Percent	Actual wt. in g.
Flour	100	1000
Baking powder	2.5	25
Shortening	60	600
Sugar	60	600
Sultana	20	200
Orange peel	10	100
Egg	20	200
Vanilla	1	10
Salt	0.8	8

Procedure

1. Sieve flour, salt and baking powder together.
2. Cut the hardened shortening in small pieces and rub in the flour lightly with finger tips. The mixture should resemble bread crumbs.
3. Add powdered sugar and mix well.
4. Add cleaned sultana and diced orange peel.
5. Whisk egg with vanilla and salt lightly. Add to flour gradually and mix to a soft but non-sticky dough.
6. Break the dough into small pieces of walnut size. Round each piece and press gently to make it slightly flat appearing. Place on baking sheet an inch apart.

7. Brush with egg white and place half cherry in the center.

8. Bake to golden brown colour.

PEANUT COOKIES

Ingredients	Percent	Actual wt. in g.
Shortening	75	750
Sugar	75	750
Salt	1	10
Egg	20	200
Vanilla	1	10 ml.
Flour	100	1000
Baking powder	1.5	15
Peanuts (Roasted, chopped)	100	1000

Procedure

1. Cream fat, sugar and salt.
2. Whisk egg with vanilla and add.
3. Sieve flour with baking powder and mix gently in the creamed mixture.
4. Add three-fourth of chopped peanuts and mix.
5. Relax the dough for about half an hour in cool place.
6. Break into small portions, top with remaining peanuts and place on greased baking sheet about an inch apart.
7. Bake at 200 deg.C for 20-25 min.

MELTING MOMENTS

Ingredients	Percent	Actual wt. in g.
Shortening	75	750
Sugar	65	650
Salt	0.8	8
Egg	16	160
Vanilla	1	10
Flour	100	1000
Baking powder	1	10
Corn flakes or Desiccated cocoanut	25	250

Procedure

1. Make the dough as usual. This dough will be somewhat sticky.

2. Dip hands in water and break the dough into small pieces and roll into crushed cornflakes or desiccated cocoanut. Place on baking sheet an inch apart.

3. Bake at 200 deg.C

NANKHATAI

Ingredients	Percent	Actual wt in g.
Shortening	60-75	600-750
Sugar	50-60	500-600
Ammonium bicarb.	0.5	5
Soda bicarb.	0.5	5
Curd	5	50
Cardamom powder	0.7	7
Nutmeg powder	0.5	5
Flour	100	1000
Pista flakes	for topping	

Procedure

1. Mix dough by creaming process.
2. Break the dough into small pieces, round each piece and press lightly. Place on baking sheet an inch apart.
3. Top with pista flakes and bake at 350 degF for 30 min.

Note:

Whole wheat flour can be used partially. In that case fat percent should be increased to about 75%.

SHREWSBURRY BISCUITS

Ingredients	Percent	Actual wt in g.
Butter	50	500 g.
Liquid Glucose	2	20
Powder Sugar	45	450
Milk Solids Non Fat	2	20
Condensers Milk	5	50
Water	7	70 ml.
Salt	0.5	5
Soda Bicob.	0.2	2
Ammonium Bicarb	0.3	3
Vanilla	0.5	5 ml.
Maida	100	1000
Baking Powder	0.2	2

Method

Use creaming method bake at 200°C for about 20 min.

COCOANUT COOKIES

Ingredients	Percent	Actual wt. in g.
Fat	75	750
Powder Sugar	80	800
Granulated sugar	15	150
Milk Solids	5	50
Eggs	12	120
Water (Variable)	30	300
Soda	0.75	7.5
Vanilla	1	10 ml.
Butter Essence	0.5	
Yellow Colour		
Maida	100	1000
Desiccated cocoanut	60	600

Method

Use creaming method. Bake at 200°C for about 20 min.

CHOCOCHIP COOKIES

Ingredients	Percent	Actual wt. in g.
Fat	30	300
Butter	22	220
Glucose	4	40
Powder Sugar	60	600
Milk Solids	3	30
Cream of tartar	0.4	4
Granulated Sugar	8	80
Corn flakes (crushed)	2	20
Condensed Milk	4	40
Egg	12	120
Vanilla	0.5	5 ml.
Chocolate Essance	0.5	5 ml.
Milk Essance	0.5	5 ml.
Water	5	50
Salt	1	10
Soda bicarb.	0.4	4
Ammonium bicarb.	0.6	6
Semi sweet chocolate (grated)	10	100

Maida	100	1000
Baking Powder	0.3	. 3
Chocolate chips	20	200
Cashew nuts (chopped)	20	200

Method

Use creaming method. Break the dough into pieces of walnut size and place on baking sheet an inch apart. Bake at 200°-C for about 25 min.

Chapter - 19

Health Breads

Introduction

Around the world, bread is the principal food and provides more nutrients than any other single food source. Among flour and its main baked products, bread is the least expensive of our staple foods. Health baking refers to the production of bakery products that meet special consumer dietary needs. For e.g. some consumers must be on sugar free or limited sugar intake diets. Others must be on a salt free or limited salt intake diet. Since a large number of consumers are thus effected, the dietetic aspect of baking has grown considerably in order to meet these needs. Manufacturers of bakery supplies have developed a number of prepared mixes to meet the baker's demand to produce dietetic baked goods. Some retails and wholesale bakers have developed their own recipes of formulas for dietetic products. The fact that these "dietetic formulas" contain no sugar (only sugar substitutes) may make them acceptable for use by diabetics but does not necessarily quality the products as "low calorie" as the formulas contain fairly normal quantities of shortening or butter, milk, eggs and so on.

Also replacing salt (NaCl) with a salt substitute does lower the sodium contents somewhat, but in most cases not significantly enough to qualify the baked products as "low sodium". Sodium is naturally present in relatively high quaantities in milk, dough conditioners, egg and even in flour. A truly hypertensive person (with high blood pressure)may require low-sodium products rather than just salt free products. Normal white bread is prepared with flour, fat, sugar, salt, yeast, milksolids etc. and the nutrient components of normal bread are given in Table 1.

Table : 1 Nutrients Composition of Bread
(per 100gm of bread)

Nutrient	White Bread	Whole meal bread
Water, g	39.0	40.0
Protein, g	7.9	8.8
Fat,g	1.7	2.7

Sugar,g	1.8	2.1
Starch & Dextring, g	47.9	39.7
Dietery fiber, g	2.7	8.5
Energy, KJ	975.0	904.0
Thiamine, mg	0.18	0.26
Riboflaving, mg	0.03	0.06
Nicotinic acid, mg	1.4	3.09
Potentialnicotinic acid, mg	1.6	1.7
Pyridoxin, mg	0.04	0.14
Folic acid, mag	27.0	39
Pantothenic acid, mg	0.3	0.6
Biotin, ug	1.0	6.0
Vit. E, mg	trace	0.2
Sodium, mg	540	540
Potassium, mg	100	220
Calcium, mg	100	23
Magnesium, mg	26	93
Phosphorus, mg	97	2.30
Iron,mg	1.7	2.05

Potential nicotinic acid is calculated as 1 mg per 60 mg trytophan

Various types of health bread suggested to meet the dietetic needs of a particular segment of population are :

a) Gluten Free Bread
b) Reduced Fat Bread
c) No Cholesterol Bread
d) No Sugar Bread
e) Low Sodium Bread
f) Reduced Calorie Bread
g) High Fiber Bread
h) High Protein Bread

A) Gluten Free Bread

Here an old proverb"one person's food is another person's poison" is most appropriate. Bread has wheat protein called gluten. It is an important nutrient then, why gluten free bread? Becuase some people especially children have allergy from gluten. They suffer from a diseases called celiac or coeliac disease. It is also known as celiacsprue, non tropical sprue or Gluten sensitive enteropathy (GSE) - a most appropriate term used for this disease. Celiac disease is condition of gluten intolerance in children, sometimes persisting into childhood. Symptoms of celiac disease are listed in Table 2.

Patients recover on a strict-free diet. Wheat, rye, barley oats are deleterious to celiac patients. Maize and rice are tolerated satisfactorily. Suggested explanation of the disease mechanism are deficiency of a specific enzyme in the intestinal mucosa or reduced efficiency of the mucosa as a barrier that normally prevents absorption of the deleterious agents. It has been alleged that gluten may be concerned in the etiology of multiple sclerosis. Consumption of gluten free diet brings benefits to sufferers of this disease. Inhalation of cereal flour causes asthma in some occupatonally exposed individuals such as millers and bakers. Also wheat is that most allergenic of all the cereals.

Table 2. Symptoms of celiac disease

1. Passange of abnormal stools
2. Abdominal distension
3. Loss of wight
4. Anemia
5. Anorexia
6. Stunted growth

It is useless to try to make a normal appearing loaf of bread that contains no gluten. Gluten provides typical form, structure and texture of bread. No other edible substance functions in the same way as gluten. But some efforts are made to develop gluten free bread. Gluten free breads can be prepared from maize starch and some non-cereal ingredients as rice bread. The best can be done to make gluten free bread is to use eggs as the structure forming ingredients and rice or corn flour as the cereal or bulking component. Corn starch can also be used to eliminate any cereal protein. Chances of success are more if piece or loaf size is kept small. Normal fermentation and proofling steps are out of question for such product. Although the addition of fermented liquid at the final mixing might be helpful, degassed beer addition enhances the bread flavour also. Gluten free breads require polymeric substances that mimic the isoplastic properties of gluten in bread doughs. Gluten free breads can be successfully formulated by incorporating gums, soy protein and egg white into non-wheat flours. Gluten free pocket type flat breads compatible with regular wheat bread in key textural attributes can be formulated from a bake mix based on pregelatinized rice flour and corn starch that incorporated methyl cellulose, gum arabic and egg albumin as a gluten replacement. Inclusion of 3g of gum arabic (with methyl cellulose levels 3.10-4, 12 g, egg albumin levels of 2.18-4. 10g) in the bake mix yielded gluten free breads that were compatible with regular wheat bread in the frequency of cracks, separation of layers, rollability, tearing quality first bite harness, masticatory hardness, adhesiveness and cohesiveness. Higher levels of gum arabic results in more cohesive products. Lower levels of (1.37g) gum arabic resulted in loaves that were less cohesive and inferior to wheat bread in rollability. All breads possessed a perceptible corn flavour, a light yellow crumb with apparent waxy patches and a faster rate of staling than that of regular bread.

B) Reduced Fat Bread

Since it is quite obvious that fats and oils with their nine calories per gram creates major problems in the designing of diets for persons desiring to reduce weight. Excess of fat causes various health disorders such as cardiovascular ailments and obesity.

Fat has become the food formulating challenge of the decade. Consumer want fat taken out of food without the taste and texture of the food being adversely effected. The reality is that fat contibutes texture and pleasing mouth feel and positively impacts flavour, intensity and perception. So the food manufacturers continually strive to meet the demands of consumers to reduce fat. They must identify systems that mimic fat's attributes (Table 3) without its disadvantages.

Table 3 Attributed of Fat contributed in baked goods

1. Flavour	2. Viscosity/Body
3. Richness	4. Texture/grain
5. Aeration	6. Tenderness
7. Shortness	8. Levening
9. Lubricity	10. Dough handling
11. Batter stability	

Fat Replacers : Fat replacers are the ingredients used to replace fat in food system. Fat repalcer should be non-toxic, cost effective and able to mimic fat without increasing calorie intake. Various fat mimetic are listed in Table 4.

Table 4 Fate mimetic

1. **Carbohydrate based** : Microcrystalline cellulose, maltodextran modified starches, oatrim, Z-trim, polydextrose, inulin, pectin, hemicellulose.
2. **Protein bases** : Soy protein hydrolysate, casein-concentrates (simplesse), whey protein concentrates, egg white powder, gelatin.
3. **Gums** : Guar, xantahn, gellan curdian.
4. **Synthetic Fat substitutes** : Sucrose polyesters such as olestra, esterfied propoxylated glycerol and polysiloxane, Trialakoxycitrate (TAC).

When fat is to be removed and replaced with water and other ingredients, a total formulation approach must be used to build in all the desired properties. The fat mimetic impart sensory characters such as creaminess and smoothness. Body cling and firmness are developed with addition of maltodextrin, corn syrups and grains. Emulsifiiers are incorporated to interact with carbohydrates and proteins and to modify tenderness, reduce set back and provide lubrication. Flavours are added to replace the flavour profiles that had been provided by fats and oils. Plant derived carbohydrate formulations for fat replacement has some benefits over protein bases substitutes, gum formulations, sucrose polyesters, synthetic substitutes. They are often more effective in reducing the water activiy in a low or reduced fat formula. These carbohydrates are hydrophilic due to a large number of hydroxyl bonds available to bind with water olecules, creating a carbohydrate water network that can mimic the texture of fat. Physical side effects some times associated with synthetic replacements are not apparent.

Plant carbohydrates are completely degestible as part of the normal metabolic process. The ideal carbohydrates fat mimetic will possess a structure to bind and orient water in such a way to provide mouthfeel like fat. Then clear the palate in same length of time as fat does. Several ways to use carbohydrate fat replacers in food are :-

i. Mimetic is simply dry blended with other ingredients. These blends are then mixed with water and used.

ii. Mimetic is slurried and sheered to prepare a cream which has fat like characters. Then cream is incorporated with other ingredients to prepare a finished food.

Recommended Fate intake 30% of total calorie need per day e.g. adult require 18000 kcal/day needs 60 gm fat (540kcal from fat).

(c) No Cholesterol Bread

Cholesterol is the chief sterol in the body found in all tissues especially liver, nerves, brain and adrenal cortex. It is synthesized in liver (endogenous cholesterol) and found in animal products (exogenous cholesterol) as egg yolk, liver and other granular organs, milk fat, butter and meats. More than 200mg/dl of cholesterol causes atherosclerotic diseases. Atherosclerotic is due to patchy deposits of various materials in the inner side of arteries. Materials are fatty substances such as cholestrol, triglycerides, phospholipids, complex carbodyrates and lipoproteins. This leads to narrowing of lumen and decresed blood carrying capaciy. sufferer should take low cholesteril and saturated fats diet. Cholesterol content of selected foods is given in Table 5.

Table 5 : Cholesterol content of selected foods, (10g edible portion)

Food Item	Cholesterol (mg)
Barley bran	0
Corn germ	0
Oats germ	0
Rice bran	0
Wheat bran	0
Wheat germ	0
Whole egg	548
Egg yolk	1602
Egg white	0
Whole milk	14
Butter	219
Lard	766

No cholesterol bread can be made simply by eliminating any animal fat or ingredients made from animal fats. Formulation changes required are minimal. Any Baker can easily make them with little or no effect on the finished product. Vegetable shortening can be used as substitute. They should have similar physical characters as animal shortening being replaced. Following points should be checked before making "no cholesterol' claim :

- emulsifiers are made from animal fats.
- Pan greases may contain animal fat
- Washes to impart glossiness to the crust may contain material with cholesterol content.

D) Sugar Free Bread

We want sugar free bread mainly for 2 purposes.

1) To reduce the calorie content for obese persons.

2) To maintain blood glucose level in blood for diabetic patients

Sugars are carbohydrates giving 4 kcal/g of food. For sugar free bread laternative sweetners are available with no nutritive value.

Alternative Sweeteners : Sweetening agents other than table sugar or surcrose syrups, honey and molasses. They are grouped as nutritive and non-nutritive sweeteners.

Nutritive : Fructose, glucose, glycine, mannitol, sorbitol, xylitol.

Non-nutritive : Low calorie sugar substitutes used for diabetics and obese persons are aspartame, saccharin, cyclamate, dulcin etc. These sweeteners are several times sweeter than sucrose. To reduce their sweetness, polydextrose as bulking agent is used. It reduces their sweetness. Relative sweetness of various substances are given in Table 6.

Table 6. Relative sweetness of various substances.

(Sweetness compared to sucrose as 100)	
Saccharin	300
Aspartame	150
Cyclamate	30

In white bread formulation, sugar is present in very small amount (1.8g) so it do not have much influence on the health of diabetics. Most of the carbohydrates in bread is in the form of' starch. Some glucose and maltose is formed in the dough after water is added, provided amylases; represent, but only a small quantity of sugar remains at the end of a normal fermentation.

E) Low Sodium Bread

High concentration of sodium in body fluids causes various diseases as hypertension or high-, blood pressure and edema. High blood pressure is due to presistent elevation of blood pressure above normal. Normal blood pressure is 120/80mm Hg. Hypertensive person suffers from dizziness. frequent headaches, impaired vision, shortness of breadth, chest pain, failing memory, In edema there is swelling of the tissues becuase of presence of abnormally large amount of fluids in tissue spaces. This is due to disturbance in the mechanisms involved in fluid exchange. In these disturbed states intake of sodium should be reduced.

The sodium content of wheat flour is very low. So, in bread, sodium is contributed try added salt, leavening acids and sodium bicarbonate. Three slices of bread contribute 1g salt, which is equivalent to 12% of the recommended intake of 3.2 g. sodium/day. Daily consumption of [3 slices of bread with the NaCl/KCl blend could reduce consumption of NaCl by 0.58% of the recommended daily intake of 3.2 g sodium/day. So 50:50 KCl/NaCl mixture can be successfully used in bread making. But yeast does not respond to KCl in same way as it responds to NaCl. So baker will have to establish new times for fermentation and proofing. Lite salt (1:1 NaCl/Kcl : alongwith additional sucrose, milk replacers, soy oils and dought conditioner in bread formula has been used successfully.

Salt in dough effects a number of processing responses but the main reason for which bakers use this ingredient is for enhancement of the flavour of the finished product-. It also inhibits fermentation. It also improves crumb colour and grain in bread.

F) Reduced Calorie Bread

Fats give 9 Kcal/gm of food. Carbohydrates give 4kcal/g of food and proteins gives 4 Kcal/g of food. so to make reduces calorie bread, we have to replace above components with non-caloric ingredients.

A low calories food must not have more than 0.4k calories/g. A food may be called as "Reduced Calorie" if the calories are reduces by at least one third that of the traditional product Becuase of the complex nature of bread and its sensitivity to formula modification the usual approaches to calorie reduction are seldom practical. Use of non digestible substances such a purified cellulose (with no calorie addition) can be done to replace flour. Corn bran or rice bran can also be used. Calorie reduction can also be done by replacing sugar with non-caloric sweeteners such as aspartame Bulking agents which do not supply energy are used as filler ingredients. Non caloric fat substitutes such as gums, pectins, sucrose polyesters can be used. Polydextrose is also used. It is a polymer of dextrose, providing only one calorie per gram.

Another approach has been tried to reduce not the calories per unit weight but the calories per serving. A serving being defined as a certain number of slices, usually two Calorie : reduction is accomplished by reducing the weight of a slice generally by making it tinner but sometimes by modigying the height or width. There is some logic to this approach because genenrally two slices per sandwich would be consumed whether the slice weighed one ounce or three quarters of an ounce Some manufacturers have tried to puff up the bread so that it has same dimensions as regular bread.

(C) High Fiber Bread

Fiber is the protion of plant material in diet which are resist ant to digestion by enzymes produced by man". Simply dietary fiber is called unabsorbed and undigested portion of the food. The components of fiber that can be chemically characterized include :

Insoluble fibers - Cellulose, hemicellulose, lignin, insoluble gums and pentosans.

Soluble fibers - Soluble germs, soluble pectin and polysaccharides.

Recommendation of total fiber consumption is 25-30g/day of which about one-fourth should be soluble. Lack of dietary fiber in the diet causes diverticular diseases, coronory heart disease, cancer of colon or diabetes, constipation. Diverticular disease is characterised by outpouchngs of the mucous membrane through gaps or weak spots in the circular muscles of colon. This results in abdominal tenderness, distention, pain in intestianl spasm Major sources ill dietary fiber supplementation of bakery foods are listed in Table 7.

Table 7. Sources of fiber suggested for Bakery foods.

	Source	%TDC (True digestible cellulose)
Cereals		
	Wheat genn	16.9
	Wheatbran	47.1
	Oat bran	17.2
	Barley	19.1
	Rice	3.1
	Millet	8.5
	Corn bran	89.02
	Purified cellulose	Close to 100% fiber on dry weight basis
	Raisins	4.43
Legumes		
	Cow pea	30.7
	Lime bran	21.2

1. Some bakers use powdered cellulose, a FDA approved purified substance derived from-wood, to provide the fiber without adding calories.
2. some opt for increased amounts of bran, the fiber source in whole wheat bread.
3. Enrichment of foods by addition of high fiber cereal grain components is another way to increase fiber in take.
4. Combination of cellulose, grain and legume fiber can also be used to increase amount of fiber in bread.

Several adjustments have to be made for benefit of quality of high fiber bread as given in Table 8.

Table 8

Effect of high fiber in bread	Compensation
1. Fibrous material dilutes the gluten protein , volume is decreased.	Addition of vital wheat gluten. Use of strong flour.
2. Fiber tends to cut gluen strands.	Addition of SSL (Sodium steroyl-2-lactylate) is helpful.
3. Fiber has high absorption and it Interferes with hydration ration of gluten protein.	A high amount of H_2O is added.
4. High amount of added water makes the product especially susceptible. to mold growth.	Adequate amount of propionate is added.
5. Care must be taken to avoid under mixing, because the point of full dough development is hard to judge in the presence of added fiber.	

H) High Protein Bread

Some people suffer from deficiency of proteins. They are recommended to eat high protein breads. To make high protein breads, the addiion of say flour to a bread flour so far has been the most satisfactory method of increasing the protein concentration in bread. Soy flour also increases the quality of the bread-protein becuase lysine is the limiting amino acid in wheat flour but not in soy flour. Addition of synthetic glycolipids increases the levels of supplementation that are possible.

Gluten powder produced commercially is also used o increase the protein contens. Deficiency of proein causes a disease called Marasmus. supplementation of protein can also he done by addition of whey extract, casein and yeast. High proein breads and protein breads must conain not less than 22% protein, while gluen bread must contain not less than 16% formulation for health breads are given in Table 9)

Table 9. Formula for health breads (On percent basis)

Ingredient	No salt added	No Fat added	Gluten Free	Cholesterol Free	High Fibre
Flour	56.7	57.9	0.0	53.6	50.3
Water	35.0	34.7	35.8	34.9	35.2
Yeast	1.1	1.2	2.5	2.7	1.2
Salt	0.0	1.0	0.8	1.3	1.0
Shortening	2.5	0.0	2.5	0.0	3.0
Dried sltim milk	1.7	1.7	0.0	2.6	2.0
Sugar	3.0	2.9	0.0	2.0	2.0
Liquid whole eggs	0.0	0.0	3.3	0.0	0.0
Diastatic malt syrup	0.0	0.6	1.2	1.3	0.5
See Notes	0.0	0.0	(1)	(2)	(3)

Chapter - 20

Chicken Patties

Spent hens refer to old and culled chickens, which have completed their productive and reproductive phase of life. Meat from such birds is tougher, less tender and less juicy due to high collagen content and high degree of cross linkages. Spent hens also have higher proportions of low value by-products than broiler. Products prepared from spent hen meat are not readily accepted by the consumers mainly due to their toughness.

An attempt has been made to improve the quality of chicken patties prepared from spent hen meat and by-products through incorporation of spray dried skim milk powder (SMP) which has long been used in processed foods as binders to improve water and fat retention on cooking and to modify rheological and other physical properties.

Raw Materials

Broiler spent hens of 50 to 60 weeks of age were procured from the Central Avian Research Institute, Izatnagar and slaughtered at the Experimental Abattoir of the Institute. The dressed hens were deboned manually and meat as well as by products such as skin, fat, gizzard and heart were collected. SMP (brand : Anik Spray ; make : Brooke Bond Lipton India Ltd., Kollkata) was obtained from the local market of Izatnagar. The average contens of moisture, protein, fat and ash in the spent hen meat and by-products mixture were 63.69, 16.15, 19.42 and 0.74% respecvely while those in SMP were 4.5, 53.6, 7.0 and 8.7% respectively. Fresh, peeled and sliced onion and garlic (3:1, w/w) were used for making condiment mix which were ground in a domestic mixer to a fine paste before use.

Preparation of Chicken Patties

Chicken patties was formulated based on the natural proportion of lean meat (60.2%), skin (21.5%), fat (15.5%) as well as gizzard and heart in the ration of 82/:18 (2.8%) as present in spent hen carcasses. Meat and by Products (4 Kg) were minced using a mincer (make : Seydelmann, Germany), added with common salt, sodium py-rophosphate and ice cold water at 2.0, 0.5 and 2.0% levels respectively and 120 ppm of sodium nitrite, chopped for 1 min in a bowl chopper (make : Seydelmann, Germany) followed by addition of calculated quantity of skin, gizzard and heart and chopping for 30 sec. Condiments (3.0%) and ice cold water (5.0%) were added to the bowl chopper and chopped for 30 sec. This was followed by addition of SMP separately at 1.0, 2.0 and 3.0% levels to the contents, chopping for 1 min, addition of 1.5% chicken masala powder (brand : MDH, Gurgaon) and 3.0% wheat flour (maida) and rechopping for 1 min.

Table 1 : Effect of differen levels of skim milk powder on physico-chemical parameters of chicken patties (mean+SE)*

Parameters	Control	Levels of skim milk powder (%)		
		1	2	3
Yield (%)	83.78±1.04	83.37±0.98	85.30±1.49	85.10+0.86
Moisture (%)	57.09±1.21	57.94±0.77	58.11±1.06	58.67+0.72
Protein (%)	13.90±0.57	13.98±0.65	14.58±0.99	15.04+0.94
Ether Extract (%)	19.17±1.33	20.82±1.09	18.90±1.25	20.49+1.14
Ash (%)	02.23±0.06[ac]	02.07±0.04[b]	02.18+0.04[bc]	02.27+0.06[c]
Shear force value (kg/cm^2)	00.60±0.03	00.60±0.03	00.57+0.04	00.63+0.04
Product pH	06.39±0.05[a]	06.49±0.04[ab]	06.51+0.04[b]	06.56+0.03[b]
Emulsion pH	06.35±0.04[a]	06.42±0.02[ab]	06.48+0.04b[c]	06.52+0.03[c]
Emulsion stability (%)	85.05±1.28[a]	86.32±1.12[ab]	86.11+0.86[ab]	88.70+1.09[b]

* Means with different superscripts row-wise differ significantly (P<0.05)

Patties were formed (each from 70 g of emulsion), moulded into round shape (diameter 7.5 cm, height 1.5 cm), placed on cooking trays presmerared with vegetable oil and cooked in a preheated hot air oven at 180+5^{0}C for 25 min. After 15 min. of cooking, patties were turned upide down adn cooking continued for another to 10 min. to attain the core temperature of 73+2°c Control patties were preapared in the same manner as described above except that no SMP was used in its prepartion.

Analysis

Chicken patties were analysed for moisture, protein, fat and ash contents employing AOAC methods, pH and shear force value using a Warner-Bratzler Shear Press (make : G.R. Elect. Mfg. Co., USA), Emulsion was analysed for pH and stability.

Sensory Evaluation

Chicken patties were evaluated for appearance and colour (AC), flavour, juiciness, texture and overall acceptability (OA) using a 8-point descriptive scale by a panel of seven judges comprising scientists of the

Institute. The judges received prior training about various desirable and undesirable properties of chicken patties. In the scale, 8 denoted extremely desirable and 1 indicated extremely undesirable.

Results and Discussion

The physico-chemical and sensory properties of chicken patties are presented in Tables 1 and 2 respectively. Level of SMP significantly ($p<0.05$) affected emulsion pH and highly significantly ($p<0.01$) influenced flavour and texture of the products.

The yield of chicken patties prepared by using SMP separately at 1.0 (I), 2.0 (II) and 3.0% (III) levels were higher than that of control which might be due to higher retention of moisture in the treated products. Addition of 3.5% SMP to frankfurter formulation resulted in increased yield of the product . Level of SMP was directly related to the contents of moisture and protein as well as pH of emulsion and the products. Hung and Zayas reported increased capacity for holding water and decrease in cooking losses of sausages batters containing nonfat dried milk (NFDM). The protein, ether extract and shear force values of the control chicken patties did not vary significantly from those of the treated products contrary to the findings of Hung and Zayas in SMP added frankfurters. Ash content of the chicken patties varied from 2.07 to 2.27% Significantly ($P<0.05$) lower ash content in I than that of control and III and lower pH of control and its emulsion vis-a-vis those of II and III were noticed. In genenral, addition of SMP to the chicken patties formulations improved the stability of the resultant emulsions. The present findings on pH and emulsion stability agreed well with the reports of Anjaneyuluet al., for chicken sausages.

The average scores obtained by chicken patties for AC, flavour, juicines and texture ranged from 6.76 to 7.07, 6.50 to 7.10, 6.88 to 7.17 and 6.69 to 7.33 respectively. Scores for flavour and texture of control differed significantly ($P<0.05$) from those of II and III while AC and juiciness of the products did not get affected significantly by the use of SMP in the product formulations. According to Anjaneyulu et al., chicken sausages containing non-fat dried milk were rated better than control with respect to flavour, texture and juiciness. Overall acceptability scores of chicken patties did not differe significantly among the treated products. The overall acceptability score of only III was significantly ($P<0.05$) higher than that of control. Leve of SMP was directly related to the scores obtained by the chicken patties for AC, flavour, texture and overall acceptability.

It is concluded that addition of 3% SMP to the chicken patties formulation resulted in better stability in emulsion, appearance and colour, flavour, texture and overall acceptability in the products as compared to control and those prepared with other levels of SMP.

Table 2 : Effect of different levels of skim milk powder on sensory properties of chicken patties (mean+SE)*

Parameters	Control	Levels of skim milk powder (%)		
	1	2	3	4
Appearance and colour	6.76+0.10	6.83+0.11	6.95+0.10	7.07+12
Flavour	6.50+0.11[a]	6.69+0.11[a]	7.00+0.11[b]	7.10+0.12[b]
Juiciness	6.88+11[a]	7.00+0.13[a]	7.17+0.10	7.00+0.12
Texture	6.69+0.11[a]	6.81+0.10[a]	7.12+0.11[b]	7.33+0.10[b]
Overall acceptability	6.62+0.11[a]	6.71+0.02[ab]	6.88+0.11[ab]	7.00+0.11[b]

Means with different superscripts row-wise differ significantly (P<0.05)

Chapter - 21

Noodles

The consumption of pasta products, particularly noodles is increasing steadily in devel-oping countries as a result of increased industrialization and urbanization, increased job opportunities for women, increased socialization, increase in number of school going children, life style and food habits of middle income group and above all better quality and availability of processed foods.

Durum wheat is the best raw material for processing into a pasta that usually has a good texture, resists surface disintegration and retains a firm structure when cooked[2]. Durum while high in total protein content among wheat flours is deficient in lysine-one of the essential amino acids. Legumes, on the other hand, are excellent sources of protein (20-40%), carbohydrates (50-60%), fat (2-3%), B coplex vitamins and minerals (2-4%) but are dificient in sulphur containing amino acids like methicnine and cystine but quite rich in lysine. It is, therefore, often emphasized that legume seed proteins are a natural supplement to cereal grain protein in producing an verall essential amino acid balance[3]. Studies conducted by various workers employing cereal pulse combinations (wheat with green gram, Bengal gram and soybean) for development of nutritious bread, biscuit and vermicelli have been successful[4,5], The noodles provide an excellent medium into which ingredients of desired nutrient density may be added as they blend well during extrusion[6].

Material and Methods

Preparation of Experimental Samples : Thirty kilograms of durum wheat (variety PDW-233) was cleaned, freed of extraneous substances and conditioned at 17 per cent moisture for 72 housrs at room temperature. Milling was done on Italian semolina mill (Namad) fitted with rotary sieve having bolting cloths of 66, 54 and 42-mesh size. The mill provided three semolina fractions viz. fine semolina, medium sized semolina and a mixture of bran and coarse semolina. Fine and mesium sized semolina was combined while semolina from bran was separated using a purifier.

The semolina so obtained was further pruified using 180 um mesh in a Retsch sifter for 7 minutes at 50 rpm to separate the flour and dried under fan until it achieved a desired moisture content of 10 per cent.

Noodles

Pulse flours were prepared from green gram. Bengal gram and soybean. Green gram (variety ML-613) was cleaned and pearled in a Barley pearler and then grounded in a stone mill to the level that it would blend well with semolina. Soybean (variety SL-295) was similarly pearled and then milled in Cemotec sample mill. the obtained flour was kept overnight in an oven at a temperature of 80-90°C to inactivate enzymes and to remove odour form flour. For defating the soyflour, a slurry of soyflour with petroleum ether in the ratio of 1:2 was made which was kept for 24 hours. The flasks were then shaken on a shaker for one hour and contents were filtered using Whatman filter paper no.1 to separate the oil and defatted flour was kept in a hot air oven at a temperature of 50-60°C till completely dry and ether evaporation occured . The procedure for obtaining Bengal gram dal flour (variety GL-769) was same as for green flour.

Preparation of Nutritious Noodles

For making nutritious noodles of 15 different combinations, semolina was supplmented with different pulse flours at 5, 10, 15, 20, and 25 percent levels with 100% semolina as the control sample. Semolina and pulse flours were weighed in required amounts and mixed well by passing through 600 um sieve. In 700g of the flour mixture, 245ml water (35%) was added and mixed thoroughly with hand so that no pocket of dry semolina was left. The mixed material was then extruded as a uniform strip in an extruder. The strip was cut into small pieces manually and again fed to the extruder in which vacuum was created; the extrusion screw was rotated to extrude the material and noodle strands were obtained through a round die fitted at the outlet. The prepared noodles, hung on aluminium rods, were dried in a drying chamber at a temperature of 37°C for 16 hours. The dried noodle strands were cut to a length of 10" with the help of scissors and packed in polythene bags after labelling to preserve them for cooking and analysis. The moisture content of each sample at the time of packaging was less than 8 per cent. Two most popular brands of noodles available in the local market were obtained for comparing them with laboratory samples.

Determination of Cooking Quality of Noodles

Ten gram of dried noodles were added to 300ml of boiling water, cooked for 12 minutes in beakers covered with aluminium foil to avoid the loss of water. After 12 minutes, the beaker was kept for 10 minutes at room temperature. Then the volume of water left in the beaker was measured to know how much water was absored by noodles. Out of that, 50ml of water was preserved in a separate beaker; dried at 105°C and weight of the residue left after drying was noted. To 100ml of tap water in a 250ml cylinder, added the boiled noodles and noted the increase in volume. With the help of a sieve, noodles were separated from water and transferred in a plate and evaluated. The criteria used for grading the cooked noodles is given in Table 1.

Table 1 : Criteria for cooking quality of noodles.

Attributes	*Score*
Stickiness	
Nil	4
Slight	3
Sticky	2
Very Sticky	1
Consistency	
Very good	4
Good	3
Normal	2
Poor	1
Clumping	
None	4
Little	3
Much	2
Excessive	1
Overall Evaluation	
Stickiness nil (4) but consistency :	
Very good (4)	10
Good (3)	9-8
Normal (2)	7-6
Slightly sticky (3) but consistency :	
Good (3)	5
Normal (2)	4
Sticky (2) but consistency	
Normal(2)	3
Poor (1)	2
Very Sticky (1) but consistency	
Poor	1

As per the final grading, noodles which got 1 to 3 marks were considered bad, 4 to 6 were considered medium while the ones which gott 7-10 marks were considered good[7].

Sensory Evaluation of Noodles

The supplemented noodles were cooked with mixed vegetables (cabbage, carrots and capsicum), spices and sauces by using the standard method and evaluated by a panel of eight judges using sensory analysis score card (9 points scale ranging from like extremely to dislike extremely). Code numbers were given to each sample so that judges may not have any bias for particular type of sample. Each sample was repeated thrice during the course of evaluation. The judges were askied to score the samples for flavour profile (colour, taste, flavour) and texture profile (hardness and adhesiveness) along with overall acceptability scores.

Mean scores of organoleptic evaluation for each character were calculated and statistically analyzed to determine the most acceptable level of pulse supplementation in the prepared nutritious noodles.

Results and Discussion

Sixteen type of noodles were prepared in the laboratory by supplementing durum semolina with green gram flour, defatted soybean flour and Bengal gram flour at 5, 10, 15, 20, and 25 percent levels. The water uptake ratio of noodles prepared from durum semolina alone (Table 2) was 5.0 while the value for noodles commercially available in the market (Sailor and Chinese vegetarian noodles) was 4.0. Addition of dal flour increased water uptake ratio by the noodles of blends from 5.0 to 6.5 highest value for noodles prepared by 20 percent supplementation of Bengal gram dal flour. A range of 5.4-7.1 in water uptake ratio has been reported for Indian durum[8].

Table 2. Effect of cooking noodles from cereal pulse combinations on water uptake ratio, volume expansion and gruel solid loss.

Sample	*Water uptake Ratio(g/g)*	*Volume expansion (ml/g)*	*Gruel solid loss (%)*
Ds	5.0	5.8	5.82
Sailor	4.0	4.8	9.20
Chinese Vegetarian Noodles	4.0	4.6	8.80
DsG5	6.0	5.2	8.60
DsG10	5.0	4.8	9.10
DsG15	5.0	4.4	9.70
DsG20	5.5	4.2	10.50
DsG25	6.0	4.2	11.04
DsG5	6.0	5.2	8.0
DsS10	5.0	4.6	8.56
DsS15	5.0	4.4	9.20
DsS20	5.5	4.4	9.90

DsS25	5.5	3.2	10.25
DsB5	6.0	5.4	7.80
DsB10	5.5	5.2	8.48
DsB15	6.0	5.2	9.04
DsB20	6.5	5.0	9.70
DsB25	6.0	4.8	10.35

Table 3: Cooking quality characteristics of noodles prepared from durum semolina and its blends with green gram dal flour, defatted soybean dal flour and Bengal gram dal flour.

Sample	*Stickines*	*Consistency*	*Clumping*	*Overall Evaluation*
Ds	4	2	3	7-6
Sailor	4	2	3	7-6
Chinese Vegetarian Noodles	4	2	3	7-6
DsG5	4	2	3	7-6
DsG10	4	2	3	7-6
DsG15	4	3	4	9-8
DsG20	4	3	4	9-8
DsG25	3	2	2	4
DsS5	4	2	3	7-6
DsS10	4	2	3	7-6
DsS15	4	3	4	9-8
DsS20	3	2	2	4
DsS25	3	2	2	4
DsB5	4	2	3	7-6
DsB10	4	2	3	7-6
DsB15	3	2	2	4
DsB20	3	2	2	4
DsB25	3	2	2	4

Ds : Durum semolina

DsG$_{5}$, DsG$_{10}$, DsG$_{15}$, DsG$_{20}$, DsG$_{25}$: Durum semolina with green gram dal flour at 5, 10, 15, 20 and 25 percent level, respectively.

DsS$_{5}$, DsS$_{10}$, DsS$_{15}$, DsS$_{20}$, DsS$_{25}$: Durum semolina with defatted soybean dal flour at 5, 10, 15, 20 and 25 per cent level, respectively.

DsB$_{5}$, DsB$_{10}$, DsB$_{15}$, DsB$_{20}$, DsB$_{25}$: Durum semolina with Bengal gram dal flour at 5, 10, 15, 20 and 25 percent level, respectively.

Noodles

The volume of wheat semolina noodles on cooking was 5.8 ml/g while the values for Sailor and Chines vegetarian noodles (4.8 and 6ml/g, respectively) were lower than sample prepared in the laboratory. These values are in close agreement with results of Singh (1994)[9] who reported that volume of wheat semolina noodles on cooking increased ranging from 5 to 9ml with an average of 6.5ml. Addition of dal flour decreased the volume increase on cooking in all three pulse supplemented noodles. This decease in volume expansion was higher when soybean dal flour was used as compared to green gram dal flour and Bengal gram dal flour.

Gruel solid loss in durum semolina alone noodles was found to be 5.82 per cent for laboratory sample while Sailor and Chines vegetarian noodles had 9.2 and 8.8 per cent, respectively. Addition of increasing level of dal flour to durum semolina simultaneously increased the gruel solid loss per cent ranging from 8.6 to 11.04 per cent, 8.0 to 10.25 per cent and 7.8 to 10.35 per cent at 5 and 25 per cent levels respectively for green gram, soybean flour and Bengal gram supplemented noodles. It has been reported[10] that pasta from soft wheat supplemented with 10-30 per cent cowpea meal had higher cooking loss (8.0-9.2%) as compared to 5.3 per cent for durum semolina.

The cooked noodles were also evaluated for attributes like stickiness, consistency and clumping and overall evaluation. The control noodles and market samples were non-sticky with score of 4, normal in consistency with score of 2 and overall evaluation score was 6-7 (Table3). Addition of green gram flour up to 20 percent level produced excellent noodles (overall evaluation score of 9-8) which were non-sicky (score of 4), good in consistency (score of 3) with no clumping (score of 4). But 25 per cent pulse supplementation resulted in slightly sticky noodles. Similarly soy flour supplemented noodles were rated as excellent up to 15 per cent level and Bengal gram dal flour supplemented noodles up to 10 per cent.

Organoleptic Evaluation of Noodles

The mean scores for colour for noodles with durum semolina with 5 per cent Bengal gram flour, DsB5, (7.0) were significantly lower (P<0.01) than DsG5 (7.71) and DsS5 (7.7) and market samples. However, differences between dal flour supplemented samples at 10 and 15 per cent levels were statistically non-significant from each other.

The mean scores for tastes of noodles with durum semolina with 5 per cent soybean (DsS5) were significantly lower (P<0.01) than control market samples as well as DsG5 (Durum semolina with 5% green gram flour) when green gram dal flour was added at 10 per cent level to durum semolina, mean scores were significantly higher than DsS10 and DsB10 noodles indicating that green gram dal flour could be first preference for enhancement of nutritional value of conventional noodles. But at 15 per cent level of pulse supplementation, non-significant differences in taste were found in all types of noodles.

While evaluating noodles for flavour, organoleptic score ranged from 7.72 to 7.88 for green gram dal blends which were regarded as superior and better in flavour, as against commercially available market samples. Similarly for DsS15 (Durum semolina with 15% soybean flour) the score of 7.5 was closer to the control noodle samples. This shows that soy flour flavour was not distinguishable or detectable due to addition of sauces in the cooked noodles. However, addition of increasing level of Bengal gram dal flour resulted in decline in score from 7.63 for DsB5 to 7.13 for DsB10 noodles.

In the texture profile, the control noodles had mean score of 2.5 for hardness which was slightly higher than the value for market samples (2.44). The firmer the bite, the better would be the texture of the noodles. When durum semolina was supplemented with green gram and defatted soybean dal and Bengal gram dal flours, mean value for hardness was increased.

The control samples prepared in the laboratory had a mean score of 2.92 for adhesiveness as they were non-sticky and the value was significantly ($P<0.01$) higher than market sample. However, increasing the level of dal flour in the noodles significantly, decreased the score for adhesiveness.

The mean overall acceptability scores for control noodles was 7.75 indicating that they were liked very much by the judges. For green gram dal and defatted soybean dal flour supplemented noodles, the scores ranged from 7.50 to 7.67 for former and 7.25 to 7.46 for latter. Some broken strands and splitting of noodles from the centre was however observed. While 5 per cent Bengal gram dal flour supplemented noodles had mean score of 7.17 which was decreased to 6.88 at 10 per cent level. The major factor for their comparatively as overall acceptability was that the product failed to retain the length of noodle strands and were broken into small pieces like seviyan after drying only.An ideal level of substituting pulse flours to wheat semolina that would optimize nutritional quality without any significant adverse effect on functional properties or product quality was found to be 15 percent for green gram and soybean and 5 per cent for Bengal gram. The noodles supplemented with pulse flours can also have acceptable cooking quality and desirable organoleptic properties on the basis of colour, taste, flavour and texture as indicated by results of sensory evaluation. The problem of splitting of noodles strands on cooking for control and supplemented noodles was observed.

Chapter - 22

Asian Noodle Technology

Asian Noodles versus Pasta

Asian noodles are different from pasta products in the ingredients used, the processes involved and their consumption patterns. Pasta is made from semolina (coarse flour usually milled from durum wheat) and water, and extruded through a metal die under pressure. It is a dried product. After cooking, pasta is often eaten with sauces. Asian noodles are characterized by thin strips, slit from sheeted dough that has been made from flour (hard and soft wheats), water and salt (common salt or alkaline salt). Noodles are often consumed in soup. Eggs can be added to each product to give a firmer texture.

The Basics

Wheat flour is the main ingredient for making Asian noodels. About three parts of flour are usually mixed with one part of salt or alkaline salt solution to form a crumbly dough. The dough is compressed between a Series of rolls to form a dough sheet. The gluten network is developed during the sheeting process, contributing to the noodle textue. The sheeted dough is then slit to produce noodles. The noodles are now ready for ;sale, or are further processed to prolong shelf life, to modify eating characteristics or to facilitate preparation by the consumer.

In the preparation of instant fried noodles, the steaming process causes the starch to swell and gelatinize. The addition of alkaline salts (kan sui, a mixture of sodium and potassium carbonates) in some Chinese type noodles gives them a yellow color and a firmer, more elastic texture.

Noodle Processing Technology

The basic processing steps for machine-made noodles are outlined in Figure 1, These steps involve mixing raw material, resting the crumbly dough, sheeting the dough into two dough sheets, compounding the two sheets into one, gradually sheeting the dough sheet into a specified thickness and slitting into noodle strands. Noodle strands are further processed according to noodle types.

Mixing Ingredients

Mixing formula ingredients is often carried out in a horizontal or vertical mixer for 10-15 minutes. Since he horizontal mixer seems to have better mixing resuls, it is more commonly used han the vertical one in commercial noodle production.

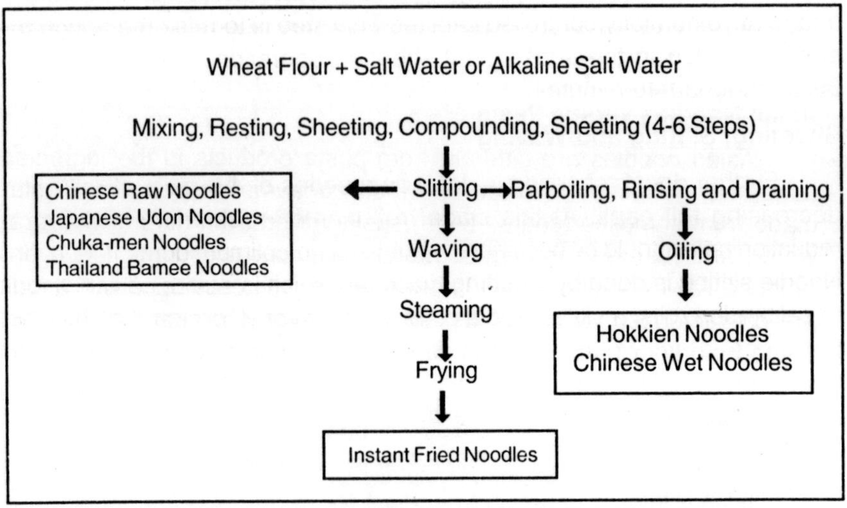

Mixing results in the formation of a crumbly dough with small and uniform particle sizes.

Since the water addition level is relatively low (vs. bread doughs), gluten development in noodle dough during mixing is minimized. This improves the dough sheetability, sheeted dough smoothness and uniformity. Limited water absorption also slows down noodle Discoloration and reduces the amount of waer to be taken out during the final drying or frying processes.

Flour proteins, pentosans and starch (especially damaged starch) determine the flour water absorption level. Variations in noodle dough water absorption among different flours is generally within 2-3%, and this is usually determined by dough handling properties and is not so sensitive to processing as is that in bread dough. However, flour particle sizes and their distribution affect the time water penetrates into the flour.

Dough Resting

After mixing, the dough pieces are rested for 20-40 minutes before compounding. Dough resting helps water penetrate into dough particles evenly, resulting in a smoother and less streaky dough after sheeting. In commercial production, the dough is rested in a receiving container while being stirred slowly.

Sheeting and Compounding

The rested, crumbly dough pieces are divided into two portions, each passing through a pair of sheeting rolls to form a noodle dough sheet. The two sheets are then combined (compounded) and passed through a second set of sheeting rolls to form a single sheet. The roll gap is adjusted so that the dough thickness reduction is between 20-40%. The combined dough sheet is often carried on a multi-layer conveyor belt located in a temperature and relative humidity controlled cabinet. This step is to relax the dough for easy reduction in the subsequent sheeting operation. The resting time takes about 30-40 minutes.

Sheeting, Slitting and Waving

Further dough sheeting is done on a series of 4-6 pairs of rolls with decreasing roll gaps. At this stage, roll diameter, sheeting speed and reduction ratio should be considered to obtain and optimum dough reduction. Noodle slitting is done by a cutting machine, which is equipped with a pair of calibration rolls, a slitter, and a cutter or a waver. The final dough sheet thickness is set on the calibration rolls according to noodle type and measured using a thickness dial gauge.

Noodle width determines the size of noodle slitter to be used (noodle width, mm=30/slitter number). The sheet is cut noodle strands of desired width with a slitter.

Noodles can be either square or round in shape by using various slitters. Noodle strands are cut into a desirable length by a cutter. At this stage, Chinese raw noodle, Japanese udon noodle, chuka-men and Thailand bamee noodle making is complete. For making instant noodles, noodle strands are waved before steaming and cutting.

Cooking Noodles

Cooking processes include parboiling, boiling and steaming. Hokkien noodles and Chinese wet noodles are usually parboiled for 45-90 seconds to achieve 80-90% gelatinization in starch. The noodles are then coated with 1-2% edible vegetable oil to prevent the strands from sticking together. Parboiled noodles have an extended shelf-life (2-3 days) and high weight gain (60-70%). They are quickly re-cooked by boiling or stir-frying prior to consumption.

Japanese udon noodles are boiled for 10-15 minutes. rinsed and cooled in running water, steeped in dilute acidic water before packing, and further steamed for more than 30 seconds in a pressurized steamer. This type of noodle usually has a shelf-life of 6 months to one year. It is also called longevity noodle. Several steps can be taken to assure optimal cooking-

- the weight of cooking water is at least 10 times that of the uncooked noodles.
- the size of the boiling pot is properly chosen,
- the pH of the boiling water is 5.5-6.0,
- the cooking time is precisely controlled to give optimal results to the product, and
- the cooking water temperature is carefully maintained at 98-100°C throughout the boiling process.

In making instant noodles, the wavy noodle-strands are conveyed to a steamer to cook the noodles. As mentioned earlier, the purpose of steaming is to gelatinize the starch and fix the noodle waves. The steaming time varies according to noodle size, but can be determined by squeezing a noodle strand beween two clear glass plates. If the white noodle core disappears, the noodles are well cooked. Steam temperature, steam pressure, and steaming time are key factors affecting the product quality.

Drying Noodles

Noodle drying can be achieved by air drying, deep frying or vaccum drying. Air drying process has been applied to many noodle types such as Chinese raw noodles, japanese udon noodles, steamed and airdried instant noodles, and others. Air drying usually takes 5-8 hours to dry regular noodles (long and straight) and 30-40 minutes to dry steamed and air-dried instant noodles. Drying by frying takes only a few minutes. Vacuum drying of frozen noodles is a newer Technology, making it possible to produce premium quality products.

For the manufacture of regular dry noodles, raw noodle strands of a certain length are hung on rods in a drying chamber with controlled temperature and relative humidity. Air drying usually involves multistage processes since too rapid drying causes noodle checking, similar to spaghetti drying. In the first stage, low temperature (15-20°C) and dry air are applied to reduce the noodle moisture content from 40-45% to 25-27%. In the second stage, air of 40° C and 70-75% relative humidiy is used to ensure moisture migration from the interior of the noodle strands to outside surfaces. In the final stage, the product is further dried using cool air.

To manufacure air-dried instant noodles, wavy noodle-strands are first steamed for 18-20 minutes a 100°C, Then dried for 30-40 minutes using hot blast air at 80°C. The dried noodles are cooled prior to packaging. Air-dried instant noodles have a low fat content, hence some people prefer them. They also have a longer shelf-life because little fat rancidity is involved. Steaming appears to be very critical to this type of noodle since it affects the water rehydration rate of the product. However, slow output of the process and lack of pleasant shortening taste and mouthfeel make the product less popular in Asia compared with instant fried noodles.

Drying by frying is a very fast process. Water vaporizes quickly from the surface of the noodles upon dipping into the hot oil. Dehydration of the exterior surface drives water to migrate from the interior to the exterior of he noodle strands. Eventually, some of the water in the noodles is replaced by oil, Many tiney holes are created during the frying process due to the mass transfer, and they serve as channels for water to get in upon rehydration in hot water. I sually takes 3-4 minutes to cook or soak instant fried noodles in hot water before consumption.

Evaluating Noodles

The evaluation (scoring)of Noodles focuses mainly on three characteristics-process performance (machining), noodle color and noodle texture. The following table indicates noodle processing steps and evaluation criteria for them. Evaluation should be done at each stage of processing since the performance of dough and noodles has an impact on end product quality. Steaming is one of the critical control points in noodle processing. The degree of starch gelatinization in instant fried noodles determines the noodle rehydration rae, firmness and visco-elasticity, and is most controlled by the seaming process. During frying, becuase the moisture content in noodles drops rapidly, starch gelatinization is very limited.

Asian Noodle Processing Evaluation

Process	Evaluaion Criteria
Mixing	Optimal water absorption; dough particle sizes are small and uniform; no big lumps.
Sheeting	Easy to sheet; smooth surface; not streaky; free of specks.
Slitting	Clean cut; sharp edges; correct noodle size.
Waving	Uniform and continuous waves.
Steaming	High degree of starch gelatinization; not sticky; good wave integrity.
Frying	Uniform noodle color; good shape; not oily; characteristic fried noodle aroma.
Paraboiling	High cooking yield; low cooking loss; good cooking tolerance
Cooking	Short cooking time; good texture tolerance to overcooking.

Noodle Colour

All noodle types require good brightness. Color can be either white or yellow depending on the absence or presence of alkali salts. Minimal noodle darkening within 48 hours is desirable. This may not be a problem for the instant noodles becuase they are dried and he color is very stable.

Noodle Texture

Contrary to colour, noodle texture characteristics are more complicated and less understood. There is a distinction in noodle bite between the Japanese type and other noodle types in that the Japanese type is softer, while others are harder of firmer. Chinese raw, wet and instant fried, chuka-men, Malaysian hokkien, Philippine instant fried and Thailand bamee noodles are hard in bite, while Korean instant fried noodles are firm in bite. the hard bite noodles require high protein flour, while the firm bite noodles require medium protein flour with strong starch. Korean instant fried noodles are somewhat similar to Japanese udon in that both require flours of high peak viscosity and large breakdown measured by an amylograph. However, the flour protein content of Korean instant noodles (bag type) is 9.0-10.5%, higher than that of Japanese udon noodle flour (8.0-9.5%). Thus, the Korean instant fried noodle is also harder.

Summary

Asian noodles have been in existence for thousand of years. They are now also becoming popular in the Western countries. Several types, mostly machine-made, are produced Worldwide. Research on Japanese udon noodles is ahed of other noodle types. Process properties, noodle color and noodle texture are the three key quality attributes in the evaluation of a wheat flour for any noodle making. Noodle process behaviour is of particular importance in moder industrial production, but this property is often ignored in laboratory evaluation. In terms of noodle color, brightness is required, and whiteness or yellowness is essenial depending on the noodle type. Noodle texture, however, is more complicated in the characterization of each noodle type, and progress can only be made to understand this property by involving Asian flour and noodle industrial representatives. Instrumental measurements of noodle color and texture are important in establishing their relationship to sensory characteristics of noodles.

Chapter - 23

Biscuits Manufacture

PRODUCT MIX:

1. Sweet Variety [Glucose],Low Count Sweet Variety, Marie / Thin Arrow Root
2. Low Count Salted, High Count Salted, High Count Sweet
3. Others.

END USE:

Biscuits are amongst the lowest cost processed foods in the country, as it is well established any time snack. Among all snack items, biscuits have certain advantages, as it is easy to use during travel or at home because of its availability, in variety of pack sizes suiting to individual tastes with substantial energy having wholesome and nutritious quality at affordable prices. Further biscuits have, in general, a good shelf life, which is higher than all other snack items mentioned above.

MARKET POTENTIAL:

The biscuit industry in India comprises of Organized and unorganized sectors. Organized sector consists of large / medium and small units manufacturing packaged biscuits. The unorganized sector consists of small bakery units, cottage and household type manufacturing facilities, which manufacture and distribute biscuit across the counter without much packaging. According to an estimate about 1.2 million Tonnes of biscuit worth more than Rs. 2200 Crores is manufactured in the country. About 7.00 lakh Tonnes of biscuits are manufactured in the organized sector and the remaining by unorganized sector.

Main varieties of biscuit marketed across the country by the major branded manufacturers are as follows :

COMPANY	VARIETIES
Parley	Glucose, Milk, Non-salt cracker, Cracker
Ampro	Glucose, Milk, Cream, Cookies, Marie

Aurofood	Marie
Bakemans	Glucose, Milk, Cream
Britannia	Glucose, Milk, Marie, Arrowroot, Sweet Cookies, Cream, Non-Salt, Cracker, Salt cracker
Nutrine	Cream, Milk
Parry's	Cream, Milk
Priya	Glucose, Milk, Cream, Snacks, Crackers, Marie

The per capita consumption of biscuits tripled from 462 gms in 1978 to 1200 gms in 1998. This is a low figure when compared With 15 to 20 kgs in developed countries. As much as 55% of the total biscuits are consumed in rural areas and about 37% of the consumption is by people with a household income of less than Rs.1000 per month. About 56% of biscuits marketed are sweet varieties consisting of glucose and Milk types followed by 19% of Marie and Thin Arrowroot in the urban markets. However the regional preferences generally vary greatly. For example, North and West have, higher shares of 70% and 65%, respectively of sweet varieties of biscuits, whereas East has the high consumption of 34% of Marie and thin Arrowroot biscuits. South is the highest consumer of 27% for milk varieties.

Urban consumer preferences for different varieties of biscuits

Variety	All India	North	East	West	South
General category					
Glucose	42	63	22	63	23
Milk	14	7	22	3	27
Arrowroot	5	1	18	0	1
Marie	14	6	16	13	21
Fancy category					
Cream	8	8	7	7	8
Non-salt cracker	6	6	5	5	7
Salt cracker	6	6	7	7	4
Wafer cream	1	1	1	1	1
Assorted and others	4	2	1	1	8

Biscuit market is growing at a rate of about 7% every year for general variety of biscuits. However the growth for cream or assorted varieties are of the range of 20% - 40%. There is a huge net work of over 9.0 lakhs retailers and 6 lakh dealers engaged in biscuit marketing. The type of outlets where biscuit is generally sold is grocer's general Stores chemists and other shops.

SUGGESTED INSTALLED CAPACITY OF THE UNIT:

The overall capacity of the unit is 4 Tonnes of biscuits per shift of 8 hours. The unit can work at least for two shifts a day progressively increasing its capacity utilization. Thus the annual capacity based on three shift operation and 300 working days will be 2400 Tonnes.

The suggested capacity allocation for different type of biscuits will be as follows:

1. Glucose varieties	0960 Tonnes per year
2. Milk varieties	0480 Tonnes per year
3. Thin Arrowroot / Marie	0240 Tonnes per year
4. Salted varieties	0240 Tonnes per year
5. Assorted and other varieties	0480 Tonnes per year
Total	**2400 Tonnes per year**

RAW MATERIAL & ITS AVAILABILITY:

The raw materials required for the manufacture of biscuits are readily available in the state. The major raw materials include sugar, wheat flour, milk powder, hydrogenated fat, oil, liquid glucose etc. The exact requirement of raw materials depends on the product mix chosen during the season, which vary depending upon the market feed back.

Approximately following quantity of raw materials are required for a typical product mix:

Maida (bakery flour)	1500 Tonnes per year
Sugar	0150 Tonnes per year
Oil / Fat / Butter	0030 Tonnes per year
Milk powder	0030 Tonnes per year

PROJECT COST:	Rs in Lakhs
1. **Land** : 4000 square meters @ Rs. 250 / m2 (Rs. 10 lakhs per acre)	10.00

2.	**Land development** : (Fencing and compound wall with gates, internal road)	2.50
3.	**Buildings** : 1200m2 @ Rs 4000 / m2	48.00
4.	Other civil works (water Tank, bore well, Machinery foundation drainage, sanitation)	4.50
5.	**Plant and Machinery:**	
5.1	Complete automatic Biscuit Plant With Rotary Moulding (For soft dough biscuits like Milk and Glucose), Rotary cutting. (For hard dough biscuits like salt and Marie) Gauge rollers, Scrap Return Conveyor, Oil spray Machine. (For salt biscuits), Stacking machine, Pulveriser Machine. (For sugar grinding), Sandwiching Machine, Cooling conveyor, Biscuit Baking Oven (Gas fired / Electrical), Planetary mixer, Electrical Control Panel etc. 4 Tonnes per shift capacity.	64.50
5.2	Gas Bank complete with LPG Cylinders Pressure Regulator necessary piping etc.	4.80
5.3	Handling equipment like, Trolleys, Pallet Trucks, Wheeled barrows etc.	1.20
5.4	Weighing Scales 300 Kg (1 No.), 10 Kg (2 Nos.), and 1 Kg, capacity (10 Nos.).	1.60
5.5	D G Set 75 Kva	2.50
5.6	Electrical panel wiring switches etc.	0.80
5.7	Erection and commissioningTotal cost of Biscuit Plant	1.50
6.	Laboratory equipment	0.75
7.	Office equipment(Telephone / computers / Fax / e-mail)	1.25
8.	Furniture and fittings	1.50
9.	Vehicles (Delivery Vans: 2 Nos.)	7.60
10.	Deposits (For power, gas cylinder, Telephone)	2.50
11.	Pre operative expenses	2.40
12.	Interest during construction	11.55
13.	Working capital margin	36.00

14.	Contingency @ 5% of fixed assets	7.55
	Total Project Cost	**148.00**

MEANS OF FINANCE:

1.	Long Term Loan from Financial Institutions and Banks (75% of capitalized cost of fixed assets limited to 2/3 of Project cost).	82.00
2.	Investment subsidy, Soft loans if any, and Equity from Promoters and Others.	66.00
	Total	**148.00**

KNOW - HOW SUPPLIERS:

Technology for the manufacture of biscuit is well-established technology and is available from experienced technical personnel Food technologists, who can be employed by the company. Technically trained persons can be recruited through the milling and baking technology division of CFTRI, Mysore. CFTRI also provides technical know-how for various types of biscuits.

International technology, know-how and training, tie-up etc. can be arranged by Cebeco India, a subsidiary of The Royal Cebeco Netherlands.

MACHINERY SUPPLIERS:

A number of machine manufacturers supply biscuit manufacturing units in India and abroad. Some of the addresses are given below:

1. Louis Reineke, Sales Manager,
   Vuurslaag BV,
   PO Box 2125,4800CC,
   Breda-Holland.
   Telephone 003176 5720404
   Fax 0031 76 76 5717077

2. Mangal Engineering Works,
   Factory Area, Patiala - 147001.
   Phones: 0175 - 212652 / 214702 / 215180,
   Fax: 0175 - 212652,
   E-mail: sales@mangal.com

3. Continental Equipment (I) Pvt. Ltd.,
   B-66, Phase-I, Okhla,
   New Delhi - 110020.

Phone: 011 - 6816297 / 98,
Fax: 011 - 6815297.

4. Mechtech Designers & Eng. (P) Ltd.,
19D, Dr. A. K. Paul Road,
Kolkata - 34.
Phone: 033 - 4581499

5. High Temp Furnaces Private Limited,
1, 2 Phase Peenya Industrial Area,
Bangalore - 560058,
Phone: 080 - 8390489 / 8390490

SUGGESTED MARKETING STRATEGY:

Major outlets for Biscuits is Grocers and General Stores. The unit has to tap these outlets through a distribution net work. The unit can appoint area wise distributors and sub agents. The product has to be popularized through proper TV commercials. The unit should also concentrate on Rural Market. Biscuits from India has already marketed in Most of the Middle East countries like UAE, Bahrain, Qatar, Oman and Muscat. New units can also tap these markets.

MAN POWER REQUIREMENT:

The project requires about 70 persons for two-shift operation out of which 45 will be required in production and remaining in other areas.

INFRASTRUCTURE REQUIRED:

12.1 **Land** : The unit require about one acre of land preferably a rectangular plot with length: width ratio of at least 1:5 to accommodate the 200 feet long Biscuit plant building.

12.2 **Building** : The total built up area required is 1200 square meter.

12.3 **Power** : The connected load required is about 50 KVA excluding Biscuit Oven. It is suggested that the oven could be gas / kerosene fired or electrical. Gas fired is preferable since it is clean and pollution free and will be able to maintain the required steady temperature in the oven. In electrically heated ovens fluctuation in supply voltage will result in uneven baking and toasting of the biscuits.

12.4 **Water** : The unit requires about 10 KL of water per day. Water is required only for cleaning, drinking and sanitation purpose.

12.5 **Fuel** : About 50 to 60 cylinders of gas will be required daily. In order to ensure constant pressure of gas and avoid sweating of cylinders it is necessary to change half the cylinders when they are half-empty with new cylinders. The Fuel required is about 300 Tonnes of LPG per year.

12.6 **Effluents** : Unit does not generate any harmful effluents. -Domestic effluent can be discharged to fields for irrigation.

COST OF PRODUCTION AND PROFITABILITY (80% CAPACITY UTILIZATION):

Sl. No.	Particulars	Cost Rs. lakhs
1.	Raw materials and Packing material cost	359.10
2.	Utilities (Power and Fuel)	52.15
3.	Wages	31.50
4.	Factory overheads	7.40
5.	Administrative Overheads	12.00
6.	Financial Expenses	33.25
7.	Depreciation	17.20
8.	Sales Expenses	172.80
9.	Total input Costs (1 to 8)	685.40
10.	Expected Sales realization	768.00
11.	Profit before Taxes	82.60
12.	Return on Investment	65%

Chapter - 24

Bread and Bun

PRODUCT MIX:

1. Bread [400gms and 800 gms loaves]
2. Bun [80 - 100 gms]
3. Other breads such as whole meal brown bread, fruit/raisin bread etc.

END USE:

Bread and bun have become very popular and almost an essential part of the urban as well as rural cuisine. Further changing food habits in the country has set the trend towards centralised and also local production and distribution of bread necessitating pre-slicing and packing. Bread has become essential part of morning breakfast. Sandwich bread with jam, butter, cheese, vegetables and fruit slices results in tasty breakfast as well as evening light snack. Bun is used for making burgers, which is a popular evening Teatime snack in many households today.

CAPACITY OF THE UNIT:

The overall capacity of the unit is to produce 500 loaves / hr (400 gms) of bread. The unit will work for single shift initially. The bakery will produce about 3000 loaves of sandwich bread of different types (Plain, milk, fruit bread, spiced /salted bread, whole wheat brown bread) and 5000 Buns of different varieties (Plain, sweet, Spiced/salted, Potato, Burger bun etc.).

RAW MATERIAL REQUIRED AND ITS AVAILABILITY:

Flours : Flour provides the structure in baked goods. Wheat flour contains proteins that interact with each other when mixed with water, forming gluten. It is this elastic gluten framework which stretches to contain the expanding, leavening gases during rising. The protein content of the flour affects the strength of dough. Bread flour is hard wheat flour with about 12% protein. Bread flour is used yeast raised bread because the dough it produces has more gluten than dough made with other flours. Sufficient gluten produces a light loaf with good volume. Slices hold together, rather than crumble. The lower gluten content flours (With 7.5%

protein) are used for cake because lower gluten content causes products to have a tender, more crumbly texture that is desirable in cake.

Sweeteners : Table sugar has many functions in bread making. In small amounts it helps yeast begin producing gas for raising yeast dough. Sugar tenderises the dough and helps the baked product to brown. Fructose, Honey, Molasses, Saccharin, Aspartame are the other sweetening agents used in bakeries.

Salt : Salt is used to enhance the flavours and sweetness of other ingredients in bread. If salt is reduced then other spices or flavourings should be increased slightly.

Leavening Agents : Baking soda produces gas for leavening when combined with an acidic ingredient such as vinegar, lemon juice, or molasses. Yeast is a living microorganism until it is destroyed by heat.

Fats : Fat, in the form of solid shortening, margarine or butter, or oil contributes tenderness, moistness, and a smooth mouth-feel to baked goods. Fat also enhances the flavour of the other ingredients as well as contributing its own flavour.

Shortening is 100% fat and is solid at room temperature. The fakeness of pastry comes from solid fat. Butter, Margarine are also used in Bakeries.

Eggs : Eggs add flavour and colour, Contribute to the structure, incorporate air when beaten, provide liquid, fat and protein to bread and can be used in cakes.

Liquids : Liquids are necessary in bread for hydrating protein, starch and leavening agent. Water, Milk or Juice can be used in the bread.

The quantity of each raw material required depends upon the type of bread. On an average following formulae can be adopted and the raw material required per day and year will be as follows:

Ingredient	Percent as per formulae	Daily (Kgs.)	Annual (Tonnes)
Bread Flour	61.30	1134	340.2
Salt	01.15	22	006.6
Yeast fresh	03.07	57	017.1
Shortening	06.90	127	038.1
Liquid Milk	27.58	510	153.0
Total	100.00	1850	555.0

Raw materials availability: All the raw materials required are available in the state. The state is large producer of wheat and the average annual production of wheat is over 75.12 lakhs Tonnes. The milk production in the state is 40.8 lakhs Tonnes of which main quantity is of Buffalo Milk. The state is also a major oils producing state in the country. Thus the raw material will be easily available.

There is very good possibility of growing hard wheat varieties such as durum wheat under custom cultivation concept. This can provide an edge to the unit in comparison to units in other states in terms of availability of superior raw material and hence quality of the products

PROJECT COST:

1.	**Land**: 2000 square meters @ Rs 250 per m^2	5.00
2.	**Land development**: (Fencing, Compound wall and Gates)	1.50
3.	**Building**: 200 square meter @ Rs 4000 per m^2	8.00
4.	**Other civil works** (Machinery foundation, water Tank etc.)	0.60
5.	**Plant and Machinery:**	
	5.1 Mixer with flour sifting arrangements with two spare bowls. 5.2 Bread dough piece moulder 5.3 Tri-Shaft ATS Oven with auto loading, turbulent heat, swing tray oven, Gas fired, with Gas bank etc. 5.4 Automatic suction Depanner [For gentle removal of bread from moulds] 5.5 Bread cooling tunnel, rack type with air washer. 5.6 Rack type Tunnel: Final Proofer. 5.7 Bread Slicer, Sugar grinder etc. 5.8 Baking Tins/Trays, Trolleys, Shovel, electrical etc.	24.80
6.	Laboratory equipment	0.40
7.	Vehicles	3.80
8.	Deposits	0.40
9.	Preliminary and preoperative expenses	0.36
10.	Interest during construction	2.92
11.	Working capital Margin	3.60

12. 1.7 Contingencies	2.22
1.8 Total Project Cost:	**53.60**

MEANS OF FINANCE:

1.	Long term loans from Financial Institutions and Banks (75% of capitalized cost of fixed assets)	37.20
2.	Investment subsidy, Soft loans if any and Equity contribution from Promoters and others.	16.40
3.	**Total**	**53.60**
4.	Debt: Equity Ratio	2.268

TECHNOLOGY SUPPLIERS:

The technology for the Bakery is available from The International School of Milling and Baking Technology at CFTRI, Mysore-570013. CFTRI also offers a diploma course and short term training program in Baking technology.

PLANT AND MACHINERY SUPPLIERS:

of the addresses are given below:

1. NBE Food Systems (P) Limited,
   B - 97/1, Naraina Industrial Area,
   Phase - I, New Delhi - 110028.
   Phone: 011-25797764,
   Fax: 011- 25797525

2. Allied Bakery Machines,
   B-12, Badarpur Border Extension,
   New Delhi - 110044.
   Phone: 011- 26946837
   Fax: 011 - 26953143

SUGGESTED MARKETING STRATEGY:

Bread may be marketed through existing distribution and Marketing Channels. Bread should be delivered fresh daily to all the designated outlets like Grocers, General Stores, Medical Shops, Hotels and Restaurants. There should be arrangements to take back stale bread left unsold from the shops. Quality will be key to success.

MANPOWER REQUIREMENT:

The total Manpower required is 18. Additional Manpower at 12 persons per shift will be required when the second and third shift production starts.

INFRASTRUCTURE REQUIRED:

1. **Land**: About half an acre of land will be required including provision for future expansion.
2. **Building**: The built up required is 200 square meters.
3. **Power**: The connected load for the unit is 30 kVA.
4. **Fuel**: Fuel is required for the Baking oven. Ovens can be built with Gas or Liquid fuel fired facility. The requirement of gas will be about 70 Kgs per day.
5. **Water**: About 5 KL of water is required for Drinking, sanitation and for the Process.
6. The unit does not generate any harmful effluents

COST OF PRODUCTION AND PROFITABILITY:

1.	Raw material and Packing material costs	56.52
2.	Utilities (Power and Fuel)	4.54
3.	Wages	4.80
4.	Factory Overheads	1.40
5.	Administrative Overheads	1.20
6.	Financial Expenses	6.51
7.	Depreciation	3.80
8.	Sales expenses	4.80
9.	Total Input costs (1 to 8)	83.57
10.	Sales realization	96.00
11.	Profit before taxes (10 - 9)	12.43
12.	Return on Investment	42.4%

Chapter - 25

Compressed Baker's Yeast

THE PRODUCTS:

Compressed baker's yeast (saccharomyces cerevisiae) is in a form of block containing 30% solids and has more shelf life than active dried yeast.

PRODUCT APPLICATIONS:

Bakers's yeast gives the characteristics light leavened crumb structure to bread by transforming the heavy dough into light porous elastic mass.

It is also responsible for dough maturity and flavor development

MARKET SEGMENTS:

Market segment is bread and bakery industry. Two forms of yeast are available : 01) Compressed yeast and 02) Active dry yeast. Active dry yeast is costlier (about five times) than compressed yeast but has only two times the fermentative action on weight basis. Therefore, small bakers always prefer compressed yeast. On account of relatively high content of moisture in compressed yeast, it must be stored at low temperature, say about 4 to 5 deg. c to prevent the loss of activity

SUGGESTED INSTALLED CAPACITY:

It is proposed to produce 1 MT of compressed backers yeast per day, i.e., 300MT per annum.

RAW MATERIAL AVAILABILITY:

The basic raw material is cane or sugar molasses which is as such available from khandsari units. The key seasonal availability of sugarcane is from Novemeber to February.

EVALUATION OF AVAILABLE TECHNOLOGY & SELECTION OF TECHNOLOGY:

The two major quality parameters for yeasts are important for its uses, i.e., viability and vitality. To achieve these two characteristics at their maximum strength, there are many ways adopted in commercial purposes. Two major factors in this regard: yeast aeration and yeast collection.

For effective aeration during production of yeast, equipments for injecting measured amounts of air or oxygen injection rate can be controlled accurately by in- line oxygen sensors.

For maximum collection of yeast during production. Specially designed cylindri conical fermenters are used, in which the yeast settles more rapidly and completely in the cone at the end of fermentation.

These advanced features of processing equipments are incorporated in plant and machinery recommended for yeast production.

MANUFACTURING PROCESS IN BRIEF:

Yeast production involves many critical steps in processing, with respect to, process control on PH, temperature and total solid content etc.. The first requirement is to prepare a proper innoculum from pure culture which will accelerate the yield of yeast from molasses.

The process starts with pumping molasses to kettles where it is diluted and sterilised. The solution of nutrients required for the growth of yeast is prepared simultaneously.

PRODUCT QUALITY SPECIFICATIONS:

IS: 1320-1981 provides detailed specifications on baker's yeast. The yeast in active dry, from contains 92% solids, whereas in compressed form it contains 30% solids. The compressed form has a longer shelf life than fresh yeast. Approximate composition of baker's yeast: moisture : 75%, protein : 13%, fat : 0.8%, minerals : 2.0%, Glycogen 7.8%, gum/ cellulose etc. 3.4%.

REQUIREMENT OF TOTAL MANPOWER & ITS COST:

Technical	10
Labour	33
Administration	09

UTILITY REQUIREMENTS & ITS COST:

Power	150 kw
Cost of Power	Rs. 32.40 Lacs
Water	8000-10000 Lts/ Day (from own Borewell)
Fuel	Lignite 2 MT/ Day
Cost of Fuel	Rs. 6.00 Lacs
Total Cost of Utility	Rs. 38.40 Lacs

PROJECT COST:

Land Requirement & its Cost	Rs. 8.00 Lacs
Civil Work Requirement & Its Cost	Rs. 30.00 Lacs
Plant & machinery: its specifications & Cost	Rs. 85.00 Lacs
Utility Equipments Requirements & its Cost	Rs. 25.00 Lacs
Other Assets	Rs. 08.00 Lacs
Furniture & Fixtures	Rs. 04.00 Lacs
Margin money for working Capital	Rs. 25.00 Lacs
Total Cost of Project	**Rs. 185.00 Lacs**

Chapter - 26

Fried Snack Foods : Sev, Bhujia, Bombay Mix, Fried Nuts and Dal

PRODUCT MIX:

1. Deep fat fried Snacks (Sev, Bhujia, Bombay Mix)
2. Fried Pulses and nuts (Moong dal, Groundnuts, Chana)

END USE:

Growing urban population, nuclear families and increasing number of working women and scarcity of domestic help, teenagers taking to novel foods, widening of media penetration and a whole of range of gadgets in the kitchen including the refrigerator have opened up a new phase for convenience snack foods. Traditional Indian snack form part of any social and family celebrations in which large scale catering to suit the regional taste are undertaken. Traditional snacks are made in homes or on cottage scale and also on large scale by specialist caterers for retailing. They are also prepared in the streets and often sold out of vending carts. These are prepared under unhygienic conditions and are prone for microbial attack. With increasing awareness about quality and its importance on health has resulted in customers looking for snacks prepared in hygienic conditions in modem machines and packaged in attractive packing.

Special snack items characteristics of Indian cuisine such as dalmoth, moong dal, and khara boondi are being increasingly made available for sale in packed condition for consumers now. Retailing of such traditional items in unit packs offers various advantages such as quick and hygienic distribution, assurance of good quality product, specified quantity, brand identity etc. Further suitable package enhances their shelf life and appeal. These fried foods having high fat content and added spices and other ingredients packed in suitable packing material do not pick up moisture and become rancid on storage unlike the product made on street side.

MARKET POTENTIAL:

Some of the snacks are identified on geographical region to which they originally belong. The traditional snacks of different regions are as follows:

Fried Snack Foods : Sev, Bhujia, Bombay Mix, Fried Nuts and Dal

North: Samosa, Sev and Bhujia, Spiced fried dal, papdi, chat, golgoppa, kachouri, boondi, puffed channa and rice, pakora and chewda.

South: Chakli, murakku, sev, kodbale, boondi, fried mixture, vada (of different types), pakora, idli and dosa (of different types).

East: Singhara, Sev, puffed Dals, flaked spiced fried Dals, salted/ spiced/roasted groundnut, chewda, and pakora.

West: Poha, batata vada, sev, fried Dals, puffed chana/rice, dhokla, khaman, spicy roasted groundnut and cashew nut, khakra and pakora.

The ready to eat snack items have ready market. Success of a unit manufacturing depends upon the product mix and selection of each product for marketing in different regions. The marketing success of some of the existing units is mainly due to proper placement of product in the market.

CAPACITY OF THE UNIT:

The overall capacity of the unit is 1000 kg per day of various snacks or 300 Tonnes per year. The annual capacity allocation for the selected varieties in the product mix is as suggested below:

- Deep fat fried Snacks (Sev, Bhujia. Bombay mixture): 200 Tonnes
- Fried Dal and Nuts (Moong dal, Chana, Groundnut.): 100 Tonnes

RAW MATERIAL REQUIREMENT AND AVAILABILITY:

The traditional ingredients used in the preparation of snacks are Potato flour, gram flour, rice flour, refined oil, Chana, HPS groundnut, Moong dal, Steamed rice, spice powders, salt, and other flavoring ingredients and chemicals to enhance the shelf life of frying medium and the product. The total quantity of raw materials required are about 325 Tonnes. All the raw materials required are locally available. Packing material required: For shorter shelf life and cheaper products like boondi, economic and flexlble pouches made of glassine/PE, HDPE and PP would suffice, but for longer storage and export purpose more functional material such as Cellophane/ PE, Polyester/PE with or without inert gas flushing are required. Newer multiweb structures such as HD/LD/HD, HD/PA/LD would be well suited for snack food packaging. All the packing films are also readily available in the country.

PROJECT COST:	**Rs. in Lakh**
1. **Land**: 4000 square meters @ Rs 250 per m2	10.00
2. **Land development**: (Fencing Compound wall with gate, internal Roads etc.)	2.50

3. **Building**: 300 square meter @ Rs 4000 per m2 12.00

4. **Other civil works**: (Machinery foundation, water Tank etc.) 1.40

5. **Plant and Machinery:**

5.1 Raw material preparation section consisting of cleaning equipment, mixing equipment, kneeder etc.

5.2 Snack Food Fryer: Multi flow fryer specially designed to meet the requirement of Snack food processing for economical production consisting of indirect heating system, continuous oil filtration, automatic temperature control, de-oiling / coolingbelt, flavour applicator etc.

5.3 Accessories like heating system, packing machine, handling equipment, oil storage etc.

5.4 Erection and commissioning, electrical etc. 36.50

6.	Laboratory equipment	0.80
7.	Office equipment	0.64
8.	Furniture and fittings	1.20
9.	Vehicles	3.80
10.	Deposits	1.46
11.	Pre operative expenses	0.74
12.	Interest during construction	5.78
13.	Working capital margin	8.78
14.	Contingencies	3.40
	Total Project Cost	**89.00**

MEANS OF FINANCE:		**Rs. in Lakhs**
1.	Long term loans from Financial Institutions and Banks (75% of capitalized cost of fixed assets)	59.00
2.	Investment subsidy, soft loans if any and Equity from Promoters and others.	30.00
3.	**Total**	**89.00**
4.	Debt: Equity Ratio	**1.967**

Fried Snack Foods : Sev, Bhujia, Bombay Mix, Fried Nuts and Dal

TECHNOLOGY SUPPLIERS:

Technology for the manufacture of Indian snack food is available from Institutions like CFTRI at Mysore, Private consultants and Machinery Suppliers. The formulae for the snacks are well known and can be adopted as it is. The machinery supplier will provide the operation of the modem Plant and machinery and the lay out of the plant.

PLANT AND MACHINERY SUPPLIER:

M/s Wintech Taparia Limited offers Snack food frying system on Turn-key basis, which include the process know-how, supply, erection and commissioning of Complete Plant, and Training of personnel.

M/s Wintech Taparia Limited,
25/1, Y N Road,
Indore - 452003. (M.P.)
Phone: 0731-433950 / 534586
Fax: 0731-430527.

There are others like M/s Nat Steel Equipment, Madras and the Hotel Kitchen equipment Suppliers who would be able to supply batch type fryers, blancher and other preparatory equipment. M/s Wintech Taparia has supplied similar Plants to M/s Hello Agro, Indore; Shivdeep Foods (Haldirams), Bikaner; MTR Foods, Bangalore and other successful companies in the snack food business. Inventure India, Pune is one of the machine suppliers for the equipments.

SUGGESTED MARKETING STRATEGY:

It is necessary to create a brand image for the product through proper advertising. The products have to be marketed through the existing marketing channels like the food chain stores, Grocers, and General stores.

MANPOWER REQUIREMENT:

About 28 persons are required for running the unit. Out of which, 16 person will be engaged in production.

INFRASTRUCTURE REQUIRED:

1. **Land**: The project requires about 1 Acre of land including future requirements
2. **Building**: The built up area required is about 300 square meters
3. **Power**: Connected load for the unit is 60 KVA
4. **Water**: The unit requires about 10 KL of water per day

12.5 **Fuel**: The fuel is required for the frying unit. About 40 Kg of LPG is required per day

12.6 **Effluents**: Unit does not generate any harmful effluents

COST OF PRODUCTION AND PROFITABILITY (90% CAPACITY UTILIZATION):

Sl. No.	Particulars	Cost Rs. Lakhs
1.	Raw material and Packing material cost	189.00
2.	Utilities (Power and Fuel)	10.37
3.	Wages	12.60
4.	Factory Overheads	3.27
5.	Administrative Overheads	12.00
6.	Financial expenses	21.67
7.	Depreciation	7.94
8.	Sales expenses	75.60
9.	Total input costs	332.45
10.	Sales realization	378.00
11.	Profit before Taxes (10 - 9)	45.55
12.	Return on investment	71.7%

Chapter - 27

Packaging for Biscuits

In the early days - and in some countries, even today biscuits are packed in bulk in big cartons and tinplate containers. The traditional form of packaging obviously has number of disadvantages. It provides no protection against environmental influences such as humidity, odours and light, resulting in spoilage or reduced shelf-life. The percentage of broken biscuits is relatively high Infestation by insects and the manual handling of loose products at the retail outlets may affect the safety of the product.

Today, market demands and consumer preferences have changed or are changing the way biscuit manufacturers package and present their products. The obvious winner is the portion packed varieties - from the 250g family pack to the convenient single-serve packets containing 2-4 biscuits.

PROTECTION PRESENTATION, INFORMATION AND CONVENIENCE

Packaging in general must meet four basic requirements.

Firstly, the right biscuit pack must give mechanical protection to the product. Either by neat portion packs in the classical endfold style, or by an air (gas) cushion as in the case of a pillow pack., products are prevented from breakages during transport and retail handling.

Ready-to-sell individually wrapped units eliminates the hygiene factor risks since the biscuits do not come into contact with any external element. The appropriate films and correct sealing prevents any infestation by insects. The result is a product which is fresh and tasty throughout its average shelf-life of 6 months.

The packet must be perfectly heat sealed in wrapping materials with the required barrier properties against light, humidity, gas and external odours.

Secondly, the packaging must appeal to the potential customers and stand out against a host of competing products on the retail shelves. Besides the brand name, the packets which display the manufacturer's name and logo, also serve as an effective advertising medium for the company.

Thirdly, customers are asking for more detailed information on their purchases. In many countries around the world, regulatory bodies are asking for basic information such as the composition of the product/material used, nutritional values, allowed additives, price information and the origin of the product to be clearly printed on the outer wrappings.

Lastly, it has become very important to satisfy consumer's demand for convenience packaging. Manufacturers must be able to provide not only the desired package size (family size or single serve / snack packs), but convenient packet opening facilities as well. These include tear tapes, zig zag or incision cuts on pillow pack fins and tin-tie reclosing possibilities.

THE WRAPPING MATERIALS

Since paper, carton and tins are losing out to flexible films or foils as the packaging medium, focus will be given to the latter.

The oldest flexible film known is cellophane. Invented in 1920,. it became the most important heat sealable wrapping material until polyethylene and polypropylene was introduced in the late 1960s. Polyethylene is not used independently in biscuits wrapping as appropriate sealing cannot be done on the standard machinery available

Cellophane became less popular when it became too expensive and new synthetic films which offer better properties were introduced.

Today, most biscuits are wrapped in BOPP film (bi-oriented polypropylene), commonly known as OPP. For the less demanding application, an OPP monofilm is sufficient. For higher quality products, Duplex OPP or OPP combinations (pearlised or metallised), such as OPP/PE, OPP/PET, OPP/PVDC, and OPP/Syrlene, in the appropriate thickness and sealing range are more effective. They offer effective barrier against gas, vapour, odour and light.

The wrapping material with the highest barrier properties is aluminium foil of, say 7 micron, which is often used in combination with PET or Syrlene.

A joint consultation between the in-house food technologist, the wrapping material producer and the wrapping machine supplier is essential to ensure that the most effective wrapping film is used.

Principally, only heat sealable films are recommended for the packaging of naked biscuits. They give better sealing results than cold sealing materials and are less problematic in case of, e.g. biscuit dust in the sealing areas.

THE PACKAGING STYLES

There several popular wrapping styles which are applied widely on variety of biscuits of all shapes and sizes.

Biscuits packed using the following two wrapping styles must be of a common size and shape with a certain consistency and rather narrow tolerances in their dimensions. Standard wrapping machines can be used.

Endfold wrapping: This wrapping style is the classic, traditional biscuits wrapper. A portion of biscuits standing on edge is roll - wrapped or fold wrapped into a heat sealable film.The longitudinal packet seal is sealed tightly in a fin seal style. The packet ends are folded neatly and heat sealed. Due to the neat and tight surrounding of the film, this packet gives utmost mechanical protection and acceptable barrier properties for hard and semihard biscuits and many other cracker types. Enfold wrapping is considered the most effective in terms of presentation by many marketing specialists - not only due to the neat and impeccable shape, but also its ability to clearly distinguish the product amongst the host of pillow pack items on the retail shelves.

Even though this wrapping style is not too common in South East Asia, more manufactures are looking into this option.

Pillow pack wrapping is the standard wrapping style for smaller biscuit packs (snack packs/ single serve packs) containing one or more piles of biscuits.

In addition, pillow pack wrapping is used for bigger packets with products standing on edge (Slug wrapping) as well. In this configuration, it often serves as a primary wrapper, to be over- wrapped by a carton to improve presentation and acceptance.

The main advantage of pillow packs on edge, is its flexibility with regard to the slug length. For instance, it allows the machine to automatically adjust the length during wrapping by means of tendency controlled check weighers. This feature ensures the highest weight accuracy. Additionally, the pillow pack's typical fin seal style sealing is somewhat tighter than the enfold wrap.

The disadvantage of pillow pack slug wrapping is its limited mechanical product protection due to its rather loose packing. Further, the presentation of products packed using the pillow pack style is considered by most to be less attractive than enfold packets.

The Odd size biscuits: Besides enfold wrapping and pillow pack wrapping , which by the way cover about 85-90 percent of all biscuit products, there are some speciality biscuits with their own unique wrapping needs. These include an assortment of small cocktail crackers filled in bags by vertical FFS,machines and cookies of uneven sizes whose tolerance do not allow a standard wrapping.The latter are automatically or manually loaded into decorated trays and subsequently over-wrapped on pillow pack machines. Biscuir assortments such as the famous Danish Butter cookies, for instance, are automatically loaded into decorated trays and subsequently over- wrapped on pillow pack machines Biscuit assortments such as the famous Danish Butter cookies, for instance , are automatically loaded into decorated tins or stand - up bags.

The product preparation stage

There are two categories of machine feeding options-manual feeding and semiautomatic or fully automatic feeding.

For both categories, the biscuits coming from the cooling conveyor must be channelled into distinct lanes by means of a channelling or dribble board, stacked vertically and positioned upright on their short edge. Stacking may be effected by a rotary stacker or over a belt edge (as in penny stacks).

Vertical stacking reduces the travel speed of the biscuits and allows easier handling down the line for both automatic or manual feeding.

Manual feeding : For manual feeding, the wrapping machine is positioned 90° to the stacking belt, with its in-feed chain stretching across the stacking belt. A team of operators then take the biscuits in the correct portion length from the stacking belt and place them into the partitions of the wrapping machine's in-feed chain.

In cases where potion packs in piles are to be produced, the respective pillow pack machine would be equipped with hoppers above its in-feed chain. These hoppers are mounted on both sides of the stacking belt, allowing the operators to load the stacked biscuits into hoppers. The machine then takes a preset number of biscuits from the hoppers, forms the piles and transfers the configurations into the wrapping section.

Semi-automatic feeding : In view of future plans for automation, or to achieve higher wrapping machine speeds, an automatic feeding/portioning machine can be linked to the wrapping machine. Such feeders can be mounted parallel to the stacking belt or at its end.

Feeders for manual loading are equipped with 4-8 channels. These channels are loaded by operators via magazines or preferably, via a so called dead plate at the end of the stacking belt. Two operators can then shift the incoming stacked product rows into the feeding channels using the dead plate.

The feeder automatically measures the required portion length and deposits the readyto-wrap configuration into the in-feed chain of the respective wrapping machine. Depending on the number of channels, usually 4-8 portions are formed and fed simultaneously. This allows, wrapping speeds of up to 120-150 packs a minute by only two attendants.

The main advantage of the semi automatic or manually assisted feeding style is its flexibility to accommodate different products produced on the same line. The feeding style is independent from the number of incoming products rows.

Fully-automatic Feeding/wrapping : In environment which require higher oven outputs and multiple shift operations amidst rising labour costs, a fully automatic application becomes necessary.

In such instances, two or more wrapping machines equipped with automatic feeding/ portioning machines are connected directly to the processing line. This means that the total number of incoming stacked product rows must match with the total number of available feeder channels. It might then be necessary to reduce or multiply the product rows coming out from the cooling belt. After stacking, the product rows are then diverted into two streams of 8 rows leading to two automatic feeders, each equipped with 8 feed channels. In such cases, the space between the stacker and the feeding machine must be calculated to ensure a buffer area for machine interruptions.

There are two possibilities for the fully automatic wrapping of sandwiches..

For small pillow packs or so-called vend packs containing 2-3 piles of 2 sandwiches, a pillow pack machine is linked-up directly to a 2 row creamer with a combiner at its exit, forming piles of 2 sandwiches. The desired packet configuration of 2x2 or 3x2 sandwiches is then automatically transferred into the wrapper in-feed chain.

In such a set up, the wrapping machine is driving the creamer.

For sandwich slug packs, a special sandwich counting feeder can be connected to a 2 or 4 row creamer. The counting feeder accepts the sandwiches, counts the preset number of products and forms the slug, which is then deposited into the in-feed chain of a wrapping machine.

Pick and place units or robot loading cells: For special products of irregular shapes or big varying tolerances, the above feeding systems are not applicable. Pick and place units are available to automatically load such products into trays.

In case of more demanding applications. e.g.for biscuit assortments, robot loading cells should be used. The robots are equipped with visual recognition feature to distinguish one product from another, and to load them into the cavity of a tray or allotted space in a tin.

Chapter - 28

Chapati Making Unit

Chapati; the flat Indian bread is made from atta, the whole wheat flour. On baking, it is slightly puffed and gives a golden brown colour with a few brown spots on the surface. Chapati is called as 'Roti' in many parts of India. The whole wheat flour is made into dough by adding water, sometimes oil, sugar and salt are added to the dough to make Chapati soft and tasty. This dough is divided into small pieces of 30 to 40 g each and flattened by rolling into a round shape of about 8" diameter with about 2 mm thickness. The weight of the dought piece, diameter and thickness vary according to the requirements of the user. This round flat uncooked piece of dough is put on a hot plate (300 to 350^{0}C) and baked on one side for about 20 seconds. This is then turned upside down and again baked on the hot plate tor another 30 to 40 seconds. It is again turned upside down on the hot plate and baked for further 20 seconds when it puffs. many people prefer direct fire for the last stage of baking to get puffing. It is interesting to note that chapati is the only bakery product which puffs without addition of yeast or baking powder. The typical way of baking Chapati had created problems to machinery manufacturers in designing the type of oven used for chapati baking.

This chapati or roti is the staple food of more than 60% of the Indian population. Earlier, chapati was not consumed by South Indians. Since last 25 years, the eating habits of Indians have changed and now chapati is being consumed in the South and the South Indian foods are becoming popular in the North. It is pleasing to know that 90% of the wheat produced in our country is consumed in the form of chapati or roti. Only 10% of the wheat produced in India is consumed in making biscuits-bread-cake and such other products.

Now, the question is - is there any scope for chapati "manufacture" the way it is done in case of bread and biscuits?

Let us see the history of bread business in western countries. Till 19th century, each housewife would bake the bread required for her family. By about 1900 to 1910, small bakeries called "corner bakers' came to the scene. These bakers would meet the requirement of the nearby community.

After the first world war, bread business started growing and the corner bakers expanded their business. It was being partly mechanised and by about 1940, western countries saw the rapid growth of this business, where large scale automatic bread producing factories came into existence.

They would produce thousand of bread loaves per hour and slowly the practice of baking bread at home came to an end. This was the time when the housewife turned into a working woman and had no time to bake bread for her family. This bread business was so established that the housewife has plenty of choice to buy bread of her liking. Will chapati business follow the same trend in India? Market experts feel that chapati business will grow the same way as bread business grew in western countries. Dr H.A.B. Parpia, a former Director of CFTRI, Mysore, also feels that chapati will be the top selling processed food product of the 21st century.

A question comes to our mind that since 'bread' has been in India for over 70 years, will chapati have a future? That chapati has a future is evident from the fact that bread has not reached the dining table of an average Indian family. Use of bread is restricted to making 'toast' or sandwiches. It has never found a place as a replacement or chapati in an average Indian meal. Many Indians feel that because'yeast' is used in making bread, it produces 'acidity' and bloating of stomach. The other belief is that 'chapati' is made from whole wheat flour which gives them nutrition and also sufficient roughage required for good bowel movement. I am not going into the merits of demerits of these agrguments. The job of a food technologist is to give a product that market wants.

Let us now see as to who are the potential buyers of this ready-to-eat chapati or the buyers of machines to make this chapati.

1. A working woman who does not have the help of mother or mother-in-law to make chapatis, and more so when the husband and children want to eat chapati at every meal. A packet of chapati reaching her door step every morning along with the milk bag would give her one hour extra sleep every day. As an earning member of the family, she is willing to pay for this chapati pack.

2. Old couples who are living by themselves, where the old lady is physically not capable of rolling chapatis. Although their requirement of chapatis is 4 to 5 a day, they would love to buy a packet of chapati every day. These old couples are in thousands in a city and they have money to spend for this essential requirement of their meal.

3. Third potential customers are the students coming to cities from villages for their education. These students cannot afford to eat in hotels or canteens for both their meals. If a packet of chapati is available, they would eat it with home-made pickle or jam which they bring from their villages. With a packet of chapati, they can have satisfactory filling by spending just 5 to 6 rupees. Their number is not in hundreads but in thousands in each big city.

4. Newly employed persons who come to the city without their families have the same problem as the student mentioned above. This number is also large in each big city.

5. Bus and train travellers are also the needy persons for a ready-to-eat chapati. A few chapatis consumed with tea or coffee can give them a satisfying feeling of fullness at a very low cost. The number of such persons is unimaginable.

6. Hostels, hospitals, training establishments and industrial canteens, where the requirement of read-to-eat chapatis is very large, are always the willing buyers of the product. Cooks employed for chapati making by these organisations dictate terms to their employers, as they fully know that if they do not roll chapatis in time, the whole system will collapse. A survey made in Mumbai with such establishments revealed the helplessness of these employers in feeding chapatis to their clients. Many of these organisations have shown interest in installing a chapatti making machine for their requirements.

7. Armed forces establishments would again be the largest potential buyers of a chapati making machin, as their requirements are in

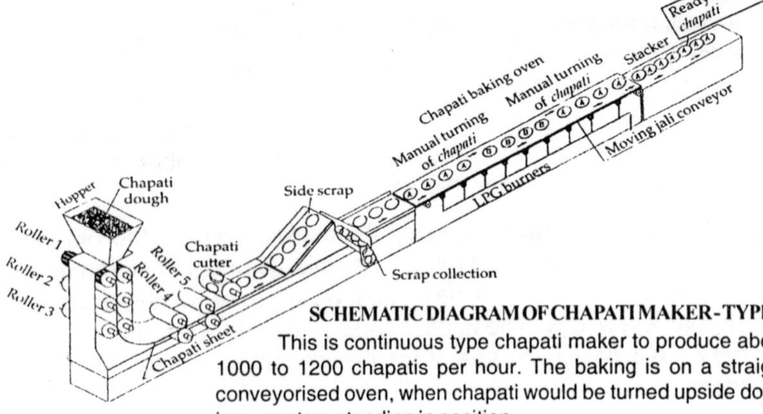

SCHEMATIC DIAGRAM OF CHAPATI MAKER-TYPE I

This is continuous type chapati maker to produce about 1000 to 1200 chapatis per hour. The baking is on a straight conveyorised oven, when chapati would be turned upside down by operators standing in position.

Chapati Making Unit

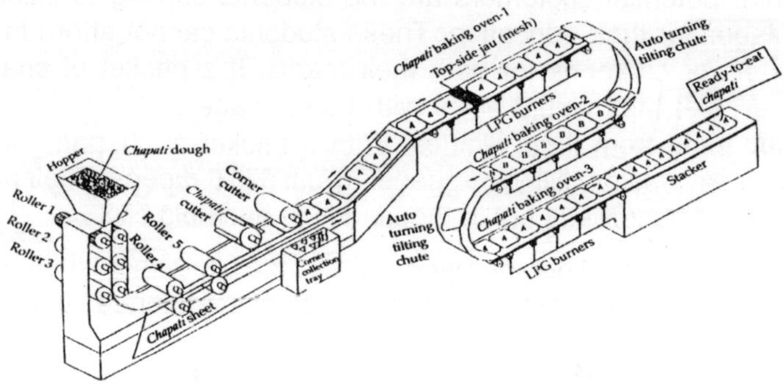

SCHEMATIC DIAGRAM OF CHAPATI MAKER - TYPE II

Type II : This is a continuous automatic chapati making and baking unit. The chapati has been shown as square or rectangular, which produce very little scrap as compared to round one. This unit would produce about 2000 chapati per hour.

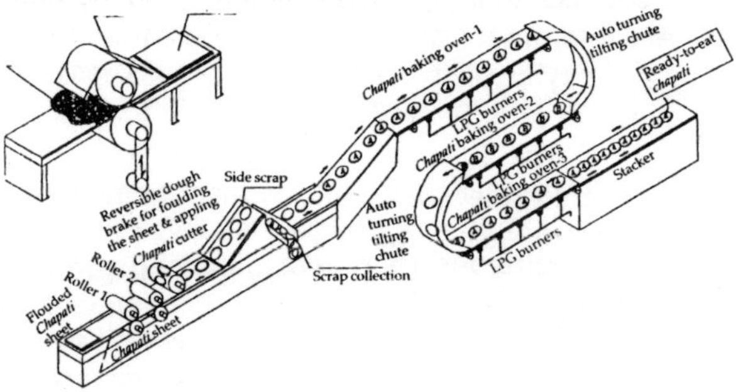

SCHEMATIC DIAGRAM OF CHAPATI MAKER - TYPE III

Type III : This also is a continuous type chapati making and baking unit. A reversible dough brake is shown on the left hand side, where sheet is formed, oil is applied between the sheet and this sheet is fed to the amin machine. This unit does not have a dough hopper as is shown in Types i and II. Chapati coming out of this unit has more oil content as compared to the other type. This chapati remains soft for a longer time. Capacity is same as 2000 chapatis per hour.

In these drawings, only single line chapati cutter is shown. This can be made to double line to double the production. i.e., 4000 chapatis per hour. This double line cutter can be had for types I and II and III.

thousands. Dr. S.S. Arya, a former Director of DFRL., Mysore, once said that armed forces would be the largest buyers of chapati making machine.

We can go on listing needy groups who are either interested in buying, a ready-to-eat chapati or a machine to make chapatis.

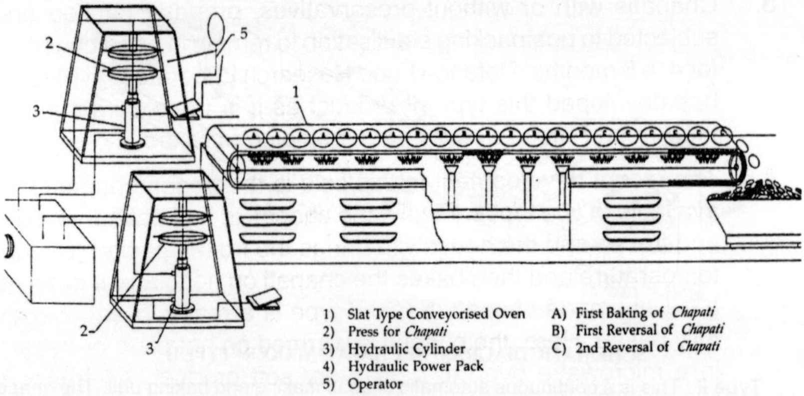

SCHEMATIC DIAGRAM OF CHAPATI MAKER-TYPE A

Type A : This is a semi-automatic machine with a capacity to make about 450 to 500 per hour. The pressing of chapati is done on an automatic press unit driven by a Hydraulic Power Pack. Two such units would work to feed the contnuous slat type conveyorised oven. This is recommended to those who want to make market trials before entering to a large scale chapati business.

Chapati-A Ready-to-eat food in disaster management : Chapati made with added soy flour skimmed milk powder, fat, little sugar and salt would be a very tasty and nutritions food with balanced proportions of fat, proteins, carbohydrates, minerals and fibres. A chapati of 35 g weight would give about 150 calories. A pack of 4 chapatis with over 500 calories could be an ideal pack for distribution in emergency situations like floods, earthquakes, rail accidents and such other emergencies. A few units to make these long shelf life chapati packs and centrally located stock piles in each state would help the authorities to reach the needy persons in the shortest time. If we make a chapati with a 4 months shelf life and store about 50,000 packs in each state, then, at any give time, we shall have a stock of millions of chapatis in the country for meeting any eventuality in India or outside the country also. There has to be a proper rotation of the stocks, where 3 months old stock is distributed to those to whom the state or central government is giving free-food. A blue print of the location of the manufacturing units, storage points, rotation pattern, cost involved to the government and distribution management can be worked out.

Now let us find out the various types of chapatis that are produced in India.

1. Oridinary chapatis which can be consumed within 36 hours.
2. Chapati with little oil to keep it soft and an added preservative to prevent mould growth, packed in polybags to last for 3 to 5 days.

3. Chapatis with or without preservatives, properly packed and subjected to postpacking sterilisation to remain in good condition for 4 to 5 months. Defence Food Research Laboratory at Mysore has developed this type of product as it is the requirement of the Armed Forces and for persons going for expeditions.

4. The recent development in this field is the frozen chapati. It is available in two types. Firstly, the chapati is half baked, packed and frozen and the housewife brings the frozen packet to room temperature and then bakes the chapati on hot plate. It puffs as a freshly made chapati. Second type is a ready-to-eat chapati fully baked. Here, the chapati is warmed on hot plate or heated in a microwave oven to get a very soft product. As freezers have reached even the grocery shops in the city, this type of frozen chapati is likely to become popular. For frozen chapati, the shelf life is very long

Mechanisation of chapati making :

If large scale requirements of chapati are there, then mechanisation of the process to make chapati is a must. Since, the last few years, the efforst have been made by Indian machine fabricators to develop chapati making machines. The first automatic chapati making machines. The first automatic chapati making machine was fabricated by M/s Om Engineering Works, Rajpur (Punjab) in the year 1985-86. This machine was fabricated on the concept and design given by the author of this article. This machine could roll over 2000 chapatis per hour and the oven for baking was a two layered type. It was installed in Pune for a party who wnated to be the first in this field of chapati making. Unfortunately, it was a commercial failure. Probably, in 1986, Pune was not ready to accept a ready-to-eat chapati. At this time, Mumbai was developing into a good market for ready-to-eat chapatis. Things have changed now. There are more then 6 semi-mechanised units in Pune who are supplying more than 50,000 chpapatis a day to Pune's industrial units and civil requirements. A large scale unit to make 4,000 chapatis an hour in likely to be operated in Pune shortly, This is going to be a three layered baking oven for proper baking of chapatis. It is now understood that if the machinery

Millennium Thoughts

Manufacturer tries to imitate the process adopted by the housewife, then he would get a product which is similar to the home-made product.

As on today, Om Engineering Works of Rajpur (Punjab) is the only fabricator who has understood the mechanisation of chapati making unit. Since they produced the first unit in 1986, they have upgraded their technology, with the result that they have now supplied a chapati making unit to Hindustan Levers for their R & D project. Hindustan Levers have started market trials to assess the acceptability of this machinemade chapati in the Mumbai market. An oil refinary in South, a cement factory in Madhya Pradesh and Godrej at Mumbai have shown interest in this chapati making machine.

Right now, there are at least five places in India, where efforts to design and fabricate a chapati making machine are going on. CFTRI, Mysore, has also developed such an automatic machine for a smaller capacity. It is expected that in the next 5 to 8 years, chapati making business is likely to grow and efficient and large capacity machines will be available to turn out 10 million chapatis per day in the first phase of this business. Once this is achieved, "sky is the limit" for this chapati business.

Let us see what a medium capacity chapati making unit would work out to :

1. **Capacity** : 4000 chapatis and hour or about 80,000 chapatis per day on 20 working hours.
2. **Space required** : 30,000 sq. ft. with 1,500 sq. ft. R.C.C. structure for the main machine and packing unit.
3. **Electric load** : About 20 H.P.
4. **Labour requirement** : 8 workers with 2 supervisors per shift.
5. **L.P.G. requirement** : About 100 kg per shift.
6. Turnover on 300 working days at Rs 1.50 per chapati as sale price : Rs. 3.6 crore
7. Net profit at 10 paise for chapati (normally it is 15 paise) Rs. 24 lakh
8. Machinery cost which includes main unit, packing machinery, gas storage facilities and other accessories. (The shed required for this is assumed to be on rental basis) : Rs. 32 lakhs.
9. **Working Capital** : Rs. 5.0 lakh
10. Pay back period on full production and sale : 18 months

As this is a highly profitable business, more and more enterpreneurs would enter food line via chapati making. A few sketches of chapati making units presented here give an idea to the readers as to how chapati is made and baked on machine.

Chapter - 29

Automatic Biscuit Making Plant

Biscuits are one of the important bakery items and can be used whole day irrespective of time. It is very common for morning breakfast and also used as a snacks.

Biscuits are generally classified into soft biscuits, hard biscuits and crackers.

Biscuit doughs are made mainly from flour, fat, sugar and water, with minor amounts of flavor, colours, and aerating agents and possibly eggs and fruits.

Obtained from the milling of wheat by the gradual reduction system. The object of milling process is to separate as cleanly as possible, the endosperm of the grain from the enveloping skins and embryo. The flour for biscuit, should be weak and low in protein content, the protein content may be 8.5 per cent of less.

Fat is used in biscuit to remove hardness and to improve the shortness of the biscuits - that is to lower the Millard reaction and polymerization particularly in alkaline conditions, and invert sugar is effective in diminishing checking in biscuits. Sugars also affect the heat denaturation of flour protein. Aerating agents commonly used are ammonium bicarbonate by itself and sodium bicarbonate with either sodium pyrophosphate or calcium hydrogen phosphate. Ammonium bicarbonate has the advantage that it leaves no residue and evolves a greater volume of gas per unit weight than any of the others but, in the absence of phosphate and sodium ions, it leaves a raw taste in the biscuits. Sodium pyrophosphate residues give a burning taste and excess sodium bicarbonate give a fine granular texture to the biscuit (which is desired) but only at the expense of a burning taste.

RECIPES FOR VARIOUS TYPES OF BISCUITS

1. Arraroot Biscuit:

Flour	2.5 Kgs.
Shortening	250 gms.
Sugar	175 gms.

Arrowroot	175 gms.
Eggs (optional)	3 Nos.
Water/milk	750 ml.

2. **Digestive Biscuits:**

Wheat Meal	2.0 Kgs.
Shortening (vanaspati)	500 gms.
Sugar	100 gms.
Eggs	4 Nos.
Sodium bicarbonate	7 gms.
Milk	1.25 Litre

3. **Honey Comb Biscuits:**

Flour	2.0 Kg.
Sugar	1.0 Kg.
Shortening	500 gms
Egg	1 Nos.
Vegetable Oil	15 gms.

4. **Almond Fruit Biscuits:**

Almonds	500 gms
Powdered Sugar	500 gms.
Eggs	3 Nos.
Flour	60 gms.
Raspberry Jam	As Requisite

5. **Soda Biscuit:**

Flour	6 Kgs.
Salt	30 gms.
Vanaspati	200 gms.
Cream of Tar Tar	30 gms.
Soda Bi-Carbonate	50 gms.
Water	2.5 Litre

6. **Coconut Biscuit:**

Maida	450 gms.
Sugar	200 gms.
Shortening	250 gms.
Eggs.	4 Nos.
Chopped Coconut	200 gms.
Water	As required.

MANUFACTURING PROCESS

Most type of biscuits use weak flours of low protein content. Good biscuit flours can be obtained if the weak varieties one chosen and they are melted in a sound condition.

The gluten of distensible natures rather them elastic protects doughs against creep.

Flour, sugar, fat, water or milk are the main ingredients whose relative proportions differ according to the variety of biscuit being made. Baking powder ponder aeration. A uniform & stiff dough is prepared by batch mixing of dough ingredients.

The dough parses through rolls where it acquires a uniform texture & thickness final contrast of thickness are achieved by passing through other rolls.

Thus, a dough sheet of uniform thickness is prepared which is passed under cutter for stamping out the biscuit shapes. these are called biscuit blank,

Biscuits are baked in a traveling oven where moisture content in the biscuit is reduced to about 3%.

The variation in proportioning ingredients is so wide spread that no limit can,really, be put. Analytical data can be referred for guidelines to some extent one type of biscuitmay contain 45 to 50% of sugar while another (water biscuits & cream crackers) contain lecithin 1% sugar. However the whole activities of biscuit manufacture can be divided in the following categories:-

1. Procurement of raw materials of required properties & their tests (if needed).
2. Mixing & Blending in a double action horizontal mixing machine (batch -by-batch).
3. Flour shifter is used for transferring flour to mixers.
4. Mixed batch of main ingredients go to automatic continuous heavy duty rotary moulding machine Here, doughs one prepared and divided before transferring to the sheeter rolls.
5. Dough sheets of inform thickness are none made form the divided dough and cut to the required sized shape of the biscuits in a Rotary cutting machine.
6. The biscuit blank are collected in boxes or conveyed on a

continuous conveyer for further treatments and the cutting wastages are automatically returned to the mixer for reprocessing into dough sheet.

7. Oil spraying machine converts the plain of light sweet biscuit in salted ones by infusing saline, contents uniformly all over the biscuit surface which in due coarse of time penetrates deeper & gets absorbed by biscuit material

8. While mixing ingredients in the mixing machine, the care is taken that finely ground/ pulverized sugar powder only is mixed. mixing is required to be fully uniform.

   A sugar grinding machine is used for this purpose.

9. As a final step, in biscuit manufacture, the biscuit blanks are placed in baking trays. The trays are either freely placed or fabricated with the wire belt continuous conveyer. The biscuits in trap one spread in such a way that one side of each biscuit is in direct contact with the baking pan.

10. After loading biscuits in the baking trap, as the loading and the conveyer is allowed to travel for ward into the baking oven chambers. The trap carrying biscuits cross oven chambers one after the other till they reach the other and of the oven where baked biscuit one unloaded automatically & collected in boxes.

11 As the biscuit travels the entire length of the baking oven (from loading end to unloading end) the biscuit gets properly baked at 270°C working temperature of the oven. After this baking only 3%of moisture is left in the biscuit.

12. The biscuit is still hot when collected from the unloading end of the oven. It is there fore, cooled on a cooling conveyer. The water jacketing system is fed with chilled water in this unit for the quick cooling of biscuit to flowing chilled water through the jacket.

13. At the end of all these biscuit mfg. processes the samples are tested in accordance with the relevant B/S - Standard of specifications.

PLANT ECONOMICS OF AUTOMATIC BISCUIT MAKING PLANT

Rated Plant Capacity	=		5.00 MT/Day
LAND & BUILDING (Land Area 800 sq.mt.) =		Rs.	16,95,000.00

PLANT & MACHINERY

1. Automatic/continuous rotary moulding & cutting machine
2. Three roll shutter
3. Oil spraying Machine
4. Mixing Machine
5. Planetary mixing Machine
6. Cooling conveyor
7. Flour shifter
8. Sugar grinding
9. Electric oven
10. Plus S.T. Packing & forwarding
11. D.G. Set
12. Distribution transformer
13. Multi-colour Flexo-printing Machine
14. Automatic Biscuit packaging Machine
15. Testing laboratory equipments
16. Delivery van & Misc. equipments e.g. tubewell weighing & measuring equipments.

FIXED CAPITAL

1. LAND & BUILDING	Rs.	16,95,000.00
2. PLANT & MACHINERY	Rs.	44,07,200.00
3. OTHER FIXED ASSETS	Rs.	4,80,000.00
TOTAL	Rs.	65,82,200.00

RAW MATERIALS

1. Wheat Flour
2. Vanaspati
3. Sugar
4. Baking Powder
5. Fats
6. Milk
7. Salt
8. Yeast
9. Miscellaneous e.g. Honey, Flavours, Colours & Fruits and Packing Materials.

TOTAL WORKING CAPITAL/MONTH

1. RAW MATERIAL	Rs.	22,10,727.50
2. SALARY & WAGES	Rs.	1,09,250.00
3. UTILITIES & OVERHEADS	Rs.	1,57,000.00
TOTAL	Rs.	24,76,977.50

TOTAL CAPITAL INVESTMENT

TOTAL FIXED CAPITAL	Rs.	65,82,200.00
TOTAL WORKING CAPITAL FOR 3 MONTHS	Rs.	74,30,932.50
TOTAL	Rs.	1,40,13,132.50

TURN OVER/ANNUM

By sales of 1500 MT. of various types of biscuits (Sweet,Salty & cream sandwiched)	Rs.	4,50,00,000.00

PROFIT SALES RATIO = Profit / Sales x 100 = 24.40 %

RATE OF RETURN = Operating profit / T.C.I x 100 = 78.36 %

BREAK EVEN POINT (B.E.P) = 33.67 %

Chapter - 30

Automatic Bread and Biscuit Unit

The project proposes to procure fully indigenous plant for manufacturing various types of biscuits, the varieties include NICE, BOURBORNE and other cream Glucose, Mini Glucose, High Count, Star etc. (both Sweet & salty).

The plant & machinery, proposed to be purchased for the manufacture of various types of biscuits for the purpose of pulverizing, mixing, rotary moulding, rotary cutting, continuous biscuit baking oven, dough brake, cooling cover, automatic biscuit packing machine & wrapper printing etc.

The total connected load required will be 180 KVA at 430V/ 3 phase/ 50 cycle of AC supply A 300 KVA transformer will be installed to disturb power.

The plant capacity of biscuit making is 2 TPD on single shifts basis. This same automatic biscuit making unit falls under small scale sector and the arrangements are adequate for B.I.S. - approval of the products. The plant requires around 500 Sq.Mts of covered area for various activities including main work shop.

PLANT ECONOMICS OF BREAD AND BISCUITS PLANT

Rated Plant Capacity = Bread = 4000 Loaves/Day
Biscuits = 750 kgs/Day

LAND & BUILDING

Land Area 500 sq.m = Rs. 13,25,000.00

PLANT & MACHINERY

1. Bread Making Unit:Flour sifter
2. Dough Kneader
3. Divider
4. Moulding machine
5. Heating Oven
6. Bread slicing & sealing machine
7. Misc. equipment e.g. vessels, trays pans, work tables, cooling rack
13. Packing equipment
14. Biscuit Making Unit: Sugar Grinder
15. Planetary type mixer
16. Automatic biscuit cutting and punching machine fitted with rotary moulder
17. Electric baking oven with conveyor
18. Tanks (PVC)

8. Bucket evevater & conveyers hoists with motors platform weighing scale.
9. Pumps motors and blowers
10. Counter scales
11. Instrumentation & accessories
12. Laboratory testing equipment (L.S.)
19. Cooling conveyor
20. Oil Sprayunit
21. Packing equipment
22. Trays trolleys & other accessories
23. Laboratory equipment
24. Instrumentation and accessories
25. Conveyers, bucket elevators tools, jigs, hoist etc. Tanks

FIXED CAPITAL

1.	LAND & BUILDING	Rs.	13,25,000.00
2.	PLANT & MACHINERY	Rs.	15,50,001.00
3.	OTHER FIXED ASSETS	Rs.	2,90,000.00
	TOTAL	Rs.	31,65,001.00

RAW MATERIALS

1. Bread:Flour
2. Fat
3. Salt
4. Dry yeast
5. Vegetable oil
6. Miscellaneous (Mis. and bread improvement)
7. Biscuit:Flour
8. Fat
9. Sugar
10. Milk Powder
11. Yeast
12. Salt
13. Ammonium carbonate
14. Miscellaneous & Packaging Expenditure

TOTAL WORKING CAPITAL/MONTH

1.	RAW MATERIAL	Rs.	4,86,545.00
2.	SALARY & WAGES	Rs.	61,625.00
3.	UTILITIES & OVERHEADS	Rs.	75,000.00
	TOTAL	Rs.	6,23,170.00

TOTAL CAPITAL INVESTMENT

TOTAL FIXED CAPITAL	Rs.	31,65,001.00
TOTAL WORKING CAPITAL FOR 3 MONTHS	Rs.	18,69,510.00
TOTAL	Rs.	50,34,511.00

TURN OVER/ANNUM

1. Bread loaves 1200000
2. Biscuit 300 Tons

Rs. 1,47,00,000.00

PROFIT SALES RATIO = Profit / Sales x 100 = 37.99 %
RATE OF RETURN = Operating profit / T.C.I x 100 = 112.39 %
BREAK EVEN POINT (B.E.P) = 28.13 %

Chapter - 31

Automatic Pineapple Biscuit Making Plant

Biscuits are one of the important bakery items and can be used whole day irrespective of time. it is very common for morning breakfast and also used as a snacks.

Biscuits are generally classified into soft biscuits, hard biscuits and crackers.

Biscuit doughs are made mainly from flour, fat, sugar and water, with minor amounts of flavor, colors, and aerating agents and possibly eggs and fruits.

Obtained from the milling of wheat by the gradual reduction system. The object of milling process is to separate as cleanly as possible, the endosperm of the grain from the enveloping skins and embryo. The flour for biscuit, should be weak and low in protein content, the protein content may be 8.5 per cent of less.

Fat is used in biscuit to remove hardness and to improve the shortness of the biscuits - that is to lower the Millard reaction and polymerisation particularly in alkaline conditions, and invert sugar is effective in diminishing checking in biscuits. Sugars also affect the heat denaturation of flour protein. Aerating agents commonly used are ammonium bicarbonate by itself and sodium bicarbonate with either sodium pyrophosphate or calcium hydrogen phosphate. Ammonium bicarbonate has the advantage that it leaves no residue and evolves a greater volume of gas per unit weight than any of the others but, in the absence of phcsphate and sodium ions, it leaves a raw taste in the biscuits. Sodium pyrophosphate residues give a burning taste and excess sodium bicarbonate give a fine granular texture to the biscuit (which is desired) but only at the expense of a burning taste.

The doughs are prepared using above mentioned in gredieuts and formed to the regulared shape by one of various processers and baked in traveling ovens to moisture content of 1 to 4 percent.

PROCESS OF MANUFACTURE

The steps involve in the production of biscuit is as follows :-

Automatic Pineapple Biscuit Making Plant

1. Preparing the Biscuit Mix.
2. Dough Making
3. Biscuit Forming & Cutting
4. Backing or Frying
5. Packing

PLANT ECONOMICS OF PINEAPPLE BISCUIT UNIT

Rated Plant Capacity = 2.00 MT/Day

LAND & BUILDING (Land Area 14400 Sq.Ft.) = Rs. 50,40,000.00

PLANT & MACHINERY

Total cost of Plant & Machinery	Rs.	86,10,750.00

FIXED CAPITAL

1. LAND & BUILDING	Rs.	50,40,000.00
2. PLANT & MACHINERY	Rs.	86,10,750.00
3. OTHER FIXED ASSETS	Rs.	4,50,000.00
TOTAL	Rs.	1,41,00,750.00

RAW MATERIALS

1. Wheat flour
2. Vanaspati
3. Sugar
4. Baking Powder
5. Fats
6. Milk
7. Yeast
8. Miscellaneous e.g. pineapple flavours, colours, & packing materials, etc.

TOTAL WORKING CAPITAL/MONTH

1. RAW MATERIAL	Rs.	12,85,900.00
2. SALARY & WAGES	Rs.	1,18,750.00
3. UTILITIES & OVERHEADS	Rs.	1,15,000.00
TOTAL	Rs.	15,19,650.00

TOTAL CAPITAL INVESTMENT

TOTAL FIXED CAPITAL	Rs.	1,41,00,750.00
TOTAL WORKING CAPITAL FOR 3 MONTHS	Rs.	45,58,950.00
TOTAL	Rs.	1,86,59,700.00

TURN OVER/ANNUM

By sale of 600 MTs of pineapple biscuits(sweet & cream sandwitched)	Rs.	3,00,00,000.00

PROFIT SALES RATIO = Profit / Sales x 100 = 23.34 %

RATE OF RETURN = Operating profit / T.C.I x 100 = 37.53 %

BREAK EVEN POINT (B.E.P) = 45.66 %

Chapter - 32

Bread Manufacturing

In the manufacture of bread the yeast is essential agent. It ferments the dough produced carbondioxide and alcohol yeast breaks the sugar into simple sugar by the Siamese and raises the dough. Mostly in bakeries compressed or active dry yeast used.

The quality of bread depends upon the activeness of yeast. As yeast in more active than less sugar remain in flour mill produce poor crust colour and less active yeast means more sugar in flour and dark colour of bread will produce so in the bread a amount of sugar and yeast is needed.

PROCESS OF MANUFACTURE

The process of manufacture of bread starts with mixing and formation. mixing and fermentation of dought is carried out by two methods (i) straight dought method and (ii) sponge dough methods.

FORMULAS :

(I) BREAD WITH OR WITHOUT ASCORBIC ACID :

Ingredients	*% of Flour (Wt.Basis)*
Flour	100
Water	66
Sugar	8.00
Yeast	3.00
Shortening	3.25
Salt	2.01
Milk (Dry)	1.00 +
Yeast food	0.525
Monocalcium Phosphate	0.145
Sodium Propionate	0.10
Oxidizing agents	-
(Potassium bromate & Potassium iodate)	0.009
Variable.	

(II) STANDARD BREAD

Flour	5000
Water	150
Milk solid	100
Acidulant	6
Yeast	100
Salt	75
Sugar	400
Monoglycerides	1.25
Water	3.450
Potassium bromate (based upon Flour wt.)	60
Potassium iodate (based uponflour wt.)	15
PPM (Part per million)	25

PLANT AND MACHINERY

1. Flour Shifter: Heavy duty fitted with automatic feeding elevator of automatic feeding elevator of sieving capacity on bag of flour (90) kg in 10 minuted fitted with 2 motors of 1 HP. Each and adjustable Aluminium hopper.

2. Water Measuring Tanks:

   Stainless Steel construction calibrated water measuring tank with visual level gauge, thermometer and two outlets valves fitted on stand. Capacity 150 litres.

3. Dough Kneading Machine:

   Heavy Duty (RVK) type with one mixing pan capacity 150 kg. flour in 15/20 minutes fitted with 5 HP electric motor (2 Nos.)

4. Extra Pens for RVK Kneader (2Nos.)

5. Single Pocket Dough Divider:

   Capacity 30 pieces/minutes app. fitted with NGEF or equivalent make 2 H.P. motor.

6. Rounder:- One bowl type dough piece rounder driven by 1 H.P. electric motor through reduction geares, having a revolving cast iron cone with stationery matching internal cast-aluminium spiral track with capacity to round upto 3500 pieces per hour and with heavy duty gear box and 1 HP motor HFEF or equivalent makes.

7. Straight through Moulder :-

   Capacity 2000-3000 leaves per hour and can also be used for twist bread purposed, fitted with 2 HP Motor (NGEF or equivalent) and driven through gear box)

8. Intermediate Providing Table:-

   Round table for first providing 8 ft. diameter with sunmica top fitted with 1 HP. NGEF or equivalent make motor

9. Travelling Oven: Capacity app. 1200 leaves per charge with an Indirect Heating system through recirculation of flues, fitted with 2 H.P. Main Motor, 3 H.P. recirculating Pan Motor, 2 HP. driven exhaust fan, Oven 2 HP. driven exhaust fan, Oven imparting top and bottom heat to baking pans in the entire cycle with capacity to bake 30000 leaves of 400 gms size per day complete with medium pressure burner. All motors of NGEF or equivalent make.

10. Tunnel-Type Final Proofer:-

    A Bread Tunnel-Type insulated final proofer, with recirculation duct on top with inline 1 HP motor driven fan/steam heater/ steam humidifier, having 1 HP. motor driven automatic rack-pusher, capable of accomodating upto 8 nos. Proofing racks for manufacturing 1,250 x 400 gm. leaves an hour.

11. Final Proof Trolleys: A set of heavy duty 12 Nos. trolleys for final proof made out of B-class GI pipe, 4 Heavy duty casters GI wheels meant for use in final proof tunnel each trolley having 8 tiers.

12. Baking Pans & Lids: A set of 1000 Moulds having 3 pans each and 400, 18 gauge MS Lids made out of 24 gauge tinplate for production of upto 1250 leaves of 400 gms size per hour.

13. Hot Leaves Collection Table: One 6 ft. Heavy Duty Structural Frame Diameter Turnatable having sunmica top driven by 1 HP. Motor, 900 RPM NGEF or Equivalent make, and fitted with reduction gear, for hot leaves collection having knockout plate form for manual depending.

14. Bread Cooling Tunnel with Pusher: A Bread cooling facility comprising of approx. 22 ft. long tunnel to accomodate 10 Nos. cooling racks, with 2 Nos. 36" size blower and exhaust

fans run by 2 H.P. motors each, having an air-washer located on top of tunnel with recirculating pump headers/nozzles/base tank and cowl for blowing air through tunnel, complete with electrical controls, and suitable for cooling upto 1,250 x 400 gm. loaves per hours.

15. Bread Cooling Trolleys: 12 Nos.

    Bread cooling Trolleys having 8 racks made of B-class GI Pipe, Heavy Duty duly Galvanised

16. Slat Conveyor: A length of salt conveyor with 1 HP, Motor drive for moulds from oven to Moulder.

17. Sliver and Sealer:- Heavy duty 4 Nos. Bread slicing machine and 4 Nos. Sealing Machine Capacity upto 600 loaves per hour, Gravity Food.

18. Boiler: Coal Fired Baby Boiler or 250 kg. Steam per hour capacity complete with all fittings.

19. Refrigerated Chest for Yeast: Refrigerated Cabinet for storing compressed yeast capacity 200 kg. with 1 HP. Motor NGEF or equ.

20. Bread Baskets: 600 Nos. made of MS plant as per Modern Food Industries (I) Ltd., design

21. Installation Charges

22. Laboratory with apart uses

PLANT ECONOMICS OF BREAD PLANT

Rated Plant Capacity = 10000 Loaves/Day
LAND & BUILDING (Land Area 668 sq.mt) = Rs. 16,56,200.00

FIXED CAPITAL

1.	LAND & BUILDING	Rs.	16,56,200.00
2.	PLANT & MACHINERY	Rs.	14,00,000.00
3.	OTHER FIXED ASSETS	Rs.	5,00,000.00
	TOTAL	Rs.	35,56,200.00

RAW MATERIALS

1. Wheat Flour
2. Salt
3. Sugar
4. Milk Powder
5. Edible oil
6. Shortening
7. Yeast
8. Wrappers & Other Misc.

TOTAL WORKING CAPITAL/MONTH

1.	RAW MATERIAL	Rs.	23,43,125.00
2.	SALARY & WAGES	Rs.	1,10,400.00
3.	UTILITIES & OVERHEADS	Rs.	2,34,400.00
	TOTAL	Rs.	26,87,925.00

TOTAL CAPITAL INVESTMENT

TOTAL FIXED CAPITAL	Rs.	35,56,200.00
TOTAL WORKING CAPITAL FOR 1 MONTHS	Rs.	26,87,925.00
TOTAL	Rs.	62,44,125.00

TURN OVER/ANNUM

1. Receipt from sales of 10,000x300 loaves of 800 gms.
2. By sale of 10000X300 loaves of 400 gm.

Rs. 3,60,00,000.00

PROFIT SALES RATIO = Profit / Sales x 100 = 6.44 %
RATE OF RETURN = Operating profit / T.C.I x 100 = 37.14 %
BREAK EVEN POINT (B.E.P) = 57.05 %

Chapter - 33

Bakery Unit (Pastries, Bread, Buns, Cake, Toffee etc.)

Pastries, Bread, Cakes, Toffies etc. comes under the bakery product. Now the advancement of age age food habits of the ready-made food. Most of all the bakery items are under the category of ready-made food. Now school going children are like to have the items like parties cakes, breads etc. for their tiffin use office going peoples like to take breads and parties products, in our daily break fast table also take. The share of bakery products even daily wages laborers also habiterated to spend their lunch by taking bread or like that baking product. By the large utilities of baking products in our life takes part the program of progress of bakery unit itself.

PROCESS MANUFACTURING OF BUNS

Theory and procedure of buns are similar to the breads only ingredients composition are different, even some excess ingredients required.

Formulations of different types of buns are given below:

NORMAL BUNS (SWEET BUNS)

Name of the Ingredients	Percentage of Ingredients
On the Basis of	
Maida	
Milk	10-12%
Shortening	8%
Sugar	10-15%
Whole eggs	5%
Yeast	8.5%
Salt	1.0%

HAMBURGER BUNS

Name of the Ingredients	Percentage of Ingredients
Maida	
Cream of Tartar	3%
Sodium Carbonate	1-15%
Shortening	15%
Sugar	40%
Egg	15-20%
Milksufficient to make dough	
Tuti Fruity	2%

GENERAL PROCESS

Sugar dissolves in part of the water, in sugar solution added all the yeast to make a yeast sugar homogeneous solution. Sodium carbonate, salt are dissolved in other part of water. Now melt the shortening ir it is solid form.

Take flour in kneading mixer added yeast sugar solution, mix homogeneously, after complete mixing added salt's solution then added shortening to the whole mixture to form a soft dough. When proper homogeneous dough has been prepared, keep the dough for one hour to make a fermented dough of well in seated volume at temperature 30°C-35°C. Then the knock back operation will start. After knock back it is pass through the divider and rounder. After warded all the rounded dough put in the mould and keep it for 40 minutes 60 minutes for final proofing. Then the dough is put in the bakery oven at the temperature of 200-300°C.

After complete baking it is takes out and keep it for looking about 2 hours. Now pack it and market the product.

PLANT ECONOMICS OF BAKERY UNIT,BUNS,CARE,TOFFEE ETC.

Rated Plant Capacity = 1243.70 Kgs/Day

LAND & BUILDING (Land Area 500 sq. mt.) = Rs. 7,00,000.00

PLANT & MACHINERY

1. Auto Siffter
2. Dough Kneader
3. Dough Grinder
4. State Convet
5. Dough Rounder
6. Dough Moulder

Bakery Unit (Pastries, Bread, Buns, Cake, Toffee etc.)

7. Diesel Rotary Rock
8. Cooling rack
9. Trolley
10. Automatic Slice
11. Cream Milk
12. Dies and Mold
13. Electrically Heating Kettle
14. Cooling Chamber
15. Packing, and sealing Machine
16. Miscellaneous Machine

FIXED CAPITAL

1.	LAND & BUILDING	Rs.	7,00,000.00
2.	PLANT & MACHINERY	Rs.	8,29,500.00
3.	OTHER FIXED ASSETS	Rs.	2,75,000.00
	TOTAL	Rs.	18,04,500.00

RAW MATERIALS

1. Flour
2. Shortening
3. Salt
4. Sugar
5. Egg
6. Milk Solid
7. Yeast
8. Butter
9. Glucose solid

TOTAL WORKING CAPITAL/MONTH

1.	RAW MATERIAL	Rs.	2,48,058.00
2.	SALARY & WAGES	Rs.	22,920.00
3.	UTILITIES & OVERHEADS	Rs.	26,100.00
	TOTAL	Rs.	2,97,078.00

TOTAL CAPITAL INVESTMENT

TOTAL FIXED CAPITAL	Rs.	18,04,500.00
TOTAL WORKING CAPITAL FOR 3 MONTHS	Rs.	8,91,234.00
TOTAL	Rs.	26,95,734.00

TURN OVER/ANNUM

1. Pastry Products: 120000 Kgs.
2. Paste 30000 Kgs.
3. Bread/Bun 99540 kgs
4. Toffee 123570 Kgs

Rs. 52,01,250.00

PROFIT SALES RATIO = Profit / Sales x 100 = 18.31 %

RATE OF RETURN = Operating profit / T.C.I x 100 = 35.32 %

BREAK EVEN POINT (B.E.P) = 49.13 %

Chapter - 34

Bakery Gel (Translucent Semi Solid Paste)

The use of emulsifying agents in bake goods (bread, cake buns) is wide spread. Generally speaking, the emulsifying agent appears to serve two purposes. In the actual preparation of the dough, the presence of the agent serves to improve the intimation of the dough, the presence of the agent serves to improve the intimate mixing of the components, and hence has a desirable effect on the quality of the final products. Secondly, in the final product, the presence of the effect of retarding staling. The exact mode of action in this latter regard is somewhat obscure, but it appears to take place as a result of the inhibition of the formation of hydrogen bonds between adjacent starch chains in the finished cake or bread.

It has been found that when emulsifier was added to a cake formula, the fat, together with the air bubbles, became more highly dispersed.

Emulsifiying agents for cakes were first offered in the 1930's. The materials permitted the baker to make cakes with higher percentages of sugar, water and fat i.e. the floor could be decreased relative to these ingredients. The surface active agent functions as an emulsifier and whipping agent making the batter easier to prepare by dispersing the ingredients and facilitating the incorporation of air bubbles. In the 1940's emulsifiers such as sorbitan monostearate and polyoxyethylene sorbitan monostearate became available as separate ingredients.

MANUFACTURING OF BAKERY GEL

(Transluient Semi Solid Paste)

Formulation (Non-ionic Type)

Fatty phase:

Polyoxyethylene (20) Sorbitan Monostearate (liquid)	-	60%
Sorbitan Monostearate (solid)	-	40%

Bakery Unit (Pastries, Bread, Buns, Cake, Toffee etc.)

Water phase		**Parts by wt.**
Citric Acid	-	0.7
Sodium Propionate	-	0.5
Water	-	5-10

∴ HLB of the above fatty phase is calculated as follow.

= [0.6 x (HLB of polyoxyethylene (20) Sorbitan monostearate) + 0.4 x (HLB of Sorbitan Monostearate)]

= [0.6 x 14.9 + 0.4 x 4.7)]

= 8.94 + 1.88 = 10.82

= This value indicate that the above product is translucent to clear dispersion when added to water with homogeneous mixing.

PLANT ECONOMICS OF BAKERY GEL

Rated Plant Capacity = 1.00 TON./Day

LAND & BUILDING (Land Area 2000 sq.mt.) = Rs. 21,45,000.00

PLANT & MACHINERY

1. Ethylene Oxide underground storage tank
2. PVC (Sintex type)water storage tank
3. Nitrogen Gas Cylinders
4. Stainless steel tank
5. Ethoxylation Reactor
6. Heating,cooling,Nitrogen inlet, Ethylene Oxide sparger,sampling facility,thermo wells
7. Charging inlet, discharge valve
8. Boiler oil fired
9. Water Chiller
10. Stainless steel tank
11. Insutrumentation & process control equipments.
12. Laboratory Equipments complete
13. Pipes, Pumps, valves,tanks,safety equipments,fire fighting equipments
14. Electrical fittings,transformers, & miscellaneous accessories
15. Weighing balance
16. Semi automatic weighing, paste filling and container sealing machine
17. Carton sealing machine
18. Tools, jigs, fixtures and accessories

FIXED CAPITAL

1.	LAND & BUILDING	Rs.	21,45,000.00
2.	PLANT & MACHINERY	Rs.	48,10,000.02
3.	OTHER FIXED ASSETS	Rs.	24,50,000.00
	TOTAL	Rs.	94,05,000.02

RAW MATERIALS

1. Ethylene Oxide Gas
2. Sorbitan Monostearate
3. Citric Acid
4. Sodium Propionate
5. Distilled water
6. Phosphoric Acid
7. Nitrogen Gas
8. Laboratory Chemicals
9. Plastic Containers
10. Cartons Corrugated Cardboard

TOTAL WORKING CAPITAL/MONTH

1.	RAW MATERIAL	Rs.	18,49,625.00
2.	SALARY & WAGES	Rs.	2,38,500.00
3.	UTILITIES & OVERHEADS	Rs.	5,34,500.00
	TOTAL	Rs.	26,22,625.00

TOTAL CAPITAL INVESTMENT

TOTAL FIXED CAPITAL	Rs.	94,05,000.02
TOTAL WORKING CAPITAL FOR 3 MONTHS	Rs.	78,67,875.00
TOTAL	Rs.	1,72,72,875.02

TURN OVER/ANNUM

By sale of Bakery Gel of 250 gms. size pack, (12,00,000 Nos.)	Rs	4,20,00,000.00

PROFIT SALES RATIO = Profit / Sales x 100 = 16.81 %
RATE OF RETURN = Operating profit / T.C.I x 100 = 40.87 %
BREAK EVEN POINT (B.E.P) = 50.43 %

Chapter - 35

Baking Powder

Baking powder is a mixture containing chemicals used for the aeration of various types confectionery. The active ingredients are sodium bicarbonate and an acid substance, which in presence of water will react with the bicarbonate to produce carbon dioxide. The relative proportions of bicarbonate and acid body must be such that the bicarbonate is fully neutralized but the residue of acid is not excessive. In addition to these two chemicals, a baking powder contains an inert filler such as starch. The acid body's mainly used in the baking powder are cream of tarter, acid sodium pyrophosphate, and acid calcium phosphate. The amount of calcium phosphate or acid sodium phosphate needed in a baking powder is about 1:3 times the proportion of sodium bicarbonate that is present, and the amount of cream of tartar required is about 2:2 times the bicarbonate content of the mixture.

MANUFACTURE OF BAKING POWDERS

The blending of baking powder is essentially a physical mixing of the various components in a large scale batch mixer and is carried out in automatic plants. However, the art is much more complex than, one might expect. The characteristics of the various components have an influence on product uniformity. The order in which mixing occurs may have an influence on the stability of the product. Blending of the sodium aluminium phosphate in commercial formula, (as in composition baking powder in table attached with it) with tri calcium phosphate should be done before addition of the other ingredients. This coats the salp and prevent reaction during storage. Similarly, incorporation of the starch with individual components tends to maintain separation until reaction is needed. Rigid specification for purity, granulation and moisture content of the components must be adhered to it a uniform stable and reliable product is to be obtained.

Variation in ingredient purity can alter the proper balance of acid to soda. Granulation is very critical, not only in terms of stability and uniformity of distribution of particles during blending, but also in the appearance of baked products. Too many fine or coarse particles would be detrimental. The proper kind and speed of blending are essential to attain and maintain proper distribution of particles. The baking powder is usually packed in airtight metal or fibre cans. However, Hermetically sealed packages are not used because of the possibility of building up high internal pressures.

Formulation :-

The first and foremost step in the manufacture of baking powder is its formulation.

	% wt.
Sodium Bicarbonate	35
Starch	24
Sodium Aluminium Sulphate	29
Acid Calcium Phosphate	12 kg

PLANT ECONOMICS OF BAKING POWDER

Rated Plant Capacity =		0.60 TON/Day
LAND & BUILDING (Land area 400 sq.mt.) =	Rs.	10,56,000.00

PLANT & MACHINERY

1. Ribbon Blender
2. Sieving set
3. Electric Motor
4. Electricity Installation charges
5. Miscellaneous

FIXED CAPITAL

1. LAND & BUILDING	Rs.	10,56,000.00
2. PLANT & MACHINERY	Rs.	1,37,000.00
3. OTHER FIXED ASSETS	Rs.	30,000.00
TOTAL	Rs.	12,23,000.00

RAW MATERIALS

1. Cream of tarter
2. Sodium Bicarbonate
3. Starch (Maize)

TOTAL WORKING CAPITAL/MONTH

1.	RAW MATERIAL	Rs.	3,05,400.00
2.	SALARY & WAGES	Rs.	32,280.00
3.	UTILITIES & OVERHEADS	Rs.	22,400.00
	TOTAL	Rs.	3,60,080.00

TOTAL CAPITAL INVESTMENT

TOTAL FIXED CAPITAL	Rs.	12,23,000.00
TOTAL WORKING CAPITAL FOR 3 MONTHS	Rs.	10,80,240.00
TOTAL	Rs.	23,03,240.00

TURN OVER/ANNUM

By sales of 180 MT of Baking Powder	Rs.	63,00,000.00

PROFIT SALES RATIO = Profit / Sales x 100 = 25.17 %

RATE OF RETURN = Operating profit / T.C.I x 100 = 68.85 %

BREAK EVEN POINT (B.E.P) = 29.25 %

Chapter - 36

Mini Flour Mill (Atta)

Mini Flour mill serve the purpose of processing wheat to convert it into Atta. Wheat grains are the seeds of the wheat plant which is able to grow in kinds of soil and under widely differing climatic conditions. The principle wheats of commerce belong to the botanical groups Triticum vulgane, Triticum drum and triticum compactum. A grain of wheat is avoid in shape fine hains.

The grains of what consists of three main parts, the enveloping skins, the embroyo and the endosperm. The relative proportions of these parts vary with the plumpness of the grain but average composition of wheat is 85% endosperm, 2.4% embroyo and 14.5% enveloping skins.

The enveloping skins are pericarp which consists of the eipdorumis, epicarp and endocarp. The percarp represent about 6% of the grain. The seed cost consisting of the tests the byaline layer which comprises about 2% of the grain. The aleuorone layer representing about 6.5% of the grain wheat show a wide range of analytical data which is not unexpected in view of the many varieties which are grown and the very different conditions under which they are cultivated. The range of data normally encountered is as follows :

PERCENTAGE

Moisture	10.0 - 17.0
Protein	8.5 - 14.0
Fat	2.0 - 2.50
Fibre	2.0 - 2.50
Mineral matter	1.5 - 2.0
Sugars	2.0 - 3.0
Starch	63.0 - 71.0

MANUFACTURING PROCESS

The milling process breaks open the wheat kernel and reduces the particles formed as to separate the outer and inner portions of the kernel. Bran and gram are almost completely separated from the white interior portions in the milling of refined flour.

Mini Flour Mill (Atta)

When the entire kernel is ground and no separations are made, the product is whole white flour. The following steps are involved in milling wheat, Wheat selection blending sieving, purifying reducing classifying and some combination of maturing bleaching and diastric or enriching treatment of the flour. It is not necessary that all these operations be performed is every flour mill. But either these operations are performed as such as or combination of these operations to serve the some purpose are performed in the flour mills.

1 Wheat selection and Blending
2. Cleaning
3. Conditioning or Tempering
4. Milling

PLANT ECONOMICS OF MINI FLOUR MILL (ATTA AND CHOKER)

Rated Plant Capacity =		22.40 MT./Day
LAND & BUILDING (Land area 350 sq.mts.) =	Rs.	13,48,500.00

PLANT & MACHINERY

1. Reel Machine for wheat cleaning.
2. Elevator Conveyor
3. Emery Rula
4. Worm Conveyor
5. Chakki
6. Pneumatic Conveyor
7. Centrifugal Machine
8. Fan Low Pressure.
9. Piple
10. Pulley/Belting/Shafts etc.
11. Motor
12. Water Dampner
13. Storage Bins
14. Plat Form
15. Tube-well with storage tank

FIXED CAPITAL

1.	LAND & BUILDING	Rs.	13,48,500.00
2.	PLANT & MACHINERY	Rs.	6,12,000.00
3.	OTHER FIXED ASSETS	Rs.	1,75,000.00
	TOTAL	Rs.	21,35,500.00

RAW MATERIALS

1. Wheat
2. Gunny bags

TOTAL WORKING CAPITAL/MONTH

1. RAW MATERIAL	Rs.	31,40,600.00
2. SALARY & WAGES	Rs.	69,000.00
3. UTILITIES & OVERHEADS	Rs.	1,24,600.00
TOTAL	Rs.	33,34,200.00

TOTAL CAPITAL INVESTMENT

TOTAL FIXED CAPITAL	Rs.	21,35,500.00
TOTAL WORKING CAPITAL FOR 2 MONTHS	Rs.	66,68,400.00
TOTAL	Rs.	88,03,900.00

TURN OVER/ANNUM

1. By selling of Atta 6586 MT
2. By selling of Chokar 146 MTS.

Rs. 4,66,30,520.00

PROFIT SALES RATIO = Profit / Sales x 100 = 10.71 %
RATE OF RETURN = Operating profit / T.C.I x 100 = 56.75 %
BREAK EVEN POINT (B.E.P) = 33.82 %

Chapter - 37

Modern Bread and Bakery Unit (EOU) (Bread, Buns, Rusk)

Modern days are changes with the advance of scientific discovery. Due to the scarcity of time now human beings changes their food habits. No body can pay much more time for their preparation of food, every body wants to get ready made fresh food, such that human being can save their time. They do not want to loss their valuable time in the preparation of daily food. By this timing now a days these different kind of food materials developed, like instant tea, instant coffee, instant milk, instant rice etc. On the above point of view bakery products are cheaper, largely accepted ready made food. Now the advancement of age use of bakery foods will gradually increases and utilization will be around the proportional of certain percentage of population increase.

PROCESS OF MANUFACTURE WITH FORMULATION

BREAD

Bread manufacturing is a process of mixing o bread ingredients and prepared a proper dough of the Ingredients, after complete making of doughing dough is divided, rounded, moulding and proofing, after proofing the products is further pass through the baking own to complete bake the product. The product i.e. bread is ready for cooling, slicing and packing for marketing.

GENERAL RAW MATERIAL :

1. Wheat Flour,
2. Yeast,
3. Sugar,
4. Salt,
5. Water,
6. Shortening agent (like vanaspati),
7. Milk or milk powder etc.

RUSK

Bread rusks are among the oldest dietetic foods and are still increasingly consumed in the country particularly by low income group people. This contains an idea of combination of nutritive substances. Due to a good keeping quality, bread rusks have been found useful in dietetics and also serve as a bread reserve.

MANUFACTURE

The process for bread rusk making is same as that for pan bread and similar or exactly some composition and procedures are used except that an additional step of roasting. These are made in different shapes and sizes depending on the local demand.

The first step is to make the bread in desired shape and size. It is baked and cooled. The loaves are then sliced and rebaked to reduce the moisture content to about 10 percent. Rebaking that is toasting plays an important role for manufacturing quality bread rusks.

Unlike bread, bread rusks should be crisp and of uniform texture. They should be free from blister and uniform golden to light brown in colour. They should be of typical agreeable odour, typical of well baked bread rusks and free from any rancidity, bitterness, mustiness, foreign flavour or odour.

FORMULATION OF BREAD RUSK

As mentioned earlier any of the bread formulation can be used for making bread rusks. Wheat flour; leavening agent like baker's yeast, hops and lactic acid ferment etc.; common salt; water and a shortening such as hydrogenated or refined edible oils are essential ingredients of bread rusks. Other ingredients like vital gluten, sugar, malt products. edible starches, vitamins, edible oil, seed flour albumin, eggs, sorbitol and milk and milk products etc. are added to add to the food value of bread rusks.

As improver a small amount of any of the following compounds may also be incorporated in the formulation.

Ammonium persulfate.
Calcium phosphate.
Potassium bromate.
Ammonium Chloride.
Calcium carbonate.

The following chemicals may be used as mould and rope inhibitor in the manufacture of bread rusks acid sodium pyro phosphate.

Ascorbic acid.
Vinegar.
Sodium diacetate.
Calcium of sodium propionate.
Lactic or acetic acid.
Acid calcium phosphate.

The amount of improvers and mould and rope inhibitors which should be incorporated in bread rusks are restricted to some maximum value and reader is advised to consult IS : 8551 - 1977 to get more information on this subject.

PLANT ECONOMICS

Rated Plant Capacity = BREAD & BAKERY UNIT

1. Bread 800 gm. 15,00,000 Pcs.
2. Bread 400 gms. loaves 18,00,000 Pcs
3. Bread 250 gm. 7,50,000 Pcks.
4. Whole Wheat Bread 400 gms. 15,00,000/-Pcs.
5. Sweet/Fruit Bun 50 gms. 30,00,000 Pcs.
6. Hamburger Bun 50 gms. 30,00,000 Pcs.
7. Cream Buns Wt. 50 gms. 30,00,000 Pcs.
8. Rusk 30,000 Kgs.

LAND & BUILDING (Land Area 1 Acres) = Rs. 39,00,000.00

PLANT & MACHINERY

Total Plant and Machinery Cost for Bread, Bun, Rusk Rs. 36,50,000.00

FIXED CAPITAL

1. LAND & BUILDING	Rs.	39,00,000.00
2. PLANT & MACHINERY	Rs.	36,50,000.00
3. OTHER FIXED ASSETS	Rs.	10,50,000.00
TOTAL	Rs.	86,00,000.00

RAW MATERIALS

Raw Materials for Bread, Bun and Rusks Rs. 20,78,950.00

TOTAL WORKING CAPITAL/MONTH

1. RAW MATERIAL	Rs.	20,78,950.00
2. SALARY & WAGES	Rs.	1,86,875.00
3. UTILITIES & OVERHEADS	Rs.	1,48,700.00
TOTAL	Rs.	24,14,525.00

TOTAL CAPITAL INVESTMENT

TOTAL FIXED CAPITAL	Rs.	86,00,000.00
TOTAL WORKING CAPITAL FOR 3 MONTHS	Rs.	72,43,575.00
TOTAL	Rs.	1,58,43,575.00

TURN OVER/ANNUM

1. By Selling Bread 800 gm. 15,00,000 Pcs.
2. Bread 400 gms. loaves 18,00,000 Pcs
3. Bread 250 gm. 7,50,000 Pcks.
4. Whole Wheat Bread 400 gms. 15,00,000 Pcs.
5. Sweet/Fruit Bun 50 gms. 30,00,000 Pcs.
6. Hamburger Bun 50 gms. 30,00,000 Pcs.
7. Cream Buns Wt. 50 gms. 20,00,000 Pcs.
8. Rusk 30,000 Kgs.

Rs. 5,75,47,500.00

PROFIT SALES RATIO = Profit / Sales x 100 = 43.12 %
RATE OF RETURN = Operating profit / T.C.I x 100 = 156.63 %
BREAK EVEN POINT (B.E.P) = 17.79 %

Chapter - 38

Roller Flour Mill

The plant will have facility to produce, maida, sooji, atta and bran. These products will be sold as per the guidance issued for Food and Civil Supplies Department of the concerned state.

The same plant can be used to process other cereals such as rice gram, dal etc. However, attempt is made have to examine feasibility and profitability of processing wheat to produce maida, Suji, atta and bran.

Flour mill serve the purpose of processing wheat to convert it into flour. Wheat grains are the seeds of the wheat plant which is able to grow is kinds of soil and under widely differing climatic conditions. The principle wheats of commerce belong to the botanical groups Triticum vulgane, Triticum drum and triticum compactum. A grain of wheat is avoid in shape and it bears at one end a number of short fine grains.

MANUFACTURING PROCESS

Processing of wheat involves three main stages as given below :-

a) Cleaning, Washing and Conditioning
b) Milling of wheat into flour.
c) Packaging & Dispatch.

The milling process breaks open the wheat kernel and reduces the particles formed so as to separate the outer and inner portions of the kernal. Bran and germ are almost completely separated from the white interior portions in the milling of refined flour.

When the entire kernal is ground and no separations are made, the product is whole white flour. The following steps are involved in milling wheat. Wheat selection, blending sieving, purifying, reducing classifying, and some combination of maturing bleaching and diastatic or enriching treatment of the flour. It is not necessary that all these operations be performed is every flour mill. But either these operations are performed as such as or combination of these operations to serve the same purpose performed in the flour mills.

COMPLETE PLANT SUPPLIERS OF ROLLER FLOUR MILLS

Sifter International,
83, Sector-6, Faridabad - 121006 (Haryana)
Ph : 5240450/5240150
E-Mail : sifter@ndb.vsnl.net.in

Septu India Pvt. Ltd.,
39 KMS, Mile Stone (Delhi),
Delhi Jaipur Highway,
Vill. Narsingpur,
Post Box No. 4,
Gurgaon - 122 001 (Haryana)
Ph : 6373010/11, 6371354
E-Mail : septu@del3.vsnl.net.in
Fax : 91-124-6322997

PLANT ECONOMICS OF ROLLER FLOUR MILL

Rated Plant Capacity =		50.00 MT/Day
LAND & BUILDING (Land Area 2000 sq.mt) =	Rs.	49,00,000.00

PLANT & MACHINERY

1. FOR CLEANING SECTION:-
   Reel Machine 1 No.
2. Aspirator Separator
3. Scourer Machine
4. Washer Whitter Machine
5. Brush Machine
6. Carter Disc separator
7. Spray Damper
8. Low Pressure Fan
9. Dust cyclone with air seal
10. Elevator system L.S.
11. Warm conveyor
12. Fabrication Material L.S.
13. Roller Mill complete in all respects
14. Plant sifter
15. Double Deck purifier
16. Bran Finisher
17. Entolator
18. Low Pressure Fan with cyclone and air seal
19. High Pressure Fan

20. Dust Collector
21. Low Pressure Fan for Dust collector
22. Warm Conveyor
23. Pneumatic systematic complete in all respects with Pneumatic cyclones, Feeders, Air seal, G.I.lifts, etc.
24. Fabrication Material Required for erection like nylon, Bolting cloths, Reduction Gears and Misc.
25. V. Belts, Nuts and Bolts, Hardware etc.
26. Electric Motor
27. Silo Bim

FIXED CAPITAL

1.	LAND & BUILDING	Rs.	49,00,000.00
2.	PLANT & MACHINERY	Rs.	53,69,000.00
3.	OTHER FIXED ASSETS	Rs.	3,90,000.00
	TOTAL	Rs.	1,06,59,000.00

RAW MATERIALS

1. Wheat
2. Chemicals

TOTAL WORKING CAPITAL/MONTH

1.	RAW MATERIAL	Rs.	88,00,000.00
2.	SALARY & WAGES	Rs.	3,02,125.00
3.	UTILITIES & OVERHEADS	Rs.	6,72,000.00
	TOTAL	Rs.	97,74,125.00

TOTAL CAPITAL INVESTMENT

TOTAL FIXED CAPITAL	Rs.	1,06,59,000.00
TOTAL WORKING CAPITAL FOR 3 MONTHS	Rs.	2,93,22,375.00
TOTAL	Rs.	3,99,81,375.00

TURN OVER/ANNUM

1. By selling Maida 9000 MT
2. BY selling Atta 3000 MT
3. By selling Suji 2250 MT
4. By selling wheat Bran 750 MT

Rs. 14,32,50,000.00

PROFIT SALES RATIO = Profit / Sales x 100 = 13.58 %
RATE OF RETURN = Operating profit / T.C.I x 100 = 48.65 %
BREAK EVEN POINT (B.E.P) = 36.51 %

Chapter - 39

Details of Plant & Machinery

BAKERY OVEN

DIESEL FIRED ROTARY RACK OVEN
al Data are on next page)

TECHNICAL DATA

Power (H.P.)	Standard	Medium	Med. Tingu	Small	S. Tingu
Blower	3.00	2.00	2.00	1.50	1.50
Gear Box	1.50	1.00	1.00	1.00	1.00
Burner	0.25	0.25	0.25	0.25	0.25
Fuel (Per Hour)	**Standard**	**Medium**	**Med. Tingu**	**Small**	**S. Tingu**
(Diesel in Ltrs.)	8.00	4.50	4.00	2.50	2.00
For Rusk Loaves	5.00	3.00	2.50	2.00	1.50
For Rusk	4.00	2.50	2.00	1.50	1.00
For Bakery Biscuit	4.00	2.50	2.00	1.50	1.00
Capacity	**Standard**	**Medium**	**Med. Tingu**	**Small**	**S. Tingu**
Bread 400 gms (Per 25 minutes)	420	216	168	108	84
Rusk Loaves 225 gms (20 Minutes)	540	336	216	168	108
Rusk Trays					
13"x21" (Trays Size)	90/120	---	---	24/36	16/24
10"x15"	180/240	90/108	60/84	45/54	30/42
Bakery Biscuits Trays					
13"x21" (Trays Size)	90/120	---	---	24/36	16/24
10"x15"	180/240	90/108	60/84	45/54	30/42
Dimesions (Appx.)	**Standard**	**Medium**	**Med. Tingu**	**Small**	**S. Tingu**
(LxWxH)	10x'8x11'	8'6'x10'	8'x6'x8.5'	6'x4'x10'	6'x4'x8.5'

Bakery Equipments

Deck Oven	**Rotary Rack Oven**
Bakery Ovens available in : (i) Large Model - 4 trays/Deck (ii) Medium Model - 3trays/Deck (iii) Small Model-2trays/Deck in Conventional and Special designs with 4 Decks, 3 Decks, 2 Decks & 1 Deck Fuel : Electric/Gas.	For electric/gas/diesel operation, made in stainless steel. Available in 2 Models : (i) Model CT3 : 10 trays Capacity. (ii) Model CT8 : 18 trays Capacity.
Spiral Dough Mixer	**Dough Sheeter**
Available in 4 models : (i) Model CM 40 - Capacity 40 kg. (ii) Model CM 60 - Capacity 60 Kg. (iii) Model CM 80 - Capacity 80 Kg. (iv) Model CM 120 - Capacity 120 Kg.	Available in : 1. floor Model (i) CSF 600 : Cylinder Length - 600 mm. (ii) CSF500 : Cylinder Length - 500 mm. 2. Table Model ; (i) CSFB 500 : Cylinder Length - 500 mm.
Cake Mixer	**Bread Slicer**
Available in 3 mdels : (i) Model 5 KMP5 -5 Lts. (ii) Model CSP 20 -20 Lts. (iii) Model CSP 40 -40 Lts.	Available in 2 Models (i) CBSL - U : for standard bread 400 gms. (ii) CBSL-J : for "Jumbo' bread

Dough Divider
Available in 2 Models : (i) CTR -30 : Semi Automatic, Capacity 30 Pleces. (ii) CTR-36 : Manual, Capacity 36 Pices.

ICE CREAM CONE MAKING MACHINE

ICE CREAM CONE PROJECT

Manufacturing of Ice Cream Cone is a very lucrative, easy-to-run and low risk business. Cones are basically made of flour and water alongwith a few other ingredients. The cost of raw material (inclusove of packing) for one standard cone as available in the market is only 8.5 paise and it is selling at 18 paise or more. Cones are eaisly sold directly to ice cream vendors.

Semi Automatic operated machine is of high capacity manufacturing of Ice Cream Cones. The machine is equipped with 4 rows of baking mould of Standard Cone diameter. The cast iron moulds are mounted in a heavy steel frame. The upper half. (The make part of the mould) which sides up and down between two steel columns is balanced by counter weights and operated by a hand lever.

In this model, the batter is thoroughly mixed in a batter mixer, a tiet and pour device is filled with a batter by manual dipping into the batter tank. The device in then placed on the mould and titled there filling each mould with exact quantity required. The mould is then closed. Heating is done automatically by electricity. The self contained heating system ensures uniform heating. When heating is complete, the mould is opened the reading cones drops down and collected and packed one unskilled worker can operate this machine. The machine can be run for 24 hours. The parameters of the machine are appened below :-

TECHNICAL DATA

Model	**E20**	**E40**	**E50**	**E60**
Electrical connected load (approx in Kw.)	6	8	9	10
Hourly unit consumption (approx in Kw.)	4	6	7	8
Production per our (in Pcs.)	600	1200	1500	1800
Weight (in kg.)	320	525	575	650
Voltage (in volts)	20/230			
Dimensions (in mm.) Length width Height	 900 850 1800			
Raw Material required	Maida, Starch, Water, Lectine, Refined Oil & Food Colour			
Workers required	3 Unskilled			
Space	400 Sq. feet for each machine			

AUTOMATIC & MANUAL WAFER BISCUITS MACHINE

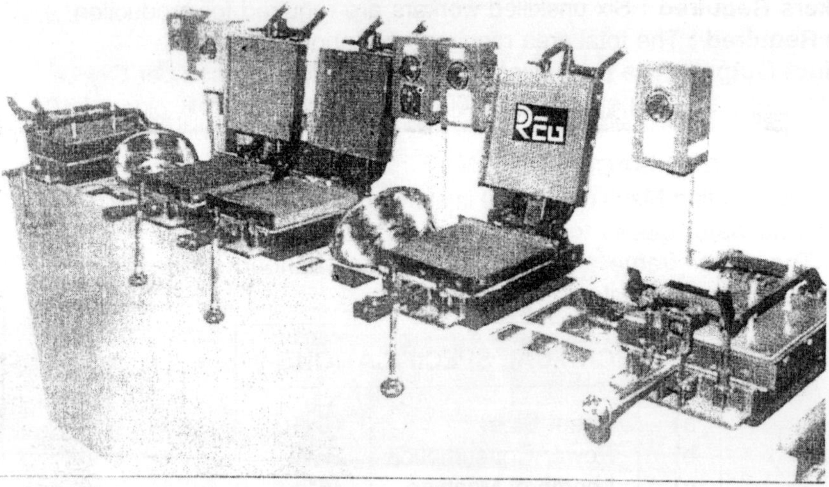

MANUAL AND FULL AUTOMATIC PLANT

Cream Wafer Plant is used to the manually operated, and production of Wafer Biscuit. The cost and operation of machines are low and economical. Machinery makers also supply the wafer baking plates with 5.10 & 15, depending upon the requirement of customers. The complete details with set of wafer plates (8 WP) production and capacity. Cream putting machine, cutting machine, packing machine and mixture machine sugar grinder ensure that production is continuous.

Better Preparation : The mixture of maida, starch, water, lactine, refine oil and food colour etc.

MIXER MACHINE WITH 2 HP

The mixture machine is ideally suited for preparing raw material into liquid for cone and wafer biscuit. The machine has adjustable shaft to mix better preparation from 10 kg. to 55 kg. The machine is fitted with 2 H.P. Electric Motor, the mixing bowl, tank and turbine are all made stainless steel and machine operation is (2KW). The better is fed to pre-heated wafer plates by a special dosing device. baking time from 1-2 minutes. The baked sheets kept to cooled and after operation for creaming and cutting and then ready to pack.

Workers Required : Six unskilled workers are required for production.
Area Required : The total area required near about 700 sq. ft.
Product Output : The production capacity is 35 to 40 cases per day i.e. 360 per day i.e. 360 per boxes 13000 to 14000 pcs. approx. pkts. of 10 Gms. each.

WAFER CUTTING MACHINE (WCM)

The Wafer Cutting Machine (WCM) is semi automatic and fitted with 2 HP Motor cuts wafer blocks to small wafer fingers of predetermined dimension. The cutter frame and feed bar can be changed to produce the different sizes of biscuits.

TECHNICAL SPECIFICATIONS		
a)	Sheet Size	10x10
b)	Power Consumption	2KW
c)	Length of Machine	46"
d)	Width of Machine	32"
e)	Height of Machine	27"
f)	Weight (Approx)	150 KG

CREAM PUTTING MACHINE (CPM)

Cream putting Machine is used for pasting a layor of cream for sandwiching the wafer biscuits. The sheet holder is designed to hold the sheet in place and allow desired cream application. It can be fitted with 2 HP electric motor and automaticy. It can be operated by an unskilled person.

CREAM MIXER MACHINE

Cream Mixer Machine is used for mix of cream and semi automatic having 3 speed system and made by special steel body. It has capacity of preparation of cream 25 kg. at a time. It also fitted with 2 H.P. Electric Motor.

TECHNICAL SPECIFICATIONS

Size of the Baking Plates	10"x10" (approx)
No. of Wafer Plates	10 Pc

Wafer Biscuit Baking Machine	
Wafer sheet Output/Hr.	2000 Pkt. P/h
Electric Heating	18 KW
Connected Load in KW	15 KW
Current Load in KW	15 KW
Dimension	
Length	8'
Width	2'
Height	4'
Net Weight	200 KG. approx.

AUTOMATIC HORIZONTAL FLOW WRAP MACHINE (FOR BISCUITS)

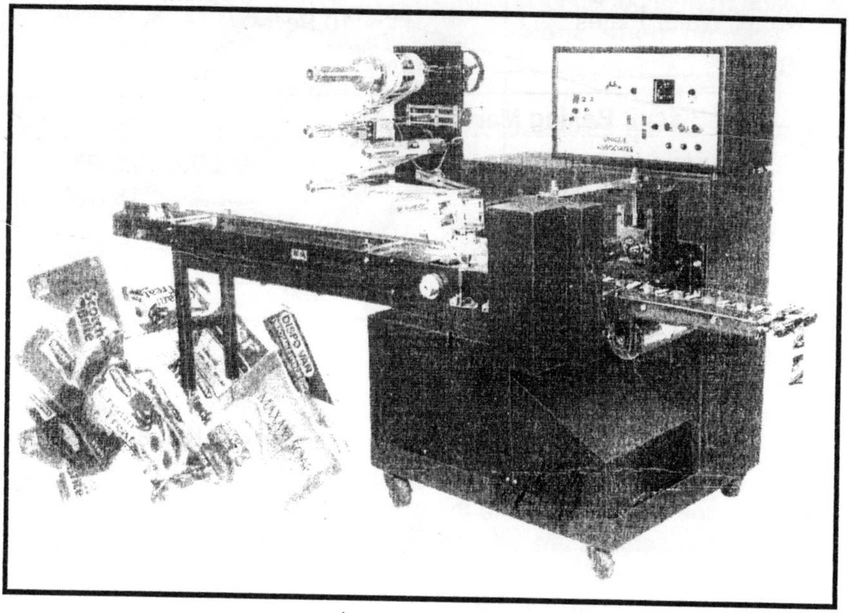

Highly Suitable for Packing of Biscuits, Chocolates, Soaps, Stationery Items, Syringes, Ball Bearing, Toys, any other Rounded, Square Shape of Solid Products.

SPECIFICATIONS

WRAPPING SIZE	Length 100 to 350 mm	Width 50 to 120 mm	Height 10 to 80 mm
PACKING MATERIAL	Any Head Sealablc Laminated Paper		
PACKING STYLE	Pillow Type		
FEEDING	Manual/Automatic		
SEALING TYPE	Continuous		
FILM CORE DIA.	ID. 70-76 mm, OD. 350 mm max.		
OPERATING SPEED	40-120 bags per minute.		
MOTOR HP	1 H.P. DC with DC Drive		
POWER CONSUMPTION	220 Volts		
OVERALL M/C. DIMENSION	L-3600, W-1500, H-1800		
NET WEIGHT	450 kg (without packing)		
GROSS WEIGHT	600 kg (with normal packing)		

BREAD MOULDS

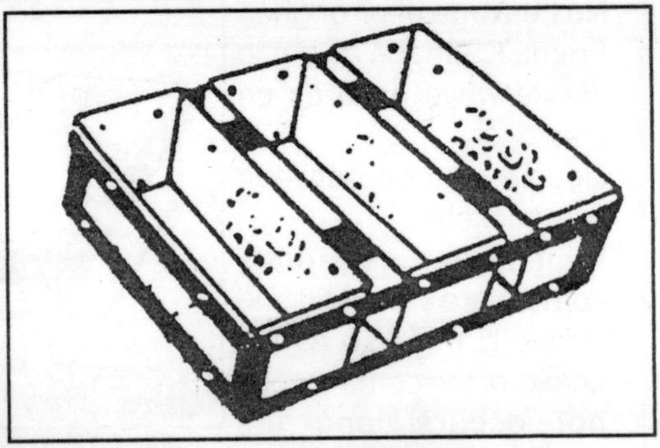

- Made from imported food grade tin plate sheet (Bright)
- Overall M.S. Channel (10MM) on top 19x3Mm Flats striping bottom
- Round Vivit Nicely placed with big rouhd head to give more durability.
- More gap (space) is proviced between two pockets, so as the bake is better.
- No leackage of oil medium
- Clamp between two pocket to provide extra durability and rigidness
- Angle are placed at corners joining the channel frame and flat frame
- Taper is provided in the moulds so as the bake comes out easily
- Mould does not touches the the ground. Frame is below its surface.
- All welded portions are smoothly grined.

ROUND BREAD MOULDS

- made from imported food grade tin plate sheet (bright)

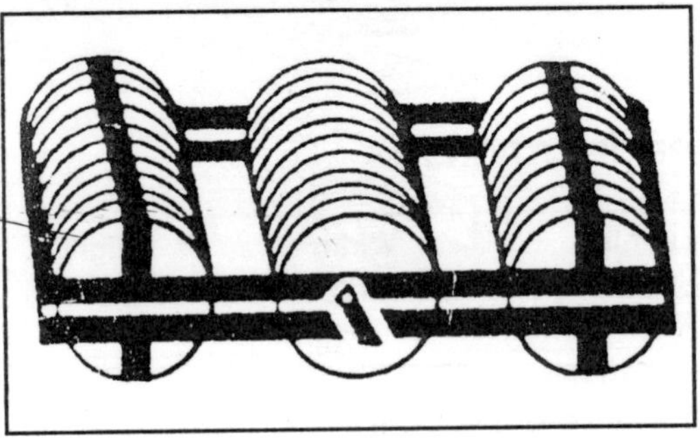

- Plane & with corrugation
- Market share can be increased by using this mould. The Bread is unique in shape
- All moulded portion smoothen & nicely grinded.
- Made by dies to provide uniform size bread.
- Corrugation provides extra durability

- 3 or 6 Pockets in a set
- Top & Bottom make on set of mould to make perfect round bread
- Riviting is done Nicely

ONE PIECE LEAK PROOF BREAD MOULDS

Made of Single Piece
without any joint in the pocket
one sheet is bended twice & Thrice to botain the specific shape.

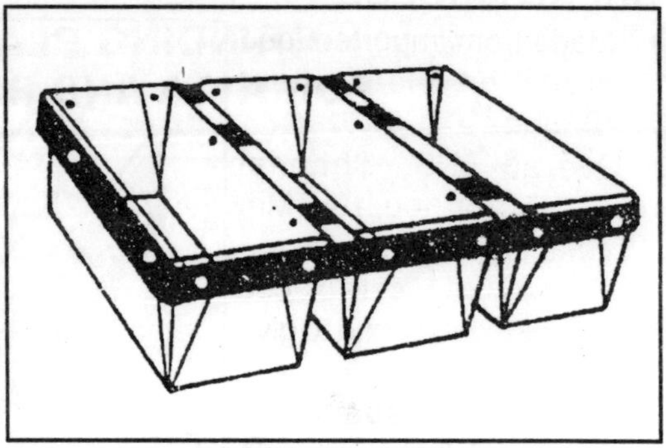

No Leakage of oil or ghee Frame KS made as not to create while hazards on conveyor Double clamps between two pockets Riviting is nicely done corners are very rigid and riviting is doen so as the unfold of the corners does not occurs long life assured uniform size of the bake is guaranteed.

SPECIAL BREAD COOLING RACKS

- Made with G.I. Pipe
- Comes with six or seven shelves with ample space to provide quick & better cooling
- Shelves are perforated so as the beard comes in contact from Bottom also.
- Heavy duty, No Maintenance, Latest Design.
- Special Wheel with Double Ball Bearing.
- Sheels for easy Movement from one place to another.

BREAD CRATE

- Made of Heavy Duty M.S. Flats, T-Angle & Angle
- Nicely Welded.
- Taper is provided, so as one crate fits to another, to consume less space
- Tailor made sizes.

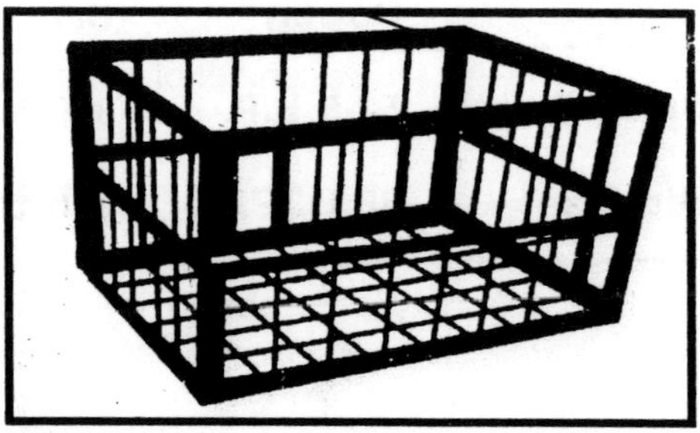

GRINDING PLANT FOR ATTA AND BESAN

GRINDING PLANT CONSISTS OF :

- One Grinder with 7.5 HP motor :
- One Roller Miils with Two Rolls with 7.5 HP motor/4 Rolls
- Five Pneumatic lifts complete with Air locks, pneumatic
- Cyclone, bends pipe with 2 HP motor & reduction gear box.
- One high pressure fan with 7.5 HP motor complete with
- Pneumatic main fold;
- One Plansifter with 2 HP motor
- Complete Control Pannel with push button Starter for Plant;
- One H.E. Cyclone of size 1000 mm of Dust Collector.

	Power	Capacity	Size
Small Plant	**52.5 H.P.**	**350 Kg. per Hour**	**19'x12.6'x6'**
Big Plant	**60 H.P.**	**800-1000 Kg. P.H.**	**26'x16.6'x7'**

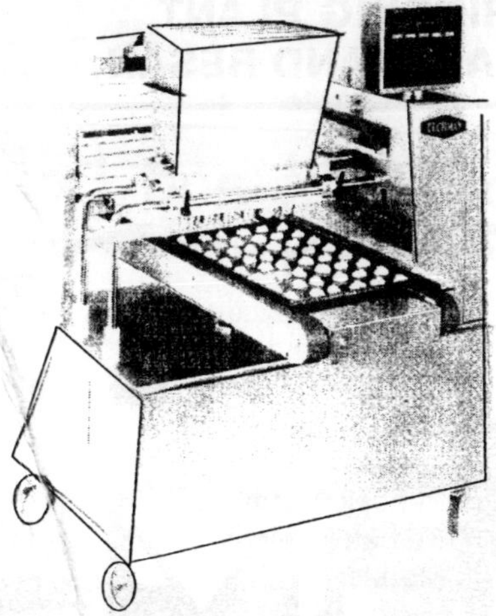

COOKIE-DROP MACHINE

Computerised machine for the automatic forming and dosing on trays of liquid, dense and hard dough.

The computer can store 99 different programs which makes product changeover simple and quick.

The easy adjustment of the parameters of each programe facilitates the operator in creating biscuits according to his fantasy.

Wire cutting device permits the production of short pastry type cookies and similar from hard dough (optional).

The machine is constructed entirely in stainless steel and food grade anticordal aluminium.

The low height of the hopper enables easy access for loading the dough into the hopper.

Particular attention has been given to quick disassembly of the parts in contact with dough, in order to effect a thorough deaning of all the parts.

Technical Data

Machine Type	Max. Prod. (Per Hour)	Power KW	OUTPUT EXITS	TRAY DIMENSION	
				WIDTH	LENGTH
CD 40	90 KG.	2 KW	6	400-460	600-660-800
CD 60	135 KG.	3 KW	9	600-660	400-600-800

Chapter - 40

Suppliers of Plant and Equipments

BAKERY MACHINE

SAS Bakery Equipments
Mr. V. V. Shaji
(Chairman & Managing Director)
No. 763, R. C. Road, Rajevgandhi Nagar, Bommanahalli
Bengaluru - 560068, Karnataka, India
Mobile:
+(91)-7204549036
+(91)-8123619283
Telephone:
+(91)-(431)-2740482

Rite Equipments Private Limited
Mr. Ramesh Babu V. C.
(Manager-Operations)
No. 31, 1st Floor, 1st Main,
Domlur Layout
Bengaluru - 560071, Karnataka, India
Mobile:
+(91)-9739992022
+(91)-9886052126
Telephone:
+(91)-(80)-43406000
Fax:
+(91)-(80)-43406060

Sun Kitchen Equipments
Mr. K. S. Siva Murugan (Partner)
No. 8/2, Nayudu Layout, Yarandahalli, Henagara Post, Near Bommasandra Industrial Area
Bengaluru - 560105, Karnataka, India
Mobile:
+(91)-9940174272
+(91)-9043007001
+(91)-9611237811
+(91)-8095933853

C. S. Aerotherm Private Limited (Customer/Presales)
Mr. Prashanth Jairam (Manager)
No. 143 H, Bommasandra Industrial Area,
Hosur Road
Bengaluru - 560 099, Karnataka, India
Mobile :
+(91)-9632221860
(Between 9 AM to 8 PM)
Phone :
+(91)-(80)-40895000.

C. S. Aerotherm Private Limited (AFTER SALES)
Mr. Deshpande
No. 143 H, Bommasandra Industrial Area, Hosur Road
Bengaluru - 560 099, Karnataka, India
Mobile :
+(91)-9243720034,
+(91)-9611195407
Phone :
+(91)-(80)-40875000

C. S. Aerotherm Pvt Limited (Purchase Manager)
Mr. Senthil Kumar
No. 143 H, Bommasandra Industrial Area,
Hosur Road
Bengaluru - 560 099, Karnataka, India
Mobile :
+(91)-9611195412
Phone :
+(91)-(80)-40895000

Deshpande Aerotherm
Mr. Senthil Kumar
Bommasandra Industrial Area, Hosur Road
Bengaluru - 560099, Karnataka, India
Mobile:
+(91)-9611195407
Telephone:
+(91)-(80)-40895000

Techno Spark Bakery Equipments
Mr. Sujithkumar (Partner)
No.67-A,SF No:515
Bharathiyar Road,

Thiruvalluvar Street Extention, Opp.Sakthi Mariyamman Kovil,Maniyakarapalayam, Ganapathy Coimbatore - 641 006, Tamil Nadu, India
Mobile:
+(91)-9843415152
+(91)-9843415122

Matrix Kitchen Makers
Mr. Mir. Mohd. Faheemuddin (Managing Director & CEO)
No. 945, 1st Main Road, 6th Cross Road, Near Shreya Hospital, Kengeri Satellite Town Bengaluru - 560060, Karnataka, India
Mobile:
+(91)-9880229452
+(91)-9632112221

Shree Shyam Agencies
Mr. Girish Purswani
A-401, Suryakiran Building, Halar Road, Valsad -396001, Gujarat, India
Mobile :
+(91) 9377967016
Telephone:
+(91)-(2632)-257016
Fax No :
+(91)-(2632)-257016

Rhombus Thermo Systems Private Ltd.
No. 136-10, Naidu Road, 6th Cross, BSK 3rd Stage, Near Balaji Kalyana Mantapa, Bengaluru - 560085,Karnataka, India
Mr. Krishna Sirdeshpande
Mobile:
+(91)-9900154181
Telephone :
+(91)-(80)-26797104
Fax No :
+(91)-(80)-26797104

Baker Enterprises
Mr. Achal Tandon (Business Partner)
23, Bhera Enclave, Paschim Vihar
New Delhi - 110087, Delhi, India
Mobile:
+(91)-9810009623
+(91)-9212447925
Telephone:
+(91)-(11)42342490
+(91)-(11)-25266238
Email:
floursifter@gmail.com
bakeryoven@gmail.com

Bharat Sales Corp.
Mr. Sandeep Kumar (Proprietor)
No. 45, G. B. Road
Delhi - 110006, India
Mobile:
+(91)-9868099126

Telephone:
+(91)-(11)-23213072
+(91)-(11)-23213070
Fax:
+(91)-(11)-23213072

Sandhu Mechanical Works
Mr. Sardar GS Sandhu (Proprietor)
WZ-105-A, Khyala Village,
Near M. L. A. House
New Delhi - 110018, Delhi, India
Mobile:
+(91)-9810264397
Telephone:
+(91)-(11)-25176924
+(91)-(11)-28336924

Ultra Worldwide Private Limited
Mr. Rajan Guglani (Director)
201, Joshi Chambers, Amehdabad Street, Iron Market,
Near Masjid East
Mumbai - 400009, Maharashtra, India
Mobile:
+(91)-9821064899
+(91)-9821038165
Telephone:
+(91)-(22)-23481424
Fax:
+(91)-(22)-23482417

Shreetech Instrumentation
Mr. Yogesh Gaikwad (Proprietor)
No. 141, Narhegaon,

Near Bharavnath Mandir
Pune - 411041,
Maharashtra, India
Mobile:
+(91)-8600994858
+(91)-9822627802
Fax:
+(91)-(20)-24391926
Email:
shreetech.instrumentation@yahoo.co.in
shreetechinstrumentation@rediffmail.com

BAKERY OVEN

Baker Enterprises
Mr. Achal Tandon (Business Partner)
23, Bhera Enclave, Paschim Vihar
New Delhi - 110087, Delhi, India
Mobile:
+(91)-9810009623
+(91)-9212447925
Telephone:
+(91)-(11)-42342490
+(91)-(11)-25266238
Email:
floursifter@gmail.com
bakeryoven@gmail.com

Uma Shankar International
Mr. Avtar Singh
K-55B, Basement, Kalkaji
New Delhi-110019, Delhi (India)
Phone :
+(91)-(11)-41058584
+(91)-(11)-41613675
Mobile No. :
+(91)-9810088622
+(91)-9871188622

Beena Equipments
Mr. Tribhuvan Panchal (Proprietor)
B - 2, Patil Compound, Opposite D - 26,
M. I. D. C., Phase - 2,
Kalyan, Shill Road, Dombivli East
Thane - 421204,
Maharashtra, India
Mobile:
+(91)-9867579735
Telephone:
+(91)-(251)-2870095
+(91)-(251)-3202797
Fax:
+(91)-(251)-2870095

Abhishek Enterprises
Mr. Bhaskar Ghule (Managing Director)
Plot No. 133, Gala No. 15, Sector No. 7,
Shivraj Industrial Premises,
P. C. N. T. D. A., Bhosari
Pune - 411026,
Maharashtra, India
Mobile:
+(91)-9766626355
+(91)-9096884642
Telephone:
+(91)-(20)-27130041

VSA Machines India
Mr. Sreekanth Yarlagadda (Proprietor)
Plot No. 117,
Sy. No. 172,
S. V. C. I. E.,
IDA, Bollaram
Hyderabad - 502325,
Andhra Pradesh, India
Mobile:
+(91)-8686031434
+(91)-9246354744
+(91)-8332892495
+(91)-8330934825
Fax:
+(91)-(8458)-279789

Gurpreet Engineering Works
Mr. S. Sharma / Mr. H.J. Singh
Guru Nanak Nagar, Nalas Road,
Near Gurudwara Sahib & Sargam Palace,
Rajpura
Patiala - 140401,
Punjab, India
Mobile:
+(91)-9256291102
+(91)-9464952354

Shreetech Instrumentation
Mr. Yogesh Gaikwad (Proprietor)
No. 141, Narhegaon, Near Bharavnath Mandir
Pune - 411041,
Maharashtra, India
Mobile:
+(91)-8600994858
+(91)-9822627802
Fax:
+(91)-(20)-24391926
Email:
shreetech.instrumentation@yahoo.co.in
shreetechinstrumentation@rediffmail.com

Orange Foodstuff Equipment Pvt Lid.
Mr. Sandeep Sinha (DGM- Sales)

No. 29, Kukreja Plaza, Below K-Star Hotel, Sector-11,
Near CBD Railway Station, Belapur
Mumbai - 400614, Maharashtra, India
Mobile:
+(91)-9769404666
+(91)-9819675666
Telephone:
+(91)-(22)-41233660
+(91)-(22)-41233661
+(91)-(22)-41233662
+(91)-(22)-41233663

Multivent Envirotech
Mr. Jitendra K Yadav / Mr. Raju P Yadav
1402 / 10, Near GIDC Office & Police Station, GIDC, Sarigam,
Tal Umergaon
Valsad - 396155, Gujarat, India
Mobile:
+(91)-9867122100
+(91)-9558556105
+(91)-8460938001

Shivang Furnaces And Ovens Industries
Mr. Dhiren Buch (Director)
No. 483, Jalaram Estate, Narol Vatva Road, Narol
Ahmedabad - 382405, Gujarat, India
Mobile:
+(91)-9327013773
+(91)-9428597582
Telephone:
+(91)-(79)-22772031
+(91)-(79)-25735849
Fax:
+(91)-(79)-25735849

Balaji Enterprises Krishna & Co.
Mr. Kailash Kenjale (Proprietor)
Paper Box, Near Hotel White House,
Mahakali Caves Road, Andheri East
Mumbai - 400093, Maharashtra, India
Mobile:
+(91)-9221838167
+(91)-9029215692
+(91)-9029445587
+(91)-8976230611
Telephone:
+(91)-(22)-26871659

Steel Ace
Mr. S. S. Sohal (Owner)
Plot No. 589, Phase - 9, A. S. Nagar
Mohali - 160059, Punjab, India
Mobile:
+(91)-9417004772
Telephone:
+(91)-(172)-2210113

Sun Engg. Works
Mr. E. Muppidathi Raju/ Mr. S. Karthick Raja (Proprietor)
Sumaithange Thottam, Sundarapuarm Road, Opp. M.M. Engg., Madukkarai Post
Coimbatore - 641105, Tamil Nadu, India
Mobile:
+(91)-9944416996
+(91)-9750944091

Shakthi Enterprises, Hyderabad
Mr. S. Govardhan Reddy / Prathap Chander Reddy (Prop.)
H. No. 23 - 63, A & B Saraswathi Nagar, Opposite Fruit Market Road, Dilsukh Nagar
Hyderabad - 500060, Andhra Pradesh, India
Mobile:
+(91)-9848073926
+(91)-9848039806
Telephone:
+(91)-(40)-24048432
Fax:
+(91)-(40)-24058226

Bread Plant
Autobake Productions
Mr. Yusuf (Owner)
No. 191, Mutton Street, Nal Bazar
Mumbai - 400003, Maharashtra, India
Mobile:
+(91)-9892908633
+(91)-7208679975
+(91)-8082432436

Arun Rega Bakery Machineries (Pvt) Ltd.
Mr. Nand Kumar
F.S.No 213, Site No 4, Sitra Kalapatti Road, Kalapatti Post
Coimbatore - 641048, Tamil Nadu, India

Mobile:
+(91)-9600965636
Telephone:
+(91)-(422)-6544899
+(91)-(422)-6458111
+(91)-(422)-6458222
Fax:
+(91)-(422)-2665633

VSA Machines India
Mr. Sreekanth Yarlaga-dda (Proprietor)
Plot No. 117, Sy. No. 172, S. V. C. I. E., IDA, Bollaram
Hyderabad - 502325, Andhra Pradesh, India
Mobile:
+(91)-8686031434
+(91)-9246354744
+(91)-8332892495
+(91)-8330934825
Fax:
+(91)-(8458)-279789

Besto Oven Industries
108, Acharya Commercial Center,
Dr C.G Road, Near Basant Cinema, Chembur
Mumbai - 400 074, Maharashtra, India
Mr. M Adil Khan
Mobile :
+(91) - 9820128427
Telephone:
+(91)-(22)-25218844,
+(91)-(22)-25568446,
+(91)-(22)-25511718
Call us
+(91)-9953357258
Email id:
besto786@yahoo.com
adil@ovenindia.com
besto@ovenindia.com
Website :
www.ovenindia.com

Besto Oven Industries
Factory 1 :
Plot No. 27,
Arkose Industrial Estate, Sajgaon,
Dheku, Tal, Khalapur
Khopoli, 410203
(M.H.), India

Asian Ovens
Factory 2 :
Site 1, Industrial Area,
B-8/2, Haripur
Jalalabad,
Lucknow Road,
Faizabad 224001
(U.P.) India.
Mobile :
+(91)-8172819222

A. G. Industries
Mr. Alok Gupta
A-108, Lok Vihar, Pitampura
New Delhi - 110034, India
Mobile:
+(91)-9868811577

A. A. Engineering
Mr. Sanjai Erat
No. 13, Om Sai Industrial Estate,
Behind Deepak Nitrate,
MIDC, Taloja
Navi Mumbai - 410208, Maharashtra, India
Mobile:
+(91)-9930768630
+(91)-9820512106
Telephone:
+(91)-(22)-27401526

Shree Shyam Agencies
Mr. Girish Purswani
A-401, Suryakiran Building, Halar Road
Valsad - 396001, Gujarat, India
Mobile:
+(91)-9377967016
Telephone:
+(91)-(2632)-257016

Uma Shankar International
Mr. Avtar Singh
K-55B, Basement,
Kalkaji New Delhi -110019, (India)
Phone :
+(91)-(11)-41058584
+(91)-(11)-41613675
Mobile :
+(91)9810088622
+(91)9871188622

Premier Equipments
Mr. K. Senniappan
77, Lakshmi Nagar,
Malumichampatti
Coimbatore - 641050, Tamil Nadu, India
Mobile:
+(91)-9443712584
Telephone:
+(91)-(422)-2675938
+(91)-(422)-2675941

Sankhla Food & Bakery Plant
Mr. Sharad Sankhla
Plot No. 64,

P.h.e.d Colony
Nagaur - 341001, Rajasthan, India
Mobile:
+(91)-9024198253
Website:
http://www.sankhlafoodandbackeryplant.com/

Chefs Equipments
Mr. Narayan Kadam
H. No. 1 - 3 - 1026/14,
Singadi Kunta,
Near GHMC Garage,
Kavadiguda
Secunderabad - 500 080
Andhra Pradesh,
India
Mobile:
+(91)-9246177685

Maanchet Machine India Private Limited
Mr. Nandha Kumar
SF No. 213,
Kalapatty Road,
Kalapatti
Coimbatore - 641 035,
Tamil Nadu, India
Telephone:
+(91)-(422)-6544899
+(91)-(422)-2669849
Mobile:
+(91)-9600965643

Super Bakers
Mr. Karmchand
Near B.O.B,
Anil Starch Mill Road,
Naroda Road
Ahmedabad - 380 001,
Gujarat, India
Mobile:
+(91)-9825033114

Uniphos Agro Industries Limited
Mr. Sandeep J. Singh
Readymoney Terrace,
No. 167,
Dr. A. B. Road, Worli
Mumbai - 400 018,
Maharashtra, India
Mobile:
+(91)-9819653097
Telephone:
+(91)-(22)-61233500
+(91)-(22)-24930681
Website:
http://www.uniphosagroindustries.com

Nk Enterprises
Mr. Nazim Khan
No. 253, Sundaram Pillai Nagar, Tondiarpet
Chennai - 600 081,
Tamil Nadu, India
Mobile:
+(91)-9952136851
Telephone:
+(91)-(44)-25922227
Website:
http://www.nkenterprisee.com

BISCUIT MAKING PLANT

O.H.P.Food Products Private Limited
Mr. Hemant Arora (Owner)
A 55, FF Complex,
Jhandewala,
Rani Jhansi Road,
Karol Bagh
Delhi - 110055, India
Mobile:
+(91)-9711436268
+(91)-9911544166
+(91)-7503969078
+(91)-7503791477
Telephone:
+(91)-(11)-27290789
+(91)-(11)-43715244
Email:
info@theindustryconsultant.com
great7532@gmail.com
ohpfood@gmail.com

Streamline Exports
Mr. Kavit Vora
No. 46, Suprabhat Building,
Office No. 2249,
Gandhinagar,
Bandra East
Mumbai - 400051,
Maharashtra, India
Mobile:
+(91)-9820244566
Telephone:
+(91)-(22)-26510410
Website:
http://www.streamline-exports.com

BBL Foods Private Limited
Mr. Lakhbir Mutchall
Santosh Nagar, Cross Roads
Hyderabad - 500059,
Andhra Pradesh, India
Mobile:
+(91)-9848050607
Telephone:
+(91)-(40)-24530680
+(91)-(40)-32436296
Website:
http://www.bblfoods.net

Raman Industries
Mr. Inderjit Singh
D- 344, Focal Point, Phase- 8
Ludhiana - 141010, Punjab, India
Mobile:
+(91)-9888782828
Telephone:
+(91)-(161)-5077393
+(91)-(161)-2673682

Ultra Worldwide Private Limited
Mr. Rajan Guglani (Director)
201, Joshi Chambers, Amehdabad Street, Iron Market, Near Masjid East
Mumbai - 400009, Maharashtra, India
Mobile:
+(91)-9821064899
+(91)-9821038165
Telephone:
+(91)-(22)-23481424
Fax:
+(91)-(22)-23482417

K K Industries, Ghaziabad
Mr. Vijay Kumar (Proprietor)
248 A, Patel Marg (Bhonja)
Ghaziabad - 201001, Uttar Pradesh, India
Mobile:
+(91)-9810777035
Telephone:
+(91)-(120)-2834097
Fax:
+(91)-(120)-2834097

Sehgal Exports
Mr. Bhalvinder Singh (Managing Director)
D-4, Focal Point
Patiala - 147001, Punjab, India
Mobile:
+(91)-9815480042
Telephone:
+(91)-(175)-2232647
Fax:
+(91)-(175)-2232647

Mangal Machines Private Limited
Mr. Lalit Kumar Dhiman (Director)
Old Factory Area
Patiala - 147001, Punjab, India
Call Us:
08373904874
Mobile:
+(91)-9878802223
+(91)-9357002223
Telephone:
+(91)-(175)-2360180
Fax:
+(91)-(175)-5013358
+(91)-(175)-5003358

Dr Tk Foods
Mr. Tej Kuchroo
E - 312, Crystal Plaza, Lokhandwala Link Road, Andhari
Mumbai - 400053, Maharashtra, India
Mobile:
+(91)-9820026518
Telephone:
+(91)-(22)-26733730
Website:
http://drtkfoods.com/

Jet Flash Economics Groups
Mr. Raj Kha Asraf Zaman Ali Shah
No. 9, Kazi Nazrul, Islam Avenue, Express I. T. Building, 2nd Floor, Kaikhali
Kolkata - 700 052, West Bengal, India
Mobile:
+(91)-9231638688
Telephone:
+(91)-(33)-25733435
+(91)-(33)-25733436

Shakti Engineering Works, Howrah
Mr. Shubhojit Chakorborty
Near Ichapur, Kamardanga Road, Santragachi
Howrah - 711 104, West Bengal, India
Mobile:
+(91)-9830219586
Telephone:
+(91)-(33)-26773480

Amrit Engineering
Mr. Amrit Preet Singh
Plot No. 139, Industrial Area, Phase- 2
Chandigarh - 160002, Chandigarh, India
Mobile:
+(91)-9815950485
Telephone:
+(91)-(172)-2641202
+(91)-(172)-5086093
Website:
http://www.amritenggwork.com

Aarti Enterprise
Mr. Vijay Thakkar
No. 5, Mahalaxmi Shopping Center, Opp. Jivanpark, N. H No. 8, Isanpur
Ahmedabad - 380043, Gujarat, India
Mobile:
+(91)-9925701625

Uniphos Agro Industries Limited
Mr. Sandeep J. Singh
Readymoney Terrace, No. 167, Dr. A. B. Road, Worli
Mumbai - 400 018, Maharashtra, India
Mobile:
+(91)-9819653097
Telephone:
+(91)-(22)-61233500
+(91)-(22)-24930681
Website:
http://www.uniphosagroindustries.com

Antriksh Automation & Engineers
Mr. P.P.S. Gill
No. 104,
Sharda Apartments,
West Enclave,
Pitampura
New Delhi - 110034, Delhi, India
Mobile: +(91)-9311214477

Industrial Bearing Corporation
Mr. Arvind Shah
No. 56/9, Sherif Devji Street, 1st Floor, Masjid
Mumbai - 400 003, Maharashtra, India
Telephone:
+(91)-(22)-23437211
Mobile:
+(91)-9819455718

Sumo Packaging Industries
Mr. Subrata Mondal
Kona Naskar Para, P. O. Kona,
Near Vivekanand Club
Howrah - 711114, West Bengal, India
Telephone:
+(91)-(33)-28473198
Mobile:
+(91)-9831521743

Mohan Lal & Sons, Patiala
Mr. Sudhir Dhiman
Abchal Nagar, Factory Area, Patiala - 147001, Punjab, India
Telephone:
+(91)-(175)-2360206

Ananta Consultancy Services Private Limited
Mr. Ashish Patel
Plot No. 36, D, Kandivali Industrial Estate,
Kandivali (West)
Mumbai - 400 067, Maharashtra, India
Telephone:
+(91)-(22)-28683991
+(91)-(22)-28697865
+(91)-(22)-28697866

Standerd Roll, India
Mr. Daljinder Singh
Naudharani Road, Near Railway Crossing
Maler Kotla - 148023, Punjab, India
Mobile:
+(91)-9781261783
Telephone:
+(91)-(1675)-257257

Standerd Roll, India
Mr. Daljinder Singh
Naudharani Road, Near Railway Crossing,
Maler Kotla - 148023, Punjab, India
Mobile:
+(91)-9781261783
Telephone:
+(91)-(1675)-257257
Website:
http://www.standerdrollindia.com

Samir Polymers
Mr. Manish Sehgal
D-4, Focal Point
Patiala - 147001, Punjab, India
Telephone:
+(91)-(175)-2232647
Website:
http://www.sehgalexports.com

Sankhla Food & Backery Plant
Mr. Sharad Sankhla
Plot 64, P.h.e.d Colony
Nagaur - 341001, Rajasthan, India
Mobile:
+(91)-9024198253

Chapter - 41

Consultants for Bakery Units

Engineers India Research Institute (EIRI)
Mr. Sudhir Gupta / Ankur Gupta
4449, Nai Sarak,
Main Road
New Delhi - 110006,
Delhi, India
Mobile:
+(91)-9811437895
+(91)-9811151047
+(91)-9818804181
Telephone:
+(91)-(11)-23918117
+(91)-(11)-23916431
+(91)-(11)-23947058
+(91)-(11)-64727385
Email:
eiriprojects@gmail.com
eiribooks@yahoo.com
eiriprojects@hotmail.com
eiri9811437895@gmail.com

O.H.P.Food Products Private Limited
Mr. Hemant Arora (Owner)
A 55, FF Complex,
Jhandewala,
Rani Jhansi Road,
Karol Bagh
Delhi - 110055, India
Mobile:
+(91)-9711436268
+(91)-9911544166
+(91)-75039[illegible]078
+(91)-75037[illegible]77
Telephone:
+(91)-(11)-27290789
+(91)-(11)-43715244

Baker Enterprises
Mr. Achal Tandon (Business Partner)
23, Bhera Enclave,
Paschim Vihar
New Delhi - 110087,
Delhi, India
Mobile:
+(91)-9810009623
+(91)-9212447925
Telephone:
+(91)-(11)-42342490
+(91)-(11)-25266238
Email:
floursifter@gmail.com
bakeryoven@gmail.com
Email:
info@theindustryconsultant.com
great7532@gmail.com
ohpfood@gmail.com

Foodees- A Group Of Consultants
Dr. Girish Gupta (CEO)
G - 17/47,
Ground Floor,
Sector - 15, Rohini
Delhi - 110085, India
Mobile:
+(91)-9810290977
+(91)-9811151444
Telephone:
+(91)-(11)-27894505
Fax:
+(91)-(11)-27894505

Sohal Engineers
Mr. Jagjit Singh
C - 57,
Wazirpur Indl. Area
New Delhi - 110 052,
Delhi, India
Mobile:
+(91)-9811163270
Telephone:
+(91)-(11)-27372847
+(91)-(11)-42473633

Chefs Equipments
Mr. Narayan Kadam
H. No. 1 - 3 - 1026/14,
Singadi Kunta, Near GHMC Garage,
Kavadiguda
Secunderabad - 500 080
Andhra Pradesh, India
Mobile:
+(91)-9246177685

Century Chemical
Mr. Ankit Agarwal
Room No. C- 517,
Bagree Market, No. 71,
Canning Street
Kolkata - 700001, West Bengal, India
Telephone:
+(91)-(33)-23580712
Mobile:
+(91)-9831380479

EIRI PROCESS TECHNOLOGY BOOKS

CHEMICAL/ DYES/ PETROCHEMICALS/ LUBRICANT/ ELECTROPLATING

01 Small Medium & Large Chemical Industries
02 Industrial Chemicals Technology Hand Book
03 Modern Technology of Organic & Inorganic Chemicals
04 Hand Book of Electroplating Anodizing & Surface Finishing Technology
05 Hand Book of Agro Chemical Industries (Insecticides & Pesticides)
06 Technology of Synthetic Dyes, Pigments Intermediates
07 Petrochemicals, Lubricants, Greases & Petroleum Refining
08 Hand Book of Lubricants, Greases & Petrochemicals Technology

GUMS, ADHESIVES AND SEALANTS

01 Technology Of Gums, Adhesives & Sealants With Formulations
02 Hand Book Of Adhesives With Their Formulaes
03 Adhesives Technology & Formulations Hand Book (Hand Book of Adhesives)
04 Technology of Glue and Adhesives with Adhesives Bonding and Formulations

SMALL SCALE INDUSTRIES/ STATIONERY/PAPER/ INKS/ CANDLES & EXPORT BUSINESS

01 Start Your Own Export Business (How To Export)
02 Start Your Own Small Business And Industry
03 Candle Making Processes & Formulations Hand Book
04 Stationery, Paper Converting & Packaging Industries
05 Modern Inks Formulations & Manufacturing Industries
06 Profitable Businesses To Start For Entrepreneurs
07 Modern Small & Cottage Scale Industries
08 Profitable Small Cottage Tiny & Home Industries

BIO FUEL & BIOPROCESSING

01 Technology Of Bio-Fules (Ethanol & Biodiesel)
02 Modern Technology Of Bioprocessing

PRINTING, SCREEN PRINTING & PACKAGING

01 Hand Book of Printing Processes Technologies & Industries
02 Hand Book Of Printing Technology (Offset, Screen, Flexo, Gravure, Inkjet & Digital)
03 Hand Book Of Offset Printing Technology
04 Screen Printing With Processes & Tech.
05 Hand Book Of Prepress
06 Hand Book Of Packaging Technology
07 Modern Packaging Technology for Processed Food, Bakery, Snack Foods, Spices and Allied Food Products
08 Hand Book Of Food Packaging Technology
09 Modern Technology of Printing Inks

PAINT, VARNISH, SOLVENTS, COATING & LACQUERS, POWDER COATING

01 Paint Pigment Varnish & Lacquer Manufacturing
02 Paint Varnish Solvents & Coating Technology

EIRI PROCESS TECHNOLOGY BOOKS

03 Paint, Pigment, Solvent, Coating Emulsion, Paint Additives & Formulations
04 Technology Of Coating, Resins, Pigments & Inks Industries
05 Manufacturing Technology & Formulations Hand Book On Thinners, Putty, Wall & Industrial Finishes And Synthetic Resins
06 Technology of Synthetic Resins and Emulsion Polymers
07 Technology of Paints and Coatings with Formulations
08 Powder Coating Technology Hand Book

PLASTIC/POLYMER PROCESS, COMPOUNDING, INJECTION MOULDING, ROTATIONAL MOULDING, PLASTIC FILM, FIBRE GLASS, PLASTIC WASTE RECYCLING, MOULDS, PET & RESINS INDUSTRIES

01 Moulds Design & Processing Hand Book
02 Hand Book Of Plastic Materials & Processing Technology
03 Injection Moulding Of Plastics
04 Plastic Processing and Packaging Industries
05 Plastic Waste Recycling Technology
06 Technology Of Plastic Films
07 Rotational Moulding Technology Hand Book
08 Plastic Compounding, Master Batches, Pet & Other Plastics
09 Synthetic Resins Technology With Formulations
10 Technology Of PVC Compounding And Its Applications
11 Hand Book of Polymer And Plastic Technology
12 Hand Book of Fibre Glass Moulding
13 Technology of Reinforced Plastics
14 Plastic Additives Technology Hand Book
15 Technology of Pet Bottles, Preform and Pet Recycling
16 Modern Technology of Extrusion & Extruded Products
17 Technology of Synthetic Resins & Emulsion Polymers
18 Technology of Plastic Additives with Processes and Packaging
19 Technology of Disposable Medical Products

BAKERY, CONFECTIONERY & BREAKFAST, PASTA & CEREALS

01 Hand Book Of Bakery Industries
02 Hand Book Of Confectionery With Formulations
03 Breakfast, Dietary Food, Pasta & Cereal Products Technology
04 Hand Book Of Modern Bakery Products
05 Modern Bakery Technology & Fermented Cereal Products With Formulae
06 Technology of Confectionery, Chocolates, Toffee, Candy, Chewing & Bubble Gums, Lollipop and Jelly Products with Formulations

AGRO CULTIVATION, ANIMAL FARMING, AGRO PLANTATION & AGRO CHEMICAL/ PESTICIDES/ FLORICULTURE & BEE KEEPING

01 Poultry Farming & Feed Formulations
02 Hand Book of Pig Farming
03 Agro Based Hand Book of Plantation, Cultivation & Farming
04 Agro Based Plantation Cultivation & Farming
05 Agro Chemical Industries (Insecticide & Pesticides)
06 Modern Bee Keeping & Honey Processing

EIRI PROCESS TECHNOLOGY BOOKS

07 Technology Of Modern Rice Milling And Basmati Rice
08 Hand Book Of Goat Farming
09 Floriculture Hand Book (Flowers Growing Technology)
10 Aloe Vera Cultivation, Processings, Formulations And Manufacturing Technology
11 Poultry Farming, Hatchery and Broiler Production

DAIRY FARM, MILK PROCESSING AND ICE CREAM

01 Hand Book of Dairy Formulations, Processes & Milk Processing Industries
02 Milk Processing And Dairy Products Industries
03 Hand Book Of Dairy Farming to Produce Milk with Packaging
04 Hand Book Of Ice Cream Technology And Formulae
05 Hand Book Of Milk Processing Dairy Products And Packaging Technology
06 Dairy Farming for Milk Production Technology
07 Commercial Dairy Farming with Project Profiles

HERBS & MEDICINAL CULTIVATION

01 Herbs, Medicinal & Aromatic Plants Cultivation
02 Aushidhi And Sungndhit Paudho Ka Vaysayik (Hindi)
03 Hand Book Of Aromatic & Medicinal Plants And Biodiesel (Jatropha)
04 Hand Book Of Medicinal & Aromatic Plants (Cultivation, Utilisation & Extraction Processed)

FOOD & AGRO PROCESSING, PRESERVATION, SNACK FOOD, DEHYDRATION, FRUIT BEVERAGE, POTATO, MAIZE, MEAT PROCESS

01 Fruits & Vegetables Processing Hand Book
02 Fruit Beverage & Processing With Mango
03 Food Processing & Agro Based Industries
04 Manufacturing Technology of Snacks Food, Namkeen, Pappad & Potato Products
05 Preservation & Canning Of Fruits and Vegetables
06 Hand Book of Food Dehydration & Drying
07 Meat Processing & Meat Products Hand Book
08 Technology of Food Preservation & Processing
09 Hand Book of Food Packaging Technology
10 Agro Based & Processed Food Products
11 Potato & Potato Processing Technology
12 Technology of Maize & Allied Com. Products
13 Technology of Food Processing Industries
14 Technology of Sweets (Mithai) with Formulae
15 Modern Technology of Frozen Food Products
16 Technology of Water and Packaged Drinking water
17 Complete Hand Book on Frozen Food Processing and Freeze Drying Technology
18 Technology of Sweets (Mithai), Namkeen and Snacks food with Formulae
19 Complete Book on Banana Cultivation, Dehydration, Ripening, Processing, Products and Packaging Technology

EIRI PROCESS TECHNOLOGY BOOKS

20 Technology of Chicken Meat and Poultry Products
21 Agro Food Processing and Packaging Technology
22 Modern Technology of Tomato Processing and Dehydration (Ketchup, Juice, Paste, Puree, Soup and Drying)
23 Modern Technology of Agro Processing and Food Packaging Products with Project Profiles
24 Start Your Own Coffee and Coffee Processing

SOAPS & DETERGENTS

01 Household Soap. Toilet Soap & Other Soap
02 Profitable Small Scale Manufacture Of Soaps & Detergents
03 Synthetic Detergents With Formulations
04 Modern Technology of Acid Slurry, Surfactants, Soap and Detergents with Formulae

ORGANIC FARMING AND FOOD

01 Hand Book Of Organic Farming And Organic Foods With Vermi-Composting And Neem Products

FISH FARMING & FISHERY PRODUCTS

01 Hand Book Of Fish Farming And Fishery Products

COSMETIC (SYNTHETIC & HERBAL)

01 Cosmetics Processes & Formulations
02 Herbal Cosmetics & Beauty Products With Formulations
03 Profitable Small Scale Manufacture Of Cosmetics (Synthetic & Herbal)
04 Hand Book Of Synthetic & Herbal Cosmetics (How to Make Beauty Products)
05 Technology Of Herbal Cosmetics & Toiletries Products With Formulae

OIL AND FATS

01 Hand Book of Oils, Fats And Derivatives With Refining & Packaging Technology
02 Technology of Oilseeds Processing, Oils & Fats and Refining

ESSENTIAL OILS & AROMATIC

01 Essential Oils Manufacturing & Aromatic Plants
02 Modern Technology Of Essential Oils
03 Technology Of Perfumes, Flavours & Essential Oils
04 Essential Oils Processes & Formulations

PERFUMES AND FLAVOURS

01 Hand Book Of Flavours & Food Colourants Technology
02 Hand Book Of Perfumes & Flavours
03 Hand Book of Perfumes With Formulations
04 Technology Of Perfumes, Flavours & Essential Oils
05 Hand Book Of Flavours Technology

BUILDING MATERIALS & CHEMICALS

01 Technology Of Building Materials & Chemicals With Processes

EIRI PROCESS TECHNOLOGY BOOKS

Complete Hand Book Of Ayurvedic & Herbal Medicines)

STEEL, S.S., NON FERROUS METALS, ROLLING MILL

01 Modern Technology of Non Ferrous Metals and Metal Extraction

02 Processing Technology of Steels and Stainless Steels

03 Modern Technology of Rolling Mill, Billets, Steel Wire, Galvanized Sheet, Forging & Castings

04 Manufacturing Technology of Non-Ferrous Metal Products

WOOD, VENEER, PLYWOOD, PARTICLE, BOARD, FIBREBOARD, BAMBOO & FOREST PRODUCTS

01 Modern Technology Of Wood, Veneer, Plywood, Particle Board, Fibreboard, Bamboo & Forest Products

BIO GAS PRODUCTION

01 Modern Technology of BIOGAS Production

WASTE BASED PRODUCTS INCLUDING INDUSTRIAL, AGRICULTURE, MEDICAL, MUNICIPALITY, ORGANIC & BIOLOGICAL

01 Technology Of Products From Wastes Industrial, Agriculture, Medical, Municipality, Organic & Biological

02 Products from Waste Technology Handbook

FOOD CHEMICALS, FOOD ADDITIVES, PIGMENTS, AROMA, SWEETENERS AND FOOD EMULSIFIERS

01 Technology of Food Chemicals, Pigments and Food Aroma Compounds

02 Modern Technology of Food Additives, Sweeteners and Food Emulsifiers

SOYBEAN

01 Technology of SOYBEAN Products with Formulae

02 Technology of Soya Milk, Tofu, Hydrlyzate and allied Soyabean Products with Project Profiles

EIRI Multiple Project Reports in CD ROM

01 92 New Lucrative Project Reports In Cd

02. 45 Infotech/It, Hospitality, Hospital, College, School & Club

03. 23 Profitable Construction Projects

04. 56 Agro Based & Food Processing Projects

05. 52 Food, Dairy, Bakery, Confectionery & Snacks Foods

06. 45 New Chemicals & Allied Project Reports

07. 100 Profitable Plastic, Polymers & Allied Projects

08. 44 Textile, Garments, Hosiery & Allied Products In Cd

09. 23 Dairy Farming (Buffalo & Jersey Cow, Dairy Products & Other Milk Processing Ind.

10. 42 Paper, Pulp & Paper Converting Products Reports

EIRI Multiple Project Reports in CD ROM

11. 31 Essential Oils, Perfumes, Flavours & Aromatic Compounds
12. 28 Surgical And Disposable Medical Projects
13. 36 Profitable Printing & Allied Projects Reports
14. 63 Profitable Packaging & Allied Project Reports
15. 99 Profitable Printing & Packaging
16. 42 Electroplating, Anodizing & Allied Projects
17. 31 Profitable Plantation & Cultivation Projects
18. 55 Profitable Products From Agro And Other Industrial Wastes
19. 35 Profitable Gums, Adhesives, Sealants And Resins Projects
20. 54 Paint, Varnish, Solvents, Lacquers, Resins, Enamel, Pigments, Thinners & Powder (54 Project Reports In Cd)
21 43 Iron, Steel, Casting, Fabrication, Wire Drawing & Rolling Mills Projects
22. 26 New Educational Projects (Schools, Colleges, Training/ Management Institute, Hostels Etc.)
23. 12 Mosquitoes Preventive Projects (Coils, Mats, Liquids, Agarbatti, Nets, Spray Etc.)
24. 21 Bakery And Allied Products
25. 67 Rubber And Rubber Goods Industries
26. 37 Aluminium And Aluminium Based Industries
27. 14 Potato And Potato Based Industries
28. 50 Electrical, Electronics And Computer Based Industries
29. 52 Cosmetics (Herbal & Synthetics) Technology Projects (52 Project Reports)
30. 10 Molasses Based Lucrative Projects
31. 24 Fruits/Veg. & Allied Food Dehydration Projects
32. 7 Power Plant Projects (Thermal, Hydro, Solar, Wind Energy And Lignite Coal Based)
33. 35 New Profitable Industries
34. 160 New Export Oriented And Profitable Projects (160 Project Reports In Cd)
35. 5 Ginger & Ginger Processing Industries
36. 13 Fish Farming And Fishery Products
37. 6 Agarbatti And Allied Projects
38. 28 Fruit Juices, Food Dehydration And Allied Products
39. 9 Tea Plantation And Processing Based Industries
40. 14 Roasted/Salted Cashew Nuts, Almonds, Namkeens, Spices Projects
41. 23 Injection Moulded Plastic Products (23 Project Reports)
42. 38 Biofertilizer, Biofuel, Enzyme, Organic Farming & Manure, Protein And Allied Lucrative Projects
43. 10 Maize & Corn Processing Projects
44. 11 Profitable Solar & Solar Based Products
45. 11 Infotech/It Projects
46. 42 Hospitality, Building Material, Power Steels, Alcohol & Other Food Products
47. 24 Soap & Detergents (Scouring Powder, Toilet Cleaner, Laundry Soap, Detergent Cake & Powder, Toilet Soap, Enzyme Based Detergents, Phenyl & Soap Coated Paper)
48. 10 Coconut And Coconut By Products
49. 22 Alcohol, Beer, Imfl, Country Liquor, Wine & Other Related Projects